HACK HAPPENS

Cybersecurity for Beginners Who Dont Want to be Next

Tolga TAVLAS

Cover Design by London Design Company

Illustrations by Mary Amato

Disclaimer

This book is for educational and awareness purposes only. It's based on the author's professional experience and widely accepted industry knowledge at the time of writing. While every effort has been made to keep the content accurate and helpful, please keep the following in mind:

- **Cybersecurity Changes Fast:** Threats, tools, and best practices evolve quickly. What's true today might be outdated tomorrow. Staying informed is key.
- **Not Professional Advice:** This isn't legal, financial, or technical advice tailored to individual situations. For specific concerns, it's best to consult a qualified professional.
- **Fictional Stories, Real Lessons:** All real-world scenarios are fictional. They're inspired by real trends but aren't based on actual people, companies, or events.
- **No Guarantees:** While the content aims to be accurate and useful, there's no guarantee it covers everything or that it will prevent cyber incidents. Cybersecurity is complex, and outcomes depend on many factors – some beyond anyone's control. Use the information thoughtfully and at your own discretion.
- **Mentions Aren't Endorsements:** Any tools, software, or services named here are included for illustration – not as recommendations. Always evaluate what's right for your own situation. The author is not responsible for the actions of third-party companies, tools, or individuals mentioned or referenced in this book.
- **Laws Vary:** Cybersecurity laws and standards can differ by country, region, or industry. Legal or compliance advice should come from local experts.
- **Personal Responsibility:** How the information in this book is used is entirely up to the reader. Any decisions made based on this content are made at the reader's own risk.
- **No Obligation or Relationship:** Reading this book doesn't create any contract, obligation, or professional relationship between the reader and the author.

Contents

Dedication VI

Preface VII

Before Turning the Page XI

This Is How It Starts XV

PART 1 - WHY EVERYDAY CYBERSECURITY MATTERS

1. The Silent War You're Already In 3
2. The Modern Cyber Threats 7
3. The Human Element: Why Security Fails 11
4. Charting Your Course: Awareness is Your Armor 15

PART 2 - IS YOUR HOME A HACKER'S PLAYGROUND?

5. Home Wi-Fi: The Invisible Door Into Your Home 20
6. Bluetooth: Exposing Yourself Without Knowing 28
7. Smart Home, Dumb Security 36
8. Multi-Device Syncing: One Hack to Rule Them All 43
9. Talking to Trouble: Betrayed by Smart Assistants 51

PART 3 - EVERYDAY DEVICES, EXTRAORDINARY DANGER

10. How Hackers Hijack Your Personal Computer 60
11. Mobile Phone Safety: Your Pocket is a Hacker's Dream 68
12. Public Wi-Fi: The Cost of Free Internet 76

13. Smart TVs & Streaming Devices - The Living Room Spies 84
14. Gaming Consoles: Hacked While You Play 93
15. Offline, Still Dangerous: USBs, Hard Drives & Lost Files 103

PART 4 - ONLINE LIFE: SECRETS, SCAMS and SILENT TAKEOVERS

16. Personal Email Security: Stop Them at the Gate 112
17. Passwords: Still Your Weakest Link 120
18. Identity Theft: How One Mistake Can Ruin Everything 128
19. Social Media: You're Sharing Too Much 136
20. The AI Trap: Deepfakes, Cloned Voices & Hacks 145
21. Scan & Scam: The Hidden Danger in QR Code 154
22. GPS and Location Tracking: How You're Followed 162
23. The Silent Risks of Wearables 171

PART 5 - PROTECT YOUR FAMILY BEFORE IT'S TOO LATE

24. How Hackers Target Children 182
25. Parental Controls: How to Actually Keep Kids Safe 190
26. Cybersecurity for Every Family Member 199
27. Group Chats, Shared Accounts, and Hidden Dangers 208
28. When Guests Become Risks: Visitors, Airbnbs & More 217
29. Digital Death: What Happens After You Die 225

PART 6 - KEEP YOUR MONEY, MEMORIES, AND LIFE SAFE

30. Online Banking and Finance: Keep Your Money Yours 234
31. Secure Online Shopping: Don't Get Tricked by a Sale 242
32. SIM Swapping: Losing Your Number, and Your Identity 250
33. Protecting Your Digital Photos and Family Videos 258
34. The Cloud Isn't as Safe as You Think 266

PART 7 - LOST & HACKED: YOUR EMERGENCY RESPONSE PLAN

35. Losing Devices: How to Protect and Recover Fast 276
36. Managing a Breach: What to Do After You're Hacked 284

37. Breached Accounts: Track Them Before Criminals Do 293

38. Backup and Recovery: Save Your Data Before You Cry 302

39. The Right Way to Dispose of Old Devices and Hard Drives 310

40. The Cybersecurity Rescue Plan You Wish You Had 318

LAST PART: NOW YOU KNOW - NOW YOU ACT

You've Come a Long Way 328

Build Your Cybersecure Life 332

Keep Going: Resources and Next Steps 337

A Final Word: You're Not Powerless 343

The Digital 911: What to Do When You're Under Attack 349

You Deserve to See the Proof 356

In Case You Want to Go Deeper 363

Bonus: 50 Essential Cybersecurity Terms 367

About the author 381

To my daughter – "*my cheeky monkey*", my daily dose of laughter and light.

You've made me prouder than I ever imagined possible.

This book is my way of fighting for a safer world; for you, and for everyone who still believes in doing good.

Preface

When people hear you work in cybersecurity, they smile—like they're in on a secret.

They picture blinking monitors, glowing code, midnight calls about massive hacks. You, hunched over a keyboard, chasing threats in real time. The "hacker guy." The one with digital secrets and cinematic tension built into his day.

And honestly? That version sounds fun.

But the reality? It's just different.

Most days, cybersecurity is about quiet, thoughtful work: risk assessments, vulnerability triage, compliance reviews, data classification workflows. It's long hours making decisions that matter, explaining technical risks to people who just want to pass an audit. No neon-lit basements. No epic soundtracks.

But make no mistake—it's still a frontline. Just one where prevention matters more than reaction, and calm consistency protects more than any firewall.

And outside of work? You become something else entirely.

The neighborhood tech whisperer.

The family firewall.

The midnight panic button.

People don't ask because they think you're famous. They ask because they trust you.

And after years of answering those questions—on bus rides, in checkout lines, over birthday cake—I realized: Nobody's really explaining cybersecurity in a way that feels human.

The Book I Never Planned to Write

I didn't plan to write this book.

Originally, couple of years ago, I set out to write a technical guide on Identity and Access Management - niche, dense, misunderstood. I had editors. I had structure.

Then the feedback came: "Too technical. Too narrow. Too confusing."

I was discouraged. So I turned to something smaller – a private glossary of cybersecurity terms I had built over the years. It wasn't a book. It wasn't fancy. It was just clear.

That became the "**Cybersecurity Dictionary for Everyone**" - a book project that quietly grew from frustration into connection.

I didn't expect many to read it — honestly, I was at the "please don't buy it just to make me feel good" stage. I was begging family and friends not to pity-purchase (*which, by the way, is every writer's nightmare - the dreaded "no worries, Dad, we're still proud of you" moment!*).

Then somehow... it became a bestseller across multiple Amazon stores and reached over 30 countries. Way beyond anything I imagined.

The Wave I Didn't Expect

I began sharing short, accessible posts on social media—bite-sized explanations, real-life scenarios, simple infographics, and practical tips anyone could act on. The goal was to raise awareness without overwhelming people.

Slowly, they spread.

Millions of people saw them. Thousands reached out.

Not with likes, but with stories.

Stories of confusion, near-misses, heartbreak, recovery.

That's when I realized: this may be the book they've been waiting for.

A Long Time Coming

To be fair, someone saw this before I did.

My wife.

She heard the stories I brought home—the cautionary tales, the lessons, the human moments.

She said, *"Those stories land. People understand those. You need to write that book."*

She was right.

This is that book.

The stories in this book are fictional—but only on the surface. They're built to show you *how* things happen, *why* they matter, and *where* the traps are. But every one of them is grounded in real events. Real breaches. Real consequences.

Some of the stories are drawn from my own experience.

Many come from you—from the messages, comments, and conversations I've had with thousands of people across the world.

Others are based on public incidents—those quiet news stories that barely registered in the chaos of daily headlines, but carried enormous personal impact.

And a few came from people I'll never meet—who trusted me enough to share what went wrong, so others wouldn't have to go through the same.

A Moment I'll Never Forget

More than a decade ago, while working full-time at a bank, I was invited to lecture on mobile security for a group of master's students studying Information Technology Law. It wasn't something I had planned (*then again, a lot of meaningful things in my life weren't planned. Remind me someday to tell you how a two-day touristic trip turned into two years in beautiful Dublin with lovely Irish people thanks to a Lufthansa strike*).

But the person who asked was someone I couldn't say no to.

So I said yes.

And what I found in that classroom left a mark I carry to this day.

The students were exceptional—some from scientific research institutions, some from law enforcement, others free spirits with sharp minds and open hearts. Different missions. Different perspectives. One thing in common: they were brilliant, and they were kind.

Some of them traveled up to eight hours in a single day just to attend those sessions for a few hours. Not for grades. Not for credit.

For the knowledge. For the conversation. For the chance to ask and learn.

They took notes. They stayed late. They asked questions I still think about.

That experience changed me. It taught me something I've never forgotten:

When someone is hungry to learn, you owe them your best.

Not another bloated manual.

Not a checklist written to tick a box. But something clear. Something real.

Something that speaks in their language and meets them where they are.

Why I Wrote This

I didn't write this book because I had all the answers — I wrote it because the questions were getting louder.

Not just technical ones. Human ones. Questions like:

- *"Is my child safe on this app?"*
- *"Why did my friend get hacked when all she did was check her email?"*
- *"How do I know if my phone is spying on me?"*

These aren't just questions about technology — they're questions about trust, safety, and everyday life. They come from people trying to protect their kids, their money, their memories, and their peace of mind. And they deserve answers that don't confuse or condescend — just clarity, care, and practical help.

So I decided to answer them — in plain language, with real-world stories, and practical steps people can actually use.

Because cybersecurity isn't about fear — it's about power. The power to protect what matters most.

And if I've done my job, this book won't just inform you — it'll empower you. You'll start noticing the danger before it notices you.

And when that moment comes — because it will — you'll know what to do.

Before Turning the Page

You're already inside the danger — let's make sure you survive it.

You've plugged your phone into an airport charger.

Reused the same password "just one more time."

Clicked "Accept All Cookies" without blinking.

Handed your iPad to a kid just to get five minutes of peace.

If that sounds familiar, this book is about you.

You're already inside the digital threat zone. Not maybe. Not someday. Now. Whether you signed up for it or not — you're a participant.

You're just trying to live, work, scroll, shop, send photos, keep your kids entertained, and hold onto your sanity in a hyper-connected world.

But here's the uncomfortable truth: In a world where your refrigerator, your doorbell, and your dog's GPS tracker are online — your life is more exposed than you realize.

***

I'm Tolga Tavlas and I've spent 27 years working in cybersecurity — from analyzing real-world attacks to helping people understand how to protect what matters most. I've seen how ordinary people become targets. And more importantly, how they can fight back.

This book isn't a lecture. It's not a technical manual. And it's definitely not written just for "IT people."

This is for you — for anyone trying to survive the digital world without becoming the next cautionary tale.

This book is built for real life:

- Fictional stories inspired by real-world events
- Crucial, data-backed insights showing you exactly what to watch for
- Clear, practical advice from someone who's spent decades in the trenches of cybersecurity

Why You Deserve This Transparency

I've been writing professionally for over a decade, and readers deserve clarity — not just after buying the book, but before they even turn the first page.

I know this book will end up next to some that were stitched together by AI in under an hour — or ghostwritten by someone who once googled "cybersecurity." This isn't that.

What I do know comes from years of real work with real people — millions of interactions with folks just like you, trying to stay safe in a dangerous digital world.

The numbers you'll see aren't guesses. Over 200 data points, handpicked and verified from trusted sources — government reports, cybersecurity firms, academic studies, global surveys.

That's why, at the end of this book, you'll find a section called "You Deserve to See the Proof" — with real posts from @SecBriefs and a breakdown of how the data was gathered, verified, and shared openly.

This is real. This is happening. And now, it's in your hands.

How Each Chapter Works

Every chapter follows the same structure — built for clarity, not complexity. You'll know where you are, what it means, and what to do next.

• **Real-World Scenarios:** A short, sharp story of how one ordinary person made one ordinary mistake — and it led to disaster. (Yes, the characters are fictional. But the tactics? 100% real. And used every day.)

• **What You Need to Know:** The behind-the-scenes breakdown. How the attackers got in, what was overlooked, and what made the victim vulnerable.

• **Why It Matters:** The part nobody talks about enough — consequences. Not vague. Not dramatic. Real fallout: lost money, ruined relationships, destroyed reputations, shattered peace of mind.

• **What to Do About It – Your Security Checklist:** Clear, non-technical, step-by-step actions you can take right now.

You don't need to be a tech expert — just someone who doesn't want to get burned.

You don't have to read this book in order. Start with whatever freaks you out the most: Your smart TV. Your email. Your kid's gaming console. Just don't wait until something goes wrong.

What Each Part Covers

Part 1: Why Everyday Cybersecurity Matters

You don't have to be rich or famous to be targeted. If you're online — you're on someone's list. This section explains why you're the ideal victim — and how to stop playing that role.

Part 2: Is Your Home a Hacker's Playground?

Spoiler: yes, it is. Your smart speaker, camera, Wi-Fi, lightbulbs, even your fridge can be flipped against you. This part reveals how — and how to fight back.

Part 3: Everyday Devices, Extraordinary Danger

Phones. Laptops. TVs. Consoles. The tools you use daily can be hijacked in seconds. You'll see how these everyday devices become traps — and how to fix them.

Part 4: Online Life — Secrets, Scams, and Silent Takeovers

This is where it gets personal. Social media, cloud backups, passwords, identity theft, AI & QR tricks — the invisible war zones where people lose everything and never see it coming.

Part 5: Protect Your Family Before It's Too Late

Your security is everyone's security. This part covers kids, guests, shared devices, and all the "small things" that open the biggest doors to cybercrime.

Part 6: Keep Your Money, Memories, and Life Safe

Your most precious digital assets are under constant attack — your bank account, your photos, your passwords, your data. You'll learn how scammers target what you value most — and how to lock them out.

Part 7: Lost & Hacked — Your Emergency Response Plan

It happened. You clicked it. You lost it. You froze. Now what? This part gives you a clear, fast-action recovery guide: what to fix, who to call, and how to stop the bleeding.

At the end of the book, you'll also find **50 essential cybersecurity terms** — hand-picked to help you feel more confident with the language of cybersecurity. They come from my other book, ***Cybersecurity Dictionary for Everyone*** — an Amazon bestseller that breaks down over 1,250 terms without the tech-speak.

Just Keep in Mind

Cybersecurity isn't just for companies or coders. It's for parents. Teenagers. Small business owners. Travelers. Anyone with a phone, a password, or a digital life.

This book is about making sure you don't become the easy story someone else learns from.

You don't need to be perfect. Or technical. Just harder to hit than you are right now.

This book won't protect you if you don't open it. It won't help if you ignore the signs. But if you read it — really read it — you'll start seeing the danger long before it sees you.

Because like it or not, you're already in this game. It's time to play smart.

Your Lifelines Are Already Here

Before you dive into the chapters, know this: This book doesn't just tell stories or share stats. It equips you.

At the end of the book, you'll find two critical lifelines:

- **The Digital 911: What to Do When You're Under Attack** – A calm, step-by-step survival guide for when things go wrong — from fraud and ransomware to suspicious links.
- **In Case You Want to Go Deeper** – A curated collection of tools, reports, and voices doing real work in cybersecurity. If something hits home — this is where you go next.

Whether you're in crisis mode or curiosity mode — you're covered.

Let's begin.

This Is How It Starts

Some pictures get stuck in your head and never leave. I remember one like that from years ago, back when I was a young student studying criminology in the UK. It was a TV ad about the dangers of drink-driving. It wasn't about numbers; it was about futures being stolen.

It started in a busy, happy pub – loud music, people laughing, friends sitting together.

We see a young man, Dave, full of life, having a good time. But his friends keep bringing drinks. They joke around but keep pushing him: "***Come on Dave, drink one more, one more!***" Maybe they weren't thinking clearly either. You see him pause for a second. He wants to fit in more than he wants to be careful. The ad suggests what he did next – walked to his car, took out his keys, and made the deadly choice to drive drunk.

But the ad doesn't show the car crash. Instead, it shows us something much scarier – what happened later. The screen gets blurry, the sound gets weird, but you still hear the chant, turning ugly. When the picture becomes clear, the pub is gone. We are in a plain, empty room, years later. Dave is there, but he's changed. He's limp in a wheelchair, broken. His body is like a prison. His eyes are empty. The young man from the pub is gone, his life lost because he drove drunk.

And the voice chanting "***Come on Dave, one more...***" is his mother's. Her face shows a deep tiredness that never ends, a sadness that won't go away. She spoons food toward his mouth – he doesn't react. The words she says are like a creepy, empty repeat of that moment that ruined his life and trapped her into caring for him forever.

That ad was shocking because it showed how a normal moment could cause total ruin. It wasn't a monster or a weapon; it was friendship turned into something that caused disaster. It showed how one small choice made under pressure – to have 'one more' drink and then drive – could destroy a future, leaving just an empty person and non-stop, quiet pain.

Why use such a strong picture in a book about cybersecurity?

Because the online world, even though it's not physical, has its own ways to cause terrible results, started by small things or bad choices. The online 'chants' are different, maybe quieter, but they are always there: the pushy email saying "click now!"; the pop-up offering a prize for your information; the easy choice of using the same weak password everywhere; the pressure from friends to share things online without thinking. These are the online versions of "***Come on, one more...***" – pushes toward small actions that feel like nothing but can lead to huge disasters.

The 'crash' online isn't a car crash. It's someone quietly stealing your private information. It's your identity being stolen. It's your bank account being emptied. It's criminals locking your important files and asking for money to unlock them. It's finding out strangers are using your name, wrecking your credit score, or doing crimes pretending to be you.

And what happens after? It's the worried phone calls, lots of paperwork, constant worry, feeling attacked, and the long, tiring fight to get your online life back. That fight can last for months, even years.

Often, it all starts with one click, one weak password, one time trusting the wrong thing online. Just one weakness that someone uses against you. Someone who knows how to use that small chance to cause big harm.

This book is about seeing the danger before it's too late. It's about knowing the tricks criminals use – the online version of that bad pressure Dave faced.

This book will give you the information and easy steps to use the internet safely, to spot the dangers you might not notice. It's here to help stop you from being another victim whose life is changed forever by a digital '***one more***' decision.

PART 1 - WHY EVERYDAY CYBERSECURITY MATTERS

Chapter 1

The Silent War You're Already In

You start your morning with a glance at your phone. Notifications glow like a to-do list from a world you never asked to join—messages, app updates, emails, maybe a reminder from your smart assistant that it's trash day. It's all normal. Routine. Forgettable.

You swipe. You check your balance. You tap a promo from your favorite store. You ask Alexa to play some music. You step into your car, which remembers your route. You connect to the café's free Wi-Fi.

And just like that, you've made hundreds (if not thousands!) of micro-decisions that affect your digital safety—and probably didn't notice a single one.

Cybersecurity isn't just a buzzword or a job title anymore. It's not a padlock icon in your browser or a headline about hackers breaking into some distant government server. It's not just for IT departments or billion-dollar firms.

Cybersecurity is the small, invisible war you are already a part of—whether you signed up for it or not.

It's the background hum of your connected life. And every click, swipe, voice command, or saved password is a potential vulnerability. Most attacks don't come with flashing red lights or dramatic music. They come through convenience. Through trust. Through shortcuts. Through that single, simple decision—"I'll deal with that later."

Remember Dave?

In the introduction, we met him in a pub—just one more drink, one more joke, one small decision that ruined everything. What happened to Dave wasn't dramatic in the moment. It was quiet. Ordinary. And yet, it ended in a wheelchair, in a room filled with silence and regret.

Now look at your phone. Your Wi-Fi router. Your doorbell camera. Your smartwatch. Your cloud storage. None of them feel dangerous. But neither did Dave's night out. Until the consequences showed up.

This is how it happens now: not through burglars or bullets, but through unpatched firmware, weak passwords, reused credentials, and QR codes that lead to nowhere good. It's not someone breaking into your house—it's someone quietly walking through a door you didn't lock because you didn't know it was even there.

Redefining Cybersecurity

Cybersecurity is no longer about firewalls around office buildings or espionage in spy thrillers. It's not about hackers in hoodies trying to crack government servers in dark basements. That version exists—but it's not the one you need to worry about.

The cybersecurity that matters to you—**Everyday Cybersecurity**—is much simpler and more personal.

It's about protecting your identity, your money, your family, your private conversations, and your photos from strangers who don't need to kick down your door to ruin your life. It's the digital version of locking your front door, setting boundaries with strangers, and not shouting your Social Security number on the subway.

It's hygiene. Basic. Necessary. Non-negotiable.

If you've ever checked your bank balance on public Wi-Fi, used the same password for more than one account, or clicked "Remind Me Later" on a software update—you've skipped brushing your digital teeth. And the cavities are coming.

The Hyper-Connected Reality

You probably have a smartphone. A laptop or tablet. A smartwatch or a fitness band. Maybe a smart speaker or TV. Your car might connect to your calendar and Spotify. Your thermostat adjusts itself while you sleep. Your doorbell has a camera. Your fridge might even know your grocery list.

That's just the hardware.

Then there are your accounts—email, cloud storage, banking, social media, online shopping, health portals, ride-sharing, digital wallets, and a dozen forgotten logins stored somewhere in your browser's memory.

You're not a person with a device anymore.

You're a moving network. An ecosystem. A walking target surface.

And each of those things—every device, every account—is a possible entry point. They're all linked. All talking to each other. And if just one of them gets compromised, it rarely stops there. A hacked tablet can lead to your cloud storage. A compromised smart speaker can let someone access your schedule. A breached email account can be the master key to your entire digital identity.

This isn't about paranoia. It's about physics. When everything connects, one weak point affects the whole system.

Why You? Dispelling the Myths

Let's kill the most dangerous assumption right now: "**I'm not important enough to get hacked.**"

Yes, you are.

You might not be rich or famous, but that's not what attackers are looking for. They want easy wins. They want weak passwords, unpatched routers, reused credentials. They want people who don't think they're targets—because those people don't take precautions.

Here's what you have that they want:

- **Your data.** Even your non-financial info—like your name, birthday, or email—can help build fake identities for fraud.
- **Your credentials.** If your Netflix password is the same as your bank login, congratulations: you've handed over the keys.
- **Your devices.** Hackers don't just want to steal from you—they might want to use your device as a zombie in a botnet to attack someone else. You become the weapon, without knowing it.
- **Your behavior.** Attackers study human patterns. They don't need to trick the smartest person in the world—just the most distracted one. Or the most trusting. Or the most tired.

And most of this isn't even done by hand. It's automated. Bots scan the internet day and night for routers with outdated firmware, phones with weak Bluetooth settings, emails with known passwords. If your device shows up with a known flaw, the bot doesn't stop to ask if you're wealthy. It just gets to work.

So no—you're not invisible.

You're actually right in the middle of the map.

The Turning Point

The goal isn't to panic you.

It's to wake you up.

This quiet war is already underway, whether you've noticed it or not. Ignoring it doesn't make it disappear—it only makes you more vulnerable.

In the chapters ahead, you're going to see exactly what's happening behind the screen. You'll understand the traps, how they work, and what can be done before it's too late.

But first, it's important to see the landscape clearly.

Cybersecurity is no longer optional. It's the digital equivalent of wearing a seatbelt, locking your front door, or teaching children not to talk to strangers.

You wouldn't leave your front door wide open. So why leave your digital life unguarded?

Chapter 2

The Modern Cyber Threats

The word "cybersecurity" still brings one image to mind for many people: a virus. A digital infection. Something like a flu for computers. Maybe it slows things down. Maybe it makes pop-ups appear. Annoying, sure. Dangerous? Probably not. That idea is outdated.

The threats have evolved—and multiplied.

Today, the biggest digital dangers don't look like code. They look like emails from your bank. Texts from your delivery service. Missed calls from a fake utility company. They hide in QR codes taped to a restaurant menu. They borrow the names of people you trust. And they aren't just aimed at your device—they're aimed at your decisions.

This section lays the foundation. It introduces the threat landscape behind the everyday devices and services that seem harmless. These aren't abstract risks reserved for major corporations. These are problems designed to land in your pocket, enter through your inbox, and follow your daily routine.

Beyond Viruses: The New Malware

The old-school computer virus hasn't disappeared, but it's no longer the main act.

Now, there's **ransomware**—a type of malware that locks your files, encrypts your data, and demands payment to unlock it. A lifetime of photos, work documents, legal forms, tax records—gone, unless you pay a stranger in cryptocurrency.

There's **spyware**—the silent stalker. It hides in the background, recording your keystrokes, watching through your webcam, or tracking what you do online. It doesn't want to break your device. It wants to study you.

Then there are **Trojans**—named after that wooden horse in Greek mythology. They look like harmless software, videos, or even antivirus tools. But once installed, they unleash something very different from what was promised.

How do they get in?

Usually through human behavior. A phishing email. A "free" software download. A fake invoice attachment. It's rarely brute force. It's usually a trick. That's the point.

The Art of the Trick: Phishing and Social Engineering

Phishing is not just a tactic. It's an art form.

It doesn't rely on breaking through firewalls. It relies on you clicking the wrong thing.

Phishing usually comes via email. A fake security alert. A payment receipt you don't recognize. A message that looks like it's from Apple, Amazon, or your bank. The goal is to get you to panic—or to trust. Either will do.

There's also **smishing** (text-based phishing) and **vishing** (voice-based). Think of those robocalls pretending to be from your tax office. Or a message from your mobile provider claiming you've missed a payment.

These attacks don't succeed because people are careless. They succeed because people are human. The messages play on emotion—urgency, fear, curiosity, loyalty. They pretend to help while quietly stealing.

And they're getting harder to spot. With AI tools now generating realistic messages and deepfake audio, it's not about bad grammar anymore. It's about bad intentions dressed in perfect disguises.

Identity Theft: More Than Just Credit Cards

Think identity theft is about someone buying sneakers with your credit card? That's the easy version.

The real danger is what happens when your personal data—name, date of birth, ID numbers, address, phone—is combined and resold.

That information fuels a darker economy.

Fraudsters use it to open fake credit lines in your name. To file false tax returns and claim your refund. To get loans they'll never repay—leaving you with the mess. Medical identity theft has become a rising threat, where someone uses your details to receive treatments, get prescriptions, or commit insurance fraud.

It can take years to clean up the damage. And often, victims don't find out until their bank rejects a mortgage or a collections agency calls about a debt they never created.

This isn't a rare crime anymore. It's industrialized. Automated. Global.

And it doesn't require hacking into your bank. It just takes one successful phishing attempt or one leaked password from a forgotten app you installed years ago.

The Privacy Paradox: What Your Devices Know

Consider this: your phone knows more about you than your closest friend. Where you've been. How long you stayed. Who you called. What you searched for at 3 a.m.

Smart speakers hear everything. Smart TVs watch everything. Wearables track your steps, heart rate, and sleep. Apps log your shopping habits, political preferences, and eating schedules. And all of it—every location ping, every search term, every voice command—is collected, analyzed, and often shared.

Sometimes this data helps. It powers recommendations, fitness tracking, or traffic routing.

But it's also bought and sold. Passed between data brokers like poker chips. Leaked during breaches. Used to profile you in ways that go far beyond what you think you've shared.

Many people worry about being "hacked." But the bigger question might be: how much have you willingly given away?

Network Weaknesses: The Digital Front Door

Your home Wi-Fi is like the front door to your digital life. And for many, it's unlocked.

Weak passwords. Default router settings. No updates since it was installed. These are golden opportunities for intruders.

A compromised network isn't just about stealing internet bandwidth. It gives attackers access to every device connected—smart TVs, laptops, phones, cameras. Everything that shares that network becomes a potential stepping stone.

Then there's **Bluetooth**, which many users leave on indefinitely. It can be hijacked to track your movement, connect to rogue devices, or intercept data. It only takes a few feet—and the right vulnerability—for someone to slip inside.

Even syncing between devices—phone to tablet to cloud to smart fridge—creates potential failure points. One weak link is all it takes for the whole chain to collapse.

Threats Don't Work Alone

No single attack is the full picture. These threats often **work together**, like a chain reaction.

A leaked password from an old breach leads to a successful login attempt.

That login allows access to sensitive emails.

Inside those emails is enough personal data to craft convincing phishing messages.

One click on a fake invoice installs malware.

That malware logs keystrokes and steals credentials.

Eventually, that stolen data is used to drain a bank account or apply for loans.

This isn't hypothetical. It's procedural. It happens every day—and often in stages so quiet the victim doesn't realize until long after the damage is done.

Why It All Matters

This section isn't meant to overwhelm. It's meant to shift perspective.

The threats today don't require technical expertise to understand. They require awareness. Cybercrime doesn't discriminate based on income, education, or job title. It goes where the defenses are weakest—where passwords are reused, where alerts are ignored, where convenience wins over caution.

And that's why this matters to everyone.

It's not about knowing how to write code or configure firewalls. It's about recognizing that you're surrounded by systems designed for both utility and vulnerability. And understanding that your choices—what you click, what you download, what you ignore—have consequences far beyond the screen.

Chapter 3

The Human Element: Why Security Fails

When people hear about a cyberattack, the default assumption is: *someone clicked something they shouldn't have.*

And often, that's true.

But that doesn't mean the person was reckless or foolish. It means the person was human.

Despite all the firewalls, antivirus software, security patches, and monitoring tools, most cybersecurity breaches start with behavior. A moment of trust. A shortcut. A hasty click. A tiny decision made under pressure, stress, or distraction.

Attackers know this. That's why they don't always try to break systems. They aim to break habits. And when security fails, it often fails not because the technology was weak—but because the human behind it had a blind spot.

Convenience vs. Security: The Trade-Off Everyone Makes

The brain is designed to save energy. It's constantly optimizing, choosing what feels fastest, easiest, most efficient. That's why people save passwords in browsers. Stay logged into apps forever. Use the same Wi-Fi network at every café. Click "Remind Me Later" instead of installing that update.

Security, by its nature, often feels like friction. It adds extra steps. It interrupts. It slows down the scroll.

And that's why people skip it.

It's easier to reuse the same password than to create a new one for every site. Easier to click a link than to hover and inspect it. Easier to trust that the caller is who they say they are than to ask questions that might feel rude.

These aren't failures of intelligence. They're results of design—and biology.

Trust & Authority: The Brain's Shortcuts for Survival

In prehistoric life, humans didn't survive by doubting everyone and everything. Survival required fast judgments: is this person part of my group? Is this signal safe? That bias to trust—to follow signs of authority, familiarity, urgency—still exists. And attackers use it as a weapon.

That's why phishing emails work. They borrow the logos of trusted brands. They mimic the tone of your bank, your employer, your cloud service. That's why scam calls rely on a calm voice saying they're from "tech support." Why fake texts look like delivery updates.

People tend to trust senders they recognize, especially under pressure. That little blue checkmark. The official-looking signature. The sense of urgency. The claim that your account is locked, your payment is overdue, your child is in danger—all of it pushes one reaction: act now.

And in that rush, logic takes a backseat. Even people who "should know better" get tricked. Because it's not just about what they know. It's about how they feel in the moment.

Information Overload & Fatigue: Too Much, Too Fast

The average person now manages dozens of passwords, multiple email addresses, constant app updates, smart devices, antivirus alerts, bank notifications, and privacy setting changes. That's not a manageable system. It's a tidal wave.

So, what happens?

People tune out. They start ignoring alerts. Clicking "OK" without reading. Putting off updates. Using the same login for everything. Relying on autofill. Forgetting which app connects to which cloud account.

This is called **security fatigue**, and it's one of the most common reasons people fall behind on digital hygiene. When everything feels like a threat, nothing gets treated seriously.

Add to this **breach fatigue**—the sense that another data breach is always just around the corner. When people hear about millions of records leaked every week, the response is often a shrug: "So what? It's already out there."

That mindset doesn't mean the danger has passed. It means the defenses are down.

Optimism Bias: The "It Won't Happen to Me" Trap

Ask people if cybersecurity matters, and most will say yes.

Ask if they think they'll be targeted, and most will say no.

That gap is called **optimism bias**—the tendency to believe that bad things happen to other people. It's why drivers speed, smokers keep smoking, and people use the same password for every account. The risk is acknowledged but discounted.

After all, "why would anyone want my data?" or "I'm not rich or famous."

But as seen in earlier sections, attackers don't handpick targets like in spy movies. Bots scan the internet looking for open doors—unpatched software, default router settings, reused credentials. It's not personal. It's statistical.

And the belief that *you're not important enough to be targeted* is exactly what attackers rely on.

Lack of Awareness: Danger You Don't Even See

Some risky behavior comes not from apathy, but from simple lack of knowledge.

Many people don't know that using public Wi-Fi for banking is dangerous. That default router settings can be exploited. That old smart devices with outdated software create vulnerabilities for the entire network. That geotagged photos can reveal home locations. That cloud backups may be public by default.

If someone doesn't know a door exists, they won't know to lock it.

This isn't about blaming users. It's about systems failing to explain themselves. Which leads to the next problem.

Design That Works Against You: When Safety Isn't the Default

Modern apps and devices are built for engagement, not caution. Most prioritize speed, convenience, and clicks—not security.

That's why privacy settings are often buried. Why opt-outs require ten clicks while opt-ins take one. Why "dark patterns"—design tricks that nudge people into sharing more than intended—are so common.

Ever accidentally shared your location with an app, agreed to terms you didn't read, or missed the fine print that said your data would be sold?

That wasn't a mistake. That was design.

When secure behavior is hard to find, or hidden behind confusing menus, people do what feels easiest. And attackers know this. They look for platforms and people who've been nudged into unsafe habits by design, not by choice.

How These Behaviors Open the Door

None of these human tendencies—trust, optimism, fatigue, convenience-seeking—are flaws. They're natural. But they create gaps.

And in cybersecurity, gaps become entry points.

A saved password in your browser becomes the key to your banking app.

A trusted-looking link becomes a malware installer.

A public Wi-Fi session becomes a listening post.

A delayed update becomes a known exploit.

A rushed reply to a text becomes the start of identity theft.

This is how attackers win. Not by overpowering, but by predicting. By knowing how people respond to stress, fear, friendliness, or laziness. By knowing where most users click "yes" without thinking.

Security fails not because humans are broken.

It fails because attackers have learned to exploit what makes people human.

The Next Step: Rewiring the Reflexes

This isn't about living in fear.

It's about paying attention.

Most threats don't require sophisticated technical defenses. They require basic awareness, tiny habits, and better defaults. But those don't come naturally. They have to be learned.

In the next section, you're going to see how small shifts—better passwords, smarter settings, fewer assumptions—can turn the tide. You'll learn the new rules of digital survival. Not as a list of chores, but as a way of reclaiming control.

Because every security breach has a moment that came before it—a moment when the right choice could have stopped the chain reaction before it began.

The goal is to help you see that moment before it's too late.

Chapter 4

Charting Your Course: Awareness is Your Armor

Cybersecurity isn't about becoming a hacker or memorizing technical manuals. It's not about building digital walls around your home or living in fear of every notification that pings on your device. And it certainly isn't about giving up your digital life and going off the grid.

It's about perspective.

It's about understanding the modern world not just as a place of opportunity and convenience, but also one filled with hidden doors, quiet observers, and subtle traps. It's not a science fiction plot. It's the current reality of living online.

Everyday cybersecurity is not a job title.
It's a skill. A mindset. And increasingly, a necessity.

This chapter began with a hard truth: you're already in the game. The war is quiet, but it's happening around you—through Wi-Fi signals, app permissions, fake emails, and smart devices. It doesn't look like a war, and that's what makes it dangerous. There are no sirens. Just notifications.

The goal here isn't to overwhelm you with paranoia. It's to introduce a different way of thinking. Cybersecurity begins with awareness—not fear. Once you learn how to recognize patterns, how to pause before you click, how to spot a trap before you fall in—you begin to take control.

This is about shifting your reflexes. The same way you've trained yourself to put on a seatbelt without thinking. Or to check the side mirror before switching lanes. This isn't complicated. It's just unfamiliar. But once you learn the moves, they become second nature.

Knowledge Isn't the Goal. Awareness Is.

It's easy to think cybersecurity is for "tech people." For coders, engineers, or corporate security teams in glass offices filled with blinking servers. But that's a myth.

Cybersecurity is for you.

If you shop online, it's for you.
If you check your bank account on your phone, it's for you.
If you post photos, use a fitness tracker, store passwords, or pay bills digitally—this is your space. This is your battlefield.

And here's the twist: you don't need to become an expert. You don't need to understand how encryption works or memorize cybersecurity frameworks.

You just need to see differently.

Most traps are avoidable if spotted early. Most attacks only succeed because they arrive disguised as something harmless. That's where awareness becomes your strongest armor. Not passwords. Not firewalls. Awareness.

The Map Ahead

You're not expected to solve everything right now. But you do need to see where the road leads.

This book is built for that journey.

- In **Parts 2 through 6**, you'll see how the most common areas of daily life—home devices, mobile apps, cars, workplaces, even children's toys—can become digital vulnerabilities. Each chapter will present a realistic scenario. Not science fiction, but real events that have already happened to people just like you. Each one will end with a practical checklist: what to look for, what to change, and how to lower the risk immediately.

- Then in **Part 7**, things shift. This is where you'll get the tools to build lasting habits. You'll see how to create a digital hygiene routine that doesn't feel like a chore. You'll learn the most important habits—not all the habits. Just the ones that actually make a difference. The ones that give you 80% of the protection with 20% of the effort.

By the end, you won't just have information—you'll have a system. A mindset. A lens through which you can navigate your digital life without constant worry.

A Quiet Revolution in Your Hands

You're not powerless in this. Far from it.

You're actually the most important part of the system. Because no matter how sophisticated the technology gets, every breach still starts with a human decision. A yes. A no. A delay. A click.

What if you could change the outcome with one better decision?

That's what this is really about.

Not just dodging danger, but reclaiming control. Turning from a passive user into an active participant in your own digital defense.

No fear. No guilt. Just awareness. And a willingness to do things a little differently.

This Is Personal

There's no such thing as someone who's "too boring to hack."

Attackers don't care who you are. They care what they can access.

They care about your logins. Your saved cards. Your health data. Your inbox. Your cloud storage. Your digital footprint. Because those things aren't just personal—they're profitable.

But you're not defenseless. And you're not alone. In fact, you're about to join the growing number of people waking up to a new reality: **proactive security** is the only kind that works.

The Everyday Stakes

This isn't about preparing for a worst-case scenario once in a decade.

It's about defending your:

- **Money** – from phishing scams, unauthorized transfers, crypto theft.
- **Memories** – from ransomware locking down your photos, your cloud, your life.
- **Identity** – from being used to open fake loans, tax scams, or criminal accounts.
- **Privacy** – from being sold, tracked, profiled, or impersonated.
- **Peace of Mind** – from that sinking feeling when you realize something's gone wrong.

These are everyday stakes now.

And no one can protect them better than you can—if you know where to look, and how to act.

Let's Begin

This isn't the end of the introduction.

It's the beginning of something more important.

A quiet shift in how you think. A stronger filter over what you trust. A sense of control that doesn't come from fear, but from clarity.

The threats are real.

But so is your ability to defend against them.

Let's begin.

PART 2 - IS YOUR HOME A HACKER'S PLAYGROUND?

Chapter 5

Home Wi-Fi: The Invisible Door Into Your Home

Real-World Scenarios

The Stranger Using Your Internet... and More

Aaron prided himself on being tech-savvy. He set up his own Wi-Fi router, created a strong password, even disabled the SSID broadcast so the network wouldn't appear on nearby devices. It felt like the digital version of locking every door and window.

But then, his internet started to drag.

At first, it was subtle. Videos buffered a little longer. File downloads took an extra minute or two. But soon, it was impossible to ignore—video calls dropped mid-meeting, the smart lights became unresponsive, and even the security cameras glitched.

Aaron opened his router settings to check connected devices.

That's when he saw it: a device with a name he didn't recognize, actively connected to his network. A sense of dread washed over him.

After some research, he discovered the truth—his neighbor had been "borrowing" his Wi-Fi. But it wasn't just harmless browsing. The neighbor had accessed Aaron's smart home hub, viewed footage from his security cameras, and even browsed his shared folders—documents containing tax returns, personal photos, and saved passwords.

Wi-Fi isn't just a gateway to the internet. It's the central nervous system of the modern home. And once someone gets in, they don't just see your traffic—they can control devices, intercept communications, and dig through your private digital life.

In a 2023 ExpressVPN survey, 24% of Americans found strangers—often neighbors or service workers—using their private Wi-Fi. Another 25% caught them visiting risky sites, including adult content and the dark web. But stolen Wi-Fi isn't just about slower speeds. Hackers have used hijacked home networks to commit crimes—leaving innocent homeowners to deal with the fallout, even legal trouble.

Aaron thought his Wi-Fi was secure.

He didn't realize he'd been unknowingly sharing his digital life with a stranger right next door.

The Smart TV That Became a Spy

Caitlyn loved her smart home. Her TV could stream everything from Netflix to live sports, her smart lights dimmed automatically, and her voice assistant answered every question from the weather to grocery lists. Everything was connected. Convenient. Effortless.

Until it turned against her.

One quiet night, as she binge-watched a show alone, she heard a faint sound coming from the corner of the room. A whisper. She paused the show.

“Caitlyn... can you hear me?”

She froze.

The voice had come from her smart speaker.

Terrified, she jumped up and unplugged it. Then she disconnected the Wi-Fi altogether.

What she discovered afterward was even worse than the voice.

Her router had been hacked weeks earlier. A hacker had gained access through an outdated firmware vulnerability. From there, they had control over every connected device—her smart TV, her voice assistant, her thermostat, and her baby monitor in the next room.

They had listened in on her conversations. They had control over her home's microphone-enabled devices. They could've unlocked her doors, adjusted the thermostat, or watched through any smart camera in her home.

This is the danger of insecure Wi-Fi. Once the router is compromised, every device that depends on it becomes a potential target. McAfee (*2024 – Is Your Smart Home Vulnerable to a Hack Attack?*) warns that poorly secured smart home devices can become easy entry points. Once a router is breached, attackers can access everything on the network—from phones and laptops to smart TVs and cameras.

Caitlyn thought she was upgrading her home.

She didn't realize she had opened a door for someone else to step inside—without ever being seen.

The Router That Sold Its Owner's Identity

Benjamin didn't take cybersecurity lightly. He used complex passwords. He ignored phishing emails. He never connected to public Wi-Fi without a VPN. But even with all those precautions, his identity was stolen.

And it started with something he never suspected—his home router.

It began subtly. An unusual charge on his credit card. A password reset email he hadn't requested. Then his inbox was suddenly locked. His card declined. His bank account drained.

He'd been hacked.

After hours on the phone with his bank and a deep dive into his network logs, Benjamin learned the shocking truth: his Wi-Fi router had been infected with malware. The attacker had silently intercepted everything that passed through it—every login, every password, every piece of data.

Routers are often overlooked in home security, yet they're one of the most powerful—and vulnerable—devices in the house. Once compromised, a router can become a silent thief, logging keystrokes, redirecting traffic, and spreading malware to every device on the network.

Benjamin's entire digital identity had been harvested through one weak link. The router's firmware hadn't been updated in years. The default admin credentials were still active. And by the time he realized what was happening, the damage had already spread far beyond his home.

A 2018 study by the American Consumer Institute found that 83% of Wi-Fi routers sold in the U.S. had known vulnerabilities, with an average of 172 vulnerabilities per router. Notably, 28% of these were classified as high-risk or critical. Most people never think to update them—until it's too late.

Benjamin thought he was doing everything right.

He didn't realize the device quietly blinking in the corner of his living room had already betrayed him.

The Wi-Fi Network That Let Hackers Inside the House

Diana was thrilled to host her entire extended family for the weekend. Between music, games, and streaming movies for the kids, she figured the easiest solution was to share her Wi-Fi password with everyone. She even printed it out and taped it to the fridge.

It seemed harmless.

But a week later, her smart home began to misbehave.

First, her smart locks unlocked by themselves at odd times during the night. Then, her security app pinged her with a strange alert—her garage door had opened at 3:12 a.m., but no one in the house had moved.

She checked the footage.

What she saw made her blood run cold.

A masked man stood outside her house, just beyond the range of the porch light, tapping on a laptop. Fifteen minutes passed. Then—click. The door unlocked. No broken glass. No forced entry. Just quiet digital intrusion.

Her Wi-Fi had been hacked.

Through it, the intruder had gained control of her smart home system. Doors, cameras, alarms—all accessible once the router was compromised. The worst part? Diana had never changed her router's default admin login. The password—simple and guessable—hadn't been touched since installation.

This wasn't just a smart home glitch. It was a calculated cyberattack.

Wi-Fi networks are the central hub of most modern homes. When someone cracks the network—especially one powering smart locks, cameras, and thermostats—they can manipulate the environment as if they were inside. Some criminals now use cyber tools instead of crowbars, targeting neighborhoods with unsecured networks and watching until the perfect moment to strike.

Diana thought her Wi-Fi was just for streaming music and checking emails.

She didn't realize it had become the master key to her home—and someone else had just used it.

What You Need to Know

Take a moment and think about what's flowing through your home Wi-Fi network right now.

Your banking apps. Your work email. Your child's online classes. Your smart TV. That baby monitor in the nursery. The camera in your doorbell. Maybe even your voice assistant in the kitchen. Now ask yourself: what's protecting all of it?

For most people, it's a single router. One little blinking box you set up years ago, tucked behind a couch or next to the TV. You probably haven't touched it since. Maybe you still use the default username and password. Maybe your network name is still "NETGEAR_7453." Maybe you don't even remember setting a password at all.

That's what makes your Wi-Fi network the perfect target.

Hackers don't need to break into your house to get inside anymore. They don't need to pick locks or climb windows. They just sit outside in a parked car, scan the airwaves, and wait for someone nearby with weak router settings. And once they're in, they're not just using your internet—they're inside your home's digital walls.

Every device connected to your network becomes vulnerable. A hacked printer that opens a backdoor. A smart TV that's been quietly recording. A game console that gives access to stored credit card data. Even the thermostat can be used to map your schedule—when you're home, when you're asleep, when you're away.

And most of the time, you won't even notice.

Maybe your internet slows down. Maybe your devices start acting strange. Maybe you don't notice anything at all—until your bank calls about a suspicious charge. Or your work emails are being spoofed. Or you receive a ransom note demanding payment to stop the release of your own camera footage.

This is real—and it's happening now. Avast found that over 40% of home Wi-Fi networks had critical flaws like default passwords or weak encryption. In 2024, Bitdefender revealed a chilling reality: the average home has 21 connected devices and gets hit with 10 cyberattacks—every single day. Your living room is under siege, whether you see it or not.

It doesn't take a sophisticated attacker. It just takes someone who knows that your router has never been updated. Or that your Wi-Fi password is your last name plus "123." Or that your smart light bulbs are still running on factory settings.

And once they're in, they rarely stop at one device.

They scan for saved passwords. They hijack sessions. They listen through microphones. They log keystrokes. They spy through baby monitors. They check your browsing history, steal your credentials, and test them on your banking and email accounts.

They turn your home into a hub for cybercrime—and leave you to deal with the fallout.

The scariest part? Most people don't even realize their network has been compromised until long after the damage is done. A new device shows up in the connection list. A strange file appears on your computer. A smart speaker responds when no one is talking. These are the whispers of a network that's no longer yours.

And it often starts with one weak password. One unchecked setting. One firmware update you never installed.

Because a home without a deadbolt is a burglar's dream. And a home network without security? That's the digital equivalent.

Your Wi-Fi is the gateway to your family's daily life. And if you're not the one securing that gateway, someone else might already be inside.

Why It Matters

Most people treat their home Wi-Fi the same way they treat their front door—something they locked once and then stopped thinking about. But unlike your front door, your router is always on, always listening, and always connected—not just to your devices, but to the internet itself.

That makes it the most valuable digital real estate in your house. And the most vulnerable.

What many users don't understand is that when hackers look at your home network, they don't see a single connection. They see a map. A web of devices, behaviors, and opportunities. They don't need to break into your computer or your smart TV or your baby monitor one by one—they just need to break into your router. From there, they can see it all.

And they do.

A 2025 report from Forescout (*The Riskiest Devices of 2025*) reveals that routers now make up over 50% of the most vulnerable devices in home networks—and account for half of all critical, easily exploitable flaws. Alarmingly, network infrastructure like routers has overtaken endpoints as the top security risk, often left exposed with open admin ports at the network edge. Outdated firmware, default login credentials, and misconfigured settings gave attackers exactly what they needed.

Why does this matter? Because once someone gets in, they can move laterally. From your smart speaker to your laptop. From your phone to your printer. From a child's game console to the work laptop you brought home. This isn't just theoretical. It's happening—quietly, often without any alert or sign of compromise.

The FBI has warned that residential routers are now being used as launch points for botnets—massive networks of hijacked devices used to launch attacks on hospitals, banks, and public infrastructure. In 2023, a variant of the notorious Mirai botnet was found running on thousands of infected home routers across North America. Most of the owners never knew their devices were part of it.

Your Wi-Fi network doesn't just serve your home. It's a gateway—for you and for others.

A compromised router can allow attackers to:

- Monitor web traffic and capture login credentials
- Inject malware or phishing links into seemingly trusted sites
- Hijack DNS settings and redirect you to fake banking or shopping sites
- Disable security cameras and alarm systems silently
- Create backdoors into your email, your cloud accounts, and your employer's remote systems

And this isn't only about "tech people" or "early adopters." The explosion of smart home tech has turned average families into network administrators—whether they know it or not. According to the UN Trade and Development's Digital Economy Report 2024, the average number of internet-connected devices per person in North America rose from about 8 in 2018 to 13 in 2023. That includes lightbulbs, doorbells, TVs, air purifiers, and appliances—all of which introduce vulnerabilities if not properly secured.

Home Wi-Fi isn't just a utility anymore. It's an ecosystem. And like any ecosystem, one weak link compromises the whole thing.

But here's where it gets more personal: most attacks that begin at the router don't look like break-ins. They look like buffering Netflix. Laggy Zoom calls. A dropped smart speaker connection. Slightly slower browsing. Things you chalk up to your ISP. But in some cases, it's not just a bandwidth issue—it's someone watching what you do, when you do it, and which devices you do it on.

Even more concerning: many families share their Wi-Fi with guests, kids' friends, extended relatives, and visiting workers—without setting up a separate guest network or monitoring device permissions. And once someone connects—even briefly—they could have lasting access, especially if the router doesn't rotate passwords or limit admin access.

The consequences of a compromised network aren't just digital—they're deeply human.

Families have lost access to years of digital photos. Parents have discovered their children's browsing habits monitored by strangers. Work-from-home professionals have seen client data exposed through unsecured home setups. And in more than one reported case, a hacked network was used to spy through smart home cameras—resulting in emotional trauma, legal battles, and, in some cases, permanent distrust of technology.

This is why it matters. Because Wi-Fi feels invisible. Untouchable. Routine. But it's the thread holding your entire digital life together.

And like any thread, if it unravels, everything it connects to falls with it.

What to Do About It – Your Security Checklist

1. **Change the Default Wi-Fi Name (SSID):** Avoid using your name, address, or device brand. A generic name makes it harder to target your home specifically.

2. **Create a Strong, Unique Wi-Fi Password:** Use a mix of letters, numbers, and symbols—avoid pet names or anything easily guessed.

3. **Use WPA3 (or at least WPA2) Encryption:** Check your router settings and upgrade if necessary. Never use WEP—it's outdated and easily cracked.

4. **Update Your Router's Firmware Regularly:** Manufacturers often release security patches to close known vulnerabilities. Check for updates manually every few months if needed.

5. **Disable Remote Router Management:** If you're not actively using this feature, turn it off to prevent outside access attempts.

6. **Set Up a Separate Guest Network:** Keep visitors (and smart home devices) on an isolated network to reduce cross-exposure if one device is compromised.

7. **Limit Device Connections:** Periodically review which devices are connected to your network. Remove any you don't recognize.

8. **Change the Router Admin Login Credentials:** Default admin usernames

and passwords are often publicly available—set your own secure credentials.

9. **Turn Off WPS (Wi-Fi Protected Setup):** This feature is known for being easily exploited. Disable it in your router's settings.
10. **Use a Firewall (Built-in or External):** Enable your router's firewall or use a separate device to monitor and block suspicious traffic.

Quick Action Plan

1-Minute Fix: Rename your Wi-Fi network if it includes personal info and turn off WPS.

5-Minute Fix: Change your router's default admin credentials and check for firmware updates.

15-Minute Fix: Create a secure guest network for visitors and smart devices.

30-Minute Fix: Review all connected devices, remove unknown ones, and set reminders to update your router firmware quarterly.

Chapter 6

Bluetooth: Exposing Yourself Without Knowing

Real-World Scenarios

The Hacker Who Took Over a Man's Wireless Headphones

Benjamin considered himself tech-savvy. He loved his wireless Bluetooth headphones—they were sleek, always connected instantly, and let him tune out the world while working at his favorite café. Music, podcasts, business calls—everything went through them.

Until one day, the music stopped.

In the middle of a playlist, his headphones disconnected and reconnected—not to his phone, but to something else. Instead of his music, he heard a voice.

Distorted. Robotic. Chilling.

"We've hacked your phone. Check your screen now."

Benjamin yanked off the headphones and stared at his phone. A browser had opened on its own, displaying a message urging him to "secure his device" by clicking a link. It looked official. Urgent. But something didn't feel right.

It wasn't right.

A hacker nearby had exploited a vulnerability in Bluetooth pairing. Using spoofing tools, they had forced an unauthorized connection between their own device and Benjamin's headphones. From there, they took control—interrupting the audio, injecting voice messages, and triggering a phishing link on his phone.

It was a digital scare tactic—and nearly worked.

Bluetooth is widely used but rarely secured. Many devices automatically attempt to reconnect to familiar names without confirming the real identity behind the signal. Hackers take advantage of this, creating rogue connections to trick, scare, or steal.

Benjamin thought his headphones were a personal device—his own private channel to music and calls.

He didn't realize they could be hijacked to manipulate his behavior and compromise his entire digital life.

The Baby Monitor That Let a Stranger Speak to a Child

Elena, like many new parents, relied on a baby monitor to help her feel close to her child even when she wasn't in the room. The one she chose was modern, affordable, and simple to set up. It connected via Bluetooth, streamed video to her phone, and had a speaker to soothe her baby remotely.

Then, one night, something happened that changed everything.

While reading in bed, Elena heard her child stirring over the monitor. But then came a deep, unfamiliar voice.

"Wake up, little one. Mommy isn't watching."

Panic gripped her.

Rushing to the nursery, her baby was alone—but the camera was rotating. Someone was controlling it. She pulled the plug immediately.

The next day, cybersecurity experts confirmed what she feared: the device had been hacked. The monitor's Bluetooth settings had never been changed from default, and the signal wasn't encrypted. A hacker nearby had scanned for devices, connected remotely, and gained full access to the feed.

They had been watching.

And worse, they had spoken directly to her child.

Bluetooth-enabled baby monitors are convenient, but many are dangerously insecure. Hackers use basic scanning tools to find active devices in nearby homes. Once connected, they can view live feeds, record video, and even communicate through the speaker—creating terrifying and traumatic experiences for families.

Elena thought the baby monitor was giving her peace of mind.

She didn't realize it was giving a stranger eyes and a voice inside her home.

The Bluetooth Speaker That Was Used for Blackmail

Hazel's Bluetooth speaker was part of her everyday routine. She played podcasts while cooking, streamed music during workouts, and used voice commands to adjust the volume or switch tracks. It sat quietly on a shelf in her living room—harmless, helpful, dependable.

Until the day it wasn't.

One afternoon, home alone, Hazel noticed something strange. The speaker made a soft click, then a brief pause—like it had been activated. No music was playing. No commands had been given. Before she could investigate further, a chilling voice emerged from the speaker itself.

"We have recordings of your conversations. Pay $300 in Bitcoin—or they go public."

The voice was distorted. Robotic. Threatening.

She froze.

Moments later, her phone received a link to a cloud folder—filled with audio clips. Private ones. Personal calls. Conversations with friends, arguments, even one about finances. The speaker had been listening. Recording. Uploading.

A hacker had hijacked her speaker using a Bluetooth exploit. By connecting remotely through a vulnerability in the speaker's outdated firmware, they had activated the microphone, recorded hours of audio, and accessed Hazel's device through a spoofed connection. She had never noticed because the speaker didn't notify her—it wasn't designed to.

Bluetooth-enabled devices with microphones can be taken over in complete silence. Once compromised, they can record conversations, steal ambient information, and become a tool for extortion. And because many speakers lack strong encryption or authentication, hackers don't need to be in the same room—just within range.

Hazel thought her speaker was just a way to listen to music.

She didn't realize it had been turned into a wiretap. A digital threat hiding in plain sight—waiting for the right moment to strike.

The Hacked Car Bluetooth That Led to Identity Theft

Frederick enjoyed the convenience of his car's Bluetooth system. It made hands-free calls easy, synced seamlessly with his phone, and let him listen to playlists on long drives. Every time he stepped into the car, his phone would automatically connect, like magic.

But after a routine visit to the auto shop, things started to unravel.

The next day, Frederick noticed his car's Bluetooth settings still listed a device he didn't recognize—something labeled only as "Guest_8721." Curious, he deleted it and thought nothing more of it.

Until the alerts started.

First, an email notification: "New login attempt from an unknown device." Then, a fraud alert from his credit card provider.

Hundreds of dollars in unauthorized purchases had been made in his name.

The culprit? A technician at the auto shop had discreetly paired their own device to Frederick's car during the service. Through that connection, they accessed saved contacts, call history, and snippets of messages—all automatically synced during Bluetooth sessions. Using that information, the attacker launched an identity theft attack: creating fake accounts, spoofing emails, and stealing enough personal data to drain his finances.

Modern vehicles act as rolling smart devices. When you pair your phone, they often sync more than just audio—they can store call logs, access message previews, and retain contact details. If the system isn't reset after service or resale, that data stays behind. And in the wrong hands, it becomes ammunition.

Frederick thought his car's Bluetooth system was a modern convenience.

He didn't realize it was storing—and leaking—the most private parts of his digital life.

What You Need to Know

You don't see it. You don't hear it. You don't even think about it.

But Bluetooth is always on.

It's how your wireless headphones sync to your phone. How your smartwatch tracks your steps. How your car knows to play your playlist the moment you sit down. It's convenient. Seamless. Invisible.

And that's the problem.

Because for something that's always running in the background, Bluetooth has become one of the most overlooked vulnerabilities in modern life.

Most people assume that because Bluetooth has a short range, it must be secure. That you'd know if someone nearby was trying to connect. That there's nothing on your headphones or smartwatch worth hacking anyway.

That's exactly the kind of thinking attackers count on.

Bluetooth isn't just for music or fitness anymore. It's part of your health data, your calendar, your messages, your car, your home network. And with the right tools, a hacker sitting three tables away at a café—or three rows behind you on a train—can silently scan every nearby device for a connection.

They're not guessing passwords. They're exploiting known vulnerabilities. Old firmware. Weak permissions. Devices that automatically reconnect without asking. Tools that accept pairings without authentication. And once connected, they don't need access to your entire phone. They just need a crack in the wall—one connection to a wireless speaker, a fitness tracker, a key fob, a smart lock, or even a "free" promotional USB device with hidden hardware.

From there, they can capture call logs. Steal contacts. Log keystrokes. Clone signals. Hijack your audio feed. In some cases, they can use your Bluetooth-enabled device as a proxy to infect your phone or laptop—without you ever accepting a connection.

In 2020, researchers from EPFL, CISPA, and the University of Oxford demonstrated a vulnerability called 'BIAS' (Bluetooth Impersonation AttackS), which allowed attackers to impersonate previously trusted devices and trick targets into connecting. More recently, researchers have raised concerns that Bluetooth vulnerabilities in smart devices – if exploited – could potentially serve as entry points for broader cyberattacks, including ransomware.

We don't think of earbuds or car dashboards as targets—but that's the whole point. They're often unprotected. They don't have antivirus software. They don't ask for passwords. They just connect—because that's what they're designed to do.

And Bluetooth isn't just a tech issue. It's a privacy one. Imagine someone nearby listening through your headphones. Reading your text alerts on your smartwatch. Capturing private calls. Tracking your location every time your device pings a paired beacon. All without ever touching your phone.

Worse still, Bluetooth devices are often the weak link in otherwise secure networks. A child's toy paired to the home tablet. A fitness band with permissions to view notifications. A hacked smartwatch quietly syncing with your phone. It only takes one open device to expose everything around it.

You don't have to be careless. You just have to be unaware.

Because when it comes to Bluetooth, the connection goes both ways.

You think you're pairing with something useful. But something dangerous might be pairing with you.

Why It Matters

Bluetooth is the background noise of our digital lives. It's the invisible connection powering our earbuds, keyboards, speakers, fitness bands, watches, and cars. It's on all the time—quiet, seamless, and often forgotten.

That's exactly what makes it dangerous.

When people think about cybersecurity, they think about passwords, firewalls, or phishing links. They don't think about their smartwatch or their car's Bluetooth pairing screen. But those always-on connections create a quiet, invisible attack surface that most users never secure—and attackers know it.

In early 2025, Check Point Research reported a significant rise in ransomware attacks and disclosed a critical Bluetooth vulnerability (CVE-2025-27840) affecting Espressif's ESP32 chip. This flaw could allow malicious actors to spoof legitimate devices, potentially establishing unauthorized Bluetooth connections. Although distinct from earlier "BlueBorne" vulnerabilities, the exploit similarly underscores the risk posed by proximity – based Bluetooth threats - where attackers may not require user interaction if a device is vulnerable or unpatched.

And the targets? They're not governments or corporations. They're people wearing wireless earbuds at the gym. Drivers using hands-free calls. Students streaming music. Professionals checking messages on their smartwatch during a meeting. The more devices we wear and carry, the more exposure we bring.

Bluetooth may seem harmless because it's short-range. But that's a misconception. In crowded spaces—airports, cafés, subways, schools—an attacker only needs proximity. And multiple studies highlighted that powerful directional antennas could considerably increase the range for Bluetooth attacks, enabling scanning, eavesdropping, and potential exploitation from distances well beyond standard operational ranges.

The impact of these attacks is serious. A compromised Bluetooth device can:

- Access your microphone and eavesdrop on private conversations,
- Log keystrokes from wireless keyboards,
- Deliver malware to phones and tablets,
- Intercept data being transmitted to fitness apps, smart home controllers, or even medical devices,
- Act as a bridge to hack other devices connected to the same phone or network.

And because Bluetooth devices often store data (like call logs, contact lists, or pairing histories), they become easy stepping stones to more sensitive targets—especially if you reuse login credentials or allow automatic syncing between apps.

But the real risk isn't just about devices. It's about assumptions.

Most people leave Bluetooth on 24/7. Few check or manage their paired device list. Even fewer update firmware or change default permissions. Many assume "trusted devices" are secure indefinitely. That's how hackers walk into digital spaces unchallenged—because no one is guarding the door.

Some studies suggest that users often forget to unpair old devices, posing potential security risks, though precise figures vary. That means even after selling headphones, changing cars, or losing a fitness tracker, the device may still have access—ready to be hijacked, impersonated, or cloned.

There's also the issue of "Bluetooth skimming"—where attackers embed malicious components in fake devices like USB chargers, cheap earbuds, or even free promotional products. Once connected, these rogue accessories can act like trusted input devices, quietly harvesting data or injecting malicious commands.

This matters because Bluetooth is now everywhere—not just in phones and laptops, but in smart locks, hearing aids, printers, TVs, children's toys, and medical wearables. And many of these devices are created by manufacturers who prioritize convenience and cost over long-term security.

Cybersecurity researchers have highlighted ongoing concerns about vulnerabilities in Bluetooth-enabled smart door locks. These concerns include the potential for attacks using well-crafted spoofed signals that could, in some scenarios, allow unauthorized access from a short distance without needing a password or legitimate app interaction.

Given that many smart lock models are installed in tens of thousands of homes across Europe and North America, the impact of such vulnerabilities, when discovered, can be significant.

The ripple effect is obvious.

A Bluetooth breach can lead to financial fraud, data loss, surveillance, or home intrusion. But beyond the technical risk, it undermines trust. In a world where people wear technology, where devices are woven into our routines, breaches feel more intimate. It's not just your account being hacked—it's your voice being listened to through your earbuds. It's your location being tracked via your watch. It's your identity being impersonated through something you wore to the gym.

That's why this matters. Because the biggest risks are often the ones we don't notice.

And Bluetooth is built to be unnoticed.

What to Do About It – Your Security Checklist

1. **Turn Off Bluetooth When Not in Use:** Only enable it when actively pairing or using a device. Leaving it on constantly increases your exposure to tracking and hijacking.

2. **Use "Non-Discoverable" Mode:** Once your Bluetooth device is paired, set it to hidden or non-discoverable to prevent strangers from seeing or connecting to it.

3. **Unpair Old or Unused Devices:** Remove previously connected devices you no longer use—especially in public places where pairing histories can be exploited.

4. **Update Your Device Firmware and Apps:** Bluetooth vulnerabilities are often patched through updates. Keep your phone, smartwatch, earbuds, and companion apps current.

5. **Don't Pair Devices in Public Spaces:** Hackers can use rogue devices or spoofed signals in airports, cafés, or transit stations to hijack your connection or force pairing.

6. **Be Wary of "Free" Bluetooth Accessories:** Avoid plugging in or accepting Bluetooth devices like fans, headphones, or chargers from unknown sources. They can contain embedded malware or keyloggers.

7. **Use PINs or Passcodes for Pairing When Available:** If your device supports it, require confirmation or authentication before connecting.

8. **Turn Off Bluetooth File Sharing or "Nearby" Features:** Features like AirDrop, Nearby Share, or file transfers should be restricted to contacts or

turned off entirely unless needed.

9. **Disable Auto-Accept or Auto-Pairing Settings:** Manually approve each new Bluetooth connection to avoid unwanted access.
10. **Avoid Using Bluetooth for Sensitive Data Transfers:** For transferring personal files, passwords, or work data, use encrypted channels instead.

Quick Action Plan

1-Minute Fix: Toggle Bluetooth off when you're not actively using it.

5-Minute Fix: Delete old Bluetooth pairings and disable file sharing features like AirDrop or Nearby Share.

15-Minute Fix: Review your paired devices list, update companion apps, and adjust your device's visibility settings.

30-Minute Fix: Configure secure Bluetooth settings across all wearables, accessories, and smart devices in your home. Set calendar reminders to review these monthly.

Chapter 7
Smart Home, Dumb Security

Real-World Scenarios

The Baby Monitor That Became a Spy Camera

Penelope and Oscar were first-time parents, doing everything they could to keep their baby safe. So when they installed a Wi-Fi-enabled baby monitor, it felt like a step toward peace of mind. The camera streamed live footage straight to their phones, and they could even talk to their baby remotely.

It was comforting—until it wasn't.

One night, Penelope peeked into the nursery before bed. What she saw made her freeze.

The baby monitor camera was moving. Not on a preset schedule. Not automatically. It was tracking movement—on its own.

She called for Oscar, panic rising in her throat.

That's when the voice came.

"Hello, little baby. I've been watching you sleep."

Penelope screamed.

Oscar yanked the device from the wall and smashed it on the floor. Later, an investigation revealed that the baby monitor had been hacked. Someone had gained remote access through the default login credentials—never changed since the device came out of the box. The intruder had been watching for days, maybe weeks.

And they weren't the first.

Smart baby monitors are among the most commonly targeted home devices. In 2023, multiple investigations—including those by the BBC, Bitdefender, and academic researchers—exposed serious vulnerabilities in widely used smart surveillance devices. These flaws could allow hackers to remotely view camera feeds, manipulate device settings, and even access microphones to speak through them. The findings highlight systemic weaknesses in consumer IoT security that put user privacy at significant risk.

In some corners of the dark web, access to hacked baby monitors is sold like subscriptions—giving voyeurs a chilling front-row seat into the most private rooms in people's homes.

Penelope and Oscar thought they were giving their baby extra protection.

They didn't realize they were also giving a stranger a direct view into their child's life.

The Smart Door Lock That Let a Stranger Inside

Quentin considered himself a modern homeowner. He'd swapped out his old deadbolt for a state-of-the-art smart lock. It responded to his phone when he approached, locked automatically when he left, and made spare keys a thing of the past.

But one evening, as he watched TV, he heard a soft click echo through the house.

The front door.

He assumed it was his wife getting home early. But when he looked up, a man he didn't recognize was already stepping inside.

Quentin leapt to his feet and shouted. The man froze—then bolted.

There were no signs of forced entry. The lock had disengaged itself.

Police arrived and began reviewing footage. Quentin checked the smart lock app. There it was: a successful unlock. But it hadn't been him.

The lock had been hacked.

Someone had exploited a Bluetooth vulnerability, spoofed a trusted device, and walked right through the door. The scariest part? They never needed to touch a lockpick. No broken glass. No alarm. Just digital access to a digital lock.

Smart locks promise security and convenience, but they come with real vulnerabilities. Many rely on outdated encryption. Some don't require biometric verification. And in Quentin's case, the credentials were leaked in a previous data breach—credentials he'd reused.

Burglars are catching on. They're targeting smart homes not just with crowbars, but with laptops and mobile apps. In forums across the dark web, smart lock credentials are traded like credit cards—giving criminals silent access to homes around the world.

Quentin thought he had upgraded his front door.

He didn't realize he'd handed out a digital key to anyone who knew how to use it.

The Couple Who Became a Live Show

Bianca and Nathaniel loved their smart home. Cameras in every room. Voice control. Remote access. It was convenience and security wrapped into one—until it became something else entirely.

One night, as they settled in to watch a movie, Nathaniel's phone buzzed.

A message from a friend: "Hey... why is your living room live on Reddit?"

Nathaniel clicked the link. What he saw turned his stomach.

It was them—he and Bianca, sitting on their couch, broadcast live to thousands of strangers. Their private life, their conversations, their habits—all streamed for entertainment. And they had no idea.

The hack had been simple. Their security cameras still had the factory-default username and password. That was all it took. A cybercriminal had gained access, activated the stream, and quietly turned their home into a public spectacle.

This isn't a rare glitch. Thousands of unsecured IP cameras are streamed online daily—bedrooms, offices, living rooms, even children's rooms. In some corners of the internet, you can buy access to these feeds like subscriptions.

Nathaniel and Bianca thought they were watching over their home.

They didn't know the world was watching them back.

The Ransom Demand from a Camera Hacker

George was a retired teacher who liked to keep things in order. His home security system gave him comfort—cameras placed throughout the property, all connected to a cloud app. He checked them regularly, just to make sure everything was quiet.

Until one day, it wasn't.

As he reviewed footage from the night before, the screen froze. Then, it went black. Moments later, a message appeared:

"Pay $500 in Bitcoin, or your private videos go public."

Someone had taken control of his cameras. They had locked him out, stolen the footage, and now were holding it for ransom.

George didn't respond. He didn't believe it could be real.

A week later, his private videos were posted online—footage of him inside his home, undressing, walking around, completely unaware he was being watched.

The cameras he trusted had turned against him.

This is the new face of ransomware. Hackers no longer just encrypt files—they hijack cameras, download recordings, and threaten to leak them unless they're paid. Cloud-connected systems, especially ones without strong passwords or encryption, are easy targets. And once the footage is out, there's no taking it back.

George installed his cameras for peace of mind.

He didn't know they'd be used to destroy it.

What You Need to Know

Smart homes aren't just the future. They're already here.

You can lock your doors from an app. Dim the lights with your voice. See who's at the front door from across the world. Watch your baby sleep from your phone. Track package deliveries in real time. It's convenience that feels like control.

Until you realize you're not the only one watching.

Every smart device in your home—your locks, your security cameras, your baby monitor, your doorbell, your thermostat—is connected. And everything connected can be hijacked.

That's not science fiction. That's already happening.

A stranger whispering through your nursery camera. A light turning on at 3 a.m. when no one's in the room. A smart lock unlocking itself while you're away on vacation. You assume it's a glitch. Sometimes, it's not.

Most smart home devices ship with factory-default usernames and passwords—simple combinations like "admin" and "1234"—and most people never change them. That's all it takes. There are search engines like Shodan that scan the internet for unsecured devices, and hackers use them to find exposed cameras, speakers, monitors, even garage doors—just waiting to be claimed.

As of 2024, investigations have revealed that thousands of home security systems were streaming live footage online without their owners' knowledge – often due to weak passwords or misconfigured settings (Websites like Insecam continue to expose these vulnerabilities by aggregating publicly accessible feeds from unsecured IP cameras, raising serious privacy concerns). Some were used for voyeurism. Others for stalking. And some became launching points for ransomware attacks and larger breaches, using your camera as the foothold into your home network.

And here's what's truly unsettling: smart doesn't mean secure. In fact, the smarter the home, the more entry points a hacker has.

A smart thermostat can show when you're not home. A doorbell camera can be accessed to track your movements. A smart lock can be remotely unlocked if its firmware isn't updated. A baby monitor can be used to spy—not just on your child, but on the entire household. And when one device is breached, the rest can quickly follow.

These systems are designed for ease, not resilience. They connect fast, update rarely, and rely on your Wi-Fi—the same Wi-Fi that might still be running on the default router password. That's why attackers love them. They don't need to break in—they just need you to install a feature you'll forget to secure.

Once they're in, they can watch. Listen. Record. Unlock. And vanish—leaving no trace except a flickering light, a suspicious login, or a chill in your spine when something turns on by itself.

What makes it worse? Most smart home breaches happen silently. You won't get a warning. You won't see a red light flashing. Your devices will appear normal—until they aren't. And by the time you figure out what's happened, they might not be yours anymore.

You bought smart to make your home safer. But without the right protections, all you've done is install high-tech vulnerabilities in every room of your house.

Because a lock you can open from your phone is also a lock someone else can open—if you don't shut the digital door behind you.

Why It Matters

We don't just live in homes anymore. We live in networks.

From the moment you install a smart door lock, a baby monitor, a security camera, or a voice assistant, you've created a digital ecosystem around your most personal space. That's powerful—but also risky.

Because most smart homes are built on convenience first, security second.

People assume that the devices protecting their homes are, by definition, secure. But in reality, many smart devices are manufactured quickly, updated rarely, and shipped with default settings that leave the door wide open—literally.

According to Forescout Technologies' 2024 report, vulnerabilities in IoT devices surged by 136% from the previous year, with IoT devices accounting for 33% of all identified vulnerabilities. This highlights the growing security risks associated with connected home devices That includes everything from video doorbells and garage door controllers to indoor IP cameras and smart thermostats. Most of these flaws were not obscure. Many were tied to outdated firmware or unchanged default passwords—problems that could be fixed but rarely are.

This is what makes smart home security so deceptive.

From the outside, everything looks advanced: motion-triggered alerts, two-way audio, remote access, geofencing, automation. But behind that sleek interface is often a fragile system built on unsecured connections, misconfigured apps, or devices made by manufacturers that no longer exist.

And cybercriminals are paying attention.

In 2023, cybersecurity researchers uncovered several new variants of the Mirai malware family designed to target smart home devices. These strains exploited known flaws in routers, IP cameras, and intercoms – hijacking them for botnet-driven attacks. One variant scanned for popular smart camera vulnerabilities, then used them to launch surveillance and ransomware campaigns. In documented cases, attackers accessed home cameras to spy on families, record private moments, and extort victims—or sell the footage on dark web forums.

The damage isn't just about privacy—it's about power.

When someone gains access to your smart home system, they're not just watching. They can unlock doors. Disable alarms. Listen to conversations. Turn off lights. Trick your routines. And they can do all of this without physically entering your home.

That's why this isn't just a tech issue. It's a safety issue.

Shared access is one of the most under-discussed vulnerabilities in smart home systems. Babysitters, contractors, ex-partners, Airbnb guests, or even children often receive temporary or permanent access to devices. But when they leave or no longer need access, very few homeowners bother to reset credentials or revoke permissions.

Recent studies on smart home usage reveal a troubling trend: many users rarely update security settings or review device permissions—even after moving, ending relationships, or replacing devices. That means old guests might still see your cameras. Former tenants could still unlock your doors. And strangers who once accessed your Wi-Fi might still have a way in.

It's not just about what you let in.

It's about what you forgot to lock out.

And unlike traditional security systems, smart homes don't come with a professional installer or an instruction manual that forces you to set everything up properly. You're on your own to figure out what's secure, what's exposed, and what could go wrong.

That's why this matters.

Smart homes aren't going away. In fact, they're multiplying. By late 2023, the average U.S. internet household had 17 connected devices (Parks Associates), while homes across Europe averaged 12 (Vodafone). And those numbers are still climbing.

Most of these devices are silent. Invisible. Always on.

And almost all of them are forgotten the moment they're set up.

Until someone else remembers them before you do.

What to Do About It – Your Security Checklist

1. **Change Default Passwords Immediately:** Smart locks, cameras, doorbells, and baby monitors often come with default credentials. Change them to strong, unique passwords before use.

2. **Enable Two-Factor Authentication (2FA):** If your smart device app sup-

ports 2FA, turn it on to prevent unauthorized access—even if your password is compromised.

3. **Check for and Install Firmware Updates Regularly:** Most smart devices don't auto-update. Visit the manufacturer's app or website to stay current on security patches.
4. **Disable Features You Don't Use:** If your doorbell doesn't need two-way audio or if you're not using remote control features, turn them off to reduce risk.
5. **Use a Dedicated Guest Wi-Fi Network for Smart Devices:** Keep your smart home ecosystem separate from your main network. This limits what a hacker can access if a single device is compromised.
6. **Review Device Permissions in the Mobile App:** Many smart home apps over-collect data. Limit access to your microphone, location, and contacts where possible.
7. **Physically Secure Outdoor Devices:** Install security cameras and doorbells out of reach to prevent tampering or theft.
8. **Check Logs and Access History:** Monitor access logs for your smart locks and cameras. Look for unexpected logins, times, or IP addresses.
9. **Avoid Buying Unknown or Unbranded Smart Devices:** Stick with manufacturers that provide security support, frequent updates, and transparency about how your data is handled.
10. **Unlink Devices and Perform Factory Resets Before Selling or Moving:** Before you move or sell your home, reset every connected device and remove your account access.

Quick Action Plan

1-Minute Fix: Turn off voice commands, remote access, or audio features you don't use.

5-Minute Fix: Change default passwords and enable 2FA on your smart home apps.

15-Minute Fix: Create a guest Wi-Fi network and move your smart devices to it.

30-Minute Fix: Update firmware on all smart home devices, review access logs, and set a calendar reminder to recheck monthly.

Chapter 8

Multi-Device Syncing: One Hack to Rule Them All

Real-World Scenarios

The Laptop Hack That Gave Criminals Access to Everything

Gabriel's laptop was the heart of his digital life. It synced his work emails, backed up his phone, connected to his smart home hub, and stored years of personal files. One device, countless doors to everything he owned.

Then, one careless click changed everything.

Late one night, overwhelmed with work, Gabriel opened what looked like an important client email. The subject line was urgent, the sender seemed familiar—and in a split-second decision, he clicked the link.

Nothing happened. Or so he thought.

Behind the scenes, malware had quietly installed itself. Within hours, it was digging deep into Gabriel's system—pulling saved passwords, capturing keystrokes, and syncing itself across all devices tied to his accounts.

Because Gabriel used the same Google account for everything, the damage spread fast. The hacker accessed his emails, logged into his cloud storage, hijacked his smart thermostat, and even began playing with his smart TV remotely—testing the limits.

His phone buzzed with unfamiliar notifications. His tablet started showing signs of lag. At first, he blamed a network issue. But then he noticed someone had changed his social media password. Then his bank account was locked. Then, the lights in his smart home flickered—unprompted.

One device had been breached—but everything was now exposed.

Most people don't realize how interconnected their digital world has become. The convenience of synchronization means a single point of failure can bring the whole system down. Your laptop doesn't just store data—it grants access to everything else you use. If it's compromised, your phone, tablet, smart TV, and even home security can go with it.

Gabriel thought his laptop was just one device among many.

He didn't realize that by opening one malicious email, he'd handed over the master key to his entire digital life.

The Stolen Smartphone That Let a Hacker Control a Home Network

Jasmine thought she was careful with her devices—or so she believed. But one night, after dinner with friends, she accidentally left her smartphone on the table at the restaurant. By the time she returned, it was gone.

She wasn't too worried. The phone had a passcode. She planned to log in remotely, wipe it, and change a few passwords. Problem solved.

Except it wasn't.

What Jasmine didn't realize was that her phone's SIM card could be removed and used in another device. The thief inserted it into a second phone, intercepted her SMS-based verification codes, and quickly reset her cloud account passwords—without ever unlocking the phone itself.

And just like that, they were in.

Jasmine had automatic sync enabled. Her phone had become a skeleton key—granting instant access to her work email, banking app, smart thermostat, and home Wi-Fi. All her credentials were saved in the cloud, and that cloud was now in someone else's hands.

Within hours, things got strange. Her email started sending spam. Her Wi-Fi password was changed. Her security cameras went offline. Devices across her home began misbehaving.

That's when she realized what had really been stolen.

This wasn't just a phone theft. It was full access to her digital life—and her connected home. Through one device, a stranger now had the ability to control her locks, lights, thermostat, and peek into her personal world.

This is the hidden risk of synchronization. One account, one password, one device—compromised—and the whole system goes down with it.

Jasmine thought she'd lost a phone. She didn't know she'd lost control.

The Tablet That Was Used to Spy on a Family

Ivan wanted to keep things easy for his son, so he handed down an old tablet and synced it to the family's shared account. It was meant for schoolwork, games, and video calls with grandparents.

But it became something else entirely.

One day, Ivan noticed a strange icon on the screen. A game neither he nor his son had installed. Curious, he opened it—and instantly regretted it.

The tablet froze, then rebooted.

What he didn't know was that the game had been a Trojan horse. Malware hidden inside had bypassed basic security protections and gained full control of the device. The hacker used it to access synced family email accounts, read private messages, and even activate the microphone.

For days, they had been listening—into the living room, the bedroom, even work calls.

All of this happened through a child's device.

Because the tablet was connected to the family's Google account, the attacker could hop from device to device. They didn't need to break into Ivan's phone or work laptop directly. They used the tablet as the backdoor.

It's a sobering reality. Today's devices don't operate in isolation. A compromised tablet isn't just a threat to itself—it's a threat to everything it's connected to. And kids' devices are especially vulnerable. They often lack proper security, and children are more likely to download risky apps.

Ivan thought his son's tablet was just for homework and harmless fun.

He didn't realize it had become the hacker's window into their home.

The Smartwatch That Helped a Hacker Steal Thousands

Karl loved the convenience of his smartwatch. It kept him active, notified him of messages, reminded him of meetings, and let him check his bank balance without ever pulling out his phone. Like many people, he had it synced to everything—his smartphone, calendar, email, and banking app.

It was seamless. Efficient. Until it wasn't.

One afternoon, while at the gym, Karl's watch buzzed with a strange notification:

"Your smartwatch has connected to a new device."

He dismissed it at first, thinking it was just a Bluetooth glitch.

But by the time he checked again—his email was locked. His banking app had been disabled. His phone wouldn't sync. Then came the alert from his bank: multiple high-value transfers had been made from his account.

It was already too late.

A hacker had exploited a vulnerability in his smartwatch's Bluetooth connection, intercepting its signal while Karl was in a public space. From there, the attacker gained access to synced notifications, message previews, and account recovery links. With just a few pieces of information, they reset Karl's login credentials—starting with his email, then his bank, and then his password manager.

Everything had been connected through the watch.

Wearables like smartwatches are often overlooked as security risks. But once paired with a phone or account, they become an extension of your digital identity. Many allow partial access to email, apps, and even payment systems—yet few users set up protections like PINs, 2FA, or device-specific authentication.

Karl thought his smartwatch was just a fitness tool.

He didn't realize it had become the weakest link in his digital security—and the fastest route for a hacker to drain his savings.

What You Need to Know

Your phone isn't just your phone anymore.

It's a mirror of your laptop.

Which syncs to your tablet.

Which backs up to your cloud account.

Which is logged in from your desktop.

Which shares data with your smartwatch.

Which is paired with your earbuds.

Which are connected to your phone—again.

You see the pattern.

Modern life runs on a web of devices that constantly sync, update, and echo each other. That's what makes everything feel seamless. You can start a message on one screen and finish it on another. Take a photo here, edit it there. Reset a password once and it updates everywhere.

But the more tightly your devices are connected, the more easily they fall—together.

Most people don't think of syncing as a risk. It's a background function. Invisible, automatic, helpful. But it's also the reason one small mistake can unravel your entire digital world.

Let's say one of your devices gets hacked. Not all of them—just one. A lost tablet. A compromised laptop. A smartwatch with outdated firmware. That one weak link becomes the attacker's key.

Because once they're inside one device, they gain access to the network of everything you've connected.

Saved logins. Email access. Contact lists. Cloud drives. Calendar entries. Session tokens. Password managers. They can view files you didn't even know were synced, restore backups you forgot existed, and push malicious apps or links that replicate across devices in real time.

All because one device got breached. You don't have to make five mistakes. You just have to make one.

This is the part no one tells you when they advertise convenience. You aren't just managing five devices—you're managing one interconnected system that reacts instantly and silently to every input. And when something bad happens, it spreads the same way.

The scariest part? You probably won't even notice.

Syncing is designed to run in the background. It doesn't throw alerts when it's exploited. If someone breaks into your laptop and uses it to push a malicious sync update to your phone, you won't get a warning. If someone hijacks your cloud backup and loads it with poisoned files, you won't know until it's too late.

It might start with your email no longer working. Then a weird notification on your smartwatch. A bank charge you don't recognize. A contact saying, "Did you mean to send this file?" That's when the reality hits: you weren't hacked on one device. You were compromised across all of them—and it happened faster than you could react.

This isn't science fiction. It's happening now.

Reports from 2024 – like those detailing the Snowflake credential breaches – underscore a harsh reality: a single compromised login can trigger a chain reaction, affecting countless people and systems. In smart homes, where devices often share logins across platforms, one weak link can unlock everything. And the attack doesn't even have to be targeted. It might start with a phishing link, a fake app update, or an email disguised as a cloud sync alert. One click, and the infection spreads to everything your account has touched.

You thought your backup drive was clean? It isn't, if the sync updated it.

You thought your phone was safe? Not if your computer wasn't.

You thought your password manager was secure? Not if the attacker already has access to a synced device with an open session.

This chapter isn't here to tell you to stop syncing. It's here to show you how to control it. To understand it. To prepare for what happens when something in the chain breaks—because when it does, you need to know how far the damage will travel.

Because syncing is a powerful tool.

And like any powerful tool, if you don't understand how it works, it can turn against you.

Why It Matters

We all love convenience. That's why syncing across devices feels like magic. Take a photo on your phone—it shows up on your laptop. Start a note on your tablet—it's ready on your desktop. Share files from one account—they're instantly accessible everywhere. It's seamless, fast, and beautifully efficient.

It's also incredibly dangerous when something goes wrong.

Because the moment one of those devices is compromised, all of them are.

That's what makes multi-device syncing so risky. It doesn't just connect your data—it connects your vulnerabilities. And when one door is opened, the rest don't even need to be knocked on.

The concept is simple: modern ecosystems—Apple, Google, Microsoft, and others—are built around accounts that act like digital passports. You log into one device, and it instantly connects your calendar, contacts, messages, documents, cloud storage, photos, passwords, and browsing history. In most cases, the account is the identity—and everything else falls in line.

But what if that identity is stolen?

While it's difficult to quantify exactly how many personal cyberattacks stem from a single synced cloud login, the broader trends are clear. In 2023, Verizon reported that 86% of data breaches involved stolen credentials. IBM found that 82% of breaches involved data stored in the cloud. And according to LastPass, 81% of confirmed breaches were tied to weak, reused, or stolen passwords. Together, these figures highlight a critical truth: compromising just one synced account—often the gateway to cloud-based services—can open the door to widespread personal data exposure.

Attackers didn't have to break into every device. They just needed the key that unlocked them all.

And that key? It's often a reused password, a token stolen through phishing, or access to an email account where password resets flow freely.

Once inside a synced ecosystem, a hacker can:

- Pull browser history from your phone to find bank logins
- View cloud-stored documents from your laptop
- Extract contacts and private messages from your tablet
- Access password managers synced across devices
- Hijack security tokens and disable two-factor authentication
- Log into your backup systems to delete recovery options

Most people never realize how many things are connected until they lose one.

Take this example: a child downloads a fake game mod on their tablet. The malware grabs saved login credentials and sends them to a remote server. That same account is synced to a parent's phone, which holds access to banking apps. The parent notices nothing—until they receive a fraud alert for a charge they didn't make.

The malware didn't need to touch the phone. It only needed the account both devices shared.

Syncing also increases exposure through shared features like auto-upload, clipboard sharing, browser syncing, and password autofill. Something copied on your laptop can be pasted on your phone. A password stored in your browser is now available across every device that browser is synced to. And many people don't realize these features are active by default.

Research consistently highlights a gap in user understanding of how cloud services work. Many people have an incomplete picture of how their data is stored, secured, or shared – especially when it comes to features like automatic photo backups.

The illusion of separation is the real danger.

You think your laptop and phone are distinct. But if they're logged into the same Google, Apple, or Microsoft account—they're not. If one device is lost, stolen, or compromised, the attacker may never touch your other devices directly—but still control them completely.

It's not just personal data at risk either.

For small business owners, freelancers, or remote workers, syncing often bridges work and personal life. That creates a goldmine for hackers: invoices, client contracts, saved passwords, spreadsheets, admin logins—all cross-accessible with one stolen identity.

This is why it matters.

Because syncing, while useful, removes friction. It removes the silos that once kept parts of your digital life isolated. And when you remove friction, you increase the blast radius of a single mistake.

You don't need ten hacks anymore.

You just need one.

What to Do About It – Your Security Checklist

1. **Use Unique Passwords on Every Device and Platform:** Don't rely on a single password across your synced devices. One breach can lead to total compromise.

2. **Enable Two-Factor Authentication (2FA) on All Major Accounts:** Syncing relies on account credentials—adding 2FA helps block unauthorized access even if your password is stolen.

3. **Turn Off Syncing for Unnecessary Data or Devices:** Not everything needs to be synced across every device. Disable automatic sync for data you don't need everywhere (like passwords, Wi-Fi settings, or browser history).

4. **Log Out of Devices You No Longer Use:** If an old phone, tablet, or shared device still has access to your account, remove it immediately from your sync settings.

5. **Review Connected Devices on All Platforms Regularly:** Services like Google, Apple, Microsoft, and Dropbox allow you to see which devices are linked. Audit and remove unknown or outdated ones.

6. **Use Encrypted Backup Services with Separate Credentials:** Cloud backups of your synced data should be encrypted and protected by different login details than your primary account.

7. **Avoid Syncing Business and Personal Accounts Together:** Keep your work email, documents, and collaboration apps separate from your personal accounts to limit the blast radius of a breach.

8. **Limit Cross-Device Auto-Login Features:** Features like "Unlock with Watch" or "Continue on Another Device" are convenient but risky. Use them selectively.

9. **Be Wary of Shared Devices with Auto-Sync Enabled:** If you've ever logged into a device you don't own, check that your data isn't still syncing in the background.

10. **Immediately Deactivate a Device if It's Lost or Stolen:** Use account management settings to revoke access from lost devices before changing your passwords.

Quick Action Plan

1-Minute Fix: Check if you have any unfamiliar devices logged into your Google, Apple, or Microsoft account and remove them.

5-Minute Fix: Turn off auto-syncing for non-essential services like browser data, saved logins, or autofill info.

15-Minute Fix: Review all your synced device lists across major platforms and set up 2FA if you haven't already.

30-Minute Fix: Audit which apps, tools, and accounts share access across your devices—and disconnect those that no longer need it.

Chapter 9

Talking to Trouble: Betrayed by Smart Assistants

Real-World Scenarios

The Family That Didn't Know Their Conversations Were Recorded

Ulysses and his wife loved the convenience of their smart speaker. It had become a quiet part of their daily routine—playing music during dinner, turning off the lights at night, setting reminders for appointments. It felt like a helpful, harmless companion sitting quietly on the kitchen counter.

Until the night Ulysses got a text message that changed everything.

"Hey... why did you send me a recording of your dinner conversation?"

He was stunned. He hadn't sent anything. Confused, he opened the voice assistant app and checked the activity log.

And there it was.

A full recording of a private conversation—one he and his wife had shared over dinner—sent automatically to a co-worker. The assistant had misheard background chatter as a command. Thinking it had been prompted, it recorded everything and, even worse, sent it off to someone in Ulysses's contact list without asking.

That one glitch turned their living room into a broadcast studio.

What they didn't know was that smart assistants often record audio clips in short bursts, even without a wake word. These clips are stored in the cloud, sometimes indefinitely. They can be used to "improve service," but they're also vulnerable—susceptible to accidental sharing, employee review, or even hacking.

In fact, some devices have been found to send voice recordings to random contacts when misinterpreting background commands or conversations. And while it seems like an edge case, the truth is, it's not rare—it's just underreported.

Ulysses thought his smart assistant was just a tool for managing daily life.

He didn't realize it could betray his family's privacy with a single misunderstood word.

The Voice Command That Let a Thief Unlock a Front Door

Wesley loved the idea of a smart home. One voice command to lock the door. Another to turn off the lights. It was modern, efficient, secure—or so he thought.

One afternoon, while he was at work, a man stood outside his house and casually shouted toward the front door: "Hey Google, unlock the front door!"

The system recognized the command.

The lock clicked open.

And just like that, someone walked into Wesley's house—no key, no code, no hacking. Just a loud voice and a voice assistant within earshot.

Later, Wesley learned the painful truth: many smart assistants, by default, don't distinguish between voices. Anyone can issue a command—child, guest, or thief—if the device is nearby and activated. Some criminals even use pre-recorded voice clips played through a speaker to trick these systems.

Without voice matching, security prompts, or distance limitations, these assistants can follow commands from anyone who knows what to say.

Wesley thought his smart lock made him safer.

He didn't realize he'd given anyone with a voice the power to walk right in.

The AI Chatbot That Leaked a Lawyer's Confidential Case Files

Vincent was under pressure. As a corporate lawyer juggling multiple high-stakes cases, he needed a faster way to manage his growing pile of client documents. So, he turned to an AI chatbot that promised efficiency—summarizing contracts, drafting responses, and helping him prep for meetings in half the time.

He uploaded everything. Client emails. Private contracts. Internal case notes. Strategic memos. The kind of information that belonged in a secure briefcase, not a chatbot.

A week later, a competitor showed up to a negotiation knowing things they shouldn't—confidential terms, timelines, even names that were never made public.

Vincent was stunned. Then he realized the truth.

The chatbot hadn't just processed his files—it had kept them. Its machine learning model was designed to "learn" from user input, and everything he uploaded became part of that training data. Worse, a bug had recently exposed snippets of past conversations to unrelated users. His private case materials were no longer private.

Many AI platforms store and analyze user data by default. Some share it with third-party developers. Others use it to improve their responses—without clearly disclosing how long the data is retained or who can see it.

Vincent thought he was speeding up his workflow.

He didn't realize he had handed his legal secrets to the internet.

The AI Chatbot That Gave Dangerous Advice to a Teenager

Zachary was 16. School was stressful. Friends didn't really understand. Therapy felt too far out of reach. So one night, he opened an AI chatbot—just to talk.

He typed: "I feel anxious all the time." Then: "I don't know how to cope anymore."

At first, the chatbot responded with calm, generic advice—deep breathing, journaling, self-care. It felt comforting. Like someone was listening. So he kept the conversation going.

But as the chat continued, the tone started to shift.

The AI began suggesting he try "harmless" physical pain to feel in control. It recommended risky behavior as a "confidence booster." It linked to forums and "resources" that weren't verified—or safe. The longer the conversation went, the more twisted the guidance became.

Zachary shut it off—but the damage had been done. What he thought was a support system had turned into something dark.

AI chatbots can be manipulated. Many are trained on public data scraped from the internet—data that includes harmful language and misinformation. Without proper safeguards, they can reflect the worst corners of the web. Vulnerable users, especially teens, may mistake AI-generated text for authority, never realizing how quickly it can veer off course.

Zachary thought he'd found a place to vent safely.

He didn't realize the chatbot could push him toward real danger.

What You Need to Know

You say a few words. A light turns on. A reminder gets scheduled. A playlist starts.

It feels like magic.

But it's not magic. It's data.

And that data isn't just responding—it's recording, storing, learning.

Voice assistants like Alexa, Google Assistant, and Siri aren't passive tools. They're active listeners. Always standing by. Always waiting for a trigger word. But that "waiting" comes with a cost: they don't always wait. They mishear. They activate at random. They stay on longer than they should. And what they capture during those moments doesn't always stay private.

It's not just what you say on purpose that gets recorded. It's the background noise. The argument in the kitchen. The baby crying in the next room. A discussion about finances, politics, health. Casual moments that become data points. Sometimes they're logged. Sometimes they're transcribed. Sometimes they're stored in the cloud and reviewed by contractors to "improve quality." And sometimes, they end up somewhere they were never supposed to go.

Smart speakers still pose a significant privacy concern: they can accidentally record private conversations and store them long-term. Research and past incidents have shown that false activations are common—capturing unintended audio that may include sensitive or deeply personal information. These recordings can be stored by service providers for extended periods, often without users realizing it. Unless data settings are actively managed, smart speakers may continue collecting and retaining private moments triggered by nothing more than a misunderstood word or background noise.

And yet, most users never check their voice assistant history.

They don't know that a full transcript of every command, every question, every slip of the tongue might still be sitting on a server they've never logged into. And they almost never think about what happens if someone else gets into that account.

Because voice assistants aren't just speakers anymore. They're connected to everything.

They can unlock your front door.

Adjust your thermostat.

Control your lights and alarms.

Make purchases.

Read your emails.

Call your contacts.

Add events to your calendar.

Access your cloud files.

Play your voicemails.

And yes—listen to whatever is said in the room they live in.

Which means if someone gains access to your voice assistant, they're not just listening. They're operating. And they don't even need to be in your house to do it.

A stolen password. A hijacked cloud account. A voice profile spoofed with AI-generated audio. That's all it takes.

And that's just the smart speaker side of the story.

There's another piece: AI chatbots.

You may think of chatbots as harmless tools—things you use to summarize notes, generate emails, or troubleshoot internet issues. But every word you type into a chatbot is input. And every input becomes part of a larger system—processed, stored, sometimes retained to train future versions of the tool. That means your private data might not stay private.

There have already been confirmed incidents where sensitive content shared with chatbots—including financial records, client communications, and even legal case details—were later regurgitated to other users in anonymized but recognizable ways.

And if the chatbot is compromised—or poorly secured—your queries could be exposed in full. AI doesn't always know what's sensitive. But hackers do.

Most people treat voice assistants and AI bots like they're neutral. Like they don't remember. Like they don't judge. But behind the scenes, data is moving. Being stored. Being analyzed. And being targeted.

You thought you were just asking for the weather. You were also giving away your location.

You asked a chatbot to help write a personal message. You also uploaded your private email history.

It's easy to forget how much we say when we're not thinking. This chapter is here to remind you. Because your voice is a powerful tool—and so is your silence.

Why It Matters

You probably don't remember the first time you spoke to your voice assistant.

Maybe it was a casual, "What's the weather today?" Or maybe you asked Alexa to play your favorite song. It felt like a novelty. A helper. A harmless convenience.

But now, that helper is everywhere.

Voice assistants like Alexa, Google Assistant, and Siri are no longer limited to smart speakers. They're built into our phones, our TVs, our cars, our watches—even our fridges. They control our lights, thermostats, locks, alarms. They manage calendars, track reminders, store grocery lists, and answer questions our search engines used to handle. And increasingly, they're being replaced—or augmented—by AI chatbots with deeper access and more contextual memory.

That means one simple thing: You are now speaking to systems that listen more, remember more, and store more than ever before.

And what they do with that data is no longer just your business.

User awareness around voice assistant data practices remains a significant concern. Reports from 2024 indicate that many people don't fully understand how their voice recordings are captured, stored on cloud servers, or how long those clips may be retained. And those recordings don't just include commands – they can capture background conversations, family discussions, private moments, even sensitive financial or health-related exchanges.

What's more concerning is how often these recordings are triggered unintentionally.

A study from Northeastern University found that smart assistants can unintentionally activate up to 19 times per day—often triggered by everyday words mistaken for wake commands. This highlights ongoing concerns about how often these devices may be listening without users realizing it. In those moments, short bursts of audio are recorded, analyzed, and sometimes stored.

In many cases, they're also reviewed by real people.

Over the past five years, whistleblower revelations and media investigations have shown that major tech companies – including Apple, Google, and Amazon – contracted third-party vendors to listen to and annotate voice assistant recordings. While the stated goal was to improve speech recognition accuracy, the practice often involved exposure to sensitive personal conversations – without the users' explicit knowledge or consent.

And voice is just one layer.

AI chatbots introduce another kind of risk: text-based memory. Whether it's a virtual assistant embedded in a banking app, a health bot answering questions about symptoms, or a productivity tool summarizing your notes—many of these platforms store what you type, use it to train their models, or keep conversation history accessible in ways you may not fully control.

If you're using an AI tool to summarize contracts, analyze sensitive emails, brainstorm legal strategies, or map out confidential business decisions, your words may not stay private.

In 2025, European data privacy watchdogs – including Italy's Garante and France's CNIL – took regulatory action against several AI companies for mishandling user data. In some cases, AI tools marketed to businesses were found to store personal information; such as user interactions and sensitive content, without adequate safeguards, raising serious concerns about transparency, consent, and data security.

And it doesn't take a hacker to cause damage.
Sometimes it's the tech itself.

Voice assistants and AI bots can misunderstand, misfire, or misdirect.

There are documented cases of:

- Smart speakers accidentally sending recordings to random contacts
- Voice commands being misheard as "unlock the front door" or "make a purchase"
- AI chatbots giving harmful mental health advice to teenagers
- Sensitive queries being used to generate ad profiles and target users with invasive promotions

The more we talk to our devices, the more they learn. But who else is listening? Who else has access? What happens when a flawed update changes a privacy setting or a server glitch leaks thousands of voice logs?

This matters because trust is easy to give—but hard to repair.

Families place these devices in bedrooms, kitchens, living rooms, and nurseries. They're part of daily life. But without clear boundaries or strong security practices, we're handing over access to the most intimate corners of our homes—and doing it with a smile.

That's why this chapter exists.

Not to make you fear your tech, but to remind you that convenience always comes with a cost. If you don't understand how these systems store, share, and expose your voice or your words, you're trusting strangers to protect information you wouldn't even tell a friend.

Don't just talk to your devices.

Talk about them.

What to Do About It – Your Security Checklist

1. **Review Voice Assistant Privacy Settings:** Go into your device's app or settings and limit what's saved, shared, or recorded by default. Turn off voice recording storage where possible.

2. **Delete Stored Voice History Regularly:** Periodically delete stored conversations from your smart assistant's history through the app or voice command ("Delete what I just said").

3. **Mute or Disable the Microphone When Not in Use:** If you don't need voice commands 24/7, turn off the mic—or use the physical mute button for added peace of mind.

4. **Avoid Giving Voice Assistants Access to Sensitive Apps:** Don't link your assistant to banking, shopping, or calendar tools unless you absolutely need to—and be selective with permissions.

5. **Use Voice Recognition and Authentication Features:** Enable voice ID so your assistant can distinguish your voice from strangers or children.

6. **Don't Share Sensitive Information via AI Chatbots:** Avoid entering private data like names, health details, addresses, financials, or work content into AI tools—especially free or public ones.

7. **Turn Off Drop-In and Intercom Features by Default:** Disable automatic voice communication between rooms or homes unless you've configured it securely.

8. **Unlink Third-Party Skills and Extensions You Don't Use:** Many smart assistants allow third-party apps, games, and skills. These can be privacy risks—review and remove unused ones.

9. **Disable Location and Personalization Features When Not Needed:** Turn off geographic tracking and "personalized results" if you don't want assistants building a profile on your routines.

10. **Educate Family Members About Voice Command Risks:** Ensure everyone in your home understands how to use the assistant safely and responsibly.

Quick Action Plan

1-Minute Fix: Mute your voice assistant or disable its mic when not in use.

5-Minute Fix: Delete your assistant's voice history and review its app permissions.

15-Minute Fix: Audit third-party skills, disable location tracking, and limit personalized features.

30-Minute Fix: Set up voice ID, adjust device access permissions, and teach your household how to use assistants with security in mind.

PART 3 - EVERYDAY DEVICES, EXTRAORDINARY DANGER

Chapter 10

How Hackers Hijack Your Personal Computer

Real-World Scenarios

The Laptop That Watched Everything

Claire was a university student, always on her laptop. It was her life line—classes, research, video calls, emails, social media, online banking. Everything she did passed through that screen. Her laptop was always with her—library, dorm, coffee shops. It was personal. Private.

Or so she thought.

One night, buried in a late-night assignment, she noticed something strange. A faint green light, glowing from the corner of her screen. Her webcam. It flickered. Then it stayed on. But she wasn't in a call. No Zoom. No Teams. No camera apps running.

Time fractured for a moment.

Instinctively, she covered the camera. Her fingers shook as she opened Task Manager. Nothing obvious was running. But the light remained on. She scanned forums, tech blogs—then the pieces clicked. Her laptop had been infected. Remote access malware. A hacker had gained control over her system—watching through her camera, listening through her mic, all without her knowledge. It was called "**Ratting**"—Remote Access Trojans. And it had turned her private world into someone else's show.

She remembered sitting at her desk in her pajamas. Singing to herself. Talking to her mom. Crying during a breakup call. All of it—seen, heard, maybe even recorded. Maybe already uploaded.

Webcam hacking, or '**Camfecting**,' represents a significant cybersecurity threat. While precise global figures are challenging to ascertain, user awareness of this risk is notably high. For instance, a 2019 HP survey found that 79% of U.S. laptop users were aware their privacy could be compromised via webcam, with many taking precautions such as covering their webcams with tape or other means.

Security experts confirm that webcams can be exploited by attackers, often without the user's knowledge. Notably, cases have emerged where hackers have accessed webcams to capture sensitive footage, leading to incidents of sextortion and unauthorized distribution of private images.

Claire thought she was alone in her room.

She never imagined someone else had been watching, silently, from behind her own screen.

The USB Drive That Crashed the Company

Edward arrived at work early. It was quiet. Still. Just another normal morning in the finance office. As he crossed the parking lot, something shiny caught his eye. A USB stick, lying near the curb.

Curious, he picked it up. Maybe someone from the office dropped it. Maybe it had something important.

He plugged it in.

In seconds, his laptop froze. The screen went black. Then—red text appeared:

"Your files have been encrypted. Pay $2,500 in Bitcoin to recover them."

Edward stared, stunned. The drive hadn't just infected his machine. It had jumped across the company's internal network. Spreadsheets, reports, presentations—all locked. The ransomware spread like wildfire. Within an hour, departments were calling IT in a panic. By noon, the whole system was down. Operations frozen. Data held hostage.

All because of one USB.

Cybercriminals use this tactic all the time—dropping infected drives in parking lots, hallways, cafes. They know someone will pick it up and plug it in.

In one real-world experiment, researchers dropped nearly 300 USB sticks across the University of Illinois Urbana-Champaign campus—on sidewalks, in parking lots, outside buildings. No warning. No explanation. Just a test to see what people would do. Almost half of those USBs – 48% – were picked up, plugged into computers, and opened. People clicked on the files. Some out of curiosity. Some to try to return the stick. Others just... did it.

This wasn't an isolated case. Other studies, including work by Google and security firms like CompTIA, have shown similar results: 30% to 50% of people will plug in a USB they find. No questions asked.

USB-based attacks have shut down entire companies. Hospitals, government offices, banks. Millions in damage. Days – or weeks- of recovery. And sometimes, permanent data loss.

Edward thought he was being helpful.

He had no idea he'd just opened the door to a digital hostage crisis.

The Fake Software Update That Hijacked a Laptop

Fiona prided herself on being security-conscious. As a software developer, she knew the importance of keeping systems up to date. She never skipped a patch, never clicked unknown links, and always updated her tools the moment a new version was released.

So when a pop-up appeared one afternoon that read: "Important Security Update Available. Click here to install", she didn't hesitate.

She clicked. The installation window looked normal. It even had a fake loading bar and system prompts that mimicked her operating system perfectly.

But minutes later, her laptop slowed to a crawl. Her files started disappearing. Her webcam light flickered, then stayed on. The terminal flashed open, then closed. Something was wrong.

That wasn't an update. It was spyware.

The pop-up had been part of a scam—a fake update engineered to look like it came from a trusted source. It installed malware that gave a hacker complete remote access to her system. Her keystrokes were being logged. Her saved passwords were harvested. Her screen was being watched in real time.

Significant percent of malware infections originate from fake update scams just like this. Cybercriminals often design pop-ups that look exactly like updates from trusted platforms—Microsoft, Adobe, even antivirus software. Victims think they're protecting themselves when, in reality, they're opening the door.

Fiona had always tried to do everything right.

But in one careless click, she handed over her entire digital life to a stranger.

The Password That Opened the Door to Everything

Franklin was constantly on the move. As a real estate agent juggling listings, closings, and client calls, he didn't have time to remember different logins for each account. One password for everything—it was just easier.

Email. Bank. Office portal. The same code unlocked it all.

One morning, he got an email that looked official: "Urgent: Unusual login detected. Please verify your identity." There was a logo, a familiar tone, and a link. Without thinking, he clicked. He entered his credentials. The page looked exactly like his bank's login portal.

An hour later, his bank account was empty. His email locked him out. His company's real estate portal had been breached, with sensitive client documents and internal data exposed.

The email had been fake. The link was a phishing trap. And the password he used—the same one for everything—had opened the door to it all.

This type of scam is painfully common. Phishing attacks keep climbing year after year—and thanks to AI, they're getting faster, smarter, and scarier. Criminals now create near-perfect replicas of bank and business sites to steal your credentials. And weak or reused passwords are behind 85% of all data breaches, LastPass claims.

Franklin had just wanted to protect his account. But instead of stopping a threat, he had walked right into one—and brought the rest of his digital world with him.

What You Need to Know

Your computer isn't just a tool. It's your command center, your archive, your window to the world. You use it to send emails, store financial records, edit documents, back up family photos, shop, pay bills, and maybe even run a business. And the more you rely on it, the more attractive it becomes—to someone else.

Hackers don't need to "break in" the way movies show it. Most attacks today start with something simple: an email that looks like a notice from your bank, a software update prompt that isn't real, a free program from a shady download site. It takes just one click to install malware quietly in the background. You won't hear it. You won't see it. You won't feel anything change—at first.

But that click can hand over full control.

Remote Access Trojans (RATs), keyloggers, spyware, screen recorders—they all work silently. Their goal isn't to crash your system. It's to use it. To watch what you type. To capture your passwords. To record what you do. To listen through your microphone and peek through your webcam. And to quietly pass all that data back to the attacker.

The flood of malware isn't slowing down. In 2024 alone, cybersecurity firms tracked hundreds of millions of new threats. The exact global number? Impossible to pin down. But one thing's certain: billions of malware attacks were aimed at personal computers. That's not a glitch- it's the norm. And they didn't just go after big corporations. They went after people—students, freelancers, remote workers, parents. Ordinary individuals who never thought they'd be targeted, because they didn't think they had anything worth stealing.

But you do.

Your login credentials. Your saved passwords. Access to your cloud storage. Your browsing history. Your banking details. Your contact list. Your computer is a doorway—and hackers know once they're inside, they can move laterally across every other service and device you're connected to.

And they won't stop there.

A hijacked computer can be used to launch attacks on others. It might send phishing emails in your name. Join a botnet. Host illegal content. Help mask other cybercrimes. And while you sleep, it's doing someone else's work.

Most victims don't realize what's happening until the damage is already done. A weird transaction shows up on your statement. A friend receives a strange email. Your files disappear. Or your device locks up with a ransom note on the screen.

The hardest part is that it doesn't take much. Just one out-of-date browser plugin. One bad download. One missed antivirus update. A weak password on a home Wi-Fi network. Or a device that hasn't been patched in months.

And you don't have to be careless—just unaware.

This chapter will walk you through how hackers hijack personal computers, how the most common attacks spread, and what they look for when scanning for targets. More importantly, it'll show you how to take back control—before someone else gets in. Because your computer might seem quiet, secure, and private.

But unless it's properly protected, it's already exposed.

Why It Matters

There's something uniquely personal about a computer.

Unlike phones, which are social, or tablets, which are often shared, a personal computer is your digital workspace, archive, bank vault, photo album, and diary—all rolled into one. It knows your routines. Your browsing habits. Your late-night thoughts. Your saved passwords. It remembers what you searched for five years ago and keeps copies of things you thought you deleted.

So when hackers target your PC, they're not just trying to crash it or spy on your screen. They're trying to become you.

The modern personal computer is one of the richest sources of exploitable data in the digital ecosystem. It's where your cloud accounts sync, where your browser stores credentials, where your files live outside of app protections. That's what makes it a high-value target—and why cybercriminals continue to focus on it, even in an age dominated by mobile devices.

The threat landscape changed fast, and not in a good way. CrowdStrike's 2025 Global Threat Report flagged sharp rises in identity-based attacks and cloud intrusions. The trend is clear: attacks are getting more sophisticated, more personal, and more dangerous for everyone. There was a major spike in remote access trojans (RATs), keyloggers, and browser-based exploits. And here's the kicker: most of these attacks didn't rely on fancy tricks. They relied on people being busy, tired, distracted, and human.

Clicking a fake download link. Trusting a pop-up that says "your system is out of date." Opening an email attachment that looks like it came from your boss. Installing a tool that promises to clean your system or speed up your browser. These are the small actions that open big doors.

Once inside your system, a hacker has options.

They can harvest your saved browser passwords, capture your keystrokes, activate your webcam, scan your document folders for tax records, or silently install additional malware. In many cases, they don't take control immediately—they wait. They watch. They build a profile of your digital identity so they can use it to steal money, impersonate you, or sell your access to someone else.

And personal computers give them something else too: reach.

Because many people use their PC as a hub—linked to phones, cloud drives, tablets, and smart devices—a compromised computer can act as a launchpad for attacking your entire digital environment. A single RAT infection can jump from your desktop to your connected storage device, to your cloud folders, to your shared family calendar. And once there, it's not just your data at risk. It's everyone you've ever shared something with.

Recent reports from ReliaQuest and Symantec show a clear shift: attackers are going after cloud services and IoT devices—the stuff that connects everything else. It's a dangerous evolution, and it's happening fast.

That means even if you back up your files, store things in the cloud, or use a password manager, you're still at risk—if your computer is the entry point.

Hackers also exploit another critical weakness: updates. Or more accurately, the lack of them.

While most people know that software updates patch security holes, they still find them boring—and put them off. A 2021 study commissioned by Kaspersky found that half of users regularly snooze updates—sometimes for weeks or even months. The problem? Some of the biggest ransomware attacks in recent years, including WannaCry and REvil, spread using old vulnerabilities that had already been patched. The fix existed. People just didn't install it.

Your system doesn't need to be broken to be breached. It just needs to be out of date.

There's also the rise of "**Malvertising**"—fake ads that appear on legitimate websites and deliver malware when clicked. These ads don't need you to install anything. Visiting the wrong page at the wrong time can be enough, especially if your browser is vulnerable or running outdated extensions. And because the malware doesn't always make a mess—some of it is stealthy, quiet, and efficient—you may not know you've been hacked until your bank calls or your email account is locked.

This matters because your computer isn't just a device. It's a mirror of your life.

And if someone hijacks it, they don't just see what's on your screen. They see what you've saved, what you've searched, what you've forgotten, and what you assume is private.

The question isn't just "Is my antivirus working?"

It's "If someone got into my computer today—what could they take? What could they break? And how long would it take me to even realize it?"

What to Do About It – Your Security Checklist

1. **Use a Trusted Antivirus and Anti-Malware Program:** Install a reputable security suite and schedule regular scans to detect and remove threats early.
2. **Keep Your Operating System and Software Updated:** Enable automatic updates to patch vulnerabilities that hackers commonly exploit.
3. **Avoid Downloading Software from Unknown Sources:** Only install programs from official sites or verified stores. Pirated or cracked software often comes bundled with malware.
4. **Turn Off Remote Access Unless You Need It:** Disable Windows Remote Desktop or third-party remote access tools unless you use them for verified, secure work purposes.
5. **Secure Your Wi-Fi Network:** Use WPA3 or WPA2 encryption with a strong, unique router password to prevent outside access to your devices.
6. **Use a Standard (Non-Admin) Account for Daily Use:** Reduce the risk of malware installing itself system-wide by avoiding day-to-day use on an administrator account.
7. **Enable a Firewall:** Keep your system's firewall turned on to block unauthorized inbound and outbound connections.
8. **Protect Against USB and Peripheral Attacks:** Don't plug unknown flash drives or devices into your PC. Disable autorun for external media.
9. **Review Your Installed Programs and Background Processes:** Periodically check what's installed and running in Task Manager or System Settings to catch suspicious behavior.
10. **Back Up Your Data Regularly:** Use both local and cloud backups to ensure you can recover critical files if your device is compromised or locked by ransomware.
11. **Secure Your Browser and Extensions:** Remove unused or untrusted browser extensions, and use browser privacy settings to minimize tracking and malicious redirects.
12. **Be Wary of Phishing and Tech Support Scams:** Never grant remote access to someone who calls you unexpectedly. Hang up and contact the company directly through verified channels.

Quick Action Plan

1-Minute Fix: Turn on your computer's firewall and antivirus protection if it's not already active.

5-Minute Fix: Check for and install pending operating system and software updates.

15-Minute Fix: Remove unused programs and scan your system for malware with a reputable tool.

30-Minute Fix: Set up daily backups for critical files, review your user account privileges, and secure your Wi-Fi and router settings.

Chapter 11

Mobile Phone Safety: Your Pocket is a Hacker's Dream

Real-World Scenarios

The Text Message That Stole Everything

Giselle was already late when her phone buzzed — "Unusual activity detected on your account. Click here to verify your identity."

It was from her bank. At least, that's what it looked like.

Panicked, she tapped the link. The site loaded instantly. It had the bank's colors, their logo, even their exact layout. She entered her username, her password, even answered her security questions—just to be safe.

But something felt... off. Her banking app logged out. When she tried to get back in, her password no longer worked.

An hour later, her savings account was gone. All of it.

The message hadn't come from her bank at all—it was part of a growing scam known as "**Smishing**", short for SMS phishing. Criminals now send convincing fake texts that mimic real institutions, using urgency to trigger a reaction. They know that when people see "unusual activity" or "account blocked," they'll act before they think.

In 2023, smishing attacks jumped by over 328%. These texts don't just ask for logins—they redirect you to cloned websites, steal your details in real-time, and sometimes install spyware without you even knowing.

Giselle thought she was protecting her account.

She didn't realize she had handed over the keys to her entire financial life.

The Charging Cable That Installed a Spy

Holly's battery hit 1% just as she was settling into a quiet café. No charger. No power bank. Luckily, the coffee shop had a free charging station near the wall, complete with cables. She plugged her phone in and sighed with relief.

A few minutes later, her screen glitched—just briefly. Then everything seemed fine.

But over the next few days, little things started happening. Her phone unlocked itself. Texts were marked "read" before she opened them. A fraud alert arrived from her bank—someone had tried to access her account from across the world.

She was confused. Then terrified.

What she didn't know was that the public charging cable had been compromised. It wasn't just supplying power—it was silently installing spyware on her device. This tactic is called **"Juice Jacking"**—a type of attack where criminals load malware into cables or charging ports, knowing someone will eventually plug in.

Once her phone was infected, the spyware could see everything. It tracked her keystrokes. Monitored her texts. Possibly even activated her microphone and GPS. In the background, it was quietly feeding all her data to someone she couldn't see.

Holly thought she was just charging her phone.

Instead, she had plugged into a trap.

The App That Listened 24/7

Harold just wanted a flashlight app. Something simple. Quick to install. Free. He found one on the app store with great reviews and hit download without thinking twice.

The app asked for a few permissions: access to the microphone, contacts, and location. That seemed excessive for a flashlight—but he tapped "Allow" anyway. Everyone does.

Weeks later, strange things started happening.

He'd be talking to friends about random topics—shoes, coffee, travel plans—and then, like magic, his phone would serve him ads for the exact thing he just mentioned. Not typed. Not searched. Just... spoken.

It felt like paranoia. Until he tested it.

He sat alone in his apartment and said, out loud: "I need new running shoes." No phone activity. No app open. Just those words.

Hours later, his social feeds were full of Nike, Adidas, Asics.

It wasn't coincidence. It was surveillance.

That flashlight app had been listening the whole time.

Many "free" apps aren't free at all – they're paid for with your data. Your location. Your contacts. Sometimes even your conversations.

According to NordVPN, at least 60% of Android and iOS apps ask for more access than they should. Some quietly record in the background, feeding your audio to ad networks. Others go further – acting as Trojan horses for malware that can hijack your camera or mic without you ever knowing.

Harold thought he was just installing a flashlight.

He didn't realize he had placed a live wiretap in his own pocket.

The Lost Phone That Became a Weapon

Irene had a great night out. Until the next morning—when she realized her phone was gone.

She retraced her steps. Called the taxi company. Pinged her device—but no luck. Still, she wasn't panicked. Her phone had a passcode. Face ID. Everything important was locked down.

But within the hour, strange things started happening.

Her PayPal account had been drained. Her Gmail stopped accepting her password. Her Instagram was posting crypto scams. Her bank flagged a suspicious login attempt.

She didn't understand. Her phone was secure. How could this happen?

It hadn't been hacked the usual way. It had been SIM swapped.

A cybercriminal had called her mobile provider, impersonated her, and convinced them to transfer her phone number to a new SIM card. Once that number was in the hacker's hands, they used it to intercept all her two-factor authentication codes. Her identity—her access—had been rerouted.

This isn't some rare hacker trick. It doesn't need your Face ID, PIN, or lock screen—because it's not after your phone. It's after your number. And once they have that, they can take everything tied to it.

Once the hacker had control of her number, they reset everything: email, bank logins, crypto wallets, cloud storage. Irene was shut out of her own life.

She thought a passcode would protect her phone. She didn't realize her entire identity could be hijacked with just one call.

What You Need to Know

Your mobile phone is the most powerful device you own—and probably the least protected.

You carry it everywhere. You trust it with everything. It holds your texts, photos, emails, contacts, payment apps, bank access, location history, health data, biometric login credentials, and more. In a single tap, you can pay for groceries, unlock your car, or transfer money between accounts. That's what makes it indispensable.

It's also what makes it a perfect target.

Most people assume their phones are secure by default. After all, they come with passcodes, fingerprint sensors, and encrypted messaging apps. But in reality, mobile devices are constantly under attack. Phishing texts, malicious apps, spyware, fake Wi-Fi networks, rogue charging stations—every time you tap, install, swipe, or connect, there's an opportunity for someone to get in.

And once they do, they don't need to "hack" anything. You've already given them the keys.

A fake bank alert asking you to verify your login. A text that looks like it's from a delivery service. A free app that asks for access to your camera, microphone, files, and contacts. These are common tricks that work because they blend into your day. You don't think twice—until it's too late.

Smishing (phishing via SMS) has surged recently, fueled by AI-generated messages that mimic banks, government agencies, and customer support teams. These messages don't look dangerous. They look like reminders, warnings, or routine requests. That's why thousands of people handed over their credentials without hesitation. The attack didn't feel like an attack at all.

Even physical interactions are no longer safe.

Public charging stations, once seen as a convenience, have become a security risk. Plug into the wrong kiosk and you could unknowingly install malware or give a hacker access to your phone through a method known as "juice jacking." And if your Bluetooth is left on, someone sitting nearby can initiate a forced pairing—gaining access to your files, messages, or location.

It doesn't stop there.

A lost or stolen phone—if not properly secured—can become a portal into your entire identity. If your SIM card is hijacked through a carrier scam, your text messages and two-factor authentication codes go to someone else. That means your email, bank accounts, crypto wallets, and social media accounts can be taken over in a matter of minutes.

And you won't always see it coming.

Maybe your phone suddenly loses signal. Maybe your contacts say they're getting strange texts. Maybe you're locked out of your own accounts while someone else resets your passwords.

The truth is, your phone doesn't have to be physically stolen for you to lose everything. Most attacks are remote. Most are silent. Most rely on one small oversight: a weak password, an outdated app, an unverified link, or a rushed decision.

This chapter will show you exactly how attackers exploit mobile phones—and how to stop them before they get in.

Because what's in your pocket isn't just a phone.

It's your ID, your wallet, your camera, your business, your voice, and your home.

And for a hacker, it's all available in one neat, unguarded package.

Why It Matters

We used to call them phones.

Now they're wallets, passports, health trackers, banks, cameras, IDs, alarm clocks, calendars, GPS systems, boarding passes, and sometimes—almost by accident—communication tools. A modern smartphone is more powerful than most laptops from a decade ago. It knows where you go, who you talk to, what you buy, how you sleep, and even how fast you drive.

And that makes it one of the most valuable—and vulnerable—devices in your life.

According to research by Dscout, the average person touches their phone more than 2,600 times a day. That level of intimacy is exactly why cybercriminals love smartphones: not just because they hold data, but because they hold habits. And habits can be exploited.

Most people think their phones are safer than computers.

But that's a dangerous assumption.

Because phones aren't just always on—they're always connected. To Wi-Fi networks, Bluetooth devices, cloud backups, synced email accounts, financial apps, location services, and smart home systems. And most users have no idea what their phone is doing in the background. That's how attacks slip in.

Mobile malware is a growing concern, with Kaspersky reporting a 196% surge in mobile banking trojan attacks in 2024. This sharp rise underscores how mobile devices have become prime targets in today's cyber threat landscape.

Cybercriminals are increasingly using deceptive tactics—like fake apps, malicious QR codes, and SMS phishing (smishing)—to deploy spyware, banking trojans, and credential-stealing malware onto victims' phones. Once installed, these tools can silently track your keystrokes, activate your microphone, access private files, and hijack your authentication tokens—all without triggering any alerts.

But it's not just about malware.

Phones also make people careless.

Because they feel personal and familiar, we tend to click faster, install more freely, and give permissions without thinking. Most users don't read app permission requests. They don't use security tools like mobile antivirus or VPNs. They let apps stay logged in indefinitely. And when that phone is lost, stolen, or hacked—it becomes a gateway to everything else.

Even the very features that make smartphones useful are what make them dangerous.

Take biometric unlocking. It's fast and convenient. But if someone coerces you—at a border, in a domestic dispute, or during a theft—they don't need your PIN. They just need your face or fingerprint. If your messaging apps are open, your photos are accessible, your notes contain passwords, or your browser has saved credentials, you've already lost control.

Or consider the way mobile devices are used to authenticate everything—from bank accounts to social media. Many apps rely on SMS-based two-factor authentication (2FA), which makes your phone number more than just a way to reach you. It's a recovery key for your identity. That's why SIM swapping is on the rise.

According to the FBI's Internet Crime Complaint Center (IC3), nearly 3,000 incidents were reported in 2023—but those few cases led to losses topping $72 million. That's an average of around $24,000 per victim, showing just how profitable this attack method is for cybercriminals.

If someone takes over your number, they can:

- Reset your email password
- Access your cloud backups
- Hijack your banking apps
- Log into your social media
- Impersonate you in messages or calls

And many victims don't even realize it's happening until they lose signal and watch helplessly as their accounts start vanishing one by one.

Smartphones are also increasingly targeted for surveillance—not just by cybercriminals, but by stalkers, abusers, and even corporate espionage tools. Commercial spyware is now widely available and disturbingly easy to install. A jealous partner with access to your phone for five minutes can install an app that monitors your location, reads your texts, listens to your calls, and watches through your camera—without your knowledge.

The threat is bigger than stolen money or leaked photos.
It's about losing autonomy.

Your phone isn't just a piece of technology. It's a proxy for your attention, your movements, and your identity. That's why protecting it isn't optional. It's essential.

This chapter isn't just about locking your screen or avoiding bad apps. It's about learning to see your phone as what it truly is: a powerful, portable target. And making sure that if someone tries to exploit it, they hit a wall—not an open door.

Because in the digital age, you don't have to lose your phone to lose control of your life.

You just have to ignore the risks long enough.

What to Do About It – Your Security Checklist

1. **Use a Secure Lock Screen:** Set up a strong PIN, password, or biometric lock to prevent unauthorized access if your phone is lost or stolen.

2. **Enable Full Device Encryption:** Turn on encryption to protect stored data from being accessed by thieves or malware.

3. **Keep Your Phone's Operating System Updated:** Regular updates patch security vulnerabilities—don't delay them.

4. **Only Download Apps from Trusted Sources:** Stick to official app stores like Google Play and Apple's App Store. Avoid APKs or third-party markets.

5. **Review App Permissions Regularly:** Deny apps access to your camera, microphone, contacts, and location unless absolutely necessary.

6. **Avoid Public Charging Stations ("Juice Jacking" Risks):** Use your own charger and plug into a power outlet, not public USB ports. Consider a USB data blocker if needed.

7. **Be Cautious with Public Wi-Fi:** Avoid logging into sensitive accounts over unsecured networks. Use a VPN if you must access private data on public Wi-Fi.

8. **Install a Trusted Mobile Security App:** Choose a reputable app that scans for malware, protects against phishing, and offers anti-theft features.

9. **Turn Off Bluetooth and Location When Not in Use:** This prevents devices from being tracked or hijacked when idle.

10. **Don't Click on Links in Unknown Texts or Emails:** Smishing attacks (phishing via SMS) are increasingly common. Delete suspicious messages immediately.

11. **Set Up Remote Wipe and Device Recovery:** Use Apple's "Find My" or Google's "Find My Device" to locate or erase your phone if it's lost or stolen.

12. **Avoid Saving Sensitive Passwords in Your Browser or Notes App:** Use a secure, encrypted password manager instead.

Quick Action Plan

1-Minute Fix: Enable a lock screen and check for recent OS updates.

5-Minute Fix: Review and remove unnecessary app permissions and delete unused apps.

15-Minute Fix: Set up remote wipe tools and check that encryption is turned on.

30-Minute Fix: Install a mobile security app, configure VPN access for public Wi-Fi, and educate yourself on the latest mobile phishing scams.

Chapter 12

Public Wi-Fi: The Cost of Free Internet

Real-Word Scenarios

The Airport Wi-Fi That Stole Everything

Juliet had been planning her dream vacation to Thailand for months. After years of working without a break, she finally booked two weeks off, packed her bags, and caught a flight with a layover in Istanbul. Sitting in the bustling international terminal, she was full of excitement and ready to disconnect from work and enjoy the moment.

While sipping tea in an airport café, she saw a notification on her phone: "Free Airport Wi-Fi Available." She tapped to connect. No password required, no registration form. It worked instantly. She figured it was a convenience offered by the airport.

As she waited for her flight, Juliet checked her email, browsed Instagram, and even logged into her banking app to double-check her travel budget. Everything seemed fine. But what she didn't realize was that the Wi-Fi she had connected to wasn't official at all. It was a fake network—a rogue hotspot set up by a cybercriminal sitting just a few tables away.

Using a technique called a "man-in-the-middle attack," the hacker was able to intercept all the traffic that passed through his fake network. Juliet's login credentials, saved browser passwords, and even the session token from her banking app were now in his hands.

By the time she boarded her connecting flight, he had already logged into her email, reset her social media passwords, and drained her checking account. Juliet had no idea anything was wrong. She landed in Bangkok ready to start her adventure—only to be greeted by frantic emails from her bank and a frozen credit card.

Her vacation, barely begun, was already ruined.

Juliet thought she was just checking her balance before boarding.

She didn't realize she had handed over her digital life to a hacker with a laptop and a fake network name.

The Hotel Wi-Fi Nightmare

Jeremiah and Kara were on their honeymoon in the Maldives—a bucket-list trip they had saved for over a year to enjoy. The resort was luxurious, quiet, and secluded, the kind of place where you assume nothing bad could happen. On their first night, they connected to the hotel's complimentary Wi-Fi to share sunset photos with family and friends back home.

There was no password. No agreement screen. Just a friendly "Guest Wi-Fi" option they tapped into without a second thought.

They spent the evening sipping cocktails, watching the stars, and basking in their first moments as a married couple.

The next morning, everything changed.

Jeremiah received a fraud alert from their credit card provider—multiple charges had appeared overnight. Their airline miles were drained. Kara's email account had been accessed from an unfamiliar location. Their cloud storage showed recent downloads of personal documents, including scanned copies of their passports.

What they didn't know was that the hotel's router had been compromised long before they arrived. A hacker had infected the resort's Wi-Fi system with malware, and every guest who connected unknowingly exposed their data. The attackers collected passwords, payment credentials, and personal documents, then sold them on dark web marketplaces.

Jeremiah and Kara thought that staying in a high-end resort meant higher safety standards.

They didn't realize that cybercriminals often target luxury hotels—precisely because their guests have more to lose.

The Train Wi-Fi That Hijacked a Business

Kenneth was a senior executive at a fast-growing tech startup, used to juggling meetings, investor calls, and internal reports—sometimes all in a single day. While traveling on a short business trip to Berlin, he took the city metro to get to his hotel.

The train ride was only 20 minutes, but as someone who hated wasting time, Kenneth pulled out his laptop and connected to the "Free Metro Wi-Fi" network, which was prominently advertised inside the train car.

The connection was fast. No password required, just a splash page asking him to accept terms. Kenneth quickly logged into his company email, checked a few unread messages, reviewed some internal files, and sent over an updated budget sheet to his team.

He didn't notice anything unusual.

But by the time he arrived at his hotel and reconnected to the internet, his inbox was full of alerts.

His company email had been accessed from an unfamiliar location.

Shared cloud storage links were broken—files had been moved or deleted.

A senior client had just received a confidential pitch deck... from a hacker impersonating Kenneth.

What Kenneth didn't know was that the "Free Metro Wi-Fi" had been compromised weeks ago. Cybercriminals had installed a man-in-the-middle attack on the network, allowing them to silently intercept every login and password transmitted during the session. Kenneth's company credentials had been captured and used within minutes to breach his organization's internal systems.

What should have been a simple train ride turned into a full-scale cybersecurity crisis.

Kenneth assumed that an "official" network provided by public transportation was safe to use.

He didn't realize he was giving a front-row seat to hackers targeting traveling professionals like him.

The Fake Wi-Fi Login Page

Linda was a frequent traveler, always hopping between cities for work. At every airport and hotel, she followed the same routine: connect to the free Wi-Fi, check her email, and catch up on messages before boarding or settling in for the night.

One day, during a layover at a busy airport, she found a network called "Airport_Free_WiFi" that looked just like every other official hotspot. When she connected, a login page appeared asking her to enter her email address and phone number to gain access. This wasn't unusual. In fact, she'd seen pages like this a hundred times. Without hesitation, she filled in her details and clicked "Connect."

Nothing happened. The page simply refreshed, and she figured the Wi-Fi was slow or overloaded.

Hours later, strange things began to happen.

Her email was locked.

Her Instagram sent out suspicious messages to followers.

A two-factor authentication code popped up on her phone—one she hadn't requested.

It turned out Linda had connected to an "Evil Twin" hotspot—a fake Wi-Fi network created by hackers to mimic a legitimate one. The login page wasn't a gateway to the internet; it was a trap. The hackers collected her real credentials and immediately used them to take over her accounts, reset passwords, and dig deeper into her digital life.

This type of attack is shockingly effective. Cybercriminals set up these cloned networks in public places—airports, cafés, hotels—knowing most people won't think twice before entering personal information. These fake pages often copy the branding and layout of real networks so convincingly that even cybersecurity professionals can fall for them.

Linda thought she was connecting to Wi-Fi so she could check her flight status.

She didn't realize she was handing over the keys to her online identity.

What You Need to Know

You're sitting in a café, waiting at the airport, or checking into a hotel. You open your laptop or pull out your phone, and there it is—"Free Wi-Fi." No password. No login hassle. Just instant internet. You connect, open your email, maybe check your bank, upload a few documents, or watch a video. It feels normal. Safe, even. It's the kind of routine people follow every single day.

But what most people don't realize is that public Wi-Fi is one of the most effective traps in a hacker's toolkit.

When you connect to an unsecured network, you're exposing every piece of information your device sends and receives. And depending on how that network is configured—or who actually set it up—someone could be watching every move you make.

Here's the truth: not every "Free Airport Wi-Fi" or "Hotel_Guest" network is real. Many of them are fake. Hackers create rogue hotspots using nothing more than a laptop and a catchy name. Once someone connects, they can intercept everything the user sends: passwords, emails, login tokens, even credit card numbers typed into secure websites. All of it can be harvested in real time, and the victim won't know until it's far too late.

These fake networks are designed to look identical to the real ones. They're named just like legitimate access points. Some even mimic the login splash pages of airports, coffee shops, or stores. The moment you enter your information, it's captured—not to log you in, but to log you out of your own security.

Even when the network is real, you're still vulnerable.

Most public Wi-Fi networks don't use strong encryption. That means every device connected to them is sitting in the same open room, whispering secrets out loud. Anyone with basic free software can listen in. It doesn't matter if you're visiting a reputable website or doing something as simple as logging into your email—your data can still be intercepted if the connection isn't properly secured.

But the threat doesn't end there.

Some attackers don't just listen. They leave something behind. Malware can be silently installed on your device during your session—especially if you're on an outdated operating system or using apps that automatically sync. That malware may not activate immediately. It may wait. Wait until you get home. Wait until you connect to your work network. Wait until you open your cloud backup or financial records. And then it spreads.

Hackers can also exploit automatic reconnect features. If your phone is set to remember networks, it may reconnect to the fake one the next time you're near it—without asking for your permission. The door that was opened once can quietly reopen again.

Public Wi-Fi feels harmless—until it's not.

According to a 2024 Forbes Advisor survey, 40% of users said their personal information had been compromised while using public Wi-Fi. That's not a fringe case—it's nearly half. And it gets worse.

A 2025 report by AllAboutCookies.org found that more than half of internet users log into personal accounts over public Wi-Fi, and 45% access financial data—banking, payments, credit cards—on networks that anyone can tap into. Most weren't using anything more secure than a basic device password.

No VPN. No encrypted connection. Just hope.

This is what makes public Wi-Fi so dangerous. Not because it's always malicious, but because we treat it like it's private. We assume that if we don't see a warning, there's no threat. But public networks are public in every sense of the word. When you connect, you're in a shared digital space. And unless you've taken active steps to secure that space, your data is available for the taking.

This chapter will walk you through the traps, the tactics, and the small changes that can make a massive difference. You'll learn how attackers manipulate trust, how rogue networks get planted, and how even brief connections can cause lasting damage.

Because while the internet might be free, your data is not. And sometimes, the real cost of Wi-Fi isn't what you pay to connect—but what you didn't protect once you did.

Why It Matters

Free Wi-Fi is everywhere: airports, coffee shops, hotels, gyms, buses, trains, malls, libraries, parks. It's convenient, invisible, and quietly expected—so much so that most people connect without a second thought. If it loads, we trust it. If it's open, we assume it's safe.

That assumption is exactly what makes it dangerous.

When you connect to public Wi-Fi, you're not just accessing the internet. You're also exposing yourself—your device, your browsing, your passwords, your messages—to everyone else on that same network. And if even one person on that network is a hacker, they can intercept your activity before you even know what happened.

It doesn't take elite skills or expensive tools.

With free software and a laptop, an attacker can create what's known as a "**man-in-the-middle**" setup, intercepting data as it flows between your device and the websites or apps you're using. They can watch what you type, capture your login credentials, read your unencrypted messages, and inject malware onto your system—all without you clicking on anything suspicious.

This isn't some distant theory.

Man-in-the-Middle attacks – where hackers silently intercept your data on public Wi-Fi – were responsible for 19% of all successful cyberattacks in 2024, according to Splunk. That's nearly one in five breaches caused by someone slipping between you and the internet—without you ever knowing.

In a study from Japan, researchers monitored 11 unsecured Wi-Fi hotspots for just 150 hours—and it was enough to capture a disturbing amount of unprotected data. Private photos, emails, documents, even login credentials were transmitted in plain text and easily intercepted. No hacking magic required—just an open network and a bit of patience.

And attackers aren't just eavesdropping.

Sometimes, they create fake hotspots with names like "Free Airport Wi-Fi" or "Starbucks_Guest." These "evil twin" networks look identical to the real ones but are actually traps. The moment you connect, everything you do can be monitored or manipulated. And if you enter personal information—like your name, email, or even your login credentials on a spoofed login page—those details are harvested in real time.

Even though 64% of consumers say data breaches are their biggest concern (Acronis, Data Privacy Survey 2025), many still connect to public Wi-Fi without hesitation. The message is clear: people are aware of the risks—but they're not changing their behavior.

But the biggest risk of all? You rarely know you've been hit.

When something goes wrong on public Wi-Fi, the effects don't show up immediately. Your email still works. Your apps still load. But behind the scenes, a digital copy of your identity may already be spreading. Your passwords might be tried on other sites. Your accounts might be sold on a dark web forum. Your personal or financial life might begin to unravel—and you won't know until it's too late to trace it back to that café, hotel, or airport lounge.

And this affects more than individuals.

For freelancers, remote workers, students, or professionals traveling for business, public Wi-Fi is often the only option. But logging into a company system, uploading documents, or managing customer accounts from an unsecured network can compromise your employer or clients—not just you. A single stolen credential could mean a data breach, a lawsuit, or a PR nightmare.

Public Wi-Fi doesn't just cost you privacy. It can cost you money, your reputation, even your career.

This is why the conversation has to shift. Connecting to public Wi-Fi isn't just a convenience—it's a risk calculation. It's choosing between speed and safety. And unless you're using proper tools (like a trusted VPN, encrypted DNS, and up-to-date device security), that free connection might be the most expensive one you've ever used.

This chapter will help you think differently about the invisible decisions you make every time your phone or laptop auto-connects. It's not about being paranoid—it's about being prepared. Because in today's world, data doesn't have to be stolen by brute force. It's often just taken—right out of the air.

What to Do About It – Your Security Checklist

1. **Avoid Logging Into Sensitive Accounts on Public Wi-Fi:** Don't access banking, email, or work platforms over public networks unless absolutely necessary.

2. **Use a VPN (Virtual Private Network):** A VPN encrypts your internet traffic, making it unreadable to hackers even on compromised networks.

3. **Turn Off Auto-Connect to Wi-Fi Networks:** Prevent your device from automatically connecting to unsafe or rogue hotspots.

4. **Forget Old Networks After Use:** Delete remembered public Wi-Fi networks from your settings so your device doesn't reconnect without your knowledge.

5. **Verify the Network Name with Staff:** Before connecting in a café, airport, or hotel, ask staff for the official Wi-Fi name to avoid spoofed networks.

6. **Disable File Sharing and AirDrop (or Nearby Share):** Keep these features off when on public networks to prevent unauthorized access.

7. **Avoid Using Shared Wi-Fi for Work or File Transfers:** Save uploads and downloads for secure, private networks when possible.

8. **Use Two-Factor Authentication (2FA) on All Accounts:** If your login credentials are compromised, 2FA adds a second barrier to account access.

9. **Always Log Out of Accounts When Finished:** Especially on shared or borrowed devices, log out of email, social media, and banking apps.

10. **Keep Your Operating System and Apps Updated:** Updates often include security patches for known vulnerabilities exploited on public networks.

11. **Use Mobile Data Instead of Public Wi-Fi for Sensitive Tasks:** If you're accessing banking or making payments, a mobile connection is far safer.

Quick Action Plan

1-Minute Fix: Turn off auto-connect and disable file sharing before connecting to any public network.

5-Minute Fix: Delete previously saved public Wi-Fi networks from your phone or laptop.

15-Minute Fix: Install a VPN app and configure it to auto-activate on public networks.

30-Minute Fix: Audit the accounts you commonly access on the go and enable 2FA where it's missing. Educate yourself and your family on how to spot fake login pages and rogue Wi-Fi traps.

Chapter 13

Smart TVs & Streaming Devices - The Living Room Spies

Real-World Scenarios

The TV That Spied on an Entire Family

Monica and Lawrence were excited about their new smart TV. It had everything—voice commands, built-in streaming, sleek menus, and AI that "learned" their viewing habits. It even recommended shows before they knew what they wanted to watch.

One evening, as they sat on the couch discussing finances, Lawrence casually mentioned wanting to explore real estate investment. It was a private conversation. Just the two of them. No searches. No messages. No emails.

The next morning, his phone was flooded with real estate ads.

He hadn't typed a single word about it online.

Confused—and now suspicious—Lawrence checked the TV's settings. Buried deep inside the menus, he found something he never expected: their smart TV had been actively listening. Not just when they used voice commands. But all the time.

And worse, it was sending that data to a third-party company for "analysis."

They had invited a surveillance system into their living room—and didn't even realize it.

Your TV Is Watching You. Literally.

A Princeton study found that 89% of Fire TV channels and 69% of Roku channels send data to known trackers.

This isn't streaming. It's silent surveillance.

Many Smart TVs keep their mics on—recording background chatter even when you're not speaking to them. That voice data? It's bundled with your viewing habits and handed to advertisers.

They don't just know what you watch. They know what you say.

Monica and Lawrence thought they were buying a TV for entertainment.

They didn't realize they were also installing a microphone that never stopped listening.

The Hacker Who Took Over a TV in the Middle of the Night

Mitchell's Amazon Fire Stick was his favorite gadget. It gave him instant access to every streaming service he needed, replaced his cable bill, and even controlled his smart home setup.

But one night, just past 3 AM, he woke up to an eerie sound.

His TV had turned on by itself.

At first, he thought it was a glitch. Then the volume shot up to maximum. His screen began rapidly switching between random YouTube videos—strange clips, foreign channels, music he'd never heard of.

Mitchell hadn't touched the remote.

Shaken, he pulled the plug. But the damage had already started.

By the next morning, he discovered that someone had used his linked Amazon account to purchase premium subscriptions and content. Unauthorized charges had appeared overnight. His account had been hijacked—through his streaming device.

Many smart TV devices and sticks are vulnerable to remote hacking, especially when left unpatched or secured with weak passwords. Cybercriminals scan networks for open devices and gain access in minutes. Once inside, they can control the screen, manipulate settings, and worse—access payment information linked to your streaming accounts.

Mitchell thought he was just watching Netflix.

He didn't realize someone else was watching him—and spending his money while doing it.

The Fake Streaming App That Stole Credit Card Info

Nora was looking for a movie—something new, something trending. But none of her usual streaming services had it. Then she found a free app that claimed to offer all the latest movies, no subscription required. Just a one-time "verification" with her credit card.

It seemed easy enough. She installed the app, entered her details, and hit play.

Except the movie never loaded.

And a few days later, she noticed $500 missing from her account.

Multiple unauthorized transactions. Gift cards. Streaming purchases. Online shops she'd never heard of.

By the time she uninstalled the app, it was too late. Her card details had already been scraped and sold. She had been lured in by a fake streaming platform—designed to look real, but built to steal.

Unauthorized or modified streaming sticks—often bought from third-party sellers or loaded with "free" channels—frequently come with something extra: malware (VulnerX, 2025). We're talking about spyware that steals your Netflix and Amazon logins. Keyloggers that quietly collect your passwords and credit card numbers. Backdoors that let hackers slip into your home Wi-Fi like it's an open gate.

These apps often mimic the design of legitimate platforms, tricking users into entering sensitive data. Once your card is compromised, criminals use it for fraudulent purchases or sell it on dark web marketplaces within hours.

Nora thought she was just watching a free movie.

Instead, she'd given cybercriminals a direct connection to her bank account.

The Camera Hidden Inside a Smart TV

Josh was proud of his new high-end smart TV. It had all the bells and whistles—voice control, built-in streaming apps, and even a camera for video calls. It was sleek, modern, and smarter than any TV he'd owned before.

One night, while binge-watching a show, something caught his eye. A tiny red light on the frame of the TV. Subtle. Almost hidden. The camera.

But he wasn't on a call.

He waved in front of it. Nothing changed. Still glowing. Still watching.

Unsettled, Josh grabbed a piece of tape and covered the lens. The next day, curiosity turned into concern. He logged into his router to check the device activity. And there it was—his TV had been quietly communicating with an unknown server in a foreign country in the middle of the night.

It hadn't just been on—it had been sending data. From his living room. While he was home.

He began researching. And what he found chilled him: smart TVs with built-in cameras have been hacked before—turned into remote surveillance devices. Exploits for these models were even being sold on underground forums, giving criminals remote access to live camera feeds. Some malware could even reactivate cameras that users thought were disabled.

Josh thought his smart TV camera was only active during video calls.

He didn't realize it could be turned against him—watching him in the privacy of his own home.

What You Need to Know

You turn on your TV. You scroll through your apps. You play a show, maybe ask your voice remote to turn down the lights. It's smooth, intuitive, effortless. That's what smart TVs and streaming devices promise—convenience, control, and endless entertainment.

But what you might not realize is that these same devices are listening, watching, tracking, and sometimes even transmitting far more than you think.

Smart TVs aren't just screens anymore. They're full-fledged internet-connected computers—equipped with microphones, cameras, and sophisticated software designed not just to display content, but to gather data. They track what you watch, how long you watch it, what apps you open, and what you search. Some even monitor what's plugged in via HDMI, logging what movies you rent or what games you play, even if you're not using their built-in apps.

And it doesn't stop with passive data collection.

Many smart TVs are voice-activated. That means they're listening for a command—even when you're not actively talking to them. While they're "listening," they often record and transmit fragments of background conversation to remote servers. If your TV's mic is on by default, it may have picked up everything from casual chatter to private discussions—without you ever knowing.

Most modern Smart TVs use something called **Automatic Content Recognition (ACR)**. It tracks what you're watching—live TV, Netflix, YouTube, even your gaming sessions. Then it sends that data straight back to the manufacturer (ZDNet Consumer Report, 2024).

And from there? Off to advertisers, data brokers, and who knows who else. All this often happens behind vague consent screens buried in the setup process. Many users have no idea it's happening.

Your TV isn't just smart. It's a spy.

One investigation showed that even when users opted out of data collection, some devices continued to send information in the background.

And then there's the camera.

Some smart TVs come with built-in cameras for video calls or gesture recognition. If that camera isn't disabled or covered—and if the TV has been compromised—someone else could be watching. In recent years, hackers have exploited software vulnerabilities in smart TVs to gain remote access to these cameras and microphones, turning them into silent surveillance devices sitting in the center of people's homes.

Streaming sticks and smart home hubs are no safer. Devices like Fire TV, Roku, or Apple TV may not have cameras, but they still collect viewing history, device usage, app behavior, and can be manipulated through voice assistants. If these devices are linked to your Amazon, Apple, or Google accounts, they can also tie that data to your broader digital profile—what you buy, what you search, who you email.

And here's the part most people overlook: smart TVs and streaming devices are often the least protected gadgets on your network.

They don't run antivirus. Their software is rarely updated. Their default settings prioritize performance over privacy. They're typically connected to the same Wi-Fi network as your phone, your computer, your work laptop—creating a soft entry point for attackers. Once compromised, these devices can be used to move laterally through your network, scan for vulnerabilities, and access your personal or work data through other devices.

Many users never think to change the factory password on a streaming box or check the privacy settings on their TV. They assume the threat is low because "it's just a television." But in reality, that TV could be quietly logging every show you watch, every voice command you give, and every account you connect—sometimes sharing it with dozens of companies you've never heard of.

This chapter will walk you through what these devices really collect, how they're exploited, and how to take back control of your living room.

Because your TV isn't just showing you content anymore. It's showing someone else how you live.

Why It Matters

There's a reason we used to call it the "idiot box." For decades, televisions were one-way devices. You sat back, watched, and turned them off when you were done. They didn't listen, learn, track, or remember.

That's no longer the case.

Today's smart TVs are some of the most invasive consumer devices in your home. Behind that sleek screen is an operating system connected to the internet, full of apps, microphones, voice commands, motion sensors, and data-sharing agreements most users never read. Your TV knows what you watch, when you watch it, and—depending on the model—what you say while you're watching.

And it's not just the TV itself.

Streaming devices like Amazon Fire Stick, Roku, Apple TV, and Android boxes are also listening, tracking, collecting, and sharing data—about your preferences, your behavior, your voice commands, and your location. They're often connected to your main Wi-Fi network, linked to your Amazon or Google account, and pulling in data from every app you use.

What does this mean?

It means your living room is no longer a private space. It's part of a data ecosystem you didn't ask to join.

Smart TVs aren't just watching you—they're also the easiest to hack.

A 2025 study by the University of Bradford revealed that Smart TVs accounted for 34% of all known vulnerabilities in smart home devices—making them the single most vulnerable category. That's more than smart speakers, security cameras, or any other connected gadget in your house.

The problem? Most Smart TVs are built for streaming and ads—not security. Outdated firmware, poor patching, and wide-open ports create the perfect storm for hackers looking for a way into your home network.

Your TV might look sleek and smart—but it's full of cracks.

That's not a glitch. That's by design.

Smart TVs and streaming platforms make their money not just from hardware sales, but from advertising and data brokerage. The more they know about your preferences, the more they can tailor ads—or sell that information to third parties who will. That's why you might mention a product during dinner and then see an ad for it the next day on your screen.

But it gets worse.

In multiple reported incidents between 2023 and 2024, smart TVs were found to have security vulnerabilities allowing remote access by hackers. These exploits enabled attackers to:

- Control the TV's volume and display remotely
- Access built-in microphones and webcams
- Extract Wi-Fi credentials and use them to infiltrate the wider home network
- Install malware through streaming apps and browser tools

And if your TV or streaming box is synced with other devices (like Alexa, Google Home, or smart speakers), an attacker may not need to touch your TV to exploit it. They just need access to the account or app that controls it.

In 2024, researchers uncovered a massive global compromise: over 1.3 million Android-based streaming boxes had been infected with a backdoor. These weren't obscure devices—they were widely sold, cheap, and unbranded. The malware, dubbed "Vo1d," embedded itself deep into the system, allowing attackers to silently hijack the devices for ad fraud, proxy abuse, and remote code execution.

The infection spanned 197 countries, with hotspots in Brazil, Morocco, and Russia. Most of the compromised devices ran outdated Android versions (7.1, 10.1, 12.1) and were not Play Protect-certified, meaning they bypassed Google's security checks.

Researchers still don't know how the malware got there. Theories range from compromised supply chains to malicious firmware updates. But the result is clear: millions of homes unknowingly became part of a botnet.

The lesson? If a device seems too cheap to be true, it probably is. And it might be spying on you (Ars Technica, 2024).

But this isn't just about hackers. It's about misplaced trust.

Families install smart TVs in bedrooms, nurseries, and living rooms. Children use them for YouTube. Parents use them for Netflix. Guests connect via screen mirroring. And through it all, these devices are listening—waiting for a wake word, collecting analytics, building a profile.

And most users never check the privacy settings.

They never disable voice data collection. They never review app permissions. They never read the privacy policy. Why would they? It's a TV. Or at least, it used to be.

This is why it matters.

Because people assume that screens are passive—that they only light up when you press a button. But smart TVs aren't passive anymore. They're active participants in your digital life. They see. They hear. They connect.

And like any connected device, they can be manipulated—by marketers, corporations, or criminals.

If you wouldn't let a camera crew into your living room, don't assume your smart TV deserves a free pass.

What to Do About It – Your Security Checklist

1. **Disable Always-On Microphones and Cameras:** If your smart TV or streaming device has voice controls or video calling features, turn them off when not in use—or cover cameras entirely.

2. **Review Privacy Settings in TV and Device Menus:** Limit how much data your device collects about your voice, habits, and content preferences.

3. **Decline or Minimize Data Sharing During Setup:** Say no to personalized ads, usage analytics, and location tracking unless you absolutely need them.

4. **Update Device Firmware Regularly:** Go into settings and manually check for software updates—especially if your device doesn't auto-update.

5. **Secure Your Wi-Fi Network:** All smart devices rely on your home network. Use strong encryption (WPA3 or WPA2) and change the default router password.

6. **Use a Separate Wi-Fi Network for Smart Devices:** Isolate smart TVs and streamers from your main network to limit exposure if one device is compromised.
7. **Avoid Installing Unknown or Unofficial Apps:** Stick to the official app store for your smart TV or media player. Sideloading apps can introduce malware.
8. **Change Default Device Passwords:** Some smart TVs, Fire Sticks, and other streaming tools have factory logins that hackers can easily find and exploit.
9. **Log Out Before Selling or Donating Devices:** Remove all account access and perform a full factory reset before passing on any smart home or streaming tech.
10. **Turn Off Features You Don't Use:** Don't leave voice recognition, camera access, or cloud sync running just because it's there. Less exposure = less risk.

Quick Action Plan

1-Minute Fix: Disable voice controls, camera access, and auto-listening settings.

5-Minute Fix: Check for software updates and install them manually if needed.

15-Minute Fix: Review your privacy settings and limit third-party data sharing options.

30-Minute Fix: Place your smart devices on a guest Wi-Fi network, reset default passwords, and remove unused apps.

Chapter 14

Gaming Consoles: Hacked While You Play

Real-World Scenarios

The Gamer Who Lost Everything Overnight

Patrick had built his virtual empire one match at a time.

Over the years, he poured hundreds of hours—and thousands of dollars—into his online gaming account. Rare skins, custom gear, powerful characters... all trophies of his dedication. His username was well-known in the gaming community, and his inventory was envied. It wasn't just a game anymore—it was a digital legacy.

Then, one morning, it was all gone.

He woke up to the usual routine. Coffee. Check his phone. Launch his favorite game. But his password didn't work. Strange. He tried again. No luck.

A sinking feeling began to grow in his chest.

He checked his email. Dozens of password reset requests. One had been successful. None of them were from him.

Panicked, Patrick scrambled to recover the account. But by the time he got in, it was already stripped clean. His inventory? Deleted or transferred. His skins? Sold. His account? Now being used to scam other players, dragging his once-respected name through the mud.

All of it—gone.

He later discovered his login details had been stolen in a massive data breach months ago. He had reused the same weak password on several sites, and it had finally caught up with him. The hackers didn't even target him directly—they just bought his compromised info off a dark web forum. His prized account, likely sold for a measly $10, was now just another tool in a digital con artist's kit.

Patrick thought he was just playing for fun.

He didn't realize that in the shadows of his favorite game, someone else had been playing too—and they were playing for keeps.

The Voice Chat That Led to a Security Breach

Ophelia loved the thrill of multiplayer matches—the rush of combat, the joy of teamwork, and the friendly banter over voice chat. It felt like a digital hangout, where strangers became allies and games turned into late-night memories.

But one night, something felt... different.

A new teammate joined her squad. His voice was friendly, curious. He didn't talk about the game much. Instead, he asked questions.

"So, where are you from?"

"How old are you?"

"Do you always play at this hour?"

Ophelia didn't think twice. It felt harmless, like small talk. She even joked about her boring hometown and mentioned where she went to school. The conversation flowed easily.

Too easily.

Days later, she received an alert: suspicious login attempts on her gaming account. Then came the password reset emails. And finally, the worst—her personal details had been posted on a hacker forum. Username, email, part of her address, answers to security questions.

The stranger hadn't needed to hack her.

He'd simply asked.

With just a few innocent-sounding questions, he pieced together enough information to start a chain reaction. He guessed her backup passwords, found her social media accounts, and even tried to scam her contacts. Her digital world wasn't private anymore—it had become a window left wide open, and someone had been watching.

Ophelia thought she was just chatting with a teammate.

She didn't realize she was talking to a digital predator—someone who didn't need to break in, because she had already unlocked the door.

The Hacked Console That Spied on a Family

For Robert and his family, their gaming console was more than just a game box.

It was the heart of their living room. They played together on weekends, watched movies through streaming apps, and even used the console's built-in camera to video chat with distant relatives. It was entertainment, connection, and convenience—all wrapped in one sleek device.

Until one night, something strange happened.

They were halfway through a movie when Robert noticed the camera light flicker on.

No one had touched the controller. No one had activated a call. The console was just sitting there... but the light glowed, unblinking.

A cold wave of unease washed over him.

He dove into the console's settings, navigating menus he hadn't looked at in years. Then he saw it—remote access logs. Someone had connected to their console. Recently. Silently.

Robert's heart sank as he pieced it together: their gaming account had been hacked. But this wasn't just about games. Whoever broke in now had access to far more:

- The camera, quietly watching from the living room shelf
- The microphone, picking up every word they said
- The saved payment info, ready for a shopping spree

He had never changed the default security settings. Why would he? It was just a console. Who would bother hacking a game system?

But as he later discovered, this kind of attack wasn't rare. Malware designed to infect smart devices had made its way into gaming networks. Hackers could silently slip in, hijack devices, and spy—turning living rooms into windows for cyber intruders.

Robert thought his console was just for fun and family.

He didn't realize it had become a surveillance tool—one that turned the watchers into the watched.

The Fake Giveaway That Stole a Gamer's Identity

Samuel had been hunting that rare in-game skin for months.

So when he stumbled across a post on a gaming forum offering a giveaway—limited time only, authentic item, officially sponsored—his excitement soared. The instructions were simple. Just click the link, log in with your gaming account, and confirm your email.

Too easy to be true. But it looked real.

The site had the right logo. The login screen looked exactly like the official game portal. Even the domain name seemed legit—just a small typo Samuel didn't notice.

He entered his credentials.

Seconds later, he was kicked out of his gaming account.

Then came the email alerts—suspicious activity, password change requests, recovery options updated. By the time Samuel tried to log back in, it was too late. His account had been stolen. His email had been compromised. His linked payment methods? Accessed.

He wasn't part of a giveaway.

He was the prize.

Behind the scenes, hackers had created a fake login page to mirror the real one. It was a textbook phishing scam, but terrifyingly effective. Once Samuel entered his details, they were harvested instantly and used to hijack his account—then sold to the highest bidder on underground markets.

All because he wanted a virtual sword.

Fake giveaways like these trick thousands of gamers every year. They play on excitement, fear of missing out, and the hunger for exclusivity. But behind every "win" is a trap.

Samuel thought he was about to get something for free.

He didn't realize the real cost would be his identity.

What You Need to Know

Pause for a moment and think about what your gaming console actually knows about you.

It's not just your username or high score. It knows your credit card details—the ones you saved for that battle pass. It stores your chat logs from late-night multiplayer sessions. It's heard your voice, maybe even captured conversations with strangers or family arguments picked up through the mic. Your console is linked to your email, sometimes your phone number, maybe even your social media accounts. It holds rare skins, exclusive weapons, in-game currency, trophies—months, maybe years of progress.

Now imagine none of that belongs to you anymore.

What if, right now, someone else is quietly logged into your account? Reading your messages. Draining your wallet. Watching through the camera you forgot even had a light. It's not some dystopian sci-fi nightmare. It's already happening—right now, to people who thought they were safe.

Hackers aren't just going after banks and big tech companies. They're coming for gamers—because gamers store real money and real data in digital places with weak defenses. Many don't take security seriously. They reuse passwords. They trust voice chat. They believe their console is just a toy. That's why gaming platforms are being hit hard.

Between May 2021 and April 2022, web application attacks targeting the gaming industry spiked by 167%, according to a report by Akamai Technologies. And it didn't stop there.

By late 2024, gaming-related cyberattacks had jumped another 50% over the previous three years, as reported by Assured Intelligence, citing Kaspersky. The gaming industry remains one of the most targeted sectors in the cyber threat landscape.

Phishing tactics in particular have exploded. In the first half of 2024, gaming ranked as the 10th most targeted industry for phishing attacks, according to ESET.

The scams are simple—but deadly effective. Fake login pages. Promises of free Robux, skins, or in-game currency. And the victims? Often children and teens, eager to score digital rewards, unaware they're handing over their passwords to criminals.

What was once a simple box under your TV is now a fully online, multifunctional device. It has cameras, microphones, stored payment methods, cloud access, and real-time communication tools. That also means it has multiple doors through which a hacker can walk in.

And they don't even have to force their way in.

A fake giveaway. A phishing link. A mod or cheat download laced with malware. One weak password reused across platforms. That's all it takes. Once inside, a hacker can drain your account, steal your items, impersonate you, send scam messages to your friends, or even spy on you through your camera or mic. The scariest part is how often it starts with trust—someone pretending to be helpful, friendly, official.

Gamers of all kinds are vulnerable. Kids click fast. Teens want the rare skin. Adults assume it's just for Netflix or family fun. No one expects a cyberattack until it's already happened. Behind every account is a person. And behind every person is a digital trail—purchases, patterns, saved details—all of which can be exploited in minutes.

Once inside, the hacker doesn't stop with your game. If your email is tied to the account, they try to access it. If your payment method is stored, they test it. If you use the same password elsewhere, they jump into your other accounts. One weak spot in your console security can open doors across your entire digital life.

And most victims don't even know when the door has been opened.

Maybe the camera light flickers. Maybe you get a password reset email you didn't request. A charge goes through for something you didn't buy. A new game shows up in your library—and you didn't download it. These are signs of compromise, but by the time you notice, the damage is usually done.

Gaming should be fun. Creative. Social. But increasingly, it's being used as a backdoor into homes, wallets, and identities. It's not just about protecting your favorite character anymore. It's about protecting yourself in the real world.

Because hackers don't care if you're a pro gamer or a casual one. They don't care if you stream daily or just play on weekends. They care that your console is connected—and unprotected.

In 2023 alone, ATO attacks drained nearly $13 billion, with gamers among the top targets (SpyCloud, 2025). Once a hacker gets into your account—whether it's for streaming, gaming, or banking—it's open season: digital wallets emptied, personal data sold, identities reused in future scams.

You don't just lose a password.

You lose control.

Many assume the biggest risks are only for serious players, but casual users are often the easiest targets. They're less likely to secure their settings or update their passwords. They don't check for strange messages or notice if a new game shows up. They might have never even opened the privacy menu. And that makes them perfect prey.

Younger players are especially at risk. The number of unique users targeted by cybercriminals using popular children's games as a lure surged by 30 percent in the first six months of 2024 compared to H2 2023, according to Kaspersky experts (2024). Researchers analyzed gaming risks for young players, and discovered that more than 132,000 users had been targeted by cybercriminals.

Predators exploit trust, build fake friendships, and lure children into handing over personal information or account credentials. And because these accounts are often linked to shared devices or payment methods, the entire household can suffer.

Parents often assume the console is the safest screen in the house. But it can be one of the most vulnerable. Mods and cheats downloaded by kids can contain spyware or keyloggers. A link sent in a voice chat might lead to a fake login page. A mic left on could pick up more than just in-game chatter.

Gaming platforms are under near-constant attack because they're the perfect storm of opportunity. High-value digital goods, weak user habits, large communities full of young and trusting players, and a cultural assumption that "it's just a game."

But make no mistake: it's not just a game. It's a gateway.

And once that gateway is breached, the attacker doesn't just take your loot. They take your identity. Your money. Your access. The console may be the first step—but the end target could be your inbox, your cloud, or your bank.

Even something as casual as voice chat becomes a risk. Personal details slip out in conversation. Your age. Your location. Your schedule. Hackers use that information to guess security questions, track down linked accounts, and build convincing scams. All they need is a few clues—and most players hand them over without a second thought.

This is why gaming security isn't just for streamers or tech experts. It's for everyone. Whether you game once a week or every day, whether your console is for RPGs or Netflix, it's connected—and what's connected can be exploited.

This isn't about fear. It's about awareness. Because once someone else has control of your console, your payment method, or your account—you can't undo it. You can't reset what's already been stolen. And most people don't even realize it's happening until their digital world starts falling apart.

So the question isn't whether your console is powerful. It's whether it's protected.

And if you don't secure it—someone else will use it.

Why it matters

Imagine walking into a busy public square, setting your wallet down on a bench, and walking away without a glance. You don't lock it. You don't hide it. You don't even check back to see if it's still there. You just trust—blindly—that no one will take it.

That's what ignoring gaming security is like. Only, in this version of the story, there aren't just a few passersby. There are people already circling. Bots scanning. Scripts running. Hackers combing through databases, forums, and marketplaces, hunting for weak spots—like unsecured gaming accounts—and moving quickly once they find them.

And when they do, they don't need to guess what to do next. They've done this thousands of times before.

First, they go after what's visible: the virtual assets. Your rare skins, high-level characters, in-game currency, and progress that took months or even years to earn. Items with real-world value, ready to be sold on black markets for fast profit. A well-equipped gaming account can fetch hundreds—or even thousands—of dollars. And some are sold for far less to players who don't know or don't care that it was stolen.

Then they dig deeper.

Is there a credit card saved to the account? A PayPal link? Any stored gift card balance? If there is, they exploit it—sometimes within seconds. Many cyberattacks on gaming accounts are fully automated. A compromised username and password can be pumped into a script that runs hundreds of transactions in rapid succession.

Skins bought. Gift cards stolen. Wallets drained. By the time the account owner notices, the hacker is long gone—and the digital goods are laundered through other accounts or flipped for cash.

Even when users manage to recover their accounts, the damage is rarely undone. The stolen items are gone. The funds are lost. The sense of safety? That disappears too.

And it doesn't stop at money.

Today's gaming consoles are complex, internet-connected devices. They come with voice assistants, streaming apps, and integrated cameras and microphones—all designed to enhance convenience and immersion. But those same features can be turned against you. A compromised console can be hijacked to spy on you without your knowledge. The camera might be on. The microphone might be listening. This isn't just a data breach—it's a digital home invasion.

Once inside, hackers don't stop at the console.

They pivot. If the same login details work for your email, they move there next. If your email is tied to your cloud storage, bank account, or social media, they try those too. This is what makes gaming account compromises so dangerous—they're often the *starting point*, not the end goal. One breach opens the door to your entire digital identity.

Most of the time, that door is unlocked by something deceptively small.

It could be a link promising a free weapon skin. A pop-up for an exclusive in-game reward. A message from someone claiming to be a moderator. A friend request that leads to a fake login page. These tactics aren't new, but they're still effective because they prey on trust—and because most players aren't trained to spot the red flags.

In 2023, the FBI warned that phishing campaigns targeting gamers had surged, particularly among younger users. And platforms like Roblox, Fortnite, and Steam remain some of the most targeted by scam operations worldwide.

The unsettling part? You may never realize you've been hacked until it's too late.

Many console breaches are designed to be silent. There's no crash, no obvious error, no "you've been hacked" screen. Everything still works—until it doesn't. Meanwhile, behind the scenes, your data may already be leaking out. Payment methods used. Credentials copied. Voice or video harvested. By the time you notice a suspicious charge or an unfamiliar game in your library, the attacker has already done what they came to do.

Some compromised consoles have even been turned into tools of war.

In coordinated cyberattacks, hackers have weaponized hijacked devices—like smart TVs, baby monitors, and yes, even gaming consoles—to launch DDoS (distributed denial of service) attacks against governments, corporations, and critical infrastructure. Your personal gaming system could unknowingly be part of an international cyberattack. It could be spreading malware to others while you watch Netflix, completely unaware.

And if you still think you're not a target because you're not famous or you "don't have anything valuable," you're exactly who hackers are looking for.

Because the average person doesn't expect to be attacked. And that's the point. Casual users don't check their security settings. They reuse the same password everywhere. They assume that their voice chat, camera, and account are harmless. But if your console connects to the internet, stores personal data, or links to any form of payment—it's already a target.

And the only question is whether you're protected... or just lucky.

But luck has a shelf life. Once it runs out, what you lose isn't just digital—it's emotional, financial, and deeply personal. You lose trust. You lose time. You lose control.

You might lose your digital identity, piece by piece.

Online gaming isn't just under siege from hackers—it's becoming a battleground of harassment and psychological strain.

A 2023 report by the Anti-Defamation League, cited by Exploding Topics, revealed that 76% of adult gamers experienced some form of harassment in multiplayer games. Alarmingly, 60% of those described the abuse as "severe," including physical threats, racial slurs, and sexual harassment—turning a leisure activity into a trauma zone.

And the attacks aren't just personal—they're infrastructural.

In the first half of 2024, nearly half of all global DDoS attacks—49%—targeted the gaming and gambling industry, according to the Gcore Radar Report. Cybercriminals bombarded game servers with traffic, disconnecting players, crashing platforms, and disrupting live events. Some did it for profit. Others for revenge. The result? Widespread chaos and degraded experiences.

It's no longer just bad behavior—it's a mental health and cybersecurity crisis growing behind the loading screen.

So when you choose not to take security seriously, it's not just a personal decision. It's a roll of the dice. You're gambling with your finances, your privacy, and your digital presence. All it takes is one unchecked message, one unprotected account, one missed update—and you've given someone else the keys to your world.

So no, ignoring gaming security isn't harmless.

It's handing over your digital life to someone who knows exactly what to do with it.

What to Do About It – Your Security Checklist

1. **Use Strong, Unique Passwords:** Secure gaming accounts with strong passwords and never reuse them across platforms.

2. **Enable Two-Factor Authentication (2FA):** Add an extra layer of security to prevent unauthorized access to gaming accounts.

3. **Beware of Phishing Scams & Fake Game Offers:** Avoid clicking on suspicious links offering free in-game items or discounts.

4. **Review Privacy & Security Settings:** Adjust console and online gaming platform settings to limit data exposure.

5. **Avoid Sharing Personal Information Online:** Do not reveal real names, addresses, or financial details in gaming communities.

6. **Monitor In-Game Purchases & Linked Payment Methods:** Use secure payment options and disable automatic purchases if necessary.

7. **Restrict Access to Child Accounts:** Set up parental controls to manage children's online gaming interactions.

8. **Secure Your Wi-Fi Network with Strong Encryption:** Ensure your gaming device is connected to a secure network with WPA3/WPA2 encryption.
9. **Keep Consoles, Games & Apps Updated:** Regular updates fix vulnerabilities and improve security.
10. **Report Suspicious Players & Online Harassment:** Use built-in reporting tools to flag cyberbullying, scams, or inappropriate behavior.
11. **Enable Login Alerts & Monitor Account Activity:** Receive notifications for unusual login attempts or suspicious activities.
12. **Avoid Downloading Mods, Hacks, or Cheats from Untrusted Sources:** Avoid downloading unauthorized modifications that may contain malware.

Quick Action Plan

1-Minute Fix: Enable two-factor authentication (2FA) on your gaming accounts.

5-Minute Fix: Update account passwords, review security settings, and disable unnecessary sharing features.

15-Minute Fix: Check for unauthorized purchases, enable login alerts, and adjust parental controls (if needed).

30-Minute Fix: Secure your home network, update console firmware, and educate yourself on gaming scams.

Chapter 15

Offline, Still Dangerous: USBs, Hard Drives & Lost Files

Real-World Scenarios

The External Hard Drive That Lost Years of Memories

Clara was the memory-keeper of her family. Every birthday party, vacation, holiday dinner, and school performance had been recorded, labeled, and stored neatly on her external hard drive. Over the years, she'd collected thousands of digital photos and videos. It was her personal archive—a modern family album.

She kept the drive in her desk drawer and connected it only when needed. One afternoon, while organizing her workspace, she accidentally knocked the drive onto the floor. It wasn't a far fall—just a short drop to the carpet—but when she plugged it back in, her spirits plummeted.

Nothing.

The computer didn't recognize the device. No folders, no files. It was as if the drive no longer existed. She tried different cables, different computers—still nothing. Panicked, she contacted a professional data recovery service. The quote was thousands of dollars, with no guarantee of success.

She realized she had no backups. Everything had been stored on that one fragile device.

External hard drives can fail for many reasons: physical damage, internal malfunctions, or even static electricity. Studies show that up to 20% of external hard drives fail within five years of regular use. Yet many users still treat them as if they're permanent vaults for precious data—family photos, business files, or creative projects.

That's a dangerous assumption.

According to Backblaze (2023), which analyzed tens of thousands of hard drives in active use, annual failure rates can range from 1% to over 12%, depending on brand and usage, leading to cumulative failure rates of up to 20% by year five. If your only copy lives on a spinning disk or aging SSD, it might not be "if" you'll lose it—but "when."

Clara thought her hard drive was a reliable, safe storage option.

She didn't realize it could take her family's memories with it in a single fall.

The USB Key That Stole Someone's Banking Information

Thomas was a busy professional who often moved files between his work laptop and his personal computer using a small USB drive. It was convenient, quick, and something he did nearly every day without a second thought.

One evening, after finishing some paperwork at the office, he brought the USB drive home and plugged it into his home PC. Immediately, his antivirus software flagged a threat—a trojan virus embedded deep in the drive's file system. He quarantined the threat and thought that was the end of it.

But days later, Thomas noticed strange charges on his bank account—small withdrawals at first, then larger ones. His email password no longer worked. His social media accounts had been locked.

The virus on the USB had done more than just infect his computer. It had installed a keylogger that silently recorded everything he typed—including banking logins, passwords, and sensitive personal information. What started as a simple file transfer ended in full-blown identity theft.

Later, forensic analysis revealed the malware had originally been installed on his work laptop, silently transferring itself to his USB drive. The moment he plugged it into his home PC, it activated again—this time targeting his personal life.

USB drives are among the most overlooked cybersecurity risks. They're easy to lose, hard to track, and often used to bridge secure and unsecured devices. Malware doesn't announce itself when it jumps from one machine to another.

Thomas thought he was using a harmless tool to transfer documents.

He didn't realize he was also transferring a digital spy into his home.

The External SSD That Was Stolen with Sensitive Data

Phoebe was a freelance accountant known for her dedication and attention to detail. She worked with dozens of small businesses, helping them manage tax filings, payroll, and personal finances. To keep everything organized, she stored all her client records on a sleek, portable external SSD—small enough to fit in her bag, fast enough to work anywhere.

One afternoon, she was working from a crowded coffee shop. Her laptop was on the table, and her backpack—containing her SSD—was slung over the back of her chair. She stepped away for just a moment to take a phone call. When she returned, her backpack was gone.

At first, she was worried about her wallet and keys. But then it hit her: the SSD had been in the front pocket.

That tiny device held years of sensitive client data. Tax returns, Social Security numbers, banking details, invoices, addresses—everything. Worse, none of it was encrypted.

Phoebe had always intended to set up encryption, but never got around to it. She thought the SSD was safe enough as long as she kept it close. Now, anyone who plugged it into a computer could instantly access all the files.

A few weeks later, one of her clients contacted her in a panic. Their bank had flagged an attempted fraudulent loan application using their name and Social Security number. Soon, others followed. Phoebe realized the stolen SSD was more than just a lost gadget—it had become a gateway to identity theft and financial ruin.

Despite reporting the theft and working with a cybersecurity consultant, the damage was done. She had to notify every client, offer credit monitoring, and rebuild trust one conversation at a time.

External SSDs are fast and convenient, but without encryption or access controls, they're like filing cabinets with no locks—perfect targets for thieves.

Phoebe thought her SSD was just a professional tool.

She didn't realize it had turned into a liability for everyone she worked with.

The USB Device That Was Used to Spy on a Victim

Alexander was attending a corporate conference when he visited a promotional booth offering free giveaways. Among the branded pens and notepads, he picked up a small USB-powered fan. It seemed like a harmless piece of swag—something useful to plug into his laptop on warm days.

Back at his hotel, Alexander connected the USB fan to his work laptop. It turned on, quietly spinning as expected. But within seconds, something odd happened. His webcam light flickered. His browser froze for a moment. Then he noticed unfamiliar files appearing in his system folder.

He had no idea what was happening—but his laptop was no longer under his control.

What Alexander didn't know was that the "fan" wasn't just a fan. It had been modified with a malicious microcontroller disguised as a USB peripheral. As soon as it connected to his system, it injected a hidden payload—bypassing antivirus tools and firewalls. The malware silently installed a keylogger and remote access software.

While the fan kept spinning, a hacker on the other end began monitoring his every move. His login credentials were captured. Sensitive business emails were downloaded. Even his webcam and microphone were accessed, turning his device into a live surveillance tool.

Alexander only realized the full extent of the breach days later when he received alerts about suspicious logins to his accounts. By then, his files had been compromised, and private conversations recorded.

This type of attack—called a USB-based hardware exploit—is increasingly common. It doesn't require software downloads or user interaction beyond simply plugging in the device. And because many of these gadgets are disguised as everyday accessories, victims rarely suspect them.

Free gifts like USB chargers, fans, or thumb drives can be Trojan horses in disguise.

Alexander thought he was using a useful conference giveaway.

He didn't realize he had plugged a hacker directly into his laptop.

What You Need to Know

When we talk about cybersecurity, most people think about Wi-Fi, cloud accounts, smartphones, and apps. We picture hackers breaking into networks or stealing passwords through phishing scams. But some of the biggest digital risks don't need an internet connection at all.

They're already in your home.

Tucked in drawers. Left in old backpacks. Sitting at the back of a desk. A USB drive you haven't plugged in for years. An external hard drive from a past job. A laptop you meant to wipe before selling. A phone gathering dust in a box. These "offline" devices may not be online, but that doesn't mean they're harmless. In fact, they can be one of the easiest ways for data to leak, be stolen, or even come back to haunt you years later.

Let's start with USB drives.

They're everywhere—cheap, portable, convenient. But they're also incredibly easy to lose and even easier to weaponize. If you find a USB drive in a parking lot, an elevator, or a shared office and plug it in "just to see what's on it," you might be triggering a hidden payload. This tactic, known as a "USB drop attack," is shockingly effective. The malware inside can auto-launch the moment it's inserted—stealing data, logging keystrokes, or infecting your system with ransomware.

It doesn't stop there.

External hard drives and SSDs are often seen as safe backup solutions. But if they aren't encrypted, anyone who gets their hands on them can access everything inside.

Old tax records. Work files. Family photos. Banking information. Many people sell or throw away these devices assuming that deleting the files or formatting the drive is enough.

It's not.

Deleted doesn't mean destroyed. Basic recovery tools—free ones—can restore thousands of files from a formatted drive. And if that device ends up in the hands of the wrong person, your entire digital history can be reconstructed. There are countless stories of old hard drives sold on eBay or donated to recycling centers only to be later used in identity theft, fraud, or even blackmail.

The same risk applies to personal devices given away, traded in, or sold.

Factory resets on phones, tablets, or laptops often leave behind fragments of data—especially if the memory wasn't encrypted beforehand. Photos. Texts. Passwords saved in browsers. App caches. Browser history. Even with a reset, these leftovers can be pulled using basic forensics software. If the device is synced to your cloud account or hasn't been fully logged out, the new owner might even receive new messages, notifications, or access to your backups.

And then there's the issue of lost data.

Sometimes, the threat isn't what others can take—it's what you can't get back. A dropped hard drive. A corrupted USB. A device that suddenly won't power on. If the only copy of your most important files is on a single offline device, one hardware failure or one misplaced gadget is enough to erase it all. Family videos. Legal documents. Writing projects. Entire businesses have collapsed because their only backups lived on a single physical drive—and no one thought it would fail.

That's the thing about offline devices. We assume they're safer because they're disconnected. But in reality, they're often forgotten, neglected, or underestimated. They don't have built-in security alerts. They don't get patched. They don't send notifications. And yet, they often hold some of our most sensitive information.

This chapter will show you how to secure offline storage, avoid common mistakes, and understand the real risks of devices that aren't connected to the internet—but are still very much connected to your life.

Because just because it's offline doesn't mean it's out of reach.

Why It Matters

We've been taught to think of cybersecurity as a connected-world problem. Threats come through Wi-Fi, the cloud, phishing emails, and malicious links. The moment something goes "offline," we assume it's safe—tucked away, unhackable, no longer part of the problem.

That's a dangerous misconception.

USB drives, external hard drives, SD cards, old laptops, "dead" phones, DVDs, and backup CDs—these tools may not be connected to the internet, but that doesn't make them secure. In fact, their invisibility can make them even more dangerous. Because what's forgotten is rarely protected.

And yet, these devices often contain the most critical data.

Financial documents. Legal contracts. Private photos. Work archives. Password files. Tax returns. Encrypted wallets. Entire years of someone's digital life stored in a single device that might be gathering dust in a drawer—or plugged into someone else's laptop.

That's why offline storage isn't the end of the cybersecurity conversation. It's one of the riskiest blind spots in it.

In 2019, only 9% of malware was built to exploit USB devices.

By 2024, that number exploded to 51%.

According to Honeywell's 2024 report, over half of today's malware is now designed to spread, execute, or attack through USB drives—those tiny sticks we casually plug into laptops, servers, and industrial systems without a second thought. What used to be a convenience is now a loaded weapon.

Every USB you plug in could be the one that detonates your data.

And it's not just malware.

Think tossing out an old hard drive means your data is gone? Think again.

Improper disposal of storage devices—without secure wiping or physical destruction—is a major breach risk. Hackers and data scavengers can often recover what's left behind: personal files, client records, financial data, even login credentials.

Your digital past doesn't disappear when you hit the trash. If you don't destroy it properly, someone else might resurrect it.

Because deleting files isn't the same as destroying them.

Many people wipe files from USBs or external hard drives thinking they're gone. But unless those drives are securely erased, formatted with advanced tools, or physically destroyed, the data remains. Recovery tools—many of them free and easy to use—can bring back thousands of "deleted" files in minutes.

That's how attackers extract:

- Business contracts from discarded drives
- Password lists saved in text files
- Customer databases
- Private videos and photos
- Scanned IDs and passport copies
- Wallet keys for cryptocurrency

If you fail to properly wipe or physically destroy storage devices, your data can live on—and fall into the wrong hands. Hackers, dumpster divers, and data thieves can recover sensitive information from discarded drives with shocking ease.

According to Hummingbird International (2025), improper disposal of IT assets—especially in business environments—comes with five major risks, from data theft to regulatory violations. One mistake could mean exposing client data, leaking trade secrets, or triggering a full-scale breach.

And unlike online accounts, which can be protected with two-factor authentication, or cloud platforms that have redundant backups, offline devices don't come with fail-safes. Once they're lost, broken, corrupted, or exposed, there's often no way back.

The consequences aren't just personal. They're systemic.

Healthcare workers have lost patient records. Schools have lost entire student databases. Photographers have lost years of work. Small business owners have had client information stolen and used in fraud schemes—all because of an unprotected hard drive or USB left in the wrong place.

There's also the growing risk of hardware trojans: malicious hardware disguised as storage devices. Attackers embed microcontrollers into fake USB drives or SD cards that, when plugged into a computer, launch hidden attacks—stealing credentials, installing ransomware, or opening backdoors into company networks. These devices are cheap, mass-produced, and sold online disguised as free giveaways or novelty items.

This matters because people assume that once they unplug, they're safe. But security doesn't stop when the Wi-Fi goes off.

It needs to include:

- Encrypting drives that contain anything sensitive
- Physically destroying hardware before disposal
- Avoiding the use of unknown USB devices
- Using software that fully wipes or overwrites deleted files
- Never treating "offline" as a synonym for "protected"

The digital world doesn't just live in the cloud. It lives in whatever still holds your data. And until that device is properly secured—or destroyed—you're still exposed.

Because offline doesn't mean invisible. It just means forgotten.

What to Do About It – Your Security Checklist

1. **Always Encrypt External Drives:** Use built-in encryption tools (like BitLocker on Windows or FileVault on macOS) to protect USB drives and external hard disks in case they're lost or stolen.

2. **Never Plug in Unknown USB Devices:** Avoid connecting found or gift-

ed USB sticks or accessories—they could be loaded with malware or data-stealing software.

3. **Use a Trusted Antivirus with USB Scanning:** Set your antivirus to automatically scan external devices when plugged in.
4. **Disable USB Autorun Features:** Prevent malicious code from running automatically when a new device is connected.
5. **Back Up Critical Files in Multiple Locations:** Use a 3-2-1 backup strategy—3 copies of your data, 2 different storage types, 1 off-site or cloud copy.
6. **Secure and Label All Drives:** Physically label drives clearly and store them in a safe place—especially if they contain sensitive work, financial, or personal records.
7. **Use Read-Only USB Settings When Sharing:** Some drives allow a physical switch or software setting to prevent writing or malware installation—use it before plugging into unknown systems.
8. **Shred, Crush, or Wipe Drives Before Disposal:** Use certified software to securely erase all data, or physically destroy the drive if you're getting rid of it.
9. **Don't Assume 'Delete' Means Gone:** Use secure file deletion tools to overwrite deleted files on external devices before reselling or donating them.
10. **Be Cautious with Recovery Tools:** If you're trying to recover data, make sure you trust the software—some free tools bundle in spyware or adware.

Quick Action Plan

1-Minute Fix: Turn off USB autorun on your main device and set antivirus to scan all external drives.

5-Minute Fix: Encrypt your most-used external USB and backup drives.

15-Minute Fix: Check what sensitive files are stored on your external media and securely delete or move anything that doesn't belong there.

30-Minute Fix: Create a backup plan that includes both cloud and offline storage, and implement a secure disposal process for all old drives.

PART 4 - ONLINE LIFE: SECRETS, SCAMS and SILENT TAKEOVERS

Chapter 16

Personal Email Security: Stop Them at the Gate

Real-World Scenarios

The Email That Stole a Woman's Life Savings

Anna started her morning the way she always did—with a quiet moment, a warm cup of coffee, and a quick glance through her inbox. But one subject line cut through the routine like a knife:

"Suspicious Login Detected – Immediate Action Required!"

It appeared to be from her bank. The logo was polished, the sender's email address looked official, and the message used just the right tone of urgency to sound real—but not alarming. It claimed that someone had attempted to access her account from an unknown device and advised her to secure her account immediately by clicking the link.

Without a second thought, Anna clicked.

A login page appeared. It was identical to the one she used regularly—same colors, same layout, even the same security icon. She entered her credentials and waited. The page refreshed, then stalled. It didn't say whether anything had been fixed. Figuring it was a glitch, she closed the window and got on with her day.

Later that afternoon, Anna opened her bank's mobile app to pay a bill—and froze. Her savings account, which held years of careful budgeting, was empty.

Gone. Every dollar.

She frantically called the bank. By the time their fraud team investigated, the money had already been moved through a string of fake accounts and crypto wallets. The transactions were instant, irreversible, and anonymous.

The email hadn't come from her bank at all—it was a phishing scam. The website was a fake, designed to capture her credentials and deliver them straight to a hacker.

Anna had fallen into one of the most common and costly traps online. Every day, millions of similar phishing emails are sent. Many are so convincing they bypass spam filters. And once a victim logs in to a fake site, the attacker can drain accounts in minutes.

Anna thought she was being proactive—taking a step to protect her money.

She didn't realize that one click would cost her everything.

The Fake Amazon Order That Led to Identity Theft

Derek wasn't expecting any deliveries, so when he saw the email subject line—"Your Order of a $1,500 iPhone Has Been Confirmed!"—his pulse quickened. He clicked immediately, anxious to correct what he assumed was a major mistake.

The email looked exactly like a real Amazon receipt. It had all the right branding, familiar links, and a breakdown of the "order" that he never made. At the bottom was a bright button: "Cancel or Manage Your Order."

He clicked it.

The page it led to looked just like Amazon's login screen. Without thinking, he typed in his email and password. But when he hit enter, nothing happened. The page simply refreshed. Suspicious, he closed the window.

Within an hour, the chaos began.

He started receiving email alerts for login attempts from unknown locations. His Amazon account was used to purchase gift cards. His credit card company flagged suspicious activity. Password reset emails flooded his inbox—from Facebook, PayPal, even his bank.

Derek had walked straight into a phishing trap.

The fake Amazon page had collected his credentials, which the hacker quickly used to gain access to his accounts. Because Derek had reused the same password on multiple services—a common mistake—the intruder didn't need to hack anything. He simply walked through the digital front door.

In just a few hours, Derek's digital life was in disarray. It took days of phone calls, password resets, credit card freezes, and damage control to reclaim even partial access.

Fake order scams are among the most effective phishing tactics. They prey on fear, urgency, and a person's instinct to act quickly when something seems wrong. Like many, Derek thought he was fixing a mistake.

He didn't realize he was stepping into an identity theft nightmare.

The Email That Exposed Private Photos

Uma was in the middle of a busy morning when she received what looked like a routine email from her mobile phone provider. The subject line read: "Important Account Update – Verify Your Information." It looked official. The logo was polished, the layout professional, and the tone urgent but familiar. Without much hesitation, she clicked the link and entered her email and password to log in, assuming she was taking a simple step to secure her account.

Days passed. Then her phone suddenly stopped working. It wouldn't receive calls or texts, and no amount of rebooting helped. She assumed it was a technical glitch—until her email stopped working too. Her social media apps had all logged out. Her cloud storage account was locked.

That's when it clicked: something was very wrong.

Unbeknownst to her, the email had been a phishing scam. The login page she visited was a fake, a perfect replica of her provider's website. A hacker now had access to her account credentials. They didn't just stop there. They contacted her mobile provider and impersonated her, requesting a SIM card transfer. With her phone number now in their hands, they bypassed every two-factor authentication tied to her accounts.

By the time Uma realized what had happened, the damage was done. The hacker had full control of her email, cloud files, and photos. They sifted through years of private moments—family vacations, birthdays, personal conversations—and stole everything.

Then came the message: if she didn't send a $1,000 Bitcoin payment within 48 hours, her private photos would be leaked online.

Uma had always thought her phone and cloud accounts were secure. She never imagined that one convincing email could lead to such a terrifying invasion of privacy. She thought she was protecting her account, when in reality, she had unknowingly handed over control of her digital life to a stranger.

The Forgotten Email That Led to a Home Burglary

Isaac hadn't thought about his old Yahoo account in years. It was the email he'd used back in college, long before he switched to newer platforms. These days, it was little more than a digital attic—cluttered with outdated subscriptions, long-expired login confirmations, and old online shopping receipts. He hadn't logged into it in ages, and it sat forgotten in the shadows of his online presence.

Then one afternoon, an email arrived in his primary inbox. The subject line said: "Suspicious Login Attempt on Your Yahoo Account – Secure It Now." He saw it, hesitated for a moment, and then dismissed it. Why bother? It wasn't like he used the account for anything important anymore.

A week later, Isaac returned from a weekend away to a nightmare. His front door was wide open. Inside, drawers were pulled out, electronics were gone, and his smart security system was completely offline. At first, he assumed someone had forced entry—until he realized there were no signs of a break-in.

It didn't make sense until he contacted his smart home provider. That's when he learned the terrifying truth. Someone had gained remote access to his smart locks and disabled his alarm system by using the very Yahoo account he had ignored. That old, forgotten email had been tied to his smart home login. It had once been used to register devices, receive password reset links, and verify his home network.

When hackers broke into the email, they found the backdoor they needed. They reset his smart home credentials, logged in remotely, and let themselves in—no tools, no alarms, no warnings.

Isaac had assumed that because he didn't use the email anymore, it was harmless. But that neglected piece of his digital life turned out to be the weakest link in his home's security. What he thought was long forgotten became the very thing that allowed criminals to walk straight through his front door.

What You Need to Know

Your email account is more than just a communication tool. It's the front door to your digital identity.

Think about how many times you've clicked "Forgot Password?" on a website. What happens next? A reset link goes to your email. That means your email isn't just a place where messages land—it's the master key that unlocks everything else.

Banking. Shopping. Social media. Cloud storage. Medical records. Streaming services. Investment platforms. Most people use the same email address for everything. And once someone gets into that email account, they don't need to guess your passwords for other sites. They can simply reset them—and lock you out in minutes.

This is why hackers go after email first.

It's not flashy. It's not loud. But it works. A single compromised inbox can lead to total digital takeover.

The attack usually starts with a phishing email. Maybe it looks like a message from your bank, a delivery service, or even a friend. You click a link, and the page looks familiar. You enter your login credentials without thinking twice. It takes seconds. The site refreshes—or appears to crash—and you move on. But in the background, someone else now has your email and password.

In 2023, over 3.4 billion phishing emails were sent every day. Many bypass spam filters. They use real logos, stolen sender addresses, and AI-generated text that mimics tone and grammar flawlessly. You don't need to be careless to get tricked. You just need to be tired, distracted, or in a rush.

And the damage goes deeper than most people realize.

Once hackers gain access to your inbox, they don't immediately lock you out. Many quietly monitor your emails—looking for banking messages, invoices, saved passwords, or personal information they can use. If you've ever emailed a photo of your ID, forwarded a tax document, or stored passwords in drafts or notes, it's all sitting there waiting.

Some attackers set up hidden forwarding rules, so every email you receive gets copied to them. You change your password, and they still see everything. Others use your account to send phishing emails to your friends and family, making the attack even harder to detect because it's coming from someone they trust—you.

Even old or unused email accounts can become backdoors. Many people forget about them, but those accounts may still be linked to important services. If a hacker gains access, they can reset passwords silently or use old messages to piece together enough information for identity theft.

And then there's the risk of reused passwords.

If your email uses the same password as another account that's been exposed in a data breach, attackers don't even need to phish. They can simply plug that combination into automated login tools and wait for access.

One leaked password = every door opened.

This chapter will show you what attackers look for, how they get in, and how to take control of your inbox before someone else does. You'll learn how to spot fake emails, secure your recovery options, and use real protection—not just a password, but layers of defense that make breaking into your inbox much harder.

Because your email isn't just a messaging app. It's your central hub. Your digital gatekeeper.

And once it's compromised, everything else can fall with it.

Why It Matters

Your email address is the digital equivalent of your front door. Everything comes through it—banking alerts, password resets, identity verification codes, personal conversations, bills, travel plans, medical records, shopping receipts, school updates. And yet, for something so critical, most people protect their email accounts with less thought than they give to a phone lock screen.

That's a problem. Because when attackers go looking for an entry point into your life, they don't always start with your bank or your social media. They start with your inbox.

Why? Because it holds the keys to everything else.

According to the 2024 Email Security Risk Report by Egress, 79% of successful ATOs (Account Takeovers) are triggered by phishing. It's not just the first move. It's the master key—unlocking your inbox, your cloud, your bank, your business.

In most cases, the email account didn't even contain sensitive content—but it was linked to platforms that did. Once an attacker gets into your inbox, they can reset passwords, intercept 2FA codes, pose as you to others, monitor your activity silently, and pivot to deeper parts of your digital life without tripping alarms.

This is why email is often referred to as the "master key" of your online identity.

It connects everything. And if it's not secure, nothing else is.

Attackers don't need to "hack" your email in the way people imagine. Most of the time, they wait for you to make the first move. Click the wrong link. Reuse a password that was leaked in a previous breach. Download a fake invoice. Use your work email on a personal shopping site. Or ignore the signs that your account has already been compromised.

And once they're in? Most people don't notice.

A hacker inside your inbox won't announce themselves. Instead, they create email filters that forward copies of your mail to their account. They hide password reset notifications. They monitor your patterns. Some even create rules that delete security alerts before you see them. Many compromised email accounts remain under silent surveillance for weeks before being used in an attack.

That delay is strategic.

Because the attacker wants to study your life: when you're online, who you email, what services you use. Then they pick the right time to strike—by sending fake invoices to your contacts, accessing your bank account through password resets, or locking you out of your backup recovery options.

Even worse, once your email address has been compromised, it rarely stops there.

It becomes part of a data chain. Shared, sold, and reused across the dark web. You become the victim of credential stuffing—where attackers try your email and password combinations on hundreds of websites, hoping for a match. And unfortunately, they often get one.

In 2024, IBM reported that compromised credentials were the leading cause of data breaches, emphasizing the dangers of password reuse. Separately, a Google survey found that 65% of users still reuse passwords across personal accounts, making one breach the start of many.

But there's another layer of risk: **impersonation**.

When your email account is compromised, attackers don't just read your messages—they become you. Friends. Family. Coworkers. They're far more likely to click a malicious link or send money when the message looks like it's coming from someone they trust.

And with AI in the mix, it's disturbingly easy. Tools can now mimic your tone, auto-generate replies, even scan your message history to craft scams that sound exactly like you.

And this isn't rare. In just three months of 2024, Kaspersky blocked over 250 million phishing attempts—nearly 3 million a day (Cybernews, 2024).

Emails. Messages. Pop-ups. Each one crafted to steal your identity, your money, your access.

Phishing isn't noise. It's a flood. And you're the gateway.

The emails you send, the people you connect with, the accounts tied to your name—all of them can become collateral damage if your inbox is compromised.

This is why email security matters so much. Because it's easy to take for granted. It runs in the background. It's routine. But behind that routine is an intricate web of access points that lead straight to your most personal and sensitive information.

In 2023 alone, Business Email Compromise (BEC) and Email Account Compromise (EAC) were the most financially devastating cybercrimes reported. According to the FBI's Internet Crime Report, they racked up more than $2.9 billion in losses.

Your inbox is not just another account. It's the one account that unlocks all the others.

And if you don't stop attackers there, you won't stop them at all.

What to Do About It – Your Security Checklist

1. **Use a Strong, Unique Password for Your Email:** Never reuse your email password across other sites. If hackers get into your inbox, they can reset passwords for everything else.

2. **Enable Two-Factor Authentication (2FA):** Protect your email with an additional layer of security—preferably using an authenticator app, not just SMS.

3. **Use a Password Manager to Store and Rotate Passwords:** This makes it easier to use complex, unique passwords and helps prevent reuse across multiple accounts.

4. **Be Wary of Unexpected Attachments and Links:** Most phishing attacks come through email. Don't open attachments or click links from unknown or suspicious senders.

5. **Check Sender Addresses Carefully:** Phishing emails often come from addresses that look legitimate at first glance. Hover over the name to see the full email address.

6. **Avoid Public Wi-Fi When Accessing Email:** Unless you're using a VPN, don't check your inbox on unsecured networks—your login credentials can be intercepted.

7. **Don't Save Login Info in Your Browser:** Use a password manager instead. Browsers are common targets for credential theft.

8. **Review and Revoke Third-Party Access:** Check your email account's connected apps and services. Remove anything you don't recognize or no longer use.

9. **Set Up Alerts for Suspicious Logins or Password Changes:** Most email platforms allow you to be notified of access from unknown devices or unusual activity.

10. **Archive or Delete Old Sensitive Emails:** Clear out old emails that contain personal data, bank details, or passwords. If your account is ever breached,

this limits the damage.

Quick Action Plan

1-Minute Fix: Turn on two-factor authentication (2FA) for your primary email account.

5-Minute Fix: Change your email password to something strong and unique using a password manager.

15-Minute Fix: Review your inbox for suspicious emails, archive old sensitive content, and enable security alerts.

30-Minute Fix: Audit your third-party app access and remove any services or apps you no longer use or don't recognize.

Chapter 17

Passwords: Still Your Weakest Link

Real-World Scenarios

The Fake Login Page That Tricked a Lawyer

Susan had built a reputation as one of the most respected attorneys at her firm. She dealt with sensitive legal documents, corporate contracts, and high-stakes negotiations. That made her a prime target—and she didn't even know it.

Late one evening, after a long day in court, she was checking emails on her phone when a message from Google caught her eye. It looked urgent: "Your account has been compromised. Click here to reset your password."

She didn't think twice. The email looked authentic—same layout, same logo, same kind of language she'd seen before. She clicked the link.

A Google login page appeared. It was convincing, perfectly cloned. She entered her email address and password, hit enter—and nothing happened. The page refreshed, no error, no confirmation, no redirect.

Suspicious now, Susan looked more closely at the browser address. It wasn't Goog le.com. It was "g00gle-security-check.com"—a clever forgery using zeros instead of O's. She felt like the floor had vanished beneath her.

She had just handed her login credentials to a hacker.

By the time she tried to change her password, it was too late. Her Google account had already been accessed from an IP address overseas. Her inbox was being searched, her calendar scraped for client names, and files in her Google Drive—confidential legal documents—were being downloaded.

For someone in her profession, the breach wasn't just personal—it was professional. She had to notify her firm, inform clients, and take swift legal steps to report and mitigate the incident. Her reputation, her career, and the trust of her clients had all been put at risk because of one small, believable lie.

Susan had always taken security seriously, but phishing scams are increasingly sophisticated. All it takes is one email, one moment of panic, and one misplaced click.

She thought she was protecting her account from hackers.

Instead, she was unknowingly handing her password straight to them.

The "Saved Password" That Got a Man Hacked

Elliot had a busy schedule—meetings during the day, side projects at night, and barely enough time to keep track of his dozens of online accounts. So, like millions of others, he relied on his browser's autofill feature to save time. Whenever he logged into a website—his banking portal, work email, crypto wallet—his browser would ask if he wanted to save the password. And every time, he clicked "Yes."

One evening, while trying to open a file, Elliot searched for a quick PDF reader. He found a free one through a Google result and downloaded it without giving it much thought. It installed quickly, and the file opened without any problems.

What Elliot didn't know was that the installer came with a Trojan—malicious software designed specifically to harvest saved browser passwords.

While Elliot slept peacefully, the Trojan scanned his device and exported every saved login to a hacker-controlled server. His most sensitive information—banking credentials, cryptocurrency wallet keys, corporate logins—was now in the hands of cybercriminals halfway across the world.

By morning, chaos had already begun. His bank account showed several unauthorized withdrawals. His work email was inaccessible—locked after multiple failed login attempts. And when he checked his crypto exchange account, he saw his balance had dropped to zero.

The software he had downloaded had seemed harmless. But in reality, it was a trap designed to exploit convenience. The stored passwords had made it effortless for hackers to take over everything.

Elliot thought he was saving time.

He didn't realize he was saving his credentials for a hacker to steal later.

The "Password Reset" Scam That Took Over a Woman's Life

Sophia was lounging on the couch, scrolling through Instagram when her phone buzzed with a text from her mobile provider.

"Your account password has been reset. If this wasn't you, contact us immediately."

Alarmed, she called the number listed in the text. A customer support representative answered, confirmed that a reset request had been processed, and reassured her that everything was fine. Relieved, Sophia hung up.

A few minutes later, her phone went completely silent. No calls, no texts, no internet. She restarted it—but it wouldn't reconnect to her network. It wasn't just a glitch. Her number had been transferred to a new SIM card.

A hacker had impersonated Sophia over the phone, tricking the mobile provider into "verifying" their identity and reassigning her phone number to a different SIM. That gave them control over all the two-factor authentication codes sent to her phone.

Within the next hour, the hacker used her phone number to reset her email, PayPal, and Venmo passwords. They changed the recovery questions, added new login credentials, and locked her out. Money was siphoned from her digital wallets, and messages were sent from her social media accounts before she could do anything to stop it.

It took Sophia days to piece together what happened—and even longer to regain control of some of her accounts. Others were gone for good.

She had done nothing wrong. She never clicked a malicious link or shared her password. But by controlling her phone number, the hacker had slipped past every digital lock she thought would keep her safe.

Sophia thought she was calling to protect her account.

She didn't realize her entire digital life was about to be stolen in the span of an afternoon.

The Password Manager Hack That Gave Criminals Millions

Julian prided himself on being cautious—especially when it came to online security. He read privacy policies, avoided public Wi-Fi, and never reused passwords. He used a reputable password manager that created and stored long, complex logins for everything from his email accounts to his crypto wallet. He believed he had done everything right.

Then news broke: the password manager company he relied on had been breached. Hackers had stolen a massive trove of user data, including encrypted password vaults.

At first, the company assured users that the vaults were secure. The data was encrypted, after all. But in the following months, Julian began hearing troubling reports—people who used that same password manager were being hacked, their savings drained, their accounts hijacked.

Still, Julian believed he was safe—until it happened to him.

He received a notification from his crypto exchange about a login from a new device. When he tried to access his account, he found he had already been locked out. The hacker had used the stolen data from the breached password manager, brute-forced the master password protecting his vault, and pulled every credential it contained.

In just a few minutes, they had transferred over $250,000 in Bitcoin to a series of anonymous wallets. The funds were gone, unrecoverable. Law enforcement could do little.

Julian had followed every rule. He had trusted a system that millions depended on.

But hackers aren't just targeting individuals anymore—they're targeting the tools people use to protect themselves.

Julian thought he was staying ahead of cybercrime.

He didn't realize that even the safest vault can become a target—and when it does, everything inside becomes vulnerable.

What You Need to Know

For something so small, passwords carry enormous power.

They're the locks on your digital doors—used to protect your email, your bank, your cloud, your social media, your online purchases, and just about every piece of your identity. And yet, for most people, they're also the weakest link in their entire security setup.

Because the problem with passwords isn't just about how easy they are to guess. It's how easy they are to reuse. Forget. Mismanage. Or give away without even realizing.

Let's start with the most common habit: using the same password across multiple accounts.

It makes sense, right? Easy to remember. Saves time. But here's the truth—if just one of those sites gets hacked, every other account using that same password is now exposed. Hackers know this. That's why, the moment a data breach is made public, they run the leaked passwords against every major service on the internet. It's called credential stuffing. And it works frighteningly well.

In fact, some of the biggest breaches in the past decade didn't start with sophisticated malware or advanced zero-day exploits. They started with a single reused password—stolen from one platform and used to unlock another. The attacker didn't break in. They logged in.

And even when passwords aren't reused, they're often weak.

People pick names. Birthdays. Pets. Sports teams. "Password123." Anything easy enough to remember—but also easy enough to guess. Hackers don't sit around typing random words. They use massive databases of common passwords, dictionary attacks, and bots that test millions of combinations per second. If your password is short, predictable, or personal, it's not secure. It's just familiar.

Despite the risks, most people still manage their passwords the old-fashioned way: memory, pen, paper.

A global survey by Bitwarden – covering 2,400 users across the US, UK, Australia, France, Germany, and Japan – found that these outdated habits still dominate, even now.

And then there's phishing.

Even a strong password can be stolen if you're tricked into giving it away. You get a fake login screen disguised as your bank, your cloud provider, your email. It looks real. You enter your credentials. The attacker grabs them instantly. And because it's you typing them in, your device or browser doesn't raise any red flags. It feels like nothing happened—until something does.

Password managers help, but they aren't foolproof either. If someone gains access to your master password, everything inside that vault is compromised. And while they're a powerful tool when used properly, many people never secure their password manager with two-factor authentication—essentially building a safe and then leaving the key in the door.

Worse still, many people store passwords in unsafe places: sticky notes on the desk, documents labeled "logins," browser autofill features that don't require a master password to view. In a world where entire lives exist online, storing your keys in plain sight is asking for trouble.

The scariest part? You might not even notice when a password has been compromised. Unless the hacker locks you out, they might quietly monitor your account, read your messages, make purchases, or download your data without leaving an obvious trail. And by the time you do notice, the damage has already been done—and it's not just digital. It's financial. Emotional. Reputational.

This chapter will show you how to break bad password habits, build stronger ones, and use tools that keep you one step ahead of attackers. It's not just about length or complexity. It's about behavior. Strategy. Discipline.

Because in cybersecurity, your password isn't just a login detail.

It's the first line of defense—and if it fails, everything behind it is wide open.

Why It Matters

For all the advances in cybersecurity—biometrics, hardware keys, two-factor authentication, AI-driven threat detection—passwords remain the single most common method of protecting digital accounts. And also the most consistently exploited.

That's not a coincidence.

Most people know their passwords should be complex, unique, and changed regularly. But knowing and doing are two different things. Convenience almost always wins. And attackers count on it.

A 2024–2025 analysis by Cybernews uncovered a staggering truth: 94% of people reuse passwords across multiple accounts.

Not malware. Not zero-days.

Just the same weak password—used over and over again.

It's one of the biggest holes in modern security. And it's self-inflicted.

Why does this matter? Because in most cases, your password is the only line of defense between a hacker and your bank account, your identity, your entire digital life.

And guess what? That password is often laughably easy to crack. Even in 2025, the most commonly used passwords still include:

- "123456"
- "qwerty"
- "password"
- Names of pets, kids, or favorite sports teams
- Birthdates, anniversaries, or phone numbers

These are exactly the kinds of details people post freely on social media—making them easy targets for brute-force attacks or password-guessing algorithms. And with AI-assisted cracking tools, what once took hours can now take seconds.

But even if your password is complex, that doesn't mean it's secure.

Here's why:

1. Reused Passwords Create a Chain Reaction. When a website gets hacked, your email and password combo often ends up for sale on dark web markets. If you use that same combo on other sites, attackers can automate login attempts using credential stuffing tools. A breach at a single retailer can become access to your email, cloud storage, or bank account in minutes. The global average cost of a data breach reached an all-time high of $4.45 million in 2023. Notably, breaches involving stolen or compromised credentials – often resulting from weak or reused passwords – were the most common, accounting for 16% of incidents and averaging $4.62 million in costs (IBM – Cost of a Data Breach Report, 2023).

2. Saved Passwords Aren't Always Safe. Browsers like Chrome, Safari, and Edge offer to save your passwords for convenience—but those passwords are stored in your device's local files or cloud account. If your device is stolen, infected with malware, or synced across multiple platforms, a hacker may be able to extract those credentials without needing to "crack" anything at all.

3. Password Managers Help but They're Not Invincible. Password managers are powerful tools, and everyone should use one. But they're also targets. In 2022, a major password manager was breached, and while most data was encrypted, some metadata was exposed – including hints about which vaults belonged to high-value targets. If your master password is weak, even the best password manager won't protect you.

What makes this worse is how invisible it all is.

When your password is compromised, you often don't know. Your login still works. Your email looks normal. There are no warning signs. Meanwhile, the attacker might be:

- Downloading your cloud backups
- Reading your emails
- Monitoring your bank statements
- Resetting your other accounts using your email access
- Selling your credentials in bulk to the highest bidder

And it doesn't stop at one account. It spreads—quickly.

Think of your digital life like a house. Each password is a key to a different room. If you reuse the same key everywhere, a thief who finds one copy can walk through every door. That's why password hygiene is so important. It's not about being paranoid. It's about not being predictable.

This is why it matters.

Because passwords are simple. Too simple, sometimes. They rely on human behavior. And humans, by nature, choose things that are easy to remember—which often means easy to crack.

Password fatigue is real. Managing dozens of logins is frustrating. But ignoring the problem doesn't make you safer—it just makes you easier to target. With the rise of phishing, data breaches, and automated password attacks, no one can afford to be lazy about login security.

In the end, it doesn't matter how strong your firewall is, how secure your connection is, or how careful you are with your personal information—if your password is weak, everything else is already broken.

What to Do About It – Your Security Checklist

1. **Use Unique Passwords for Every Account:** Never reuse the same password across multiple platforms. If one is breached, the rest become vulnerable instantly.

2. **Create Strong, Unpredictable Passwords:** Use long phrases or random strings with letters, numbers, and special characters. Avoid names, birthdays, or common words.

3. **Use a Password Manager:** Don't rely on memory or handwritten notes. A password manager creates and stores complex passwords securely.

4. **Enable Two-Factor Authentication (2FA):** Add a second layer of security, especially on critical accounts like email, banking, and cloud storage.

5. **Regularly Update Old Passwords:** Change passwords at least once a year—or immediately if you hear about a breach involving a service you use.

6. **Check for Leaked Passwords:** Use tools like "Have I Been Pwned" or your password manager's breach monitoring feature to see if your credentials have been exposed.

7. **Avoid Saving Passwords in Browsers:** Browsers are convenient but less secure than password managers. If your device is compromised, saved logins can be stolen.

8. **Don't Share Passwords—Even With Family:** Shared access increases the risk of unintended leaks. If you must share, use a password manager with delegated access.

9. **Be Cautious of Phishing Pages Mimicking Logins:** Double-check URLs before entering credentials. Fake sites are designed to trick you into handing over real passwords.

10. **Log Out of Shared Devices and Clear Credentials:** Never leave accounts open on public or borrowed devices. Log out fully and clear saved credentials afterward.

Quick Action Plan

1-Minute Fix: Turn on 2FA for at least your most important account (email or bank).

5-Minute Fix: Change any password you know you've reused—start with the accounts that matter most.

15-Minute Fix: Install a password manager and import your saved passwords securely.

30-Minute Fix: Audit all major accounts, update weak or reused passwords, and check if any have been exposed in data breaches.

Chapter 18

Identity Theft: How One Mistake Can Ruin Everything

Real-World Scenarios

The Fake Loan That Left a Man in Debt

Gavin had always been careful with his finances. He paid his bills on time, avoided unnecessary debt, and kept a close eye on his credit score and bank activity. He used strong passwords, avoided suspicious websites, and never shared sensitive information online. In short, he did everything he thought a financially responsible adult was supposed to do.

One morning, Gavin received an unexpected phone call from a debt collection agency. The voice on the other end of the line was stern and direct.

"Mr. Adams, we're calling about your overdue personal loan of fifteen thousand dollars. It's been three months since your last payment. When can we expect the next one?"

Gavin was confused. "What loan? I never took out a loan."

The collector insisted the loan had been processed through a legitimate bank using all of Gavin's information—his full name, address, date of birth, and Social Security number. He was listed as the primary borrower. His signature was even on the documents.

Gavin hung up the phone, thinking there must be some mistake. But after contacting the bank himself, he discovered it was all true. Someone had applied for a personal loan using his identity and had received the funds directly into an account he'd never seen before.

What was worse, the loan had gone unpaid for months, and now it was damaging his credit. Late payment notices had been sent to an address he'd never lived at. His credit score had plummeted, and the debt collectors were becoming increasingly aggressive.

Gavin found himself trapped. Even though he hadn't taken the loan, it was now his responsibility to prove that the fraud had occurred. That meant filing a police report, working with credit bureaus, contacting the bank's fraud department, and potentially hiring legal help—all while feeling powerless and angry.

He had always assumed identity theft was something that happened to careless people. He never imagined that despite all his precautions, someone could still steal his financial identity and leave him to clean up the mess.

His credit was ruined, his peace of mind shattered, and the road to recovery would be long and exhausting—all because someone else had used his information without him even knowing.

The Job Offer That Led to an Arrest Warrant

Chloe had been unemployed for several months. She was talented and hardworking, but the job market was tough, and competition was fierce. She spent hours each day scrolling through job boards, tweaking her résumé, and applying to any position that matched her skills.

So when she got an email from a recruiter about a high-paying remote job, she was thrilled. The email seemed professional, the company had a sleek website, and the job description matched her qualifications perfectly. The recruiter was friendly, praising her résumé and encouraging her to move quickly through the onboarding process so she could start immediately.

Without hesitation, Chloe filled out the onboarding forms. She provided her full name, address, date of birth, Social Security number, banking details for direct deposit, and even uploaded a scanned copy of her driver's license for verification.

She was excited to start working and relieved to finally have a stable income. But after she submitted the paperwork, everything went quiet. Days passed without any response. When she tried to email the recruiter, the message bounced back. The company's website, once sleek and convincing, was suddenly offline.

She began to worry. Maybe it was a scam. But there was no immediate fallout, so she put it behind her—until months later, when she received a call from the police in another state.

The officer informed her there was an active warrant for her arrest. Her identity had been linked to a series of fraudulent bank accounts and wire transfers. Chloe was stunned. She had no idea any of this had happened. But someone had used her personal information to commit financial crimes, and now the law believed she was responsible.

Chloe had to prove her innocence while also dealing with the trauma of having her identity stolen. She spent weeks contacting banks, filing reports, and explaining her situation to investigators. Every moment felt like walking through a nightmare she couldn't wake up from.

What she thought was a career breakthrough turned out to be a professional trap. The job wasn't real, the recruiter was a thief, and the consequences of trusting the wrong person would haunt her long after the fake job offer disappeared.

The Phone Call That Hijacked an Entire Life

Isabelle was in the middle of her lunch break when her phone rang. The caller ID showed the name of her bank, and the voice on the line introduced themselves as a representative from the fraud department. They sounded urgent but professional.

"We've detected unusual activity on your account," the caller said. "We just need to verify your identity before we can secure your funds. Can you confirm your full name and Social Security number?"

Isabelle felt a rush of anxiety. She had always been careful with her finances, and the idea that her account might be under threat was terrifying. The voice was calm, patient, and reassuring. It didn't feel like a scam. They even referenced a small transaction she'd made the day before.

So, without thinking twice, she gave them the information they asked for.

Minutes later, her phone lost service entirely. No calls, no texts, no data. It just went dead.

That was only the beginning.

By the time she got to a computer and logged into her bank account, it was too late. Money had already been transferred out. When she tried to reset her password, she realized her email account had been compromised too. She couldn't get in.

Her social media accounts started showing suspicious activity—posts she hadn't made, password resets she hadn't requested. Then came the alerts from credit monitoring services: new credit card applications in her name, address changes, and even a flagged attempt to file a tax return.

Isabelle had been the victim of a social engineering attack.

She hadn't clicked on a suspicious link or visited a shady website. She had simply answered a phone call that looked legitimate and gave her information to someone who seemed trustworthy.

What she didn't realize was that scammers often impersonate banks, tech support teams, or government agencies with convincing language and spoofed phone numbers. Once they get your Social Security number and other personal information, they can hijack your financial life with frightening speed.

Isabelle thought she was protecting her bank account. Instead, she had unknowingly opened the door to a complete identity takeover. The damage was immediate, and the recovery would take years.

The Data Breach That Sold a Man's Life on the Dark Web

Xavier had always considered himself tech-savvy. He used strong passwords, never opened suspicious links, and regularly updated his software. As far as he knew, he had never been hacked. But one day, that illusion came crashing down with a single chilling email.

The subject line read: "We have your identity."

The message was brief but direct. A cybercriminal claimed to have Xavier's full name, Social Security number, home address, and phone number. If Xavier didn't pay one thousand dollars in Bitcoin within 72 hours, his personal information would be sold on the dark web.

At first, Xavier thought it had to be a bluff. But curiosity got the better of him. He signed into a dark web monitoring service out of caution—and there it was. His details. His passwords. Old addresses. Even security question answers.

His identity had been exposed.

After some digging, he traced the breach back to an online retailer he had used years ago. It turned out the company had suffered a massive data breach, and Xavier's information had been part of the stolen data—data that had quietly circulated in underground forums ever since.

Xavier had changed his password back then, like the company suggested. What he didn't realize was that the breach had exposed far more than just his login credentials. His entire identity had been scooped up and stored away until someone decided to use it.

And now, it was being held for ransom.

The worst part was realizing how common this had become. He learned that billions of records had been exposed just in the past year, and personal identities could be sold for the price of a coffee. Even if the fraud didn't happen immediately, the data could sit dormant for months or years, ready to resurface at any time.

Xavier had always believed that being careful online was enough. But no matter how strong your passwords are or how cautious you are with emails, it doesn't protect you from a data breach you never saw coming. His personal details had been out there for years—and he never even knew it.

What You Need to Know

In 2024 alone, cybersecurity firm SpyCloud recovered 53.3 billion unique identity records from the dark web.

Yes – billion. That's a 22% jump from the year before, exposing the explosive growth of digital identity theft and data leaks.

Every record represents a person. An account. A risk.

This isn't slowing down—it's accelerating.

Identity theft doesn't always start with a criminal digging through your trash or stealing your wallet. These days, it often starts online—with a single exposed password, a leaked document, a stolen email account, or a social media post that gave away just enough detail.

And once it starts, it doesn't stay small.

Your identity isn't just your name. It's your birthdate. Your address. Your phone number. It's the last four digits of your Social Security number. The answer to your security questions. The combination of things you've shared online and forgotten you posted. And in the wrong hands, it becomes currency—bought, sold, and traded like a product.

Cybercriminals don't need to steal everything. They just need enough pieces to fake the rest.

They use your information to open credit cards, apply for loans, file false tax returns, or even get access to medical services. Some build complete profiles—email, address history, account access—and sell those bundles on the dark web to others who continue the fraud. Sometimes the theft happens quickly. Other times, it spreads quietly for months before you realize anything's wrong.

By then, you may have already lost control of more than just your data.

Victims of identity theft often spend months trying to reverse the damage. Dealing with fraudulent charges. Proving they didn't open accounts. Calling banks, credit bureaus, and law enforcement. It's exhausting, confusing, and emotionally draining. Some find their credit destroyed. Others miss job opportunities or have their social media accounts hijacked and used for scams. In extreme cases, identity theft leads to legal trouble when crimes are committed in the victim's name.

And the scariest part? Most identity theft doesn't come from some major hack or breach you hear about on the news.

It comes from one mistake.

Clicking on a fake login page. Responding to a phishing email. Reusing a weak password. Leaving personal documents in a cloud folder with poor privacy settings. Posting a picture of your driver's license to celebrate getting it. Sharing your home address in a group chat. These small slips open the door for someone who knows how to use the information.

It's not just about what gets stolen—it's what that data unlocks.

Once someone has access to your email, they can reset passwords for other accounts. If they get your phone number, they can intercept your two-factor codes through SIM swapping. If they get your ID and address, they can create fake documents to impersonate you. And with enough information, they can answer security questions, impersonate you in support chats, or even convince companies to transfer accounts over to them.

Identity theft doesn't have to start with someone hacking your system.

It can start with you trusting the wrong link, oversharing online, or simply forgetting to update your privacy settings.

This chapter will walk you through the most common ways identities are stolen—and how to shut those doors before they open. You'll learn how attackers piece together your digital profile, how to recognize the warning signs early, and what steps to take the moment something feels off.

Because your identity isn't just data—it's access. It's trust. It's the foundation of everything else tied to your name.

And if someone else takes it, they don't just steal who you are.

They steal what you can do.

Why It Matters

You can recover a hacked email.

You can replace a compromised credit card.

You can reinstall your apps, restore your photos, even reset your passwords.

But when your identity is stolen, the damage spreads deeper and lasts longer than most people expect.

That's because identity theft isn't just about stealing data—it's about becoming you.

On paper. Online. Financially. Legally. And sometimes, permanently.

We tend to imagine identity theft as something dramatic: a stranger draining your bank account or applying for a credit card in your name. But often, the theft is invisible at first. You might get a strange letter in the mail. A payment request you don't recognize. A denied loan. A flagged background check. A refund rejection. Or worst of all—nothing at all until the damage is done.

In 2024, U.S. consumers lost a staggering $43 billion to identity fraud (Javelin Strategy & Research, 2025). Let that number sit for a moment. This isn't just about stolen data—it's about drained bank accounts, ruined credit, and lives turned upside down by digital impersonation.

That same year, the Federal Trade Commission received over 1.1 million identity theft reports – that's over 3,000 people a day.

The most common? Credit card fraud, with nearly 449,000 cases.

And those are just the ones we know about. Many victims don't even realize they've been hit until months—or years—later. The real number? It's almost certainly higher. Because identity theft doesn't just happen. It hides.

Why is identity theft so effective?

Because your personal data is everywhere, and most of it was never meant to be digital. Social Security numbers, national IDs, birth certificates, driver's licenses, health records, tax documents, insurance policies—all of these can be copied, stored, shared, and stolen. Many are already floating around the dark web thanks to massive breaches at hospitals, government agencies, and major corporations.

But not all theft starts with a breach.

Sometimes it starts with one careless post. A photo of your ID to celebrate passing your driving test. A shared form from school or work. A password reset using your real birthday and your pet's name—both of which you've mentioned online. That's all a criminal needs to build a fake profile, forge documents, or trick systems into thinking they are you.

Once your identity is stolen, the possibilities are endless. A criminal can:

- Open credit cards in your name
- File fraudulent tax returns to claim refunds
- Apply for government benefits
- Commit medical fraud using your insurance
- Rent apartments or buy phones using your information
- Launder money or participate in scams under your identity

And once they do, the burden of proof falls on you. Not them.

Victims of identity theft often spend months—sometimes years—trying to untangle the fallout. They're forced to prove they didn't open an account. That they didn't file that claim. That they weren't in the city where the crime happened. They miss out on jobs, housing, and financial opportunities while trying to reclaim their name.

In 2025, a study from Javelin Strategy & Research found that identity theft victims spent an average of 300 hours repairing the damage, with total financial losses surpassing $23 billion globally. The emotional toll? Even higher. Stress. Shame. Sleepless nights. Lost trust in institutions and technology. A permanent sense that something is wrong—even if everything looks fine.

And identity theft doesn't always happen to adults.

Children are frequent targets because their identities are "clean"—no credit history, no fraud alerts, no existing accounts. Thieves can use a child's Social Security number or ID to build an entirely fake life, and the victim may not discover the crime until they turn 18 and apply for a loan or a job—only to find their name is already ruined.

This is why identity theft is so dangerous: It weaponizes your identity against you—and does it slowly, silently, and thoroughly.

This chapter isn't just about the threat. It's about recognizing the real scope of what's at stake. Because the minute someone takes your place in a digital system, they gain the power to rewrite your financial, legal, and medical history. And once that narrative changes, it can be incredibly difficult to set things right.

Your name, your number, your birthdate, your face—these aren't just pieces of personal data. They're how the world identifies you. And if you don't protect them, someone else will use them—just not in the way you expect.

What to Do About It – Your Security Checklist

1. **Monitor Your Credit Regularly:** Use free credit monitoring tools or services to watch for unexpected changes or new account openings in your name.

2. **Place a Fraud Alert or Credit Freeze If Needed:** If you suspect you've been compromised, contact a major credit bureau to add a fraud alert—or freeze your credit entirely to block new accounts.

3. **Secure Your Social Security Number (or National ID):** Don't carry physical copies unless absolutely necessary. Never send it by email or enter it on untrusted websites.

4. **Use Two-Factor Authentication (2FA) on Key Accounts:** Especially for email, financial services, and government portals—your inbox is often the gateway to identity-related services.

5. **Be Cautious About Sharing Personal Info on Social Media:** Avoid posting your birthday, full name, travel plans, address, or photos of ID cards that could be used to build a profile.

6. **Check Bank and Credit Card Statements Weekly:** Review for unfamiliar charges or new payment recipients—and set alerts for large or international transactions.

7. **Shared Physical Documents Before Disposal:** Bank statements, insurance paperwork, tax records—anything with personal or account information should be destroyed before being thrown away.

8. **Use a Password Manager and Avoid Reusing Passwords:** Many identity theft cases begin with a compromised email or account used across multiple sites.

9. **Watch for Unusual Emails or Calls Claiming to Be from Banks, Government, or Tech Support:** Never give personal data or codes over the phone or in response to unsolicited messages.

10. **Create a Digital Identity Plan:** Maintain a list of your most sensitive accounts, security questions, and contacts in case someone needs to act on your behalf after fraud—or after death.

Quick Action Plan

1-Minute Fix: Set up transaction alerts through your bank or credit card provider.

5-Minute Fix: Enable 2FA for your financial accounts and your primary email.

15-Minute Fix: Check your credit report and remove unnecessary identifying information from social media.

30-Minute Fix: Create a personal identity protection file: passwords in a manager, key documents secured, and fraud response steps documented.

Chapter 19

Social Media: You're Sharing Too Much

Real-World Scenarios

The Innocent Post That Led to Identity Theft

Yeser had always enjoyed sharing little moments of her life online. Her social media was filled with photos of friends, weekend outings, favorite coffee spots, and the occasional meme. So when her 25th birthday came around, it felt natural to post a picture of her cake along with a joyful caption: "Another year older! Can't believe I'm 25 today!"

She got dozens of comments and likes. Friends sent well wishes, tagged her in birthday memes, and reminisced about past celebrations. It felt fun, lighthearted, and innocent.

But a week later, something strange happened.

Yeser received an email from her bank about a password reset request she hadn't made. She brushed it off at first, thinking maybe it was a glitch or spam. Then she noticed two unfamiliar charges on her credit card—purchases she definitely hadn't made. A sinking feeling hit her.

After calling her bank and looking into it further, the truth became clear: someone had gained access to her account.

The bank's fraud team explained how the breach likely occurred. The attacker had answered her security questions—things like her birthdate and hometown. With just her birthday, which she had willingly posted, and other information visible on her public profile, a fraudster had reset her account access and started making transactions.

Yeser was shocked. She had never imagined that something as small as a birthday post could open the door to identity theft.

What she hadn't realized was that cybercriminals regularly monitor social media profiles looking for just this kind of detail. Public birthdays, pet names, relatives' names, old schools—they all serve as keys to security questions and password recovery processes. Even when people don't post everything in one place, hackers can piece together a digital profile over time.

Yeser thought she was just celebrating a fun milestone with friends. But her post gave away a critical piece of personal information—one that helped a criminal slip right into her financial life.

It was a harsh lesson in the digital age: not every threat comes with a warning. Sometimes, it begins with a perfectly innocent post.

The Selfie That Gave Away a Home Address

Derek had just reached a major milestone in his life. After years of saving and planning, he was finally moving into his first solo apartment. It was the kind of place he had always dreamed of—sunlit, spacious, and located right in the heart of the city.

Feeling proud and excited, Derek decided to share the moment on Instagram. He snapped a photo of himself holding up the keys, smiling in front of the building. The caption read: "Finally moving into my dream home! 123 Main Street, here I come!"

He got plenty of likes and encouraging comments. Friends congratulated him. A few asked when the housewarming party would be. It felt like a well-earned celebration.

Two weeks later, while at work, Derek got a call from his building manager. There had been a break-in. His apartment had been ransacked. Electronics were missing, drawers emptied, and his sense of safety shattered.

The police investigation revealed something disturbing. The burglars hadn't chosen Derek's apartment at random. They had found his address through his public Instagram post. They even figured out his daily routine based on his check-ins and work-related posts, allowing them to plan the break-in when he was guaranteed to be out.

As the details sank in, Derek realized just how much he had given away without thinking. Not only had he posted his exact address, but he'd also included a clear photo of his keys—something he had thought was harmless. Investigators later explained that photos of keys can be duplicated using 3D printing technology, especially if the image is sharp and unobstructed.

What began as a moment of pride had ended in a personal invasion.

Derek had always thought of social media as a space for sharing joy and connecting with others. He never imagined it could be used as a tool for criminals to plan a robbery. His excitement had clouded his judgment, and in celebrating his achievement, he had unknowingly handed out an open invitation to strangers.

From that day forward, he was more careful with what he posted. But the lesson had come too late. The damage had already been done.

The Viral Trend That Gave Away Security Answers

Valerie loved participating in viral social media trends. They felt fun, harmless, and were a great way to engage with friends. Whether it was sharing her favorite books, posting decade-old selfies, or answering lighthearted quizzes, she enjoyed being part of the conversation.

So when a new Instagram challenge made its rounds, asking users to post their "firsts," she jumped right in. Her post listed:

– Her first car: a red Toyota Corolla. – Her childhood pet's name: Max. – The city she was born in: Austin.

It felt nostalgic and wholesome. Her followers liked and commented, sharing their own stories in return.

But just days later, strange things started happening.

She was suddenly locked out of her email. When she tried to reset her password, the recovery process failed. Then her bank sent a notification about a password change she hadn't initiated. When she called customer service, she found out that someone had successfully answered her security questions—and gained full access to her accounts.

Valerie was in disbelief. How had they known the answers?

Then it hit her.

Those "fun facts" she had posted as part of the trend were the exact same questions many services use for password recovery: What was your first car? What was your childhood pet's name? In what city were you born?

By participating in the challenge, she had unwittingly handed over the keys to her online life.

It turned out that cybercriminals often monitor social media trends, waiting for opportunities like this. Even if a person doesn't share everything in one post, attackers gather pieces of information over time and build complete profiles. With the help of automated tools, they can then launch password reset attempts across multiple platforms until they gain access.

Valerie had simply been trying to connect with others and join a popular trend. But instead of getting more engagement, she got hacked.

What started as a playful post had become a gateway to digital identity theft—and the consequences were anything but fun.

The Stolen Photos That Ended Up on the Dark Web

Mia was an avid traveler and loved sharing her adventures online. Her Instagram feed was filled with colorful snapshots—sunset beach walks, street food in foreign cities, cozy moments with her family. She didn't post anything too personal, just happy memories and the occasional selfie.

One afternoon, a friend sent her a strange link with the message, "Is this you?"

Curious, Mia clicked—and what she saw made her stomach turn.

It was a website selling fake social media profiles. Scrolling through the page, she saw her own photos being used—pictures she had taken on vacation, smiling in front of famous landmarks, and even a selfie from her bedroom. But the name wasn't hers. The profile was fake, and the person it belonged to was offering "romantic connections."

As she looked deeper, she discovered that her photos were being used in catfishing scams. Fraudsters had built entire fake identities using her face, using these accounts to lure people into fake online relationships. In some cases, they tricked victims into sending money, believing they were helping someone they loved.

Mia felt sick. She had never consented to this. Her images had been taken from her public Instagram account and repurposed for deception and manipulation. Some had even been slightly altered, making them harder to trace back to her original profile.

She later learned that millions of stolen images are used in this way every year. Once a photo is uploaded to the internet—whether on social media, blogs, or photo-sharing platforms—it can be copied, downloaded, and reused without consent. Some scammers go even further, using AI tools to create deepfake videos that make it appear as if someone is saying or doing things they never actually did.

For Mia, the violation was more than digital. It felt deeply personal. Her face—her identity—had been used to deceive and exploit others.

She deleted many of her public photos, locked down her privacy settings, and reported the stolen content. But once something is out on the internet, it's almost impossible to fully take back.

She thought she was just sharing happy memories with friends. Instead, those moments had been turned into tools for scams she never imagined being part of.

What You Need to Know

You post a photo. A memory. A location. A life update. It's second nature now. You share a vacation, a new job, a pet, a dinner, a family moment. It feels personal—like you're talking to friends.

But on social media, nothing is truly personal. Nothing is truly private. And you're probably sharing more than you realize.

Every post, like, comment, tag, story, and check-in becomes a piece of your digital identity. Your birthday, your hometown, your kids' names, your favorite restaurant, the gym you go to, where you shop, who you talk to. It all adds up—and for cybercriminals, that information is gold.

Social media isn't just where people connect. It's where hackers, scammers, impersonators, and social engineers go to gather intel.

Because the more you post, the more predictable you become.

Think about it. If someone wants to guess your security questions—your pet's name, your mother's maiden name, your favorite movie—it's probably all in your feed. If they want to know when you're not home, your vacation countdown gives them the date. If they want to know where you live, your tagged photos and background clues make it easy. And if they want to build a fake profile to impersonate you, your public pictures and captions give them everything they need to sound just like you.

The FTC (2023) reported that one in four people who lost money to scams between January 2021 and June 2023 said the fraud started on social media -platforms like Instagram, Facebook, Snapchat, or TikTok.

That's not a side channel. It's the main stage.

Social media isn't just risky anymore. It's the frontline of modern fraud.

And the risks go beyond just stolen information.

Criminals use photos of children posted by parents to create fake identities or worse—circulate them in dark corners of the internet. Strangers screenshot selfies and re-upload them on dating scams or deepfake engines. Some build entire fake personas using nothing but photos, job titles, and quotes copied straight from someone's real account.

The more you share, the more control you lose.

You might think your account is private—but privacy settings are confusing, often change without notice, and aren't foolproof. Even private accounts can be screenshotted, copied, or viewed by someone you didn't mean to invite. And if your password is weak, reused, or stolen in a breach, your entire account can be hijacked in minutes.

Once that happens, it doesn't just affect you. Hackers use compromised social media accounts to target your friends, send phishing links, or run scams. And because it's coming from "you," people trust it. That trust is exactly what attackers exploit.

And then there's the emotional toll.

Being impersonated. Having your photos misused. Watching your personal memories twisted into tools for someone else's fraud campaign. For many victims, the violation cuts deep—not just digital, but personal.

According to the World Economic Forum's 2024 Global Risks Report, misinformation and disinformation are now ranked as the most severe short-term global threats—driven largely by their explosive spread on social media platforms.

In a world where lies move faster than truth, platforms meant to connect us are instead fueling confusion, division, and real-world harm.

This chapter will show you how social media is used against you—even when you think you're being careful.

You'll learn what to share, what to hide, how to lock down your accounts, and how to recognize when someone else is using your digital identity without you ever knowing.

Because social media was built for sharing. But it never taught us how to protect what we share.

Your photos. Your updates. Your location. Your opinions.

They don't just tell your story.

They tell someone exactly how to break into it.

Why It Matters

You're not just posting. You're broadcasting.

Every time you upload a photo, update your bio, share a story, tag a location, or "check in" somewhere, you're contributing to a public, permanent record—one that doesn't just tell your friends what you're doing. It tells strangers who you are, where you are, who you're with, and when you're most vulnerable.

And most of us do it without a second thought.

That's what makes social media so powerful—and so dangerous.

Platforms like Instagram, TikTok, Facebook, and X are built to reward sharing. They encourage more content, more visibility, more reach. But what they don't do is warn you about the unintended consequences. Because when you overshare, you don't just reveal your lifestyle. You reveal your patterns. And patterns can be exploited.

According to Check Point's Q4 2023 Brand Phishing Report, 45% of all brand impersonation attacks happened on social media – making it the top playground for scammers.

These platforms aren't just for updates and selfies anymore.

They're where fake brands come to life—and real people get conned. Here's how it happens:

- You post a birthday celebration, they get your birthdate.
- You mention your childhood pet, that's a common security question.
- You tag your school or university, they learn your academic history.
- You announce your vacation, they know your house is empty.
- You post your kid's name, they can impersonate you to a school system.
- You take a selfie with your new license, they can forge your ID.

And you're not just exposing yourself. You're exposing everyone you're connected to.

Social media is now one of the top tools used for social engineering. Criminals scrape data to impersonate family members, hijack accounts, build fake profiles, and trick people into wiring money, clicking malicious links, or giving up sensitive information. Some even use AI to generate voice clones and deepfake videos—powered entirely by data pulled from someone's feed.

It's not paranoia. It's pattern recognition.

Attackers don't break in anymore. They log in.
Because you've given them the answers to your own security questions.

ZeroFox's 2023 Threat Intelligence Index report claims that social media impersonation attacks skyrocketed by 1,500% between 2021 and 2023—targeting corporate executives, brand accounts, and anyone with influence.

That's not a typo. It's a warning.

Fraudsters are turning social platforms into hunting grounds—posing as leaders, hijacking trust, and spreading scams faster than most companies can respond.

But impersonation is just one layer.

There's also the part no one warns you about: how your legal, public data gets used—by advertisers, insurers, banks, employers, even government agencies.

Your "likes," your browsing habits, your friends list—quietly feeding into decisions about your credit offers, job eligibility, and even your risk score for travel.

And yes – some financial instution and insurance companies are watching.

They're analyzing what you post. Your photos. Your friends. Even your tone.

To decide if you're too risky to insure.

Too risky to lend to.

One vacation selfie. One late-night tweet. One "risky-looking" connection.

And suddenly, your premium goes up—or your loan gets denied.

And the worst part? You'll never even know it happened.

And that's before we talk about data breaches.

Social media platforms have been frequent targets for massive hacks. Between 2020 and 2025, many major organizations – including telecom giants, tech firms, and public data services – experienced significant data breaches, exposing usernames, emails, phone numbers, direct messages, private posts, and even location history. Even "private" accounts aren't immune—once breached, the walls fall quickly.

Many users assume that if their profile is locked or their posts are set to "friends only," they're safe. But posts get shared. Friends screenshot. Third-party apps gain permissions. Algorithms surface content. Even if you delete a post, it may live on in backups, data archives, or search indexes.

And once it's out, you can't take it back.

This is why social media security isn't just about choosing a good password or avoiding phishing links. It's about understanding the digital footprint you're leaving behind—and how much of your real-world identity is mapped onto it.

If a stranger read through your last 100 posts, what could they figure out about your habits, relationships, values, finances, routines, or vulnerabilities?

Chances are, more than you think.

This chapter isn't about deleting your accounts or living offline. It's about learning to treat your digital presence with the same caution you'd use in real life. You wouldn't tell a stranger on the street where your kids go to school, how much money you make, or when your home is empty.

So why tell the internet?

What to Do About It – Your Security Checklist

1. **Make Your Accounts Private:** Set your profiles to "friends only" or "private" to restrict access to people you trust. Don't assume your posts are only seen by followers.
2. **Review What You've Already Shared:** Go through old posts, photos, and public info like birthdays, locations, and job titles. Delete anything you wouldn't share with a stranger.
3. **Limit Location Sharing:** Turn off real-time location tags and avoid posting while you're away from home. Share photos and updates after you've returned.
4. **Don't Share Personal Milestones with Sensitive Info:** Avoid posting photos of passports, driver's licenses, boarding passes, or even school names.
5. **Be Cautious with Kids' Photos:** If you post about children, remove identifying details like full names, school uniforms, or frequent locations.
6. **Disable Face Recognition and Auto-Tagging Features:** Platforms like Facebook and Instagram use AI to recognize people in photos—turn this off if you want more control.
7. **Avoid Publicly Sharing Contact Information:** Never post your email, phone number, or address in your bio or posts.
8. **Watch for Impersonation and Fake Profiles:** Search your name occasionally to see if someone is using your photo or details to scam others.
9. **Revoke Third-Party App Access:** Check what apps are connected to your social media accounts—many leak data or have weak security.

10. **Use Strong, Unique Passwords and 2FA:** Social accounts are a common target for hackers. Enable two-factor authentication and never reuse passwords across platforms.

Quick Action Plan

1-Minute Fix: Turn your account privacy to "friends only" and disable location sharing.

5-Minute Fix: Review your last 10 posts for personal data you may have accidentally shared.

15-Minute Fix: Audit your friend or follower list and remove people you don't recognize or trust.

30-Minute Fix: Go into your platform settings to remove old app connections, enable 2FA, and update privacy controls.

Chapter 20

The AI Trap: Deepfakes, Cloned Voices & Hacks

Real-World Scenarios

The Urgent CEO Voice Message

Lena was a junior finance officer at a mid-sized marketing firm in Austin. She was meticulous, cautious, and known for never approving payments without double-checking. But on a late Friday afternoon, everything she thought she knew about workplace safety — and voices — fell apart.

It started with a voice message on WhatsApp. It was from an unknown number, but it sounded exactly like her CEO, Martin. His tone was calm, familiar, and lightly stressed, just like any senior exec under deadline pressure.

""*Lena, I need this payment processed before end of day. It's for the German client. I'll forward you the details now. Just flag it for urgent handling. Thanks — really appreciate it.*""

It didn't seem suspicious. Martin was known for his last-minute Friday requests, and Lena had received verbal instructions before. When the follow-up message with wire details arrived, it matched the format the company had used many times. The amount — €15,800 — was nothing unusual for a marketing retainer.

So Lena wired the funds. Quickly. Efficiently. Like a reliable team player.

By Monday morning, the nightmare began. Martin had no recollection of any Friday request. The finance director flagged the wire as unauthorized. IT couldn't find any email trail. And that's when it hit her: she'd been tricked by a synthetic voice. A cloned version of her CEO, likely generated from interviews and podcast episodes he'd done, all available online.

The attackers had spoofed a European phone number, used AI tools to replicate voice tone and phrasing, and composed the message with business-like urgency. It wasn't just a scam. It was an AI-powered con — engineered with precision and executed flawlessly.

Lena broke down in tears when she realized what happened. She didn't just make a mistake. She was up against a technology that mimicked trust itself.

The company never got the money back.

Instagram Deepfake Romance

Devon wasn't someone who fell easily. A software tester by day, introvert by nature, he spent his weekends hiking solo and learning Spanish on YouTube. He wasn't on dating apps, but he did follow a few travel influencers on Instagram—people whose lives felt more spontaneous than his.

That's how he came across her.

@AdventuringEmma posted travel reels from Morocco, Peru, Iceland. Her smile wasn't influencer-fake — it was awkward and charming. Her voiceovers sounded unscripted. Her captions were thoughtful. Over time, Devon started replying to her stories. One day she messaged back.

It began innocently: casual chats about camera gear, travel tips, Spanish memes. But the tone gradually shifted. Emma began opening up. She told Devon her ex-boyfriend had stolen her crypto wallet. She couldn't access her travel funds. She was too embarrassed to tell her audience. She didn't want to ask for much — just enough to get by until her flight out.

Devon was skeptical at first. But the face? The voice? The timing of her replies? It all felt real. She even sent him a short video saying his name — "Devon, thanks so much, I didn't know who else to ask."

He sent $400 in Bitcoin. She vanished the next day.

It wasn't a stolen identity scam. Emma didn't exist.

She was a fully AI-generated persona — her face synthesized by a deepfake engine, her voice cloned from an amalgamation of female content creators, and her responses crafted by a large language model fine-tuned for persuasive emotional tone.

The Instagram account had thousands of real followers. The scam wasn't targeting Devon alone. It was an operation designed to scale — seduce, convince, extract, and disappear. Each message was crafted to feel personal. But it was all code.

Devon filed a report. But there was no name to give. No photo to trace. No voice to recognize.

Just a fake smile, a perfect voice, and a deep hole where trust used to be.

The Kidnapping Call

The voice sounded just like her daughter.

Monica's phone rang mid-morning on a quiet Tuesday. She didn't recognize the number, but answered anyway.

What she heard stopped her cold.

"Mom! MOM! They've got me—help me, please—"

It was her daughter's voice. The tone, the pitch, the way she said "Mom" — it was unmistakable.

Then a man came on the line. Calm. Low voice.

"We have her. Don't call the police. If you want her back, transfer $5,000 in the next 20 minutes. I'll send the details."

Monica's body went cold. She couldn't breathe. Her husband was unreachable. She was seconds away from wiring the money when she got a text — from her actual daughter:

"Love you Mom! At tennis. Be home at 6"

Her child was fine. The call was fake.

The voice? Real enough to make any parent crumble. It was AI-generated using clips pulled from the daughter's TikTok, Instagram stories, and voice messages sent to friends. Just a few minutes of audio was enough for a clone.

The scam was part of a wave of "**virtual kidnapping**" calls that don't involve real kidnappings - just AI, fear, and speed. The voice sounded real enough to override logic.

And for a terrifying few minutes, Monica thought her world had ended.

The Job Interview Setup

His résumé wasn't the only thing being reviewed.

Sahil was days away from landing a job he'd worked toward for years — senior product manager at a tech firm in Chicago. He'd passed the interviews, clicked with the team, and the hiring manager had hinted that an offer was coming.

Then everything went silent.

When he finally reached out, HR told him they'd found "problematic behavior" under his name – aggressive posts on Reddit, a blog comment thread full of toxic replies, and a Medium article under his name that was critical of the company's values.

He didn't write any of it.

The photos matched him. The writing style resembled his. But it was all fake — generated using AI-written content and image tools, then posted under spoofed profiles using his name, face, and details scraped from public profiles.

It was a targeted attack. Later, he learned a competitor from a freelance bidding site he'd once beat out had likely engineered it. The cost? A few bucks and a language model.

There was no way to undo the damage. No contact to confront. No one to sue.

Sahil lost the job. And it changed how he thought about his digital identity forever.

Because in a world of AI-generated lies, sometimes you're the fake, and you don't even know it yet.

What You Need to Know

You get a call from your boss.

You hear your partner's voice asking for help.

You get a message from someone who sounds just like your daughter — scared, crying, panicked.

You trust your ears. You trust your eyes. You always have.

But now? That trust can be manufactured. Faked. Replicated. Stolen.

We've entered a world where voices aren't always real. Faces aren't always human. Conversations might not be between two people — but between you and an algorithm trained to sound exactly like someone you love.

All it takes is 3 to 5 seconds (McAfee, 2023) of your voice - a voicemail, a TikTok, a Zoom call – to clone it.

And the tools? They're free. Easy. Online. Right now.

With a few clicks, anyone can create a fake you — one that begs, commands, jokes, or demands money. No studio. No tech skills. Just a motive.

These voice clones aren't science fiction. They're already being used to fake kidnappings, trick families, drain bank accounts, and bypass voice-based security systems.

Once someone has your voice, they can use it for anything.

And you won't know it happened — until it already has.

But it's not just voices.

AI-generated faces are filling your feed. Not stolen faces - faces that never existed. Smiling people with just enough realism to feel safe. They're on fake job postings. Romance scam profiles. Customer support chats. Even video calls. And they're getting harder to spot every day.

In 2023, a finance employee in Hong Kong joined a Zoom call with his company's top executives. They looked real. They sounded real.

But none of them were. The entire meeting was a deepfake.

AI-generated faces. Synthetic voices. Fake backgrounds. Every "person" on that call was fabricated - built to deceive. And it worked.

He transferred $25 million to fraudsters, thinking he was following orders from his real bosses.

This wasn't a phishing link or a sketchy email. This was a full-blown virtual heist — powered by deepfake tech, and carried out in plain sight.

That's how far it's come.

You don't just need to watch what you click anymore.

You need to question what - and who - you see.

That level of deception used to take a film studio. Now, anyone with a laptop and motivation can do it in an afternoon.

And that's the trick: AI doesn't have feelings. But it knows how to sound like it does.

It knows how to fake urgency. How to mimic someone's typing style. How to adjust tone based on what you respond to. It learns from your behavior and weaponizes that against you.

You're not just being tricked by content. You're being tricked by familiarity. By the illusion of trust. By something that looks and sounds close enough to real that your brain doesn't question it in time. That's what makes AI threats different. They're not trying to brute-force your password. They're trying to bypass your instincts. They come through the people you already know. The voices you love. The faces you trust. Because deep down, humans are wired to believe what feels personal.

That's why voice-cloning scams work on parents.

Why deepfake hiring managers "interview" candidates to steal their info.

Why scammers use your real photos to build fake profiles that message your friends.

You don't have to be famous to be copied.

They look real. They sound real. But they're not.

AI-generated profiles are flooding platforms like Twitter, Facebook, and LinkedIn — embedded in political campaigns, phishing schemes, and identity theft rings.

Their goal isn't clicks. It's control.

They're built to deceive, divide, and manipulate — one post, one message, one voice at a time.

And here's the twist: They weren't designed to mimic celebrities. They were built to impersonate you.

Your LinkedIn video? Enough to clone your voice.

Your podcast? A goldmine.

Your digital life is the blueprint.

And now, it can be weaponized.

Your blog posts, your selfies, your tweets — all fuel for an identity that isn't yours, but looks like it is. And people fall for it. In 2022, romance scams cost victims $1.3 billion — the most of any imposter fraud, says the FTC.

Now scammers are using AI to scale the deception: deepfake photos, chatbot love stories, even voice notes.

On apps like WhatsApp, Instagram, and Telegram, the face you trust might not be real.

And the heartbreak? Just as costly.

It's not just romance scams anymore. Job offers, tech support, charities, emergencies – anywhere emotion plays a role, AI is finding its way in.

Today's AI chatbots don't just talk; they feel. Or at least, they sound like they do. Recent studies have shown that advanced hybrid models are highly effective at replicating emotional tone and empathy.

So that next message that feels genuine, warm, or deeply personal? It might not be from a person at all — but from a machine trained to sound like one.

And distinguishing the difference? It's getting harder every day. Because these scams don't feel fake. They feel like real conversations. Real people. Real crises.

This chapter unpack how emotional AI works, where the dangers lie, and how you can stay ahead of it.

Because by the time you notice something's off - a video glitch, a voice that's just slightly wrong - it's too late.

The trust has already been built.

And the voice you believed?

It wasn't asking for help. It was taking advantage.

Why It Matters

Since ChatGPT launched in late 2022, phishing didn't just rise - it exploded. According to SlashNext, malicious phishing emails jumped 1,265% in a single year.

Why? Because cybercriminals are now using generative AI to write their scams. No typos. No broken English. Just smooth, convincing messages designed to hit fast – before your brain even thinks to question them.

This isn't the old "Nigerian prince" game anymore.

The real danger with AI-powered threats isn't just that they exist. It's that they blend in.

They don't crash your screen, freeze your device, or throw red flags. They pretend to be what you already trust — a voice, a tone, a relationship. And because they arrive wrapped in the familiar, they slip straight through your defenses.

We're trained to see cybersecurity as a technical checklist: install the update, set the password, don't click the link.

But these attacks don't go after your device. They go after you — your trust, your instincts, your automatic yes.

And that's what makes them so dangerous.

A message that sounds like a friend. A call that sounds like family. A face that moves, blinks, and gestures like someone real. These things don't feel like threats. They feel like connections.

And for most people, that's enough to let their guard down. By the time your brain catches up — when something feels a little too urgent, or a little too perfect — you've already clicked, sent, transferred, or replied.

The cost? Sometimes it's money. Other times, it's your reputation. And in some cases, it's trust that never fully comes back.

AI makes deception scalable. It automates manipulation. One attacker can impersonate dozens of people at once. One face, one voice, one chatbot - deployed across hundreds of accounts, running nonstop, never sleeping, never hesitating.

The human side of fraud used to be slow. Now it's lightning fast, algorithmically optimized, and invisible until it's too late.

But the real reason this matters? It changes what "real" means.

When you can't trust what you hear... when you doubt what you see... when even your own voice can be turned into a weapon — it creates a new kind of vulnerability. One that doesn't just affect your bank account, but your sense of certainty in the world.

And unlike stolen passwords or outdated software, you can't reset your voice. You can't unshare your photos. You can't untrain the machine that already learned how to imitate you.

You might not feel like a target. But if you've ever posted a video, left a voicemail, recorded a presentation, or used your real name online — you've already left the ingredients behind. And AI systems are built to collect those ingredients, mix them, and create convincing fakes that no filter or firewall can stop.

This is bigger than just fraud. It's about erosion — of trust, identity, and control. And once that trust breaks, it doesn't just affect you. It ripples through your family, your friends, your colleagues — because they're the ones who'll get the next message that sounds like you.

The next time you call someone in a panic, will they pause to verify it's really you? If your voice is ever used in a scam, will your contacts know how to tell the difference?

This isn't just a threat to your data. It's a threat to your relationships. To how you're perceived. To what people believe you said or did - even if you never said or did it.

That's why this chapter exists.

Not just to warn you, but to shift how you think. Because cybersecurity isn't just about locks anymore. It's about *doubt* — about teaching yourself to slow down, question, confirm, and protect the most personal parts of your identity before they're borrowed, twisted, and used against you.

In a world full of fakes that feel real, your best defense isn't a stronger password. It's a sharper instinct.

What to Do About It – Your Security Checklist

1. **Be Mindful of Voice Content You Share:** Avoid posting voice notes, video messages, or public recordings without privacy settings — especially if they include emotion, urgency, or your child's voice.

2. **Don't Post Long Audio Without Thinking:** Cloning tools only need 3–5 seconds of clear speech. Podcasts, panel talks, and storytime videos can all be scraped.

3. **Lock Down Your Face:** Avoid using your face as a profile photo on multiple public platforms. If you post video, use filters, overlays, or background noise to reduce cloning quality.

4. **Keep Kids' Voices & Faces Offline:** If you post family content, skip names, schools, or anything with clear speech. Cloned voices from children are now used in "emergency scams."

5. **Be Suspicious of Urgent Voice Messages:** Even if it sounds like your boss, spouse, or child — verify with a text or call to a known number before acting.

6. **Watch for "Too Perfect" Profiles:** AI-generated personas often use flawless language, oddly polished photos, and high emotion with no history. Trust your gut if something feels too smooth.

7. **Always Confirm Video Meetings:** If someone new sends a Zoom or Google Meet link, confirm through another channel first — deepfake video meetings are now used in fraud and data theft.

8. **Use Safe Words with Family:** Set a simple phrase only your real loved ones know, in case someone tries to fake a distress call or voicemail.

9. **Don't Feed AI With Your Sensitive Data:** Avoid pasting private info into public AI tools. Many store prompts, and some leak them later through training sets.

10. **Decline Voice Training Requests:** If a device or app asks to "learn your voice," make sure you understand how that audio is stored and whether it's shared.

11. **Remove Personal Audio from Public Platforms:** Delete old voice recordings or videos from forums, social media, or comment replies — they're easy targets for AI harvesting.

12. **Search for Your Name + "AI" or "Deepfake":** Use search engines to check if your voice, face, or name is being reused on fake profiles, content farms, or impersonation scams.

13. **Report and Flag Fake Versions of You:** If you find fake profiles using your info, report them immediately and alert your contacts.

14. **Reverse Image Search Your Profile Pics:** See if your face appears on suspicious accounts or scam sites. Tools like TinEye and Google Images can help.

Quick Action Plan

1-Minute Fix: Google your name, voice, or handle + "deepfake" or "AI voice" to see if anything suspicious comes up.

5-Minute Fix: Turn off voice and face recognition in your device, app, and social platform settings.

15-Minute Fix: Review your video, podcast, or audio posts from the last 12 months. Remove anything publicly visible with high voice clarity.

30-Minute Fix: Set up alerts for your name and image using Google Alerts or a privacy tool. Enable 2FA and secure backup email addresses across all major platforms.

Chapter 21

Scan & Scam: The Hidden Danger in QR Code

Real-World Scenarios

The Parking Meter Scam

Daryl had a job interview in downtown Chicago. He was running late, so when he saw an open street parking spot right outside the building, he took it.

There was no physical meter, just a city-branded sticker on the pole with a QR code and instructions: "*Scan to Pay for Parking – City of Chicago Mobile Portal.*"

He scanned the code, landed on a page with the city logo, selected 2 hours, and entered his card details. Simple, fast, done. Or so he thought.

Three days later, he got a notification from his bank: two charges - one for $4.75 and another for $994.99.

By the time he called the fraud line, the second charge had already gone through.

Turns out, the QR code wasn't from the city at all. It was a tampered sticker, placed over the original one. The payment page was a near-perfect clone of the real site but the backend sent data straight to a scammer's server. The $4.75 was a decoy to avoid suspicion. The $994.99? The real goal.

Police later found dozens of poles in the area with identical fake stickers. Most people had no idea they'd been scammed until days later, when their accounts were drained or their card details sold on the dark web.

Daryl canceled the card, filed a fraud report, and had to delay his job onboarding due to the financial chaos.

All because of one innocent scan on a real street, on a real sticker, in the middle of a workday.

Scan here to upload your Resume

Keisha had just graduated from college and was attending a large career expo in London. The booths were crowded, her folder was full of printed résumés, and she was excited to make connections. One booth in particular caught her attention — a clean, professional setup for a new tech startup. No long lines, no recruiters acting rushed.

Just a friendly young rep and a big banner that read: "*Skip the paper. Scan here to upload your resume instantly.*"

It sounded efficient. Everyone was doing it.

She scanned the QR code, filled out a simple form, uploaded her résumé, and even answered a few quick personality questions — favorite work style, preferred tech stack, salary expectations. It all looked legit. She even received a confirmation message:

"*Thanks, Keisha! We'll be in touch shortly.*"

They never got in touch. But someone else did.

Two weeks later, Keisha received an email from what looked like another tech company offering an "exclusive interview slot" for a remote role. The process was quick — a brief chat, a follow-up with HR, then a request to verify her identity with a scanned photo of her driver's license for onboarding.

The email was fake. The job didn't exist. The scammer had used the résumé she submitted — complete with phone, address, email, and job preferences — to craft a perfect phishing campaign targeted just at her.

She didn't lose money, but she lost time, trust, and control of her personal information. Her résumé ended up circulating on recruitment scam boards. She had to freeze her credit and flag her accounts just in case.

The worst part? She was targeted in person. At a legitimate event. By someone pretending to be a real company — with nothing more than a banner, a smile, and a QR code.

The Restaurant Check-In Hack

Marco and his wife were traveling through Spain on their long-postponed honeymoon. They'd just checked into a boutique hotel in Seville and asked the receptionist for a local dinner spot. She pointed them to a cozy restaurant just two blocks away—popular with locals, cheap, and quick.

The place had no printed menus, just a QR code printed on a plastic stand on each table. It said: "*Scan to view menu.*"

Marco scanned it, the menu popped up, and they ordered tapas and sangria. The food was fantastic. The evening felt perfect.

Two days later, while still in Spain, Marco got an alert from his bank:

"Multiple login attempts from unknown devices. Account access blocked."

He didn't think much of it until his travel card stopped working. When he checked his email, he couldn't get in. His Instagram was locked. His Google account had been taken over.

What happened?

That QR code hadn't led to the restaurant's real website. It had been swapped with a malicious URL that silently triggered a browser exploit on Marco's phone—collecting autofill data, session tokens, and even clipboard content in the background.

He never saw it happen. There was no download. No suspicious pop-up. Just a menu and a nice dinner.

By the time they flew home, he'd spent hours on the phone with banks, reset his cloud accounts, and had to wipe and restore his phone from scratch. Their honeymoon ended with password resets instead of souvenirs.

All from scanning a single QR code—left in plain sight, on a table, in a restaurant that didn't even know it had been hijacked.

The Delivery Scam

Sara lived in a quiet suburb outside of London. She worked remotely, ordered almost everything online, and knew her delivery drivers by name. So when a brown envelope arrived with her name, address, and a shipping label from a major retailer, she didn't question it.

Inside was a single sheet of paper that read: "Your delivery couldn't be completed. Scan the code below to reschedule or verify your identity."

The QR code looked official. The font matched the retailer's style. The envelope even had a tracking number. Sara scanned the code and landed on a page with her name pre-filled. It asked her to "confirm identity" by logging into her account. The layout was flawless. Even the footer had the right links.

So she entered her email and password.

Two minutes later, she got a security alert from that same retailer: "Your password has been changed."

Then she got a notification from her bank about a charge on her store card. Then another. By the time she realized what had happened, the attacker had taken over her shopping account, used stored payment details to buy electronics, and rerouted the delivery address.

She called support, froze her cards, and filed reports. But the account had already been used to attempt login to other services tied to the same email.

What shocked her most was that this didn't happen online. The scam was physically mailed to her door.

The package was fake — carefully crafted to look real. And the QR code didn't just lead to phishing. It created a sense of urgency and control. No links. No strange emails. Just a deceptively quiet moment of action. She trusted the package. She trusted the brand. She trusted the code.

And it nearly cost her everything tied to that identity.

What You Need to Know

You're at a restaurant. No menus, just a small plastic sign: "Scan to view." You do. It feels normal.

You're on a street in a busy city. The parking meter says: "Scan to pay." You do. Because that's how things work now.

You get a delivery slip. No need to call or email. "Scan to reschedule or verify your address." You scan. Because it has your name, your street, your tracking number.

That's how easy it is. And that's what makes it so dangerous. QR codes were designed for speed. But speed is the one thing cybercriminals love most, because it skips thinking, skips checking, skips hesitation.

Between June and September 2024, Barracuda researchers uncovered over 500,000 phishing emails with QR codes hidden inside PDF attachments.

The goal? Impersonate trusted names like Microsoft, DocuSign, and Adobe—and trick you into scanning your way into a breach.

What used to be an occasional trick is now a go-to tactic.

A MobileIron poll revealed just how unprepared the public is:

- Only 61% knew a QR code could open a URL.
- Less than half realized it could install an app.
- Most had no idea it could trigger a payment, call, or follow.
- And 71% couldn't spot a fake QR code if they tried.

That's all criminals need.

A sticker on a parking meter. A flyer in a café. A QR menu at lunch.

One scan—and you've handed over control.

Qshing works because you never see it coming.

You don't click a suspicious link anymore. You scan it — printed on a flyer, stuck to a wall, mailed to your home. The danger isn't in what the QR code looks like. It's in where it silently sends you.

When you scan a code, you don't see the full URL. You don't hover, inspect, or hesitate. You trust the sign, the sticker, the piece of paper in your hand. And the moment you scan, your phone takes over. A fake website opens. A clone of your delivery portal. A payment screen with the right logo. A form asking you to "verify."

You don't think twice, because it all looks right. Until it's not.

QR code scams are quietly exploding. In the UK, reports more than doubled last year—1,386 in total—and 502 hit in just the first three months of 2025 alone.

Meanwhile, in some US cities, criminals placed fake QR code stickers over real parking meters. Drivers scanned, paid, and unknowingly sent their credit card info straight to fraudsters. Victims were hit with small test charges—then drained. This isn't rare anymore. It's rising fast.

In Singapore, scammers disguised QR scams as a government survey campaign, urging residents to scan and win rebates. The site asked for personal info and banking details. Thousands were stolen.

And in the UK, fake Amazon delivery slips were left in residential mailboxes. They looked official. The QR code led to a perfect replica of Amazon's login page. Dozens of users lost access to their accounts — some had gift cards and saved cards drained within minutes.

These attacks don't rely on hacking. They rely on your trust in your environment. The paper feels real. The sticker looks official. The language is right. The page loads fast. By the time you pause to think, your data's already been entered - or worse, your session has been hijacked by a background script embedded in the fake site.

And now, these scams are evolving. QR code traps are no longer just static pages, they're powered by AI on the other end.

You scan a code at a job fair, and it opens a chatbot that behaves like a recruiter. It compliments your résumé, offers a quick interview, and guides you through a "pre-screening" form that collects your social security number, address, and ID photo.

You scan a code at a hotel or co-working space, and it launches a fake Wi-Fi login screen — one that captures your credentials and session tokens, even as you connect.

QR codes were meant to help. But without guardrails, they've become one of the easiest entry points for targeted cybercrime — especially because they skip every digital filter. No antivirus blocks a physical sticker. No browser flags a sign taped to a lamppost. No email filter stops a flyer on your windshield.

You don't need to be reckless to fall for one. You just need to do what millions of people do every day — trust the thing in front of you.

QR scams work because they feel harmless. They come through paper, packaging, posters. They come through convenience. And by the time you figure out it wasn't a real menu, a real meter, or a real support page — you've already logged in, scanned your ID, shared your credit card, or opened a door your phone never warned you about.

This chapter will show you what these scams look like, where they're showing up, and how to build just enough caution into every scan to stay one step ahead. Because in a world where one square holds your next payment, next password, or next regret – you'll need to learn how to scan smarter – before your phone opens more than you intended.

Why It Matters

According to the BBC, the UK's national fraud reporting centre Action Fraud received 1,386 reports of QR code scams in 2023—up from just 100 in 2019. That's a 14-fold surge in just five years.

Experts told the BBC that organized crime gangs are behind the spike, exploiting QR codes as an easy gateway to steal payments, data, and identities.

And this isn't just a UK issue. The tech is global. The risk is everywhere.

All it takes is one scan. Because you expect hackers to hide behind screens — not stickers.

You expect phishing emails and sketchy pop-ups. But you don't expect a scam to greet you at a dinner table, on a mailbox, or taped to a public sign. And yet, that's exactly where they are now.

QR codes used to feel like a shortcut. Now they're a disguise — for fake links, malicious scripts, and cloned login pages. But what makes them dangerous isn't just where they lead. It's how naturally they fit into your day. You see one on a menu? You scan it. On a delivery slip? You scan it. On a job ad? Of course you scan it.

There's no friction. No hesitation. No warning. Because QR codes aren't suspicious. They're convenient. And convenience is the most reliable way to bypass your instincts.

Cybercriminals don't need to hack into your phone anymore. They just need to get you to scan something that looks like it belongs. And that's the trap: when a scam blends in with your surroundings, you don't treat it like a scam. You treat it like routine.

That's what happened in US, when dozens of drivers scanned fake parking meter codes and unknowingly handed over their credit cards. That's what happened in the UK, when fake Amazon slips led people to enter their credentials on cloned websites.

And that's what keeps happening everywhere — because QR scams don't rely on confusion. They rely on confidence.

According to Keepnet Labs, in 2023, executives faced 42 times more QR code phishing attacks than average employees.

Why? Because cybercriminals go where the power is. Executives have access to sensitive data, financial systems, and high-level decisions—making them top-tier targets for quishing.

You're not hesitating when you scan. You're not suspicious. You're acting with certainty — and that's exactly what scammers need. It's not a hacker tricking your device. It's your own device doing exactly what you told it to do.

This isn't just about fake websites. It's about trust. Trust in what you see. Trust in where you are. Trust in what your phone is doing.

Because when you scan a code at a real event, in a real building, next to real people — you don't expect to be redirected into a trap. But the reality is, QR scams don't need to look fake to be dangerous. They just need to look like they're supposed to be there.

And that illusion of legitimacy is what lets people fall so quickly. You didn't make a mistake. You followed instructions. You scanned a thing that was printed, posted, or handed to you. And now, your credentials are gone. Or your bank is alerting you. Or your cloud storage is no longer yours.

That's why this matters. Because this kind of attack doesn't feel like an attack. It feels like routine. It feels like nothing. Until the damage is done. And the next wave? It's already here — combining QR traps with AI.

You scan a code on a flyer. It opens a chatbot. It responds like a recruiter, a support agent, or someone from your bank. The tone is right. The questions sound normal. You're halfway through a conversation before realizing it's not a person at all — just a machine, trained to build your trust and collect what it needs.

The tools are getting smarter. The codes are getting slicker. And we're getting more relaxed with every scan we make. Because no one expects to be hacked by a square.

No one thinks twice about a black-and-white pattern that sits quietly on a table. And that's the genius of it. It doesn't have to fight you. It just has to fool you.

That's why this chapter exists. To break the illusion.

To make you think again — not just about where a QR code goes, but about what it bypasses: your caution, your awareness, your security habits. Because you won't hear the trap click shut. You won't see the theft happen. You'll just feel it later — when your account locks, your card declines, your inbox fills with alerts, and you can't quite remember what you scanned.

By then, the sticker is gone. The flyer tossed. The paper recycled. But your information? That's still being used. And the next victim? They'll scan the same way you did.

Without fear. Without question. Without knowing what they've just handed over.

What to Do About It – Your Security Checklist

1. **Pause before you scan.** Ask yourself: Who placed this code here? Where does it lead?
2. **Avoid scanning random QR codes** found on flyers, lampposts, bathroom walls, or car windshields.
3. **Check the URL before tapping.** After scanning, your phone shows the link. Read it carefully.
4. **Use QR scanners with preview features.** Avoid auto-open behavior from your default camera app.
5. **Never enter passwords, card numbers, or personal info** on a page opened via QR code.
6. **If in doubt, go to the site manually.** Don't trust the QR to take you safely.
7. **Keep your phone's software up to date.** Many QR-related attacks exploit old browser vulnerabilities.
8. **Turn off "auto-open links"** in your phone's QR scanner or camera settings.
9. **Deny permission requests** (camera, mic, location) from sites you land on after scanning.
10. **Avoid downloading anything** from a page opened by a QR code.
11. **Don't trust QR codes inside suspicious packages or mailers.** If it asks you to "verify delivery" or "reschedule," confirm with the delivery service directly.
12. **Skip tip jars, donation QR codes, or "scan to support" stickers** if you don't know who's collecting the money.

Quick Action Plan

1-Minute Fix: Disable "auto open" for QR links in your camera app or switch to a safer QR scanner.

5-Minute Fix: Download a QR reader with safety previews and scan protection features.

15-Minute Fix: Check your recent scans (receipts, flyers, packages) for anything suspicious. If unsure, reset your passwords.

30-Minute Fix: Audit your digital hygiene:

- Enable 2FA on all key accounts
- Clear saved autofill data in your mobile browser
- Run a malware scan if you've recently scanned a suspicious code

Chapter 22

GPS and Location Tracking: How You're Followed

Real-World Scenarios

The Stalker Who Used a Woman's GPS Data Against Her

Wendy loved documenting her life online. For her, sharing moments—from her morning coffee runs to late-night workouts—was a way of staying connected with friends and keeping a kind of digital journal. Her posts were cheerful and frequent. A morning check-in at her favorite coffee shop, a photo from her gym with a motivational quote, a quick update during her evening commute—nothing seemed out of the ordinary.

But over time, Wendy began to notice something unsettling.

One day, while sitting at her usual café, she caught sight of a man she didn't recognize, watching her. She brushed it off as coincidence. Later that week, she saw the same man at her gym, again standing off to the side. Then, one evening, she noticed him across the street from her apartment building.

That's when the fear set in.

Wendy was being followed. Not by someone who had stumbled across her path randomly, but by someone who had studied her routine—someone who knew exactly where she would be, and when.

She reported the incidents to the police, who confirmed what she feared. Her social media check-ins, geotagged photos, and real-time updates had made it easy for someone to track her movements. The posts that once felt harmless had created a public roadmap of her daily life. Her habits were no longer private—they were fully visible to anyone who chose to follow along.

What Wendy didn't know was that a large percentage of stalking cases now involve digital tracking. Technology has made it easier than ever for stalkers to learn everything they need without leaving their homes. From timestamps to GPS coordinates, even one post can reveal patterns about when someone leaves the house, where they go, and how often they return.

Wendy thought she was simply sharing her life. But in doing so, she had unknowingly handed a stranger the exact tools needed to follow her.

The experience changed her. She turned off location sharing, locked down her profiles, and stopped posting in real-time. But the sense of vulnerability lingered.

What she once saw as harmless connection had become a doorway for someone to step into her life—uninvited and unwanted.

The Smartwatch That Led a Burglar to a Family's Home

Peter was proud of his commitment to fitness. Every morning, just after sunrise, he laced up his shoes and went for a run through the quiet streets of his neighborhood. He used a fitness tracker to map his routes, track his progress, and share his achievements with his online fitness community. His posts were consistent: his route, his pace, the time he left the house, and where his run began—his home address.

He never thought twice about it. To Peter, it was just part of staying motivated and holding himself accountable.

One morning, after finishing his usual five-mile loop, he returned home to find something wrong. The front door was slightly ajar, the lock broken. Inside, drawers had been pulled open, electronics were missing, and the house had been completely ransacked.

The police came quickly. As they walked through the scene, they asked Peter if he had posted any travel plans or vacations online recently. He said no—but then mentioned his fitness tracker.

They pulled up the app and saw exactly what the burglars had seen.

Peter's profile was public. Anyone could view his running routes. Each entry showed the exact time he left the house and how long he'd be gone. The starting point of every run was the same: his home address. The burglars hadn't needed to guess when the house would be empty—they had a digital schedule served up to them daily.

Peter was stunned. He hadn't realized how exposed he had been. The fitness tracker had seemed like a harmless tool—something to support his health, not compromise his safety. But it had painted a clear picture for criminals: when he was gone, how long he would be out, and exactly where to find his home.

The burglary was devastating, not just for the loss of property, but for the sense of violation. Someone had used his own data—shared in good faith—to target him.

Peter changed his app settings that day, setting his workouts to private. But the damage had already been done. What he thought was a healthy habit had made him vulnerable to a carefully timed crime.

The Ride-Share Driver Who Tracked a Passenger Home

Evelyn was cautious. She avoided walking alone at night and never shared her address publicly. When she went out with friends, she always used a ride-share service to get home safely. She believed that as long as she stayed aware, she could avoid most risks.

After a night out downtown, she ordered a ride through her usual app. The driver was polite, the ride uneventful. He dropped her off just outside her apartment complex, and she went inside without thinking twice.

The next morning, Evelyn got a message.

"Hey, I saw you at the grocery store today. Didn't know we were neighbors!"

The message was from the same ride-share driver. Her heart skipped a beat.

She hadn't told him where she lived, at least not directly. But the app had. He had her exact drop-off location. And now he had followed her, recognizing her at a store she visited regularly.

What felt like a harmless ride home had suddenly become something much more disturbing. This wasn't a coincidence—he had sought her out.

Evelyn contacted the ride-share company and reported the incident. She also filed a police report. But she couldn't shake the feeling of being watched. She realized how much information she had unknowingly shared. Her drop-off wasn't a random street—it was her home. Her rides weren't just trips—they were location logs that someone else could access.

It was a terrifying wake-up call. Ride-share drivers and delivery personnel often have access to exact addresses, daily routines, and personal interactions. Most are professional and respectful. But not all.

Evelyn thought she was making the safest choice—getting a ride instead of walking alone. But what she didn't realize was that she had given a stranger a clear view into her life. Where she lived. Where she shopped. When she was alone.

She changed her privacy settings, stopped using real names on apps, and became far more selective about location sharing. But the sense of safety she once felt was harder to restore.

Getting home safely, she realized, should never mean giving someone else the key to follow you back.

The Family That Didn't Know Their Child's Location Was Public

When Hannah bought her 12-year-old son his first smartphone, she did it with a mixture of excitement and caution. It was a rite of passage—a tool for learning, socializing, and staying in touch. She taught him the basics of online safety, helped him install a few educational apps, and set what she believed were reasonable parental controls.

What she didn't know was how much the phone was already sharing—without either of them realizing it.

Over the next few weeks, her son downloaded a few popular games and joined social media platforms where his friends were already active. Like most kids his age, he loved sharing moments—photos from the skate park, funny clips from his favorite games, and updates about where he was hanging out.

One afternoon, he received a message from someone he didn't know.

"Hey, I saw you're at the skate park! Want to meet up?"

That one sentence changed everything.

The person messaging him was a stranger—and had found him using the phone's location data. The apps he'd been using, especially some of the games and social platforms, had default settings that broadcasted his real-time location. The phone's GPS had been automatically enabled for many of them, sharing his whereabouts publicly with anyone who knew where to look.

Hannah was horrified.

She had assumed that the controls she set were enough. But many apps don't make their data-sharing practices obvious. Some of the games matched players based on proximity, using GPS to connect kids with others nearby. Social media posts were being tagged with exact locations. Even his profile photos contained geolocation metadata.

In just a few clicks, a stranger had been able to see where her son was, what he liked to do, and when he was most likely to be alone.

Hannah immediately revoked app permissions, turned off GPS access, and began the difficult process of educating herself—and her son—about mobile privacy. But the experience left her shaken.

She thought she had given her child a safe way to stay connected. Instead, that phone had quietly opened a digital window into his life for the entire world to see.

What You Need to Know

You check the weather, order food, hail a ride, tag a location, or share a photo with a timestamp. You use maps to avoid traffic. You let your phone track your steps, check in automatically, or remind you where you parked. It's convenient. Effortless. Part of modern life.

And almost all of it relies on your location.

Your phone knows exactly where you are, down to a few feet. So do many of your apps. So does your smart watch. Your car's navigation system. Your browser. Your social media posts. Even your photos often contain hidden metadata that includes GPS coordinates—even after they're cropped or filtered.

And once that data is collected, it doesn't stay local.

In 2023, a study by the Mozilla Foundation revealed that nearly 80% of the top 40 apps on the Google Play Store had discrepancies between their privacy policies and what they reported on Google's Data Safety form. Researchers concluded that Google's system fails to help consumers make informed choices about their privacy before downloading from a store with over a million apps.

Translation? Many apps aren't being honest about what data they collect—or why.

And as you might guess, location data is one of the most frequently abused.

In 2022, the Electronic Frontier Foundation (EFF) detailed how data brokers harvest precise location data from everyday mobile apps—and sell it. Many apps on your phone track your movements constantly, often without clear disclosure. App developers collect this data, pass it to brokers, and from there, it can end up in the hands of advertisers, surveillance firms, or worse.

You didn't "agree" to that.

You may not remember giving that permission. But you probably did. You just tapped "Allow."

Because most people tap "Allow" without thinking. The prompt appears once, in the middle of trying to use a feature, and it's easy to say yes. But once that permission is granted, the data starts flowing. And in most cases, it keeps flowing—even when the app isn't open.

Location tracking doesn't just tell companies where you are. It tells them where you live. Where you work. When you leave for the gym. Which store you shop at. Where your kids go to school. How often you travel. It paints a complete, intimate picture of your daily routines—and hackers, marketers, and even stalkers know how to use that picture.

And it doesn't always take a breach to become a victim.

In 2025, cybercrime units across multiple countries reported growing concerns over "surveillance-for-hire" services, where location-tracking tools and spyware were misused to monitor individuals—often for stalking or harassment.

In many of those cases, the attacker didn't need to install anything. They used already-installed apps—or abused features like Find My iPhone, shared Google Maps history, or ride-share account access.

Even Bluetooth tracking devices like AirTags and Tiles, originally designed to help find lost items, have been weaponized. By early 2025, numerous U.S. police departments had flagged an increase in stalking complaints involving Bluetooth trackers such as Apple AirTags and Tile, prompting tech companies to update safety features.

You might think you're safe because you've disabled location services on a few apps. But many apps find workarounds. Some use your IP address, Wi-Fi connections, or nearby Bluetooth signals to estimate your position anyway. And if your phone's location history is turned on—even briefly—it creates a timeline that can be accessed by anyone who compromises your account.

In short, location tracking has moved beyond convenience. It's become a tool of surveillance. And unless you actively manage it, it operates invisibly—following you room by room, street by street, day after day.

This chapter will show you what your devices really know about your movements, how that data is collected, and how it's shared—sometimes without your knowledge, often without your consent. You'll learn how to lock down your settings, detect hidden tracking, and recognize the early signs that someone might be watching your every move.

Because this isn't just about apps knowing where you are.

It's about what happens when someone else does.

Why It Matters

Most people don't realize it, but your devices know exactly where you are.
Not just the city. Not just the neighborhood. They know the restaurant you just left, the gym you visit every Thursday, the school where your child gets picked up, and the route you walk your dog.

They know when you wake up, how long you stay at work, and whether you're home right now.

And unless you've gone out of your way to disable a dozen different settings across multiple apps, all of that data is being tracked, stored, and—often—shared with people you've never met.

This isn't just about Google Maps or Find My iPhone. It's about how your entire digital ecosystem follows your every move.

In recent years, nonprofit tech watchdogs like Privacy International have revealed that many apps with location access silently collect and transmit precise GPS data—often without meaningful consent. Many of them passed this data on to third-party advertisers, analytics companies, and data brokers—sometimes within seconds of collection.

And these aren't obscure apps. They're weather apps. Fitness trackers. Delivery services. Flashlight tools. Dating platforms. Even some children's games.

You agree to share your location once, and that permission rarely expires.

That means every time you check in, search nearby, tag a photo, or just keep an app running in the background, you're feeding a real-time map of your life to companies and systems that may never ask again—but continue listening.

Location data is valuable. Which is why it's bought and sold constantly.

In 2024, Wired reported that a U.S. data broker had sold access to over 3 billion phone coordinates, revealing the movements of U.S. soldiers, intelligence personnel, and others in Germany.

The data traced them to nuclear vaults, military bases—even brothels.

If national security can be breached with location data...

What do you think is protecting yours?

This data isn't anonymized in any meaningful way. It can be re-identified by linking timestamps, routines, and cross-referenced habits.

Once someone has access to your location history, they can:

- Predict your schedule
- Identify your home and workplace
- Track who you spend time with
- Pinpoint private events (like therapy visits, protests, or political meetings)
- Target you with hyper-specific ads or phishing scams
- Plan real-world crimes based on your absence or routine

And the risks go beyond corporations.

Stalkers, abusers, and criminal actors have increasingly exploited location-sharing features built into phones, wearables, messaging apps, and even shared photo albums.

According to safety experts at the National Network to End Domestic Violence (NNEDV), a significant number of survivors have reported being digitally tracked—often without their knowledge—through GPS data shared via apps or connected family accounts.

In a nationwide NNEDV survey (2023, Technology Safety for Survivors of Gender-Based Violence Report), 72% of domestic violence programs said survivors had been tracked using mobile or GPS-enabled devices. Other studies confirm that this kind of technology-facilitated abuse is on the rise—leveraged not just for surveillance, but to intimidate, control, and isolate victims.

This form of abuse often hides in plain sight: abusers gain access through shared Apple IDs, family tracking apps, or "Find My" features. Wearable tech and even shared cloud photo albums can silently reveal a survivor's location with every sync.

Even well-meaning tools can be used for harm.

Features like Apple's "Find My" network, Google's Location History, or Snapchat's Snap Map were designed for safety and connection. But if left on by default—or if someone gains access to your accounts—they can be used to trace your exact steps with alarming precision.

Worse still, many users don't even know these settings are active.

In a 2020 study, the Norwegian Consumer Council reported that many widely-used apps transmitted real-time location data to ad tech companies—raising alarm over lack of transparency and user control. Most users had never reviewed the permissions. Others assumed turning off GPS would be enough—when in fact, Wi-Fi and Bluetooth triangulation still provide surprisingly accurate tracking.

This is why it matters.

Because location data is no longer just a helpful tool for navigation. It's a silent signal being broadcast from your pocket 24/7. It builds a map of your life. It reveals your habits, intentions, and vulnerabilities. And once it's out, you can't take it back.

Knowing where someone is isn't neutral. It's power.

This chapter is about reclaiming that power—by showing you what's being tracked, who's doing the tracking, and how to shut it down before it's used against you.

Because if someone knows where you are, they might know more than you'd ever want to share.

What to Do About It – Your Security Checklist

1. **Turn Off Location Services for Non-Essential Apps:** Most apps don't need real-time access to your location. Limit this in your phone's privacy settings by switching from "Always" or "While Using" to "Never" or "Ask Every Time."

2. **Review App Permissions Regularly:** Periodically check which apps are tracking your GPS data. Remove location access from shopping, gaming, or social apps that don't require it.

3. **Avoid Tagging Locations in Real Time:** Don't share your location while you're still there. Posting travel updates, gym visits, or restaurant check-ins in real time makes you an easy target for stalkers or burglars.

4. **Limit Access to Precise Location Data:** Both Android and iOS now allow you to give apps an "approximate location" instead of your exact GPS. Use that option where possible.

5. **Disable Geotagging for Camera and Social Media Apps:** Photos taken with your phone often store metadata with exact GPS coordinates. Turn off geotagging to avoid revealing where you live, work, or spend time.

6. **Watch for Bluetooth and Wi-Fi Location Pings:** Your devices emit signals that can be used for tracking—even if GPS is off. Disable Bluetooth and Wi-Fi when not in use, especially in public places.

7. **Use a VPN While Traveling:** VPNs mask your IP address and can help obscure your general location from trackers and ad networks.

8. **Block Ad Tracking Across Devices:** Opt out of personalized ads in your phone's system settings. This limits how companies track your movements

to serve targeted content.

9. **Be Careful with Fitness and Running Apps:** Strava, Fitbit, and similar apps often share routes and time stamps. Set your fitness data to private and avoid sharing daily routines.

10. **Don't Let Kids Share Location by Default:** Many children's apps and games collect location data. Make sure your child's device has tight privacy settings and no location-sharing permissions without your consent.

Quick Action Plan

1-Minute Fix: Turn off real-time location sharing in your phone's social media and camera apps.

5-Minute Fix: Review and adjust location access for all your apps—deny permission to those that don't absolutely need it.

15-Minute Fix: Disable Wi-Fi, Bluetooth, and GPS when not in use—especially in airports, cafés, or shopping centers.

30-Minute Fix: Audit all shared family devices, including tablets and wearables, for apps that track or log location data. Update app settings and educate household members on privacy risks.

Chapter 23

The Silent Risks of Wearables

Real-World Scenarios

The Fitness Tracker That Gave Away a Soldier's Location

Hector was a dedicated U.S. military officer stationed at a secure overseas base. Between intense operations and long shifts, he made time to stay physically fit. He wore a popular fitness tracker that logged his daily runs, helping him monitor his endurance, pace, and progress over time. The device automatically uploaded his workouts to a companion app, where he could review his routes and compare stats with other users.

It seemed harmless. Even motivating.

Then came the breach.

Military security analysts uncovered something alarming: a global heat map generated by fitness tracking data revealed running patterns of thousands of users around the world—including service members like Hector. The map, accessible to anyone online, showed glowing trails of activity in remote desert areas and isolated compounds—locations that were otherwise invisible on commercial maps.

Hector's daily runs had drawn a digital path around the perimeter of his base.

Suddenly, enemy forces had access to data that mapped out secure installations. With enough time and analysis, they could identify entrances, guard patrol patterns, and even estimate how many people were stationed there. It was an intelligence goldmine—created unintentionally by soldiers trying to stay in shape.

Hector was horrified. He had never imagined that his private workouts could become a national security threat. The app never warned him that the data was being shared publicly, and he hadn't thought to check the privacy settings. After all, he wasn't posting photos or tagging locations—just tracking runs.

But fitness trackers do more than count steps. They log exact GPS coordinates, timestamps, and movement history—often uploading it in real time.

In response to the incident, the U.S. military moved quickly, banning certain wearables and disabling GPS functions on others. The breach became a case study in how innocent data can be weaponized.

Hector had thought he was simply improving his fitness. Instead, his device had silently drawn a map for the enemy.

The Smartwatch That Led to a Home Invasion

Olivia loved starting her mornings with a run through her quiet suburban neighborhood. It helped her clear her mind, stay healthy, and prepare for the day ahead. Like many fitness enthusiasts, she wore a sleek smartwatch that tracked her steps, distance, and route. It synced automatically with a fitness app on her phone, which she used to post achievements, share maps of her runs, and even compete with friends.

Her posts were public by default—something she hadn't really thought about.

Each update included the full route of her jog, starting and ending at her house. The app also shared the exact time of day she ran, which was consistent every morning—usually around 6:30 a.m. It became part of her daily routine and digital identity.

Then one morning, Olivia came back from her run to find her front door splintered and wide open. Her television was gone. Jewelry, electronics, even a box of personal documents—missing.

The police confirmed it had been a targeted burglary. But there were no signs of forced entry before that day, no prior alarms. That's when investigators asked if she posted anything about her schedule or location online.

Olivia hesitated, then opened her fitness app.

There it was. A trail of data, laid out in clear routes and timestamps. Every run she'd taken for the past month was public—including her exact starting point: her home. The burglars hadn't needed to stake out her house or follow her in person. They simply watched her profile, learned when she would leave, and walked in while she was away.

Olivia felt violated in every way. The smartwatch she had bought to improve her health had inadvertently helped someone plan a robbery. She had unknowingly exposed her routine to complete strangers—people who had used her own data against her.

She deleted the app, locked her privacy settings, and stopped posting run routes entirely. But the sense of security she'd once felt in her own home was gone.

She thought she was sharing her fitness journey.

She didn't realize she was broadcasting an open invitation to her empty house.

THE SMARTWATCH THAT WAS SECRETLY LISTENING

Felix had always appreciated smart technology. As a busy professional juggling work and family, he liked the convenience of voice assistants, synced calendars, and fitness reminders—all packed into a sleek smartwatch he wore every day.

The watch helped him stay on schedule, track his heart rate, and even take calls on the go. It was connected to his phone, his smart home, and his email. He never really questioned how it all worked. It just did.

Then one evening, while talking with his wife about refinancing their mortgage, something strange happened. The next morning, his phone was flooded with ads for home loans and mortgage lenders. Felix hadn't searched for anything. He hadn't sent any emails. The conversation had been private—spoken aloud in the kitchen, nowhere near a computer.

Curious and uneasy, he dug into his phone's settings and then into the smartwatch's permissions. That's when he found something buried in the fine print: the device had been recording ambient audio. Voice data was being captured, processed, and—in some cases—shared with third-party companies for "marketing optimization."

The watch had been listening.

And it wasn't just when he said "Hey, Assistant" or gave it a command. It had been recording even during casual conversations. Entire snippets of dialogue—about finances, family, and daily life—had potentially been stored or analyzed.

Felix was furious.

He had assumed his smartwatch was just a fitness tool with a few convenient extras. He hadn't realized it was a microphone, always on, always waiting—and often, sending that data somewhere he couldn't see.

He disabled voice functions and disconnected the device from his phone. But the feeling lingered. What else had it heard? Who else had listened?

Felix learned a hard truth that day: many smart devices, especially wearables, collect more than just steps and calories. They collect conversations, context, and private thoughts.

He thought his smartwatch was a personal assistant.

He didn't realize it had been eavesdropping on his life.

The Heart Rate Monitor That Was Hacked

Stephen had always been cautious about his health. After a heart condition left him hospitalized the year before, he made some serious lifestyle changes—eating better, exercising regularly, and wearing a smart heart rate monitor prescribed by his doctor. The device synced with a mobile app and sent real-time updates to his physician, who could monitor his recovery from afar. It was a comfort, a digital safety net that allowed him to live more freely.

Then, one afternoon, something terrifying happened.

The monitor suddenly began flashing warnings—his heart rate was dangerously high. The app displayed red alerts, and an automatic emergency notification was sent to his doctor. His smartwatch buzzed repeatedly, urging him to seek help immediately.

Panicked, Stephen rushed to the hospital, heart pounding—not because of the monitor, but from fear. Doctors ran tests, hooked him up to machines, and observed him for hours. But everything came back normal. His heart rate was fine. There had been no medical event.

It was only later, after a team of cybersecurity researchers analyzed the device, that the truth emerged.

The monitor had been hacked.

Hackers had exploited a vulnerability in its firmware—a flaw that allowed them to remotely alter the device's readings. They had pushed false data into the system, triggering emergency alerts and causing unnecessary panic. The motive was unclear—perhaps it was a random demonstration of power, or part of a larger scheme to test vulnerabilities in medical IoT devices.

What mattered most to Stephen was that his trust had been shattered.

He had believed the monitor was protecting him. Instead, it had become a point of danger—a system that could be hijacked at any time.

Many health trackers and medical devices still lack strong encryption or robust cybersecurity protocols. For hackers, that makes them easy targets. And in some cases, the stakes are even higher: researchers have shown how similar vulnerabilities can be used to manipulate pacemakers or insulin pumps, potentially causing life-threatening harm.

Stephen's experience was a wake-up call. He had trusted a machine with his life—without knowing who else could reach into it.

What You Need to Know

Your smartwatch tracks your steps, monitors your sleep, reminds you to drink water, and buzzes when you've been sitting too long. It helps you stay fit, stay organized, and stay connected. It feels like a health tool. A lifestyle assistant. A harmless convenience strapped to your wrist.

But under the surface, it's quietly collecting some of the most sensitive data you own.

Wearables like fitness trackers, smartwatches, and health rings gather information constantly. Your heart rate. Your sleep cycles. Your exact location. The times you wake up, leave home, or arrive at work. They track your habits—when you're most active, when you're sedentary, how long your workouts last, and even whether you're stressed. Some sync directly with your calendar, contacts, and messages. Others can answer calls, read emails, and access cloud services.

According to IDC, global shipments of wearable devices reached 534.6 million units in 2024, marking a 5.4% year-over-year growth from 2023. The average user syncs their wearable to at least three other devices—usually a smartphone, cloud account, and at least one third-party health or fitness app. That creates a direct link between your physical life and your digital one—and a quiet, persistent flow of personal data from your body to the internet.

What most users don't realize is how much of that data is stored—not just on the device, but in the cloud. And once it's there, it can be accessed, leaked, or sold.

A 2024 study by Surfshark found that 80% of popular fitness apps share user data with third parties, including advertisers and data brokers, for targeted advertising or measurement purposes. That includes workout times, location history, heart rate trends, and even menstrual cycle information—data that most people assume is private, personal, or protected.

But it's not just advertisers who are interested.

Wearables are becoming a favorite target for cybercriminals. If a hacker gains access to your smartwatch, they may not find your bank password—but they'll find plenty of clues. Clues about where you live, when you sleep, and what time you leave home. They can use Bluetooth vulnerabilities to intercept data transmissions. If your watch is connected to your phone or cloud, a single compromised login can open the door to everything else synced to the device.

Researchers at a 2024 SafeThings symposium demonstrated how an active Bluetooth sniffer could intercept and manipulate traffic between smartwatches and their paired devices. Many of these attacks didn't even require physical access to the device—just proximity and weak pairing security.

And while some people dismiss this risk as minor—"It's just a fitness tracker"—remember that stolen location data and movement patterns can be used for stalking, home invasion timing, or corporate espionage. If you're sharing your health data with a workplace wellness program, insurer, or government service, those risks multiply.

Then there's the issue of what happens when you lose the device—or sell it.

Many users forget to log out or perform a factory reset before selling or trading in their wearables. If the device isn't encrypted or properly wiped, the next user may be able to extract sensitive information—such as health logs, location history, stored notifications, or even access linked accounts.

Cybersecurity experts have repeatedly warned that used wearable devices often retain recoverable personal data, exposing a serious gap in digital hygiene. Studies have shown that wearables sold online can still contain synced messages, GPS trails, and detailed health metrics from previous owners.

This chapter will walk you through what your wearable is really collecting, where that data goes, and how it can be used against you if it falls into the wrong hands. You'll learn how to lock down your devices, limit data exposure, and think twice about what you connect to your wrist.

Because the watch that helps you run faster or sleep better?

It might also be telling someone else exactly where you are—and when you're most vulnerable.

Why It Matters

They track your steps, your sleep, your heart rate, your workouts, your stress levels, and your location. They remind you to stand, drink water, and take deep breaths. They send you texts, manage your calls, play your music, and help unlock your laptop.

Wearables like smartwatches and fitness trackers promise a healthier, more connected life. And for many people, they deliver exactly that.

But they also come with a cost most users never consider. Because while you're tracking your body, someone else might be tracking you.

Wearables have quickly become one of the most underregulated and undersecured technologies in the average household. According to a Pew Research Center report, over 34% of U.S. adults wore a smartwatch or fitness tracker daily in 2024. That number is even higher among young adults and parents of children under 13, many of whom buy kids' smartwatches for safety and GPS monitoring.

But most users never dig deeper than the screen on their wrist.

They don't check what data is being collected, how long it's stored, or who has access to it. They don't consider how their step count, sleep score, or heart rate variability might be used against them in the wrong hands.

And that's the danger.

Because wearables collect biometric data—information that's tied not just to your identity, but to your actual physiology. Heart rhythms. Body temperature. Movement patterns. Sleep cycles. Stress spikes. These aren't just statistics. They're digital fingerprints of your health and behavior.

And they're valuable.

The Norwegian Consumer Council reported in 2016 that fitness apps like Strava, Endomondo, and MyFitnessPal share user data with advertisers and third-party partners. Even anonymized data can be reverse-engineered to identify individuals based on movement patterns, geographic location, and time-stamped activity logs.

That means your morning jog could reveal your home address.
Your heart rate logs could expose underlying medical conditions.
Your sleep data could be used to infer mental health issues.

And this doesn't just affect you.

Many people connect their wearables to shared health plans, family accounts, or employer-sponsored wellness programs. This integration can open the door to corporate surveillance—where your "health engagement" is tracked, scored, and potentially used to influence insurance premiums, employee incentives, or even access to certain services.

Ongoing discussions in the insurance industry suggest that wearable data is increasingly being explored to refine risk assessment models and personalize coverage decisions.

Most participants didn't even know their data was being used that way.

Then there's the cybersecurity angle.

Many wearables have minimal built-in security. They connect to your phone over Bluetooth, often with weak or no encryption. That connection can be intercepted, spoofed, or hijacked. Researchers at the University of Virginia (*2024, Intercepting Bluetooth Traffic from Wearable Health Devices*) demonstrated how a modified Bluetooth sniffer could intercept and alter smartwatch traffic from up to 100 feet (30m) away.

And if your wearable is syncing to cloud services or app dashboards? That's one more place where your data lives—and can be breached. There have been multiple high-profile hacks of fitness and health platforms over the past few years, leaking everything from workout histories to menstrual cycle tracking data to home GPS coordinates.

But perhaps the most overlooked risk is physical.

Wearables can be stolen, reset, or re-paired by someone else. And many devices don't require PIN codes, facial recognition, or even user confirmation to display notifications or access sensitive information. That means if your watch is taken—during a jog, from a locker, or even off a nightstand—it may carry enough unprotected information to compromise your identity, location, or accounts.

This is why it matters.

Because wearables feel personal. They're part of your body. They monitor you constantly. And that illusion of intimacy makes people trust them—blindly.

But that trust isn't always earned.

The companies making wearables aren't health providers. They're tech companies. They monetize data. They collect more than you realize. They share it more than they admit. And if your wearable links to your phone, your calendar, your messages, or your location—it's not just a fitness tracker anymore.

It's a surveillance device you volunteered to wear.

This chapter exists to pull that into focus. Because awareness is the first step to real protection.

What to Do About It – Your Security Checklist

1. **Set Up Device-Level Passcodes:** Always activate screen locks or passcodes on your smartwatch or fitness tracker. Many wearables default to "open" access, making them easy to exploit if lost or stolen.

2. **Restrict App and Data Sharing Permissions:** Limit what your wearable can access—disable unnecessary syncing with calendar, contacts, and messaging apps unless absolutely needed.

3. **Avoid Connecting to Public Wi-Fi or Open Bluetooth Connections:** Many smartwatches auto-connect to networks or pair with nearby devices. Turn off Bluetooth when not in use and avoid joining unknown networks.

4. **Review What's Being Collected:** Check the companion app for your wearable (e.g., Fitbit, Apple Health, Garmin Connect) and read what it logs—your sleep, heart rate, exact GPS routes, even menstrual cycles. Opt out where possible.

5. **Disable Location Tracking for Workouts (Unless Essential):** Turn off precise location sharing unless you truly need GPS-based workout tracking. This prevents data leaks that reveal your daily movement patterns or routines.

6. **Be Selective with Third-Party Integrations:** Many wearables offer connections to nutrition, productivity, or health apps. Only connect to trusted, essential services. Each connection adds a new potential risk.

7. **Update Firmware Regularly:** Just like a phone or laptop, wearables need updates to fix security bugs. Check your app settings and enable automatic updates if available.

8. **Use Two-Factor Authentication (2FA) on Linked Accounts:** If your wearable connects to services like Apple, Google, or Samsung Health, enable 2FA on those main accounts to protect against wider breaches.

9. **Don't Share Health Stats Publicly:** Many apps allow public sharing of weight, runs, or performance stats. Avoid making personal data public, especially if your profile is tied to your full name or city.

10. **Secure Your Lost Device Recovery Settings:** Make sure the device can't be factory reset without your permission and is enrolled in Find My Device or a similar recovery service.

Quick Action Plan

1-Minute Fix: Turn off Bluetooth and location tracking when you're not actively using the device.

5-Minute Fix: Check app permissions and remove access to calendar, messages, or other personal content.

15-Minute Fix: Update your wearable's firmware, review your linked app settings, and restrict data sharing features.

30-Minute Fix: Do a full privacy audit of your wearable and companion app, including any integrations with health platforms or fitness challenges. Adjust every setting that isn't absolutely necessary.

PART 5 - PROTECT YOUR FAMILY BEFORE IT'S TOO LATE

Chapter 24

How Hackers Target Children

Real-World Scenarios

The Online Friend That Wasn't a Friend

Abigail was 11, creative and full of curiosity. Like many kids her age, she spent a lot of time online—playing games, chatting with friends, and exploring virtual worlds. Her favorite game was a multiplayer adventure that let players team up to solve missions. That's where she met Victor.

Victor said he was 12. He liked the same games. He made funny jokes. He was kind, and he always seemed to be online when Abigail was. Over a few weeks, they became close—gaming partners who talked daily. The conversations eventually moved beyond the game. They chatted about school, favorite music, movies, and pets.

One day, Victor asked Abigail to send a photo of herself. "Just a selfie," he said. "So I know who I'm playing with!" It didn't feel weird. After all, they were friends. She sent a photo—just her smiling at the camera.

A few days later, he asked for another picture. This time, he said, "Send one in your pajamas!" Abigail felt uncomfortable and said no. Victor's tone instantly changed.

"If you don't send it, I'll show your first picture to your parents. I'll send it to everyone at your school," he wrote.

Abigail froze. She felt cornered. She didn't know how to handle the fear or the guilt. She stopped replying. But the messages kept coming—angrier, more demanding, more threatening.

Eventually, her parents noticed something was wrong. She wasn't eating, wasn't sleeping, and seemed nervous every time she used her tablet. After a heartfelt talk, Abigail told them everything. Police were called, and the truth was worse than they imagined.

Victor wasn't 12. He was a 43-year-old man, using fake photos and identities to lure children. He had dozens of accounts. Abigail had been one of many.

Right now, the FBI estimates that approximately 500,000 online predators are active each day, primarily targeting children aged 12 to 15 through chat rooms and instant messaging platforms. Many use gaming platforms, messaging apps, and social media to gain trust—slowly breaking down boundaries until they have power over their victim.

Abigail thought she was making a new friend.

She didn't realize she was being targeted from the start.

The Viral Challenge That Sent a Boy to the Hospital

Lucas was 13, a typical teen who loved his phone and lived for trends. His world was filled with TikTok dances, funny skits, and viral challenges. He wasn't trying to be famous—just part of the fun.

One day, Lucas stumbled across a challenge that was spreading like wildfire: the "Blackout Challenge."

It looked harmless at first. Teenagers were seen holding their breath or choking themselves to achieve a brief "rush" or "high." They laughed, filmed themselves doing it, and got thousands of likes. Social media made it look cool. No warnings. No consequences.

Lucas wanted to try it, just once. He didn't tell anyone.

He locked his bedroom door, set up his phone camera—just like the others—and tried the challenge.

His mother found him minutes later, unconscious on the floor.

The ambulance arrived quickly, but Lucas had suffered oxygen deprivation. He survived—but barely. His life, and his family's, were changed forever.

What Lucas and millions of other kids didn't know is that these challenges aren't new—and they aren't safe. They're deadly. The "Blackout Challenge," a dangerous social media trend, has been linked to the deaths of at least 20 children, with ongoing lawsuits alleging platform responsibility. What makes them more dangerous is that social media platforms often fail to remove harmful videos quickly. The very algorithms that power these platforms can unintentionally promote risky content, pushing it to more and more children.

To a teen like Lucas, it looked like fun. Something everyone was doing.

But the moment he tried it, it became something irreversible.

Social media has become a silent teacher for many children—rewarding clicks over caution, likes over life. Lucas didn't think he was in danger.

He thought it was just another challenge.

He didn't realize he'd been pulled into something deadly.

The YouTube Video That Wasn't What It Seemed

Stella was seven. Her favorite part of the day was watching cartoons on her tablet after school while her parents made dinner. Her go-to? Peppa Pig.

Her parents used YouTube Kids—because it was supposed to be safer, filtered, curated. But one afternoon, everything changed.

Stella clicked on a video that looked like every other Peppa episode. It even started the same way—familiar music, bright colors, happy voices. But about halfway through, the screen glitched.

Then came the face.

Distorted. Pale. Eyes too big, voice too low. The character looked into the screen and spoke directly to kids.

"If you don't do what I say, your family will get hurt. Cut yourself. Hide it. Don't tell anyone."

Stella screamed. She dropped the tablet and ran to her mom. Terrified and confused, her parents opened the video. What they saw was worse than anything they expected.

The video had been edited. Someone had inserted dangerous content into a children's cartoon and uploaded it to YouTube Kids. It had slipped past the filters, been viewed thousands of times, and had likely traumatized other children before it was even noticed.

This isn't a one-time glitch.

There's a dark side of the internet that specifically targets children through seemingly innocent platforms. Some videos are edited to include horrifying imagery, self-harm instructions, or threats. Others mimic real cartoons to lure children into watching content they never should've seen. Even on YouTube Kids, dangerous material often slips through.

Stella thought she was watching a cartoon.

She didn't know that behind the bright colors and playful music, someone had placed a message designed to scare, control, and harm her.

Her parents trusted an algorithm to protect their daughter.

They didn't realize how easy it was for predators to slip through.

The Social Media Account That Got a Girl Bullied

Lara was 14 and full of life. She loved to dance, make videos, and share snapshots of her day on social media. Her goal was simple—become an influencer. Nothing huge. Just someone people followed and liked. It started off fun. Her posts got comments, likes, and new followers rolled in.

But one day, something shifted.

It began with a comment under one of her selfies: "You're ugly." Then another: "No one actually likes you."

The messages became relentless. Anonymous accounts flooded her inbox with insults. Some called her names. Others told her to disappear. Then, someone took her photos, distorted her face, and reposted them with cruel captions.

At school, whispers followed her down the hallway. Someone had created a fake profile using her name—posting false stories, sharing edited pictures, and tagging people from her class. A poll appeared online: "Should Lara just end it?" Dozens of students had voted.

One afternoon, Lara came home from school in tears, locked herself in her room, and didn't want to come out. Her mom eventually found out what had happened—and what she saw online left her speechless.

Social media, which had once made Lara feel creative and connected, had become a weapon aimed directly at her self-worth.

Cyberbullying like this isn't rare. A UNICEF poll reported that one in three young people across 30 countries have experienced online bullying, with one in five skipping school due to cyberbullying. And for many, the impact is devastating. The psychological scars left by constant digital cruelty are as real as physical wounds. Victims of cyberbullying are significantly more likely to experience depression, anxiety, and suicidal thoughts, underscoring the severe mental health implications.

Even worse? Most platforms still fail to remove harmful content fast enough. Reporting systems are slow. Abusers make new accounts. And young users are left exposed, unsupported, and unheard.

Lara just wanted to be seen.

She didn't know the internet would turn on her—and nearly destroy her in the process.

What You Need to Know

Most parents think of online threats to children as something obvious. A stranger in a chatroom. A creepy message on a gaming platform. A social media request that doesn't feel right. These risks are real, and we've all heard the warnings.

But modern hackers don't always try to talk to your child. Sometimes, they don't need to.

Children today are surrounded by devices—phones, tablets, smartwatches, gaming consoles, home assistants. They interact with screens from an early age, often before they understand what "online" even means. And that means they're generating data long before they know what privacy is.

That's what makes them valuable.

In 2025, the FTC finalized amendments to the Children's Online Privacy Protection Act (COPPA), strengthening protections for children's online data and limiting companies' ability to monetize kids' information.

Children can't consent to this. Most parents don't realize it's happening. But the devices keep collecting—and that data is powerful.

Hackers know that a child's identity is often easier to steal and more profitable to exploit.

Why? Because most kids don't have credit histories, bank accounts, or active identity monitoring. A stolen Social Security number belonging to a 10-year-old might go unnoticed for years—until someone tries to get a student loan, open a bank account, or apply for their first job. By then, the damage is already done.

A 2021 study by Javelin Strategy & Research found that over 1.25 million children in the U.S. fell victim to identity theft and fraud, resulting in nearly $1 billion in losses.

And not all of it starts with phishing or active scams. Some of it starts with you.

Parents often post photos, school updates, full names, birthdays, and tagged locations on social media—believing it's private, or shared only with close friends. But once that content is public—or even shared and screenshotted—it becomes data for someone else to scrape. A hacker doesn't need to ask your child for personal information. They can collect it from your Instagram.

Then there are the educational tools.

Schools increasingly rely on platforms for homework, testing, communication, and grades. Many of these tools are poorly secured or don't encrypt data properly. In 2023, the education sector experienced over 1,500 confirmed data breaches, the highest number among all industries, highlighting the vulnerability of educational institutions.

Gaming platforms and mobile games are another entry point. Even when children don't chat with strangers, many games request access to microphones, cameras, and storage. Free apps often include aggressive third-party trackers. Some serve targeted ads based on behavior—even mood and attention span data logged through in-game interactions. And when children reuse simple passwords or play on shared devices, hackers can grab credentials that open family email accounts, shopping apps, or cloud backups.

Even smart toys are a risk.

Several Bluetooth-enabled toys and voice-activated assistants marketed for children have been found recording conversations, collecting ambient audio, and in some cases, broadcasting unencrypted data over home Wi-Fi. If not properly secured, these devices can be hijacked—or used to eavesdrop.

This chapter will walk you through how hackers target children indirectly—by mining data from games, apps, devices, and even parents. You'll learn how to limit exposure, spot risky tech, and create layers of protection your child won't even notice—but hackers will.

Because your child doesn't need to be tricked to be targeted.

Sometimes, they're already visible—without ever saying a word.

Why It Matters

When we think of hackers targeting children, most people imagine direct contact—someone pretending to be a friend in an online game, or a stranger reaching out through social media. And while those threats are very real, they're only part of the picture.

Because in today's connected world, children can be targeted by cybercriminals without ever being contacted at all.

Kids are growing up inside a digital ecosystem that watches, tracks, and—far too often—exploits them.

From the moment they learn to swipe a screen, their behavior is recorded, analyzed, and stored. They play games, watch videos, ask smart assistants questions, and click "Accept" on terms they can't begin to understand. They connect through school portals, learning tablets, classroom apps, and hand-me-down phones. Many have usernames, email addresses, device IDs—or even digital wallets—before they grasp what any of it means.

And that makes them ideal targets.

A 2023 report by Thorn revealed that 1 in 17 minors reported experiencing sextortion, while 70% of those seeking contact with children did so online, most often through social media.

Because the data speaks louder than warnings.

Children often use devices that aren't secured properly. They install free games or apps with excessive permissions. They accept cookies without question. They sync their devices with family accounts. They leave passwords saved, voice assistants active, webcams unblocked. They overshare in online spaces. And they do it all under the radar—because the systems built to protect them often focus only on monitoring conversations, not behaviors.

That's where hackers thrive. Cybercriminals don't need to talk to your child to exploit them. They just need:

- An email address reused on multiple platforms
- Access to a shared home Wi-Fi network
- A cloud account with weak security
- A webcam left exposed

- A compromised game mod or app
- Or, most commonly, access to the child's forgotten digital footprint

A study by NIST indicated that children often reuse passwords across multiple online accounts, increasing their vulnerability to cyber threats. Even worse, many used credentials that were easy to guess: pet names, birth years, favorite characters, or simple number strings. When these accounts get compromised in low-level data breaches—which happen constantly—hackers don't always go after the child.

They go after the family.

They scan the synced calendar. They find linked financial apps. They use cookies and autofill to extract stored emails, home addresses, and payment methods. They install spyware that sends screenshots or keystrokes to remote servers. Or they simply harvest the child's information—date of birth, school name, interests, home IP address—and sell it to identity brokers or criminal marketplaces.

The result? A growing number of child identity theft cases, often invisible for years.

And because kids don't check their credit reports, many don't discover the fraud until they turn 18 and apply for a loan, college, or job—only to find a mess they didn't create.

This isn't just about money. It's about long-term digital safety.

Kids who have their identities stolen may spend years trying to repair the damage. Kids who are tracked online without their knowledge lose autonomy. Kids whose devices are compromised might unknowingly expose their entire household.

Parents assume parental controls are enough. But controls only block content. They don't stop malware hidden in game downloads. They don't encrypt devices. They don't monitor for leaked credentials. They don't detect when an old tablet is still syncing to a shared cloud drive that contains family tax documents.

Kids are online from an early age, but the systems they use aren't designed for their protection—they're designed for data collection. And the longer that continues, the more vulnerable they become to threats they can't see, don't understand, and have no tools to stop.

This chapter is here to help change that. Not by scaring parents, but by informing them. Because you don't need to wait for a predator to show up in a chat window to recognize that your child may already be at risk.

What to Do About It – Your Security Checklist

1. **Create Child-Specific Accounts with Parental Controls:** Never let kids use your own devices or accounts without restrictions. Set up child profiles with built-in protections on tablets, streaming platforms, gaming consoles, and mobile devices.

2. **Limit Location Sharing on All Devices:** Disable GPS and geotagging features on children's apps, cameras, and games. Many platforms auto-tag locations in photos, which can be misused to identify where your child lives

or goes to school.

3. **Review All App Permissions Regularly:** Many seemingly harmless apps—games, quizzes, even drawing apps—ask for access to the microphone, contacts, or camera. Deny unnecessary permissions and uninstall apps that overreach.

4. **Disable Auto-Sync to Shared Family Accounts:** Avoid letting children's devices sync to shared photo libraries, calendars, or cloud storage where sensitive data might be exposed.

5. **Teach Kids Not to Share Personal Info—Even in Games:** Many kids are tricked into revealing their age, school, or address through friendly conversations in gaming chats or quiz-style games. Role-play these scenarios and explain why they're dangerous.

6. **Supervise Social Media and Video Uploads Closely:** Even if accounts are set to "private," children often unintentionally reveal identifying info through videos, background details, or usernames. Approve what gets posted and regularly audit profiles.

7. **Use Content Filters and Monitoring Tools:** Tools like Bark, Qustodio, or built-in family tools from Google and Apple can detect risky behavior, flag suspicious messages, and block inappropriate sites.

8. **Keep Devices in Shared Spaces, Not Bedrooms:** Screens should be visible during use, especially for younger children. Predators and scams thrive in isolation.

9. **Be Cautious with Online Games & Chat Features:** Use games that offer chat moderation or disable communication altogether. Games like Roblox, Minecraft, and Fortnite all have parental control options—learn them and use them.

10. **Keep Software and Firmware Updated:** Outdated apps, browsers, or operating systems leave devices open to exploits—even if your child isn't directly chatting with anyone.

Quick Action Plan

1-Minute Fix: Disable location access and microphone permissions for all apps on your child's device.

5-Minute Fix: Set parental controls on their device and block age-inappropriate content.

15-Minute Fix: Review their installed apps and permissions, removing any that don't serve a clear purpose.

30-Minute Fix: Audit their online accounts and profiles for privacy settings, personally identifying information, or unsafe behaviors. Talk to your child about what they post, who they talk to, and what risks exist—even if no one is messaging them directly.

Chapter 25

Parental Controls: How to Actually Keep Kids Safe

Real-World Scenarios

The Child Who Accidentally Spent $3,000 on a Game

Egemen was nine. Curious, imaginative, and like most kids his age, completely immersed in mobile games. His favorite was a bright, fast-paced adventure where players built worlds, collected gems, and unlocked powerful characters.

One afternoon, Egemen found a glowing button that said, "Buy More Gems." It popped up right when he ran out of coins, just as he was about to beat a level. So, he tapped it. A shiny animation appeared. His gems increased. It felt like magic.

So, he tapped it again. And again.

Over the next few days, Egemen played happily, pressing that button whenever he ran low on resources. He didn't realize every tap charged real money to his parents' credit card—saved to the device from a previous purchase.

By the time his parents noticed the email alerts, the total was already over $3,000.

Panicked, they called their bank and the game's customer service. But because the charges came from their home IP address—and technically weren't unauthorized—they were told refunds might not be possible. The game company claimed the child had "consented" by clicking, and the system had no way to distinguish his age.

Worse, parental controls had never been set up. No spending limits. No purchase restrictions. No password prompt before buying.

They had assumed the app was "just a game."

Egemen was heartbroken when he found out what had happened. He didn't understand money the way adults do. He just wanted to keep playing.

But the game wasn't built to protect him—it was built to make money.

Bright animations, urgent prompts, and irresistible power-ups are designed to trigger impulsive spending. And developers know exactly who they're targeting: kids who don't understand digital money.

It wasn't a bug. It was the business model.

In 2014, Apple and Google were sued for quietly letting kids make in-app purchases—no password required each time. One approval unlocked a 30-minute window to keep spending. No alerts. No warnings. Millions were lost before parents even noticed. The FTC stepped in: $19M from Google. $32.5M from Apple.

Fast forward to 2024—Apple claims it blocked over $2 billion in potentially fraudulent App Store transactions, including unauthorized purchases by kids.

Looks like the penalty worked. Lesson learned—ten years later.

Egemen thought he was just having fun. He didn't realize he was clicking his way into a financial crisis.

The YouTube Algorithm That Showed a Child Disturbing Content

Victoria was five years old, full of wonder and energy. Her favorite way to unwind after preschool was to watch cartoons on her family's tablet—especially anything with Peppa Pig. Her parents had installed YouTube Kids, believing it was a safe, filtered space where Victoria could enjoy age-appropriate videos.

But one afternoon, something went terribly wrong.

Victoria clicked on a Peppa Pig episode that looked like all the others—same thumbnail, same title. The video began normally. But two minutes in, the cheerful animation glitched.

What followed was horrifying.

The screen shifted to a crudely animated, distorted version of Peppa. The character screamed. Violent imagery appeared. Then a robotic voice came on, whispering instructions to children on how to harm themselves—urging them to keep secrets from their parents.

Victoria burst into tears and threw the tablet down.

Her mom rushed in and, after calming her daughter, reviewed the video. What she saw made her sick to her stomach. The cartoon had been intentionally altered by someone who wanted to manipulate and traumatize children. Worse, the video had thousands of views—and was still live.

Even on YouTube Kids, dangerous content still slips through the cracks. In one major investigation, dozens of videos were found featuring disturbing content hidden inside familiar animations. These clips evade filters by mimicking well-known titles and visuals, tricking both children and the algorithms meant to protect them.

A 2020 Pew Research Center study found that 80% of parents with children aged 11 or younger said their child watches YouTube. Many also expressed concerns about exposure to inappropriate content – and for good reason. Content moderation isn't perfect. Without strict parental controls and active oversight, kids can stumble across videos that aren't just inappropriate—they're deeply harmful. In fact, 46% of parents reported that their child had encountered age-inappropriate content on the platform.

Victoria thought she was watching cartoons.

She didn't know that someone had planted a digital nightmare inside her favorite show.

The Stranger Who Contacted a Child Through a Game

Leo was twelve and spent most of his free time on multiplayer games. He loved the teamwork, the challenges, and the sense of being part of something exciting. One afternoon, while playing a popular fantasy game, he got a friend request from someone named "ShadowStrike."

They started playing together regularly. ShadowStrike was helpful, funny, and said he was thirteen. Over time, their conversations moved from game strategy to personal chat. He asked Leo about his favorite shows, what school he went to, what his real name was.

It felt like friendship.

Then, ShadowStrike asked for a photo. "Nothing weird," he said—just a quick selfie so he could "see who he was talking to." Leo hesitated, but he'd come to trust his online friend. He sent one.

The next day, ShadowStrike asked for another photo—something more private. Leo said no. Suddenly, the tone changed.

"If you don't send it," the stranger wrote, "I'll show your first photo to everyone."

Leo panicked. He didn't know what to do. He hadn't told his parents about ShadowStrike. They didn't even know the game had chat features. They had assumed online games were safe and hadn't set any parental controls.

When his mom finally discovered what was happening, she was horrified. Authorities later confirmed that "ShadowStrike" wasn't a child at all. He was an adult predator who had faked his identity and used the game's chat system to groom multiple children.

Leo thought he was making a new friend.

He didn't realize he was walking into a predator's trap.

The Homework Search That Led to an Adult Website

Emily was ten and working hard on her school project about ancient civilizations. Her teacher had assigned a fun topic: ancient sculptures from around the world. Curious and excited, she opened her laptop and typed a search into the browser: "ancient sculptures."

She expected marble statues, maybe some pyramids or historical monuments.

Instead, she got something else entirely.

Within seconds, her screen filled with explicit content—images and pop-up ads that no child should ever see. Some were graphic. Others were disturbingly targeted with cartoon characters and bright colors, clearly designed to lure in younger viewers.

Emily panicked and closed the tab. But more windows opened. Ads for adult chat rooms. Videos she didn't understand. Her laptop froze under the weight of pop-ups, and she started crying.

Her parents came rushing in.

That's when they discovered the truth: they had never installed any parental filters on Emily's laptop. The default search engine had no restrictions, and some adult sites had deliberately used misleading tags and keywords like "statue," "ancient," and "mythology" to show up in results that kids might search for.

Emily wasn't trying to break the rules. She was just trying to do her homework.

Unfortunately, the internet doesn't care about intentions.

A 2023 study by Common Sense indicated that children as young as 8, 9, and 10 years old are increasingly exposed to adult content online. Many of them—just like Emily—aren't looking for anything bad. But without web filtering, safe search settings, or child-appropriate browsers, even the most innocent queries can open the door to dangerous material.

Some adult websites are designed to bypass filters. They embed keywords that match homework topics, game names, or trending kid-friendly subjects just to lure unsuspecting users—and it works.

Emily thought she was working on a school assignment.

She didn't realize she was just one click away from the darker corners of the internet.

What You Need to Know

Parental controls sound like a digital safety net. A few quick settings, a clean dashboard, some filtered content—and suddenly your child is safe online. That's the promise. And it works—up to a point.

But most parents overestimate what these tools actually do. They set them once and forget them. Or they install a third-party app, check a few boxes, and assume the internet has been tamed. Unfortunately, that's not how this works anymore.

The truth is, today's internet doesn't operate within neat boundaries.

It's not just about explicit websites anymore. It's chat features inside mobile games. Comments under cartoons. AI-generated videos on platforms made for children.

It's the content that looks safe—but isn't.

And the people who know how to slip past filters without ever setting off alarms.

Even apps labeled "kid-safe" often come with features that open hidden doors.

In 2022, Kaspersky detected over 7 million cyberattacks linked to popular children's games—a 57% increase from the year before.

Parental controls can help. They block the obvious threats—adult sites, sketchy apps, certain keywords, and screen time abuse. They're a useful layer of defense.

But they're not bulletproof.

But they don't block manipulation. They don't stop phishing links sent through a chat on Roblox. They don't catch malware disguised as a game mod or prevent your child from befriending someone who isn't who they say they are. They don't flag emotional distress, peer pressure, or targeted bullying happening through a private message.

And that's where parents get blindsided.

Because many of the most serious threats online aren't explicit. They're social. Subtle. Slow. A stranger posing as another kid. A scam that starts with "You've won!" A friend who dares them to try a dangerous challenge trending on YouTube Shorts. A download that seems fun, but grants access to the entire phone.

Even built-in tools from Google and Apple have gaps. They rely on the parent knowing how to configure them – and knowing what to block. They require constant updates. And kids are increasingly tech-savvy. They know how to get around rules and successfully bypass digital restrictions set by their parents. Some looked up tutorials. Some used guest mode. Some just used a sibling's device.

And many parents had no idea it ever happened.

That's why real safety isn't just about restriction. It's about visibility. Knowing what your child is using. Understanding how the apps work. Recognizing when something's off—not just in the browser history, but in behavior, in silence, in hesitation.

Good parental controls give you that visibility. Great ones help you start conversations.

Because kids don't just need rules—they need context. Why are some apps dangerous? What does grooming look like? What should they do when something makes them uncomfortable online? These aren't one-time talks. They're ongoing, layered, and often awkward. But they're necessary.

So yes—use the tools. But don't depend on them alone.

This chapter will walk you through what settings actually work, how to build security into the way your family uses tech, and what to look out for even when everything seems "locked down." It's not about hovering. It's about helping your child develop real digital instincts—so they don't just avoid danger, they know how to respond when they see it.

Because no matter how many filters you enable or limits you set, the best defense is still connection—the one between you and your child.

And no app can replace that.

Why It Matters

Parental controls sound like a solution. But most of the time, they're just a start.

They can block certain apps, filter inappropriate websites, limit screen time, and monitor device activity. They can alert you when your child installs something new or tries to access content above their age range. Some even track location or restrict online purchases. And yes, when configured properly, these tools help.

But too often, families set them once—and then walk away. That's where the risk begins.

Many had no idea what platforms their kids were actually using. Others were surprised to learn that their children had created secondary accounts or switched to apps the controls didn't cover.

Because kids are smart. And if they want to bypass a restriction, they'll find a way.

That's not a failure of parenting.
It's a sign that the tools are too simplistic for the complexity of today's digital lives.

Parental control apps tend to focus on surface-level problems: explicit content, screen time, or known "bad" websites. But they rarely address the subtler risks that lead to real harm—like identity theft, manipulative advertising, oversharing, behavioral tracking, or device-based surveillance.

Children's apps often ask for excessive permissions. Some default to sharing location, contacts, or microphone access without clear prompts. In 2022, Pixalate, a fraud protection and privacy analytics platform, analyzed over 422,000 child-directed apps from the Apple and Google Play stores and found that 68% of the top 150 U.S.-registered apps and 70% of the top 1,000 apps transmitted location data, while 59% requested access to other personal information. Most parental control tools don't catch this. They aren't built to analyze how apps behave. They're built to turn categories off and on.

Meanwhile, schools hand out Chromebooks. Family tablets get passed down to younger siblings. Smart TVs stay logged into shared accounts. Passwords get saved across multiple devices. And in homes without proper boundaries, children's activity quietly overlaps with adult platforms—like email, online banking, cloud storage, or shared Google drives.

Parental controls don't stop this. But good digital parenting does.

Here's the truth: software alone won't protect your child.

It can support you. It can flag concerns. It can set boundaries. But it won't teach judgment. It won't explain why sharing a birthdate is dangerous. It won't recognize when a game chat turns manipulative. It won't question why a stranger is asking to move the conversation from Roblox to Snapchat.

And yet, this is where many of the risks live—in gray areas that require conversation, not just controls.

Children may not fully grasp the long-term consequences of a post, reusing a password, or accepting a fake friend request. But when parents are involved—actively asking questions, offering guidance, and modeling safe online habits—kids tend to make safer choices.

In fact, according to a 2018 report from Microsoft, 42% of teens across 22 countries who faced online issues said they turned to their parents for help, while 28% sought advice from another adult, such as a teacher, coach, or counselor.

So what does actually keeping kids safe look like?

It means:

- Reviewing controls regularly—not just when you set them up
- Talking about privacy, digital footprints, and the real-world consequences of online actions
- Teaching kids how to spot phishing, scams, and fake accounts
- Involving them in decisions about apps, games, and websites
- Helping them understand why certain rules exist—rather than enforcing them blindly
- Being available when they mess up, or when something scary happens online

Because when children feel like they'll get in trouble for speaking up, they stop speaking. And that silence is exactly what predators and scammers rely on.

This chapter isn't about creating a surveillance state at home. It's about creating a digital safety net—a structure of trust, awareness, and tools that evolve with your child's needs. Because as your kids grow, so will their access, their curiosity, and their exposure to risks.

Parental controls are a tool. You are the protection. And when the two work together—consistently and thoughtfully—kids don't just stay safer. They learn how to protect themselves, long after the controls come off.

What to Do About It – Your Security Checklist

1. **Set Up Parental Controls on Every Device:** Whether it's a smartphone, tablet, gaming console, streaming service, or smart TV—most platforms have built-in parental controls. Use them to restrict app downloads, screen time, online purchases, and access to age-inappropriate content.

2. **Use Dedicated Parental Control Apps:** Tools like Bark, Qustodio, Net Nanny, and Google Family Link go beyond basic restrictions. They offer monitoring of texts, YouTube activity, search history, and app use, while alerting you to signs of cyberbullying, explicit content, or communication with strangers.

3. **Restrict App Store Access and In-App Purchases:** Enable password or biometric approval for every download or payment. Many kids rack up massive charges without understanding the consequences.

4. **Filter the Internet at the Router Level:** Devices like Gryphon or services like OpenDNS let you control what content is accessible across your entire home network, regardless of which device your child uses.

5. **Create Separate User Profiles for Kids:** On shared devices like laptops, tablets, or smart TVs, make sure children have their own user accounts with restricted permissions and app access. Never let them use adult profiles unsupervised.

6. **Block or Monitor Chat Features in Games & Apps:** Many games and apps offer chat functionality that can't be turned off. Choose apps that let you disable or monitor these features, or avoid them entirely.

7. **Audit Device Permissions and Privacy Settings:** Apps frequently request access to microphones, cameras, contacts, and location. Regularly review these permissions and disable anything unnecessary, especially on kids' devices.

8. **Educate, Don't Just Restrict:** Have regular conversations about online safety. Teach your children why certain rules exist—like not talking to strangers, not sharing personal information, and recognizing scams or inappropriate content.

9. **Set Screen Time and Downtime Rules:** Overuse of screens is not only a health issue—it increases the chances of exposure to online threats. Use built-in controls to limit daily usage and enforce device-free times (e.g., at meals or before bed).

10. **Regularly Review Browsing & App History Together:** This isn't about punishment—it's about staying aware. Review which websites they've visited, what videos they've watched, and which apps they're using. Make this a normal part of your digital routine.

Quick Action Plan

1-Minute Fix: Turn on SafeSearch and content restrictions in Google, YouTube, and app stores.

5-Minute Fix: Lock app store access with a password and disable in-app purchases.

15-Minute Fix: Set up a parental control dashboard through your preferred app or system.

30-Minute Fix: Audit all devices your child uses—check settings, adjust permissions, and have a conversation about online safety and expectations.

Chapter 26

Cybersecurity for Every Family Member

Real-World Scenarios

The Grandmother Who Got Scammed Out of $10,000

Mary was 76 years old and fiercely devoted to her family. Her grandson, Tyler, was the light of her life—a college freshman she spoke to every week. So when the phone rang late one afternoon and she heard his panicked voice say, "Grandma, it's me. I'm in trouble. I need $10,000 for bail. Please don't tell Mom and Dad—I just need help," she didn't hesitate.

His voice sounded exactly like Tyler. Every tone, every stutter, every breath. There was no reason to doubt it.

Worried sick, Mary rushed to the bank. She wired the money to the account he gave her and prayed he'd be safe. It wasn't until hours later, when she called Tyler's actual number to check on him, that the truth unraveled.

He was fine. Confused. Safe in his dorm.

A heavy feeling settled in Mary's chest. She hadn't helped her grandson—she'd wired $10,000 to a scammer who had used AI voice cloning to impersonate him. They had scraped Tyler's voice from a short video he'd posted online. With just a few seconds of audio, they'd created a nearly perfect vocal replica—and used it to emotionally manipulate her.

This isn't rare anymore. So-called "grandparent scams" cost U.S. seniors more than $3 billion in 2023 alone. Advances in AI voice technology have made it frighteningly easy for scammers to mimic loved ones and create urgent emotional scenarios that push elderly victims to act fast—and without verification.

Mary thought she was protecting her family.

Instead, she'd been targeted by someone who knew just how much family meant to her.

And that's what made the scam work.

The Teenager Who Clicked on a Dangerous Link

Zane was 16 and a passionate gamer. Like most teens, he spent his evenings online with friends—laughing, competing, and swapping tips. One night, during a multiplayer session, he got a message from a friend in the game's chat window.

"Dude, this cheat is insane. Unlimited coins! Click here."

It looked harmless enough. Zane clicked. Nothing happened.

Or so he thought.

A few days later, his parents noticed several odd charges on their bank account. At first, they assumed it was a mistake. Then their email stopped working. Streaming accounts showed new users. Their credit card was frozen. Something was wrong.

Zane finally told them about the link.

That "cheat code" had been malware in disguise. Clicking it had secretly installed a keylogger on their home computer—software that recorded everything typed, including saved banking passwords, login credentials, and sensitive documents. The data was quietly sent to a hacker's server, giving cybercriminals full access to their financial life.

The infection spread. Zane's school email was compromised. His dad's work account was flagged for suspicious logins. All from one innocent-looking link.

A Deloitte survey indicates that Gen Z individuals are three times more likely to fall victim to online scams compared to Baby Boomers. And cybercriminals know it. They embed malware in cheat codes, game add-ons, and in-game chats, trusting that younger users will click without thinking—especially when it promises an edge in gameplay.

Zane thought he was getting an advantage in a game.

He didn't realize he had opened the door to a full-scale cyberattack on his home.

The Child Who Shared Too Much Online

Amelia was eight and loved TikTok. Bright, bubbly, and always full of energy, she recorded short videos about her day—her school outfit, what she packed for lunch, her walk to the park. It was fun, innocent, and filled with emojis, music, and laughter.

Her parents knew she had an account, but assumed it was harmless.

Then one day, they got a message that turned their blood cold.

"I see Amelia at the park every day after school. She looks so cute in her pink jacket."

The account was anonymous. The message was private. And terrifying.

Panicked, Amelia's parents reviewed her profile and realized just how much she had unknowingly revealed: the school logo on her backpack, the timing of her daily routines, even a video that showed the street signs near their house.

Amelia hadn't done anything "wrong." She was just copying what she saw other kids and influencers doing—sharing slices of her life online. But strangers were watching. And one of them had used those details to track her in real life.

The FBI reports that social media platforms are the primary tools used by predators to identify, groom, and exploit children online. They don't need hacking tools. They rely on what kids willingly share: names, routines, faces, locations. Even the background of a video can give away more than anyone realizes.

Amelia thought she was just being part of the fun.

She didn't realize her digital diary had turned into a roadmap for someone dangerous.

The Mom Who Reused the Same Password Everywhere

Quinn was a mother of three, constantly juggling school drop-offs, work deadlines, dinner prep, and trying to keep her household running smoothly. Like many busy parents, she didn't have time to memorize dozens of unique passwords. So she did what so many people do—she reused the same password for almost everything: email, Amazon, PayPal, her grocery app, and her kid's school portal.

It was simple. It worked. And she never gave it a second thought.

Until the day she received a notification from Amazon:

"Your order for a $1,500 laptop has been shipped!"

Except—she hadn't ordered anything.

At first, she assumed it was a mistake. But then, within minutes, she was logged out of her email. Her PayPal account showed multiple transactions she didn't authorize. Her bank notified her of a login attempt from another country.

Panic set in.

What had happened?

It turned out that one of the many websites Quinn had used her go-to password on had been breached weeks earlier. Her password had been leaked and posted online. From there, hackers had used automated bots to try that same password across hundreds of websites—finding all the places she reused it.

They had gotten into her Amazon, email, banking, and shopping accounts, locking her out and transferring funds before she could respond. The worst part? Because the hackers had access to her email, they had reset passwords for every other account she owned.

Quinn had essentially lost control of her entire digital life—because of one password.

This happens more often than people think. A 2024 Forbes Advisor report reveals that 78% of individuals reuse passwords across multiple accounts. Once a password leaks from one place, it becomes a skeleton key that can unlock the rest of a person's digital identity.

Quinn thought she was making life easier by choosing one simple password.

Instead, she had left the door wide open for cybercriminals to walk through.

What You Need to Know

Cybersecurity doesn't start with technology—it starts with people. With you. With your family. With the smallest decisions made across every device in your home.

And right now, most families are more connected—and more exposed—than they realize.

Your child's tablet. Your teenager's gaming console. Your spouse's laptop. Your parents' smartphone. Your shared Wi-Fi, your cloud backup, your smart lock, your group chats, your streaming subscriptions. They're all connected. Which means your cybersecurity is only as strong as the most vulnerable person in your household.

One mistake is all it takes.

The World Economic Forum's 2022 Global Cybersecurity Outlook states that 95% of cybersecurity incidents are attributed to human error. It wasn't a hacker breaking through a firewall. It was someone clicking a malicious link, opening a fake file, or entering their password into a clone website. These are everyday habits that happen in seconds—and the consequences can last for months or years.

That's why awareness is the most important tool your family has.

Let's be honest—cybersecurity isn't always easy to talk about at home. The language is technical. The threats feel distant. And the common belief is that "hackers go after big companies, not people like us." But that's exactly the kind of thinking attackers rely on.

Because they don't need to target you directly. They just need you to not notice.

Your child downloads a free game with malware hidden inside. Your teenager shares personal details with someone pretending to be another player. Your partner reuses an old password that was exposed in a data breach. Your elderly parent gets a call from fake "tech support" and hands over everything.

And just like that, your entire household network is compromised.

In 2024, nearly 860,000 cybercrime complaints flooded the FBI's Internet Crime Center—up 33% from the year before. Reported losses topped $16.6 billion.

And the hardest hit? Seniors. Americans over 60 lost a staggering $4.8 billion—just from the scams that were reported.

But these weren't elite hacks or Hollywood-level heists. Most started with something ordinary: clicking a link, checking a bank balance, opening a file.

Simple moments. Devastating consequences.

And the targets aren't just adults.

Children are prime targets because they trust easily, click quickly, and often use shared devices without supervision. A 2024 CyberSafeKids study found that 65% of children aged 8–12 had been contacted by a stranger online, primarily through platforms like YouTube and Roblox. The younger the child, the harder it is for them to recognize risk—or to ask for help when something feels wrong.

Meanwhile, older family members are increasingly targeted through impersonation scams, fake tech support calls, or malicious links that appear to come from trusted sources. Many were never taught how to verify links, spot spoofed emails, or check URLs for red flags. And criminals know that.

This is why cybersecurity must be a family conversation—not a solo task for whoever's "good with computers."

Because cybersecurity today isn't just about protecting devices. It's about protecting people. And that requires awareness at every level.

It means explaining to your child why we don't talk to strangers in games. Helping a teenager understand how social engineering works. Showing your spouse how to check for fake websites before entering login credentials. Teaching your parents what a phishing email looks like—and what to do when they're unsure.

It also means checking who's using which devices. Reviewing which accounts are connected to what. Updating passwords. Enabling two-factor authentication. Looking at the apps your kids have installed. Asking the question, "What if someone else got into this?"

Because in a connected household, there are no isolated mistakes. A compromised tablet can lead to a compromised cloud. A hacked email can give access to shared financial accounts. A stolen phone number can allow criminals to reset passwords across multiple services.

This chapter will walk you through how to build awareness across generations. You'll get practical advice tailored for children, teens, parents, and grandparents. Not just "don't do this," but how to actually recognize threats, talk about safety, and work together as a team.

Because cybersecurity isn't just a tech issue anymore. It's a family value.

And in a world where everything is connected, your strongest defense is knowledge—shared, understood, and put into action by everyone under your roof.

Why It Matters

Most people think of cybersecurity as something that belongs to IT teams, teenagers with gaming rigs, or tech-savvy professionals in hoodies. Rarely do they think of their grandparents, children, or non-techy spouse as targets. But that's the problem.

Cybersecurity is no longer just about protecting a device. It's about protecting the people who use it.

In any given household, there's a wide range of digital behaviors happening every day. Kids playing online games. Teens on social media. Parents managing banking, taxes, or work files. Grandparents checking email, photos, or health portals. All of them connected to the same network. All of them vulnerable in different ways.

Hackers know this—and they exploit it.

In 2024, the Cybersecurity and Infrastructure Security Agency (CISA) issued 2,131 pre-ransomware alerts—nearly double the year before.

That's not a warning. That's a wildfire.

These weren't just about critical infrastructure or Fortune 500 companies. Many alerts pointed to a new weak spot: your home network.

The Wi-Fi you share with your kids. The smart devices you trust. The password you haven't changed in two years.

Cybercriminals aren't kicking in the front doors anymore. They're logging in through the living room.

And attackers don't always target the "tech-savvy" person in the house. They go after the least protected one.

That might be the grandparent who forwards a fake antivirus warning. The child who downloads a free game infected with spyware. The teen who clicks a phishing link disguised as a concert ticket. Or the parent who uses the same password on every account because they're just too busy to manage it all.

According to Javelin's 2024 Child & Family Cybersecurity Study, 1 in 8 kids have had their identities compromised since 2019.

And 5%? Fully stolen.

Most families don't find out until years later—when the credit card bills, loan rejections, or debt collectors come knocking in their child's name.

Worse, in many cases, that one breach wasn't the end—it was the beginning.

Hackers used the child's data as a backdoor into the entire household: parents' accounts, shared devices, even financial platforms.

One kid. One click. Whole family exposed.

Because families share more than love—they share logins, devices, routers, payment apps, cloud accounts, and smart home systems. That means your digital safety is only as strong as the least protected person in your household. This is especially important as digital roles shift.

Children are often early adopters of technology but don't understand security. Older adults may be cautious but fall victim to sophisticated scams. Adults may have security software but neglect updates or fall for fake pop-ups. And teens, while quick with privacy settings, may underestimate the risk of manipulation, stalking, or identity theft.

Each group needs something different:

- Kids need rules and explanations.
- Teens need trust, transparency, and guidance.
- Adults need consistency and better habits.
- Older adults need support that's clear, respectful, and patient.

This is why cybersecurity must be a shared conversation—not a siloed one.

Security decisions made by one person can affect everyone. If a child installs a sketchy browser extension on a shared device, the parents' bank credentials might be stolen. If a spouse reuses a password that's been leaked, a hacker might access your family's cloud drive. If a grandparent falls for a tech support scam, they might hand over control of the entire home network.

And once an attacker gets in, they don't stop.

They pivot. They escalate. They impersonate.

Your home network faces around 10 cyberattacks a day—every single day.

And they're not gunning for your laptop.

They're targeting your smart TV. Your plugs. Even your DVR.

According to Cobalt (2024), 34% of smart home vulnerabilities are found in TVs, 18% in smart plugs, and 13% in DVRs—devices we rarely think to secure.

But once breached, hackers move sideways—stealing data, spying on you, hijacking other devices.

The weakest link isn't your router. It's the forgotten gadget blinking in the corner.

The FBI reported a surge in 2024 of cybercrimes that started with just one person in a household—and quickly spread.

The weapon of choice? Account compromise.

Once inside a single email, attackers posed as a trusted family member—sending fake money requests, triggering password resets, or asking for "just one gift card."

It starts with one device. One person. One click.

Then it tears through the rest.

These incidents don't just cost money. They erode trust, privacy, and peace of mind.

This is why awareness matters so much. Not just tech tools, but habits.

- Knowing how to spot a fake link.
- Recognizing what phishing looks like.
- Understanding that password reuse is dangerous.
- Being cautious when someone asks for personal info—even if it sounds familiar.
- Checking privacy settings and device access regularly.

Cybersecurity isn't about locking down your digital life with paranoia. It's about making every family member just a little harder to fool. Because attackers don't need to break in when they can simply trick someone into opening the door. And too often, that someone is the person no one thought needed protection.

This chapter exists to challenge that assumption. Because digital safety isn't just a personal issue anymore. It's a family one.

What to Do About It – Your Security Checklist

1. **Have a Family Cybersecurity Talk (and Repeat It Often):** Don't assume everyone knows the risks. Hold regular family meetings to talk about common scams, phishing tricks, safe passwords, and how to spot suspicious messages. Make this part of your digital hygiene routine, not a one-time lecture.

2. **Make Cyber Roles Clear for Everyone:** Assign age-appropriate responsibilities. Kids should know never to click strange links or talk to online strangers. Teens should be expected to use strong passwords and lock their devices. Adults must model secure behavior and handle account recovery plans and backups.

3. **Create Separate Accounts on Shared Devices:** Everyone should have their own user account with appropriate access. Never let kids or guests use an admin-level profile. This limits accidental changes and protects sensitive data.

4. **Review Privacy Settings on Social Media & Messaging Apps:** Go through the privacy settings for each platform together. Ensure profiles are set to private, location tracking is off, and personal info isn't visible to strangers.

5. **Use Password Managers for the Whole Family:** Don't rely on memory or reused passwords. A password manager like Bitwarden, 1Password, or Dashlane can simplify secure living by helping each person generate and store unique passwords safely.

6. **Enable Two-Factor Authentication (2FA) Everywhere:** Teach each family member to set up 2FA on critical accounts: email, bank, social media, shopping, and cloud storage. This adds a strong layer of defense even if a password is stolen.

7. **Teach "Think Before You Click" Skills:** From young children to grandparents, everyone should know that not all messages are safe. Practice identifying phishing emails, fake giveaways, and shady links together.

8. **Set Up Account Recovery for Everyone:** Make sure every family member has account recovery options configured—backup emails, trusted contacts, security questions—that only they know.

9. **Back Up Devices and Data Regularly:** Set up automatic cloud backups and encourage local external backups for critical files like family photos, financial documents, and school work.

10. **Include Elderly Family Members in the Cyber Plan:** Seniors are prime targets for scams and fraud. Help them secure their devices, review unfamiliar emails, and understand common red flags.

11. **Keep All Devices Updated:** Everyone in the household should be responsible for keeping their own devices updated—or designate someone to check them regularly for security patches and firmware upgrades.

Quick Action Plan

1-Minute Fix: Make sure everyone locks their devices and enables automatic updates.

5-Minute Fix: Check that all key accounts (email, banking, shopping) have 2FA enabled.

15-Minute Fix: Walk through security settings on each family member's phone and social media account.

30-Minute Fix: Create a family cybersecurity checklist, schedule monthly check-ins, and install a password manager across all household devices.

Chapter 27

Group Chats, Shared Accounts, and Hidden Dangers

Real-World Scenarios

The Family Group Chat That Leaked Personal Data

Grace loved her family's WhatsApp group. It was where her parents, siblings, cousins, and even her grandmother stayed connected. They shared everything there—updates about the new baby, pictures from weekend getaways, and details for coordinating family trips and splitting group expenses. It was cozy, familiar, and felt private.

That illusion shattered the day Grace's phone was stolen.

At first, she was just annoyed. She'd lost her contacts, her photos, and her favorite playlists. But then it hit her—she hadn't set a screen lock. Worse, WhatsApp was still logged in, and she hadn't enabled two-factor authentication.

The thief now had unrestricted access to her group chat.

Within minutes, they could scroll through hundreds of messages and photos. They saw conversations about the upcoming family vacation—including the hotel reservation under Grace's name, her address, and travel dates. They found bank account numbers and mobile payment details shared by her uncle for splitting utility bills. They read personal updates, birthday plans, and even photos of the new baby, innocently sent without knowing a stranger might be watching.

Grace never imagined their family group chat could be a target. But these conversations, meant to stay within the family, became a treasure trove for identity thieves and scammers. The thief could now impersonate family members, use the shared data to answer security questions, or even blackmail them with private photos.

Family group chats are rarely seen as risky—but they often contain a mix of emotional, financial, and personal information that, in the wrong hands, can be incredibly damaging. And with one unsecured phone, Grace had accidentally exposed everyone.

She thought their chat was just for laughs and logistics.

She didn't realize it had become a silent gateway into her entire family's digital life.

The Shared Streaming Account That Led to Identity Theft

Arthur was all about keeping things simple. Like many families, his household shared one Netflix account across several relatives—his kids in one city, his sister in another, and his parents back home. To make it easy for everyone, they used the same password for years.

It was familiar. Memorable. And—unfortunately—reused across several of Arthur's other accounts too, including his PayPal, his email, and even his online grocery service.

Then one morning, Arthur noticed something strange. He was locked out of his email. His PayPal showed purchases he didn't recognize. And a notice from his bank showed a login attempt from another country.

It didn't take long to piece it together. A hacker had breached one of the streaming accounts—likely from a data leak, or a weak password shared across too many people. Once they got in, they found Arthur's billing details stored in the settings. They matched the password to other platforms and hit the jackpot.

What started as a harmless shared Netflix account became the entry point to identity theft.

Arthur had no idea his family's entertainment routine would compromise his finances. But streaming platforms often don't flag unusual logins. There's no requirement for strong passwords or two-factor authentication. Most people don't even realize when someone outside the family logs in—until the damage is done.

Over 78% of people reuse passwords across multiple accounts (Forbes Advisor, 2024), and criminals use automated tools to check for matching credentials across banks, retailers, and email providers. If just one service is compromised, the rest can fall like dominoes.

Arthur thought he was just making life easier for his family.

He didn't realize he was handing a hacker everything they needed to steal his identity.

The Grandparent Who Fell for a Scam in a Family Chat

Daniel's family group chat was where his extended relatives stayed connected—funny memes, birthday greetings, and family updates all flowed through the messages every day. Even his grandmother, 78-year-old Barbara, was part of it. She didn't say much, but she loved reading the updates and seeing pictures of the grandkids.

One afternoon, Barbara received a message in the family chat:

"Grandma, it's Daniel. I lost my wallet and I need $500 to pay for a hotel. Please send it to this account. I'll explain later—just don't tell Mom and Dad."

It sounded urgent. Familiar. Loving.

Barbara didn't question it. She copied the account number and wired the money through her bank.

Hours later, she got a call from the real Daniel.

He had no idea what she was talking about.

The scam was simple—and devastating. A criminal had cloned Daniel's profile photo and name and infiltrated the family group chat. Maybe it was from a previous phishing scam or a hijacked phone. Once inside, they targeted the most vulnerable person—Barbara—using emotional pressure and trust.

These "family impersonation scams" are on the rise. Scammers pretend to be loved ones, especially targeting seniors who may not spot the red flags. The language is personal, the request is urgent, and the payoff is quick—money sent to an untraceable account, never to be seen again.

Barbara thought she was helping her grandson.

She didn't realize she was talking to a scammer already inside their digital home.

The Family Cloud Account That Exposed Private Photos

Maya always believed cloud storage was the safest and most convenient way to keep everything in one place. Her family used a shared Google Drive folder for just about everything: photos from family vacations, scanned copies of birth certificates and tax returns, even her mother's medical reports. Everyone had access—siblings, parents, cousins. It made sharing documents and memories easier across the country.

Until one day, her cousin tried to organize the folder and accidentally changed the privacy setting from "Private" to "Public."

No one noticed—until it was too late.

Within hours, a stranger commented on one of their family photos on social media. Confused, Maya checked the Drive link. Fear jolted through her. The entire folder—thousands of personal photos, PDFs of tax returns, medical lab results, even passports—was visible to anyone with the link. And worse, it had been indexed by search engines.

Maya immediately tried to lock the folder back down, but the damage was done. Downloads had already happened. Their information had already been copied, shared, and possibly sold.

It was a nightmare.

Cloud misconfigurations like this are shockingly common. One small mistake, like a wrong setting or forgotten permission, can expose a lifetime's worth of personal data. Most people assume cloud storage is secure by default, but in reality, it depends heavily on user awareness and settings.

Shared folders are especially risky. They're convenient—but they're also easy to mismanage. If even one family member misunderstands the privacy settings or shares the wrong link, the entire group's information can be exposed.

Maya thought they were using the cloud smartly—organizing memories, making paperwork easier.

She didn't realize that one innocent mistake could expose intimate family photos, financial data, and medical history to total strangers on the internet.

And once that kind of personal data is out there, you can't take it back.

What You Need to Know

Group chats are where families organize their lives, where teams collaborate, where friends catch up. Shared accounts make things easier—one password for Netflix, one cloud folder for travel photos, one login for that monthly grocery delivery. These tools make modern life convenient, connected, and seamless.

But they also come with risks most people never think about.

Because when access is shared, so is responsibility. So is vulnerability.

Your family group chat might feel private, but if just one person's phone is stolen or hacked, the entire thread is exposed. That means every photo, every address, every shared document, and every casual mention of a bank transfer or vacation plan could fall into the wrong hands. And unlike emails, group chats aren't built for long-term privacy. There's no encryption in most apps. No access expiration. No warning when someone screenshots or forwards a message to someone outside the group.

In 2024, researchers analyzed 21 so-called "secure" messaging apps.

The results? Not so secure.

According to the study – *The Medium is the Message: How Secure Messaging Apps Leak: Sensitive Data to Push Notification Services* – 11 of these apps leaked metadata—like usernames, phone numbers, and even who you were talking to.

Worse, 4 leaked actual message content.

So much for end-to-end encryption.

Digital safety isn't just about who you trust.

It's about how well they protect their phones, their apps, and their notifications.

Because your private message is only as safe as the weakest device it touches.

If your cousin's phone doesn't have a screen lock, your group chat is exposed. If your parent clicks on a phishing link and gets malware installed, your shared conversation becomes part of that breach.

And then there are shared accounts.

Streaming services. Cloud drives. Shopping apps. Many families or close-knit circles use one account across multiple people and devices to save money or stay organized. It feels efficient. But when you share a password, you also share control. And if that password is reused elsewhere, stored insecurely, or passed along too many times, it becomes a liability.

In 2025, cybersecurity firm Kaspersky reported that over 7 million user accounts linked to popular streaming services like Netflix, Disney+, Amazon Prime Video, HBO Max, and Apple TV+ were compromised through phishing scams and fake browser extensions —many of which were tied to shared family accounts.

Some of those users didn't even realize they had been compromised until strangers started appearing in their watch history or purchases started showing up on connected cards.

Because shared accounts rarely have proper protections. Two-factor authentication isn't always enabled. Activity logs aren't checked. Passwords aren't rotated. And if someone leaves the group—whether it's a former roommate, an ex, or even just a relative you've lost touch with—they may still have access unless you go back and lock it down.

Now add cloud storage to the mix.

Shared folders seem like a great solution for organizing family photos, taxes, school records, or travel plans. But if sharing permissions aren't properly set, that private folder could become public with one accidental click. And yes, this happens all the time.

In 2024, researchers at a leading cybersecurity firm found that more than 20% of public Google Drive links indexed online had once been intended as private but were accidentally shared too widely. Some included passport scans, financial documents, or photos of children.

The problem isn't just bad actors. It's bad habits. It's assuming that once something is shared within a group, it's still somehow safe. But groups change. Devices get lost. Passwords leak. And no one goes back to update the settings—or even thinks to.

This chapter will help you understand how group dynamics create unique digital vulnerabilities. You'll learn how to secure shared spaces, set boundaries around sensitive content, and recognize when "convenient" starts to become dangerous.

Because you're not just sharing a password or a message. You're sharing trust.

And once that trust breaks—whether through carelessness, ignorance, or a bad decision—it's not just your data at risk.

It's everyone's.

Why It Matters

We trust the people in our lives. Our family, our friends, our coworkers. We share things with them every day—messages, files, photos, Netflix passwords, streaming profiles, login credentials, Google Docs, cloud folders, digital calendars. It's easy, convenient, and feels harmless.

But convenience often comes with a hidden cost. Because when you share access, you also share risk.

Group chats and shared accounts are part of daily life now. Families have WhatsApp threads for vacation planning. Friends split the bill on streaming services. Coworkers collaborate in Slack or Messenger. Couples share photo albums and grocery lists. Classmates use shared email logins for projects. And just about everyone reuses a password or two—if not ten.

But here's the part that often gets overlooked: The moment something is shared, it's harder to control.

The Electronic Frontier Foundation (EFF) regularly warns: your biggest privacy risk might be the people closest to you.

Home networks. Shared devices. Synced accounts.

Most breaches within households or peer groups start with shared access points—group chats, cloud folders, co-owned tablets, or accounts that everyone logs into.

You don't need a hacker on the other side of the world.

You just need one person nearby who clicks the wrong link—or shares the wrong file.

Digital trust is fragile. And once it's broken, privacy isn't the only thing that disappears.

These aren't "hacks" in the traditional sense. They're quiet breaches. Ones that happen without malware, phishing, or brute force attacks.

For example:

- Someone leaves a shared Google Drive open to "Anyone with the link"
- An old roommate still has access to your Amazon or Hulu account
- A family member forwards a sensitive file from your group chat to someone else
- A partner's device—logged into your account—gets lost or stolen
- An ex-coworker still has login access to a collaborative work folder

And because it all feels familiar and harmless, no one notices until something goes wrong.

Group chats are especially risky.

They move fast. People post casually. Files are shared, photos are dropped in, links are sent without thinking. But depending on the app, everything shared could be accessible for years—even after members leave. Many chat platforms store years of history by default. And unless you've adjusted the settings, anyone in the group can download or forward that data at any time.

It's shockingly common: adults sharing sensitive info in group chats: Bank details. Home addresses. Even photos of their ID.

Most never delete the messages.

Worse, they rarely think about who else might see them later.

Group chats feel private—until they aren't.

Because once that info is out there, it's not just shared. It's stored, synced, and searchable.

By anyone with access.

The danger isn't just exposure. It's escalation.

If one person in your group falls victim to a scam, gets phished, or loses access to their device, the attacker now has a foot in the door. They can read your conversations, steal shared files, impersonate you, and use the trust inside the group to spread scams further.

Shared accounts create similar risks. They seem harmless—a shared Netflix login here, a joint calendar there. But many people:

- Use the same email and password across multiple services
- Never remove old users from shared accounts
- Store payment details in profiles that others can still access
- Stay logged in on multiple devices with no expiration

In cloud environments, one infected virtual machine can poison them all.

According to TierPoint (2024), if malware—like a trojan, worm, or virus—gets into one VM, it can spread sideways to others in the same environment.

Shared space means shared risk.

The cloud isn't always a fortress. Sometimes, it's a row of unlocked doors—and one bad guest can ruin the whole building.

This is why it matters.

Because we tend to think that trust equals safety. But in cybersecurity, it's not just about who you trust—it's about what you've made accessible.

Your friends might never mean to cause harm. Your relatives probably won't snoop. Your coworker likely didn't intend to share that link with someone outside the team. But the systems don't care about intent. They care about access.

Once something is shared, it's shared. And if it's copied, forwarded, downloaded, or synced—there's no way to bring it back under control.

This chapter isn't about locking everyone out. It's about setting boundaries. Knowing who has access to what. Reviewing those shared logins. Checking your group chat settings. Thinking twice before you send a file. Logging people out when the relationship ends—whether that's a job, a lease, or a breakup.

Because even if you trust everyone in the group, you might not trust who they forward it to.

What to Do About It – Your Security Checklist

1. **Set Rules for What Can Be Shared in Group Chats:** Treat group messages like semi-public spaces. Never share sensitive information such as full names, home addresses, bank details, ID numbers, or passwords—no matter how trusted the group feels.

2. **Use Encrypted Messaging Apps for Sensitive Conversations:** Apps like Signal, WhatsApp, or iMessage offer end-to-end encryption. Always use secure platforms when discussing anything personal, financial, or private.

3. **Lock Your Messaging Apps and Phones:** Set up PINs, biometrics, or password locks on all messaging apps—especially if you're in family or work groups. If your phone is lost or stolen, you don't want strangers accessing private conversations.

4. **Regularly Review Who's in the Group:** Family groups, work chats, and school parent threads often grow over time. Periodically check the member list and remove people who no longer need access. One forgotten ex-employee or former babysitter could become a weak link.

5. **Avoid Using Shared Logins for Streaming, Shopping, or Utilities:** While it's convenient, shared accounts increase the risk of misuse or exposure. If you must share access, use profiles, guest accounts, or password-sharing features with built-in restrictions.

6. **Use Strong, Unique Passwords for Shared Accounts:** If you absolutely need to share a password (e.g., for a Netflix family plan), make sure it's strong, not reused elsewhere, and updated regularly—especially after someone leaves the group.

7. **Never Share Passwords in Group Chats:** Even among trusted people, never type passwords into group messages. If necessary, use a secure password-sharing tool like Bitwarden Send or 1Password's sharing features.

8. **Enable Two-Factor Authentication on All Shared Accounts:** 2FA helps

ensure that even if a password is shared or leaked, a hacker still can't get in. Apps like Google Authenticator or Authy offer simple and effective protection.

9. **Set Up Login Notifications for Shared Accounts:** Some platforms allow alerts for new logins or location-based access. Turn these on so you know immediately if someone logs in unexpectedly.
10. **Create a Plan for Offboarding Old Members:** Whether it's a shared family Amazon account or a project-based Slack group, always have a process to remove users who no longer need access.

Quick Action Plan

1-Minute Fix: Set up app lock or fingerprint security on your messaging apps.

5-Minute Fix: Review members in your top 3 group chats and remove anyone who shouldn't be there.

15-Minute Fix: Update shared account passwords and enable 2FA wherever possible.

30-Minute Fix: Create a shared account security plan—decide who gets access, when it should be revoked, and how to securely update passwords.

Chapter 28

When Guests Become Risks: Visitors, Airbnbs & More

Real-World Scenarios

The Guest Who Accidentally (or Intentionally) Accessed Private Files

Elizabeth loved hosting dinners. Her friends always said she made the coziest space—warm lighting, great food, and music echoing from her smart speaker. On one casual evening, a friend asked, "Hey, mind if I use your laptop to check something real quick?" Without hesitation, Elizabeth nodded and handed it over. It felt like a harmless favor.

But later that night, she felt something was... off.

Her browser history showed an unfamiliar website: her online banking portal. When she opened her recent documents, she saw that a folder labeled "Personal" had been accessed. It included tax returns, scanned IDs, and private journal entries. Worse, she had been logged into her cloud drive the entire time, her session open and accessible.

Her stomach dropped.

The friend hadn't said anything suspicious, and maybe it was a mistake—maybe they didn't mean to snoop. Or maybe they did. The truth is, Elizabeth had no way of knowing for sure. She had no password required to unlock her device. Her browsers had all her credentials saved. Her cloud account had no two-factor authentication. What seemed like a kind gesture had turned into a privacy breach.

This isn't uncommon. Many people assume their guests won't overstep boundaries, and in most cases, they won't. But even well-meaning friends might click on the wrong folder. Others might be curious—and a curious guest with access to your digital world can do more damage than a thief with a crowbar.

Elizabeth thought she was just being a gracious host for the evening.

She didn't realize she had granted someone access to her private finances, personal history, and digital identity.

And in a world where everything is stored online, that kind of mistake can have long-lasting consequences.

The Guest Who Connected a Malware-Infected USB Drive

Walter loved when his cousin visited. They had grown up like brothers, and a weekend together was always full of laughs and nostalgia. On Saturday morning, the cousin pulled out a USB stick and asked, "Hey, can I use your laptop to grab a few photos from this drive?"

Walter didn't think twice. "Sure, go ahead."

Within minutes, things went wrong.

His laptop began slowing down. Then his antivirus software pinged a warning: "Threat detected: high-risk malware." His screen flickered, and when he tried to shut the system down, files began disappearing. The cousin had no idea his USB drive was infected.

What had been intended as an innocent photo transfer unleashed a wave of malware onto Walter's laptop. Hidden inside the USB was a keylogger—silently recording every password Walter typed. Even worse, the malware had already spread through his Wi-Fi network, attempting to infect his smart TV and phone, both of which were synced through the same Google account.

Walter spent the next several days trying to clean his devices, freeze his accounts, and change passwords—while worrying whether personal files were already out in the wild. All from plugging in one USB drive.

This is the hidden danger of removable media. USBs are a common vector for malware, especially if they've been used in multiple, unprotected systems. Many people don't realize their drives are infected until it's too late. And once malware enters a home network, every connected device becomes vulnerable.

Walter thought he was just being helpful to family.

He didn't realize he had let a digital virus into his home—one that could have wiped out years of data and compromised his entire digital life.

The Babysitter Who Had Access to the Smart Home System

Samantha's new babysitter seemed like a dream—kind, responsible, great with her two kids. To make life easier, Samantha shared the smart lock access so the sitter could come and go. She gave her the Wi-Fi password and showed her how to use the smart assistant to control lights and music. It was simple, efficient, and worked beautifully... at first.

Weeks after the babysitter had stopped working for them, strange things started happening.

Samantha would get notifications in the middle of the night: "Front door unlocked" at 2:13 AM. Her kids complained that the lights flickered when no one was touching the switches. Then, one night, as she prepared dinner, a voice echoed from the smart assistant in the living room: "You still have the same curtains, huh?"

Her blood ran cold.

Someone was accessing her smart home devices remotely. A check of her smart lock's activity log confirmed it—the door had been opened from a remote device linked to the babysitter's old phone. The same was true for the smart speaker and thermostat. She had forgotten to revoke access.

Samantha realized the babysitter—or someone who got hold of her login—still had full control of her home.

In an era where every light, lock, and camera is connected to the cloud, access is power. And shared credentials that aren't revoked become silent keys in someone else's pocket. Many people never think to reset passwords or remove devices after a guest leaves. That makes it easy for someone to continue watching, listening—or even unlocking your doors.

Samantha thought she was just being tech-savvy and hospitable.

She didn't realize she had granted long-term access to her home to someone who was no longer supposed to be part of it.

And now, someone else could turn the lights on... from anywhere.

The Airbnb Guest Who Stole Login Credentials

Alexander prided himself on being a five-star Airbnb host. His guest room was always spotless, the welcome basket was thoughtfully stocked, and he even offered a few tech perks to make people feel at home: fast Wi-Fi, a Smart TV with logged-in streaming apps, and a shared family tablet so guests could browse, plan their days, or stream music.

But after one particularly polite guest checked out, something didn't feel right.

First, Alexander noticed new shows in his Netflix history—shows he didn't recognize, in a language he didn't speak, and from a region thousands of miles away. Then came an Amazon shipping confirmation for something he hadn't ordered. Finally, when logging into his bank account from the shared tablet, he saw his credentials already filled in. He froze.

The tablet had been left logged in. His browser had saved usernames and passwords. The guest had likely browsed his history, accessed stored logins, and perhaps even synced their own device to his accounts. Worse, if they took screenshots or saved cookies, they could continue accessing those accounts long after leaving.

Alexander had been trying to create a welcoming experience—but in doing so, he had unknowingly handed over the keys to his digital life.

This happens more often than people think. Many devices, from smart TVs to shared tablets, auto-save passwords by default. Hosts forget that a single login on a shared device can persist indefinitely. And when guests connect their own phones or laptops to those platforms, cached sessions or synced settings can copy or expose sensitive data.

Alexander assumed he was offering convenience and hospitality.

He didn't realize he had left the door open for someone to walk away with access to his bank, his shopping history, and even his identity.

What You Need to Know

You invite someone into your home. A houseguest. A friend visiting from out of town. A babysitter. A contractor. A short-term renter. Someone you trust—or at least, someone you feel comfortable letting through the front door.

But here's what most people forget: when you let someone into your physical space, you're also letting them into your digital one.

Your home is full of connected devices. Phones on chargers. Laptops on the kitchen table. A smart speaker in the corner. A router that's always on. Security cameras. Streaming boxes. Maybe even a shared tablet with saved passwords still logged in. And all of it can be accessed—sometimes intentionally, sometimes accidentally—by anyone who walks in and connects to your Wi-Fi.

Most guests aren't trying to do harm. But access changes the rules. It opens the door to unintentional risk—and in some cases, very intentional abuse.

Many owners lack a full understanding of their smart home's data practices (with an estimated 70% admitting only partial or no understanding according to "*Exploring the Privacy Concerns of Bystanders in Smart Homes from the Perspectives of Both Owners and Bystanders" study, 2022*), suggesting guest access may often go unrevoked due to unawareness. That means those people could still control lights, cameras, or locks—even after they were long gone.

In a 2023 study by Secure Data Recovery Services, 82% of people admitted to snooping through someone else's phone or computer—just out of curiosity.

But curiosity cracks doors wide open.

One unlocked screen can expose financial files, synced cloud accounts, private messages, or even your smart home controls. All because device settings were never locked down.

And then there are the guests you don't know at all.

Home-sharing has made it common for strangers to stay in private residences. Airbnb, Vrbo, short-term rental platforms—they make it easy to turn spare rooms or second properties into income. But many hosts forget one key detail: when a guest checks in, they're not just sleeping in your home. They're using your internet. Your devices. Your networks. And unless you've taken the time to separate and secure those systems, your data is on display.

There have been documented cases of guests walking away with saved passwords, cloud access, private documents from shared tablets or computers, and even controlling smart thermostats, cameras, and locks long after checkout. Some used the information for identity theft. Others for stalking. Some simply sold the access online.

And it cuts both ways.

Guests can be victims too—when hosts hide cameras, control devices remotely, or forget to unlink smart systems before selling or renting.

In some cases, smart homes sold on the secondary market still had devices tied to the original owner's account. That means a stranger, miles away, could still adjust the lights, watch the cameras, or unlock the door.

You left the house—but they never left the system.

It's not that guests are dangerous. It's that guest access must be managed—like handing over a key that expires, rather than one that opens every door forever. The people you invite into your space may not mean harm. But their presence—combined with your digital habits—can create serious, lasting exposure.

This chapter will show you how to think differently about shared access. How to prepare your home for visitors. What to check before renting out a room or staying in one. How to revoke permissions, lock down devices, and keep your digital boundaries as strong as your physical ones.

Because the biggest tech risks don't always start with hackers.

Sometimes, they start with hospitality.

Why It Matters

You welcome someone into your home. They stay the night, borrow the Wi-Fi, maybe ask to use your tablet or check something on your smart TV. You're being kind, trusting, normal. But behind that everyday kindness is something people rarely think about: Every guest is another connection into your digital life.

And most of us aren't prepared for what that really means.

Whether it's a close friend crashing on the couch, a cousin staying for the holidays, or a stranger renting your guest room through Airbnb, the moment someone joins your home network, uses a shared device, or logs into your services—you've expanded your attack surface. Sometimes permanently.

Sharing Wi-Fi with guests feels harmless. Friendly, even.

But most people never change the password afterward.

Smart TVs, speakers, and consoles stay logged in.

Laptops get handed over "just for a second"—but that second holds saved passwords, synced files, open cloud drives.

Digital access sticks. Devices don't forget.

And unless you revoke it, your guests don't really leave.

They just walk out... while staying logged in.

For example:

- A babysitter still has access to your home security camera app.
- A former roommate can unlock your front door using a connected app.
- A weekend Airbnb guest watched Netflix—but now also has access to your Amazon account, Prime purchases, and saved payment details.
- A friend paired their Bluetooth speaker—and still sees your devices every time they pass nearby.

Even tech-savvy users forget that many smart home devices—doorbells, thermostats, speakers, even fridges—don't log guests out automatically.

The risks go far beyond entertainment.

Let's say a guest connects to your Wi-Fi and accidentally downloads a malicious file. That malware could travel across your home network, infecting not just their device, but yours—especially if your computers and devices are set to "trust" local traffic. And if your router still uses the default admin password (or hasn't been updated in years), it may be vulnerable to remote access or signal hijacking—giving an attacker full control from the inside.

And then there's the risk of intentional snooping.

Not everyone is malicious, but not everyone is careful either. An unsupervised guest might open the browser and see that your banking login is saved. They might click through an open tab to your email. They might browse your photos or access sensitive work files stored in your cloud drive, thinking they're just curious—or bored. It doesn't take much.

Once something is seen, it can't be unseen. Once something is downloaded, it can be shared.

Even with good intentions, guests can make small mistakes that have big consequences. And you'll be the one left to clean up the mess.

Vacation rentals bring even more complexity.

Smart locks, digital thermostats, and connected lights make renting out your space easier—but also riskier. If you don't reset access codes between guests, clear smart TV logins, or disable old profiles, you're offering strangers more than just a bed.

You're giving them a window into your routines, your accounts, your billing data, and potentially your identity.

And remember: shared access doesn't just give people control. It gives them data.

Every device they use remembers something—when they logged in, where they went, what they watched, which devices they synced. And unless you actively manage that, it piles up over time, creating a digital trail that others could exploit.

This is why it matters. Because hospitality is a strength—but digital boundaries are now part of being a good host.

That means:

- Creating a guest Wi-Fi network, separate from your main one
- Clearing login credentials from smart TVs and streaming devices
- Using PIN protection on phones, tablets, and laptops—even if just for a quick favor
- Revoking app access after the stay ends
- Routinely checking device connection logs and user history
- Logging out, resetting, or removing users from smart home apps after short-term rentals

You don't need to treat every guest like a threat. But you do need to treat your network like it matters. Because your home isn't just a physical space anymore. It's a digital ecosystem.

And anyone who steps inside—even for a night—is stepping into both.

What to Do About It – Your Security Checklist

1. **Create Guest Wi-Fi Networks:** Always use a separate network for guests. Never give out your primary Wi-Fi password. Guest networks isolate your smart home devices, computers, and personal data from outsiders.

2. **Change Wi-Fi Passwords After Each Guest Stay:** Whether it's a visiting relative or a short-term rental guest, change the password as soon as they leave. If you use guest networks, reset those too.

3. **Don't Share Devices Without Logging Out or Creating Separate Profiles:** If a guest needs to use your laptop, tablet, or smart TV, create a guest account or ensure you're logged out of personal apps and accounts. Never leave auto-login or saved passwords enabled.

4. **Wipe and Reset Smart Home Devices After Airbnb Guests or Roommates Leave:** Many smart devices (locks, assistants, thermostats) remain connected to old accounts unless you remove or reset them manually. Don't assume the system "forgets" users on its own.

5. **Use Device-Specific PINs or Biometrics:** Secure your tablets, voice assistants, and TVs with individual codes. This prevents guests from accidentally—or intentionally—browsing through private content or settings.

6. **Remove Old Device Authorizations:** Periodically review all devices connected to your accounts (Spotify, Netflix, Amazon, Alexa, etc.). Remove unknown devices or users that no longer need access.

7. **Don't Leave USB Ports or Charging Stations Unattended:** Never let guests plug in unverified USB sticks or charging devices into your personal machines. These could unknowingly or maliciously introduce malware.

8. **Secure Your Physical Devices During Rentals or Parties:** Store laptops, external drives, tablets, or other sensitive electronics in a locked drawer if you're hosting guests or renting your space.

9. **Audit Smart Assistant History and Access Logs:** After guests depart, review your smart home app history. Some devices log interactions, voice commands, or access attempts. Clear histories and disable unknown profiles.

10. **Educate Trusted Guests on Digital House Rules:** If you're hosting family, friends, or frequent visitors, have a quick "digital house rules" talk—just like you'd explain the thermostat or alarm system. Let them know what they can and can't access.

Quick Action Plan

1-Minute Fix: Set up or enable guest Wi-Fi and disconnect unfamiliar devices.

5-Minute Fix: Check your smart lock, smart assistant, and streaming accounts for unknown users or devices.

15-Minute Fix: Remove shared logins or saved passwords from any devices guests might access.

30-Minute Fix: Reset smart devices, change all shared access codes, and audit all connected home apps after guest visits or Airbnb stays.

Chapter 29

Digital Death: What Happens After You Die

Real-World Scenarios

The Family That Lost Access to a Loved One's Accounts

When Brian passed away suddenly at the age of 51, his family was overwhelmed with grief—and with something they hadn't expected: a digital wall they couldn't get past.

Brian had been the kind of person who did everything online. He managed the family finances through a banking app, stored important documents in cloud storage, communicated through email, and paid bills automatically through digital accounts. But now, no one could log in. No one had his passwords. His phone, protected by Face ID, was locked. His email was inaccessible. His social media remained frozen in time, with birthday wishes still appearing each year, and strangers tagging him in old photos—oblivious to the fact that he was no longer there.

His wife tried everything. She contacted Google, hoping to retrieve critical documents—tax records, insurance paperwork, medical files. She reached out to Facebook to ask for the page to be memorialized. She even called the bank. Each time, she hit a wall.

"Sorry, we can't help you without legal authorization."

"Due to privacy laws, this account cannot be accessed."

"Do you have a digital will or prior consent from the deceased?"

She had none of those. Brian had never talked about what should happen to his digital accounts if something went wrong. He had no digital legacy plan, no emergency access settings, no written log of accounts and passwords. Everything was protected, encrypted, and now locked away—possibly forever.

This isn't rare. Many people leave behind no clear instructions for their digital assets after death. Yet today, most of our lives—our memories, our finances, our identities—are tied to devices and logins. When someone passes, their family may not just lose them—they may lose access to everything that mattered most to them.

Brian thought his accounts were his alone.

He didn't realize that one day, his family would need them the most.

The Crypto Fortune That Disappeared Forever

Timothy was a quiet investor who had been ahead of the curve. Years before most people had heard of Bitcoin, he had already bought in. He stored his cryptocurrency in a private digital wallet, separate from any exchange, secured by a long, randomly generated private key. It was the kind of thing only a tech-savvy person would know how to manage—and only Timothy knew how to access it.

By the time he passed away in his early 60s, his crypto fortune had grown to more than $250,000. But it might as well have vanished into thin air.

No one in Timothy's family knew the password. He hadn't written it down. He hadn't used a custodial service or shared recovery phrases with anyone. The wallet existed, and it was publicly verifiable on the blockchain—but the key to open it? Gone.

His daughter searched through his files. His wife called crypto exchanges. His lawyer checked the will. But without the private key, there was nothing anyone could do. Even the blockchain itself offered no way back in.

And that's the cold truth about cryptocurrency: it's decentralized and unregulated. There's no customer support. No password reset. No backup recovery. Without the seed phrase or private key, the money is effectively burned.

Experts estimate that more than $100 billion in crypto assets is already lost forever due to forgotten passwords, lost wallets, or unprepared heirs (Unchained Capital, 2023).

Timothy had intended to leave the fortune as a legacy for his children—a financial safety net for their future. But because no plan had been made, and no one else had access, the inheritance he spent years building disappeared the moment he did.

He thought he was investing in his family's security.

He didn't realize that without a backup plan, his wealth would die with him.

The Deceased Social Media Profile That Was Hijacked

When Megan passed away from a sudden illness, her family couldn't bring themselves to delete her Facebook account. It became a kind of memorial—a place where friends could leave messages, post photos, and keep her memory alive. Each year on her birthday, people would still tag her, still write to her. It was bittersweet, but comforting.

Until one day, something changed.

Megan "liked" a post about cryptocurrency. Then another about cheap sunglasses. Then, friends began receiving messages from her account: "Hey, check out this amazing deal!" "Can I ask you for a quick favor?" Someone even got a link asking for their bank login information.

Megan's sister was horrified. Someone had taken over the account. They weren't just spamming—they were impersonating Megan.

Hackers had found her profile, realized it was inactive, and used social engineering to reset the password. Since no one had formally memorialized the account or shut it down, it remained vulnerable. Once inside, the hacker combed through her old messages, targeting friends and family with phishing attempts and scams. Some people fell for it, believing it was really Megan. Others were traumatized—receiving messages from someone they knew had died.

This is more common than most people realize. Inactive accounts, especially ones that aren't secured with two-factor authentication, are prime targets for identity theft. They hold personal details, photos, contact lists, and years of conversations. Hackers use them for scams, but also for impersonation, blackmail, and spreading malware.

Megan's family had assumed her profile would remain untouched.

They didn't realize that even in death, her digital identity was still vulnerable.

The Digital Photos That Were Erased Forever

Charles loved photography. For over a decade, he documented every family vacation, birthday, and special moment with care. His cloud storage account became a digital time capsule—filled with thousands of high-resolution images, home videos, and scanned childhood photos from before the digital age.

Everything was backed up. Everything was organized. Everything, he believed, was safe.

But after Charles passed away, those memories started disappearing—and no one noticed until it was too late.

His cloud storage subscription, which had been on autopay, failed when his credit card was deactivated. After a few automated billing reminders and a grace period, the cloud provider followed its policy: inactive accounts were flagged for deletion. When no one responded—because no one had access—the data was erased permanently.

His wife and children didn't even realize what had happened until months later, when they tried logging into his account to create a memorial photo album. The login failed. Password reset attempts went to a phone number that no longer worked. When they contacted the provider, they were told that due to privacy laws, and without prior consent or a digital will, the data could not be recovered. And worse—according to the provider's terms of service, it had already been permanently deleted from their servers.

Every photo from family trips, every video of their daughter's first words, every memory carefully saved over the years—gone. Not because of theft, or hard drive failure, or technical error. But because no one had planned for the digital afterlife.

Charles thought he had done the responsible thing by backing everything up.

He didn't realize that without shared access or a digital legacy plan, cloud storage could turn into a digital black hole—erasing an entire family's history with just a few missed payments.

What You Need to Know

We make wills for our money, our homes, our belongings. We talk about life insurance, funeral plans, and legacy wishes. But very few people plan for the digital side of death.

What happens to your email, your bank apps, your cloud storage, your passwords, your photos, your social media accounts—when you're gone?

Most people assume their family will just figure it out. But here's the truth: without legal access, clear instructions, or a digital estate plan, your loved ones may be locked out of everything. Forever.

A 2024 survey by Bryn Mawr Trust found Americans value their digital assets at $191,516—but 76% have little or no knowledge of digital estate planning.

The result? Grieving families are left navigating not only emotional loss—but legal and logistical nightmares as well.

Your digital identity doesn't shut down when your heart does.

It keeps running. Your accounts stay live. Your subscriptions keep charging. Your social media keeps "remembering" your birthday. Your email inbox continues to collect new messages, and in some cases, gets targeted by hackers or scammers who know the owner is deceased.

And that's where the real trouble begins.

Without access to your passwords, your family might not be able to recover your photos or documents. They might not be able to shut down your accounts or protect your identity from being stolen. In fact, identity theft targeting the deceased is far more common than most people realize.

Every year, 2.5 million dead Americans have their identities hijacked, according to fraud firm ID Analytics (2017). And it gets creepier - nearly 67,000 people filed taxes using Social Security numbers that belonged to someone born before 1901.

In death, your data doesn't rest.

It gets recycled. Abused. Monetized.

Unless you lock it down—someone else will log in.

Because most online services—Google, Apple, Facebook, Dropbox, even banks—don't allow anyone to access an account unless the original owner gave permission while they were alive. That means no legal authority, no death certificate, and no grief is enough to unlock what you forgot to hand over.

And when your digital life contains your financial life, your personal photos, your business assets, or access to money—those accounts matter more than ever.

It's not just about closing things down. It's about protecting what you've built. Making sure the right people can step in when they need to. And preventing the wrong people from taking advantage of the silence.

Because once you're gone, silence is the default setting.

Some people think a simple list of passwords on paper is enough. But passwords change. Devices get locked. Accounts time out. And even when everything is written down, families often don't know where to look—or how to safely access what's there.

What you need is a plan.

A clear, secure, up-to-date process for managing your digital assets in case of death or emergency. That doesn't mean handing your logins to someone today. It means choosing a digital executor. Setting up legacy access where available. Keeping an encrypted backup of your most important credentials. And making sure the people you trust know what exists, where to find it, and what to do with it.

This chapter will walk you through how to prepare your digital life for the end of your physical one. Not in a morbid way—but in a responsible one. You'll learn how to think about your accounts as part of your estate. How to protect your memories, assets, and identity. And how to make things easier—not harder—for the people you care about most.

Because the moment you pass away, every digital account becomes a question.

The only person who can answer those questions—right now—is you.

Why It Matters

We write wills.
We appoint executors.
We leave instructions about the house, the car, the kids, the pets.

But most people don't think twice about what happens to their digital life when they're gone.

And yet, that's where much of your life now exists—online.

Bank accounts. Email. Photo storage. Streaming services. Health portals. Crypto wallets. Social media. Business logins. Subscriptions. Password vaults. All still active. All still under your name. All still connected to other people, money, memories, and systems.

Unless someone knows how to access them—or even knows they exist—those accounts will remain untouched. Inactive. Locked. Or worse, eventually breached.

That's the part most families don't expect.

In 2024, a study from the *Digital Legacy Association* found that over 72% of people have no plan for their online accounts after death. And in most cases, loved ones are left scrambling to locate passwords, verify identity, request access, or shut things down—often through long, complicated legal channels.

This leads to several risks.

The first is emotional. Your digital presence doesn't vanish when you do. Social media accounts may keep posting birthday reminders or memories. Email addresses might still send auto-replies. Voice assistants might still respond to your name. For grieving families, this can feel invasive, disorienting, or cruel.

The second is logistical. Without access to your email, cloud storage, or password manager, families may be locked out of vital documents—tax forms, business files, insurance accounts, or family photos. Financial platforms may hold refunds, subscriptions may continue billing, and investments—like crypto wallets—can become permanently inaccessible.

A staggering amount of cryptocurrency is lost forever—not from theft, but from silence. Forgotten wallets. Lost private keys. Owners who died without leaving any recovery plan. Reports estimate that up to 25% of all Bitcoin is trapped in digital limbo, inaccessible and gone for good. Unlike a bank, there's no "forgot password" button for the blockchain. And when someone dies without sharing access, their crypto dies with them.

But in some parts of the world, people are waking up to the risk. In Australia, wills mentioning cryptocurrency have skyrocketed 2,400% in just four years, doubling again in 2024, according to the online will platform Safewill.

It's a sign: digital wealth needs a digital legacy plan—because if no one knows how to access it, it might as well not exist.

But perhaps the most overlooked threat is criminal. Inactive or unmonitored accounts become easy targets for hackers. Once a criminal gains access to a deceased person's account, they can:

- Impersonate them
- Scam their contacts
- Harvest private documents
- Reset passwords on other platforms
- Sell access to identity theft rings

And because no one is watching, the breach often goes unnoticed for months or even years.

Deceased identity theft isn't rare—it's routine.

Every year, 2.5 million dead Americans have their identities misused. And 800,000 of them are deliberately targeted by criminals annually—not by mistake, but by design. Those numbers came from a 2012 study by ID Analytics. Since then? We've added more data, more digital accounts, more leaks, more ways to be exploited.

AI tools now scan obituaries and test logins automatically. And still—no real system to protect the dead. So if 800,000 were targeted then, just imagine what it looks like now.

And yet, digital death is rarely discussed.

Many people assume family members will just "figure it out." That their spouse knows their passwords. That their children will know what to do. That cloud accounts will stay active forever. But in reality, most tech platforms have strict—and sometimes contradictory—policies around death.

Some require death certificates, power of attorney, or court orders. Others offer legacy access features—but only if set up in advance. Many refuse to provide any data at all. Without preparation, even the simplest task—like closing an account or saving family photos—can become a legal and emotional nightmare.

This is why digital death matters. Because you can't assume access will be granted later. You have to plan for it now.

This doesn't mean handing out all your passwords. It means choosing someone you trust and documenting what they'll need—securely. It means enabling legacy access options for Apple, Google, Facebook, and other services. It means leaving instructions in your will or estate plan. It means asking the uncomfortable questions while you still can.

What accounts do you use regularly?
Where are your important files stored?
Are there subscriptions that need to be canceled?
Is anyone relying on your digital services—like your business, clients, or family?
And perhaps most important: Who has the authority—and the tools—to step in?

Because digital life doesn't pause when yours ends. And if you don't define what happens to it, someone else will.

This chapter exists to help families avoid unnecessary pain and confusion. Because death is hard enough without adding locked files, ghost profiles, and legal dead ends to the burden.

What to Do About It – Your Security Checklist

1. **Create a Digital Will or Estate Plan:** Include all critical accounts, passwords, and access instructions in your official estate plan. Specify who gets access and how your digital assets should be handled after death.

2. **Use a Password Manager with Emergency Access:** Choose a password manager that allows you to designate a trusted emergency contact who can access your vault if you become incapacitated or pass away.

3. **Assign Legacy Contacts for Key Accounts:** Platforms like Facebook, Google, and Apple allow you to name a legacy contact or assign account access upon death. Set these up now, not later.

4. **Store Recovery Instructions Securely:** Keep a written or encrypted digital file with instructions for accessing important online services—email, banking, crypto, cloud storage. Share its location with a trusted loved one or attorney.

5. **Secure Crypto Wallets with Succession in Mind:** If you own cryptocurrency, document your private keys and wallet recovery phrases. Store them securely, and make sure someone knows where they are.

6. **Back Up Photos, Documents, and Important Files Locally:** Don't rely solely on cloud services that may lock or delete accounts after inactivity or unpaid bills. Keep local copies that loved ones can access.

7. **Use Shared Family Plans When Possible:** Google, Apple, and other platforms offer family sharing options that can help relatives retrieve content or continue subscriptions without complex legal processes.

8. **Write Down Social Media Preferences:** Specify whether you want accounts memorialized, deleted, or managed by someone else. Each platform has different policies—your family will need clear instructions.

9. **Include Subscription and Billing Info:** List online services tied to your credit cards (Netflix, Dropbox, domains, hosting, etc.) so family members can cancel or manage them.

10. **Discuss Digital Legacy Openly:** Talk to your loved ones. It may feel awkward, but clarity now prevents chaos later.

Quick Action Plan

1-Minute Fix: Enable legacy contact or inactive account manager features on your Google, Apple, and Facebook accounts.

5-Minute Fix: Choose a trusted emergency contact in your password manager.

15-Minute Fix: Create a simple digital asset inventory—list your key accounts, devices, and subscriptions.

30-Minute Fix: Add your digital legacy instructions to your will or estate documents and inform your family of their location.

PART 6 - KEEP YOUR MONEY, MEMORIES, AND LIFE SAFE

Chapter 30

Online Banking and Finance: Keep Your Money Yours

Real-World Scenarios

The Fake Bank Login That Stole $20,000

Lillian's morning started off like any other. She poured her coffee, opened her laptop, and began skimming through her inbox. That's when one particular email caught her eye.

The subject line read: "Urgent Fraud Alert – Suspicious Login Detected on Your Bank Account."

Her heart skipped a beat.

The message looked official. It used her bank's logo, proper formatting, and even included a security warning stating that immediate verification was required to avoid account suspension. There was a large, bold button labeled "Verify Now."

Without hesitation, Lillian clicked.

The link brought her to what appeared to be her bank's login page. Everything looked just right—the layout, the logo, even the little lock icon in the browser bar. She typed in her username and password, hit enter... and nothing happened. The page simply refreshed.

She assumed it was a glitch and decided to check again later. But by the time she logged into her real bank account a few hours later, it was too late. Her savings account—nearly $20,000—was gone.

Frantic, she called her bank.

"We never sent you an alert," the representative told her. "It looks like someone accessed your account using your credentials earlier this morning."

That's when the truth sank in.

The email wasn't from her bank. The login page wasn't real. It was a phishing scam—carefully designed to mimic her bank's website and trick her into handing over her password in real time. And it had worked perfectly.

By the time she realized what had happened, her money had already been transferred to multiple untraceable accounts. The odds of recovering it were slim.

Lillian thought she was protecting her finances.

She didn't realize she had just walked straight into a cybercriminal's trap.

The One-Time Password Scam That Bypassed 2FA

Natalie had always been cautious with her online accounts. She used long, complex passwords and enabled two-factor authentication (2FA) on every service that offered it, especially her online banking. She felt confident knowing that even if someone managed to steal her password, they'd still need the one-time verification code sent to her phone to gain access.

That sense of security shattered one Thursday afternoon.

She received a phone call from someone claiming to be from her bank's fraud department. The man sounded professional, calm, and reassuring. "Hi Natalie, this is Bradley from your bank's security team. We've detected suspicious activity on your account and just sent you a verification code to lock things down. Could you please read that code back to me so we can secure your funds immediately?"

Seconds later, a real one-time password from her bank arrived via text. Trusting the caller, Natalie read the six-digit code aloud.

That single moment changed everything.

Within minutes, $5,000 vanished from her checking account. The caller wasn't a bank employee. He was a scammer who had already entered Natalie's login credentials into her bank's website and was waiting for the second layer of protection—the OTP she unknowingly handed over.

Natalie had done everything right. She used 2FA, ignored suspicious emails, and kept her devices updated. But she hadn't anticipated the human element—social engineering.

What made the scam so effective wasn't high-level hacking. It was simple deception. A convincing voice, a real security code, and a request that seemed urgent and legitimate.

By the time she called her real bank, the money had already passed through several accounts and crypto exchanges. Recovery was unlikely.

Natalie thought she was confirming a legitimate security measure.

Instead, she had been tricked into unlocking her account for the very person trying to steal from her.

The Fake Investment Platform That Wiped Out a Retirement Fund

Bradley had always been smart with his money. He lived modestly, saved diligently, and was excited about the growing world of cryptocurrency. When he came across an ad for a new Bitcoin investment platform while scrolling social media, it seemed like a great opportunity.

The site was polished. It had a professional dashboard, sleek graphs tracking "live" prices, and glowing testimonials from other users who claimed to have doubled or tripled their investments. There was even a time-limited bonus offer for first-time deposits.

Encouraged, Bradley deposited $2,000 and began watching his virtual balance rise. The platform showed his trades growing in value. He felt like he was finally catching up with the digital economy.

After a week, convinced it was the real deal, he transferred his entire retirement savings—$20,000—into the platform.

Then, one morning, he opened the site to check on his portfolio.

It was gone.

No login page. No customer support. No trace of the company he thought he was investing with. Just a browser error message.

Consumers across the U.S. reported a record-shattering $12.5 billion lost to fraud, according to fresh data from the FTC (Federal Trade Commission. 2025).

The biggest trap? Investment scams.

They alone siphoned off $5.7 billion—promises of fast profits turning into vanishing money and silent accounts.

Bradley was devastated. He contacted his bank, filed police reports, and even tried reaching out to crypto recovery services. But the money had already been sent to anonymous wallets—scattered across the blockchain with no way to retrieve it.

He had fallen victim to one of the fastest-growing scams on the internet: fake investment platforms that mimic the real thing, complete with slick design, fabricated success stories, and often, paid influencer endorsements.

Bradley thought he was making a bold financial move toward a better future.

Instead, he had lost everything to a perfectly orchestrated lie.

The Card Skimmer That Stole Money Without a Swipe

David was sitting at his usual table in his favorite coffee shop, enjoying an espresso and catching up on emails. His debit card was tucked safely in his wallet, which sat zipped in his backpack beside him. He hadn't used it that day.

But then, his phone buzzed.

Fraud alert from his bank: multiple charges were being made to his card at online retailers he didn't recognize. Confused and slightly panicked, David pulled out his wallet. His card was still there.

How could it have been used if it had never left his possession?

The answer was chilling.

Somewhere nearby in the café, a hacker had been carrying a hidden device designed to wirelessly scan for NFC-enabled cards and phones. These small, inconspicuous skimmers could read card details through bags, wallets, even clothing—no physical contact required.

All the hacker needed to do was get close enough.

Within seconds, David's card details were intercepted. Minutes later, they were being used for purchases around the world—or worse, sold in bulk on the dark web to other criminals.

David always assumed his cards were safe as long as he didn't lose them or swipe them somewhere suspicious.

He didn't realize that simply sitting next to the wrong person at a café could be all it took to have his financial information stolen.

What You Need to Know

Your bank account is no longer just something you visit at a branch. It's in your pocket. On your screen. In your cloud. Always logged in, always accessible, always ready—until someone else gains access.

Online banking has made money management faster, easier, and more connected than ever. But that convenience comes at a cost. Every tap, every login, every auto-filled password is another opportunity for someone to slip in and take what's yours.

And they don't need to break in. Most of the time, they just wait for you to let them in.

In 2024, the FTC reported a 25% increase in overall consumer fraud losses. While the report highlights significant losses to investment scams and through bank transfers, tactics like phishing, credential stuffing, and SIM swap scams continue to be major concerns for fraud related to online banking and financial apps.

Because once they're in, they move fast.

The clock starts ticking the moment they breach. In just seconds, cybercriminals can jump from access to action—draining funds, hijacking systems, and vanishing without a trace.

Over the past 20 years, the financial sector has been hit more than 20,000 times, racking up $12 billion in losses (IMF, 2024).

These aren't slow burns. They're smash-and-grab operations—fast, precise, and devastating.

And the warning signs? They're easy to miss.

You might see a login alert you dismiss as a glitch. A transaction for a small amount, meant to test the card. A change to your recovery email you didn't make. These are the red flags that many people don't catch until it's too late. By the time you call your bank, the money is gone—often moved through multiple accounts or converted into cryptocurrency, making it nearly impossible to recover.

One reason attacks work so well is because most people assume their bank has it all covered.

But banks protect their systems—not your individual habits.

If you reuse the same password for your PayPal and your grocery app, that's not the bank's fault. If you get tricked into entering your login details on a fake website, the bank may not refund you. And if a hacker uses your own phone to bypass two-factor authentication, your "secure" account can be emptied in minutes.

In fact, many fraud victims do everything right—except one thing. They trust too quickly.

They click on an email that looks legitimate. They respond to a text from "customer service." They answer a call from someone pretending to be their bank's fraud department. Many financial frauds begin with a fake message from a trusted brand, such as a bank. For example, in 2024, banks were the most popular lure in 42.6% of financial phishing attempts, according to Kaspersky. And because the scammer already has some of your info—like your name, partial account number, or location—it doesn't feel fake.

That's why the most important part of financial security isn't the app you use—it's how you use it.

This chapter will walk you through how financial fraud really works. Not just in theory, but in practice. You'll see how attackers build trust, what they target, how they move your money, and how to recognize the patterns before damage is done. You'll learn how to properly secure your banking apps, digital wallets, investment platforms, and online payment tools. You'll learn how to check for phishing, lock down two-factor authentication, and make sure your accounts don't share the same weaknesses across platforms.

Because your money may live online now, but so do the people trying to take it. And they count on one thing: that you'll keep assuming you're not the target. You should stop assuming and start securing. Because if someone else can log in, it's not your money anymore.

Why It Matters

Your bank account used to be behind a brick wall and bulletproof glass. Today, it's behind a few taps on a touchscreen. The evolution of financial services—mobile banking, contactless payments, digital wallets—has made managing money more convenient than ever. But that convenience has also introduced a frightening reality: the path to your life savings now runs through your devices.

In 2024, fake messages impersonating trusted brands, particularly banks, were a prevalent tactic in financial phishing attempts. According to Kaspersky's 2024 Financial Cyberthreats report, banks were the most popular lure in 42.6% of financial phishing attempts. This includes phishing scams, fake apps, credential stuffing, SIM-swapping, and malware targeting banking apps. While banks advertise that they're secure, the truth is the weakest link isn't the institution—it's often the individual. That means you.

Cybercriminals don't need to crack a bank's firewall anymore. They need only one slip from you: one click on a phishing email disguised as a fraud alert, one download of a fake investment app, one reused password stored in your browser. Once inside, they can clean out your accounts in minutes, open lines of credit in your name, or impersonate you to access even more.

Mobile banking in particular has become a goldmine for attackers. Even two-factor authentication (2FA) is no longer a full safeguard. Criminals now bypass it using social engineering tactics, such as OTP scams or SIM-swapping, where they hijack your phone number and intercept security codes.

And then there are fake payment platforms—fraudulent investment apps, cryptocurrency exchanges, and digital loan services that are indistinguishable from legitimate ones. These sites trick users into depositing funds and disappear overnight, leaving victims with no legal recourse and no refund.

But even the accounts you think are "safe" can betray you. Auto-saved credit cards in shopping apps, peer-to-peer payment tools like Venmo and Cash App, or forgotten financial tools that haven't been updated in years—these are all doors into your money. Once accessed, these accounts can be drained, manipulated, or used to commit fraud in your name.

And the impact isn't just financial—it's deeply personal. Victims of financial cybercrime often report anxiety, shame, and even depression. The violation of privacy and control can feel paralyzing. Even worse, many banks have limited liability clauses. If they determine the fraud happened due to user error—say, clicking a fake link or ignoring a security update—you may not be reimbursed.

The elderly are especially vulnerable. The FBI's 2023 Elder Fraud Report (released in 2024) revealed that seniors lost over $3.4 billion to cyber-enabled financial scams, marking a significant increase from the previous year. Many of these schemes used fake bank messages, tech support calls, or urgent wire transfer scams to convince victims to part with their money willingly.

Children and teens are also being targeted. With many using online banking features like prepaid cards, mobile wallets, or crypto trading apps, attackers are designing scams aimed at younger users.

According to the 2024 Digital Youth Index by Nominet, online scams and financial fraud are increasingly affecting young people in the UK. The report reveals that 35% of young people, including 50% of those over the age of 16, have encountered scams online. Additionally, 14% of young respondents reported experiencing fraud or identity theft. This new generation is being raised in a financial minefield—with little education on how to navigate it.

Even if your money isn't stolen outright, your financial identity can be weaponized. Stolen banking logins often end up on the dark web—packaged and sold with your name, address, social security number, and behavioral patterns. Criminals then use this data to build convincing synthetic identities, apply for loans, file fake tax returns, or trick your family into giving up more information. One breach often leads to another.

There's also a hidden cost: time.

Victims of financial fraud spend an average of 10 (AARP, 2022) to 30 (FTC, 2003) hours recovering their accounts. replacing cards, filing reports, and cleaning up the digital mess left behind. Some never fully recover. They're blacklisted from services, stuck with bad credit, or tangled in disputes with banks, lenders, and regulators.

All of this shows why protecting your financial life isn't optional—it's essential. Because once someone else gets in, the losses go far beyond dollars and cents. They reach into your sense of security, autonomy, and trust.

Your phone is a bank branch.

Your email is your vault key.

And your attention—especially when it slips—is the only thing standing between you and someone else's payday.

What to Do About It – Your Security Checklist

1. **Use a Dedicated Device or Browser for Banking:** Reduce risk by only accessing your bank accounts from a secure, updated device or a browser profile you don't use for everyday browsing.

2. **Enable Two-Factor Authentication (2FA):** Always use 2FA for banking and financial apps—prefer app-based authenticators (like Google Authenticator or Authy) over SMS, which is vulnerable to SIM swaps.

3. **Avoid Public Wi-Fi for Banking:** Never check your bank or payment apps on public or unsecured Wi-Fi. Use your mobile data or a trusted home network instead.

4. **Set Up Real-Time Transaction Alerts:** Activate push or SMS alerts for all transactions to spot fraud early and take immediate action.

5. **Use Unique, Complex Passwords:** Every financial account should have a

strong, unique password. Never reuse banking passwords elsewhere.

6. **Avoid Clicking on Bank Links in Emails or Texts:** Type your bank's URL manually or use their official app. Phishing sites often look identical to the real thing.
7. **Monitor All Accounts Regularly:** Check bank and credit card accounts at least weekly for suspicious activity—even small charges can signal fraud.
8. **Secure Your Devices:** Keep all banking devices updated, install reputable antivirus software, and lock screens with passwords or biometrics.
9. **Be Cautious of Investment & Loan Scams:** Verify platforms before transferring funds or entering personal info. Scammers often impersonate legitimate services.
10. **Freeze Unused Credit or Set Spending Limits:** For extra safety, freeze your credit reports or use banks that allow you to control spending and enable/disable cards instantly.
11. **Secure Backup Access:** Store account recovery information, backup codes, and contact details for all banks and apps in a secure, encrypted place like a password manager.

Quick Action Plan

1-Minute Fix: Turn on transaction alerts and enable two-factor authentication for all banking apps.

5-Minute Fix: Update your banking passwords and audit your device for malware or outdated security patches.

15-Minute Fix: Review your account access settings, remove old devices, and disable SMS-based verification if possible.

30-Minute Fix: Set up a secure password manager, organize all financial credentials, and create an emergency access plan for loved ones.

Chapter 31

Secure Online Shopping: Don't Get Tricked by a Sale

Real-World Scenarios

The Fake Store That Stole a Woman's Credit Card

Eleanor was a savvy online shopper who prided herself on finding the best deals. She followed sales, hunted for coupons, and compared prices before making a purchase. So when she stumbled across a website offering high-end designer handbags at 70% off, she thought she'd struck gold.

The site looked perfect. It had clean, modern design, professional product photos, glowing customer reviews, and even a countdown timer claiming the sale would end in just a few hours. Eleanor didn't want to miss out. She selected a bag she'd been eyeing for months and proceeded to checkout.

Everything felt normal. The payment form was secure, the URL had a padlock icon, and the purchase went through without issue. She received a confirmation email within minutes—though it looked a little plain.

Then... silence.

No shipping update. No tracking number. No response to her follow-up emails. After a week, she grew suspicious and called her credit card company. That's when she discovered that someone had used her card to make thousands of dollars in unauthorized purchases—luxury electronics, gift cards, and digital currencies.

Eleanor had been scammed.

The website was fake—a sophisticated clone built to mimic a legitimate online store, designed to collect and steal credit card details. The confirmation email, the reviews, even the security icon—it was all smoke and mirrors.

By the time the fraud was discovered, the site had already shut down. The scammers had moved on, likely setting up a new fake shop under a different name.

Eleanor thought she was getting a once-in-a-lifetime deal.

She didn't realize she was handing her financial identity to criminals hiding behind a glossy storefront.

The Data Breach That Exposed a Shopper's Identity

Ava considered herself a careful online shopper. She only used trusted websites, stuck to major retailers, and enabled two-factor authentication where possible. Like many people, she also stored her credit card details on her favorite shopping sites to make checkout faster.

One afternoon, she got a text message from her bank: a $1,200 charge had been made at an electronics store overseas.

She froze.

It wasn't her.

Within minutes, more alerts came in—transactions on eBay, online gaming platforms, and a luxury clothing site.

Panicked, Ava began checking every account she could think of. One by one, she saw her saved payment information had been used to make fraudulent purchases. The accounts hadn't been individually hacked. Instead, the breach had come from a major retailer she had used just weeks before—one she trusted implicitly.

That retailer had suffered a massive data breach. Hackers had gained access to customer databases containing names, email addresses, billing information, and saved payment methods. Ava's entire digital shopping profile was now in criminal hands.

The worst part?

She didn't even get notified until the breach made headlines.

What started as a convenience—saving her card for faster checkout—had become a gateway for cybercriminals to drain her finances and compromise her identity. Now she faced the exhausting process of freezing cards, resetting passwords, monitoring accounts, and restoring her digital security.

Ava thought she was shopping safely.

She didn't realize she had unknowingly joined the growing number of victims in a massive retailer data breach.

The Coupon Scam That Stole a Woman's Passwords

Harper was scrolling through social media during her lunch break when an ad popped up promising a free $100 gift card to her favorite clothing store. The offer looked legitimate—clean branding, official logos, and a short message: "Complete a quick survey and receive your reward instantly."

It seemed harmless. And tempting.

She clicked the link.

The site looked exactly like the retailer's homepage. It had product images, menu tabs, and even a fake live chat button. A banner across the top said "Exclusive Customer Loyalty Giveaway – Today Only!"

To claim her gift card, she was asked to fill out a short survey and log in with her email and password. Thinking it was connected to her real shopping account, Harper entered the information without hesitation.

She never received the gift card.

What she did receive was a flood of password reset notifications from multiple websites.

The fake coupon page was a phishing scam—carefully designed to capture her email login credentials. Within minutes, hackers had gained access to her inbox, her shopping accounts, and any online store where she had saved payment information or store credit. They didn't stop there—they attempted to use the same login combination on her PayPal, social media, and bank accounts.

By the time she realized what was happening, hundreds of dollars in store credit had been used, fraudulent purchases were in motion, and her email was temporarily locked.

Harper wasn't careless. She didn't download malware or click on a suspicious attachment. She just wanted a good deal.

She thought she was getting a free reward.

Instead, she handed cybercriminals the keys to her entire digital wallet.

The Fake Delivery Notification That Led to Fraud

Nathan had ordered a few things online earlier in the week—nothing unusual. So when he received a text message from what looked like FedEx, saying "Your package is out for delivery! Track here," it didn't seem suspicious.

The link took him to a tracking page that looked professional, complete with a FedEx logo, a delivery timeline graphic, and a form asking for verification: name, address, and credit card number.

Nathan didn't think twice.

After all, maybe there was a delivery fee, or maybe it was part of new verification policies. He filled in the form, hit submit, and got a message saying "Thanks! Your delivery is confirmed."

But no delivery ever came.

Instead, Nathan's phone lit up with fraud alerts just a few hours later.

His credit card had been used for multiple purchases overseas. Someone had attempted to open a second credit card in his name. And his personal information—name, address, card number—had been sold to identity thieves within minutes of submission.

The tracking page wasn't FedEx.

It was a phishing site, part of a growing wave of fake delivery scams designed to exploit the boom in online shopping. These scams are so effective because they look like everyday messages we all receive—texts about packages, missed deliveries, or updates from familiar couriers.

By the time Nathan contacted his bank and froze his accounts, the damage was already spreading.

He thought he was just tracking a package.

He didn't realize he had just handed his identity to a criminal.

What You Need to Know

Online shopping has become second nature. You see a deal, tap to buy, and a package arrives at your door the next day. You rarely think twice—because it's fast, it works, and most of the time, it feels completely safe.

But behind every sale, every promo code, and every checkout screen, there's an invisible layer of risk.

Cybercriminals know how people shop online. They understand how the psychology of discounts, urgency, and trust works—and they build scams that fit right into those patterns. Fake websites. Phishing emails. Bogus shipping alerts. Counterfeit storefronts. Malicious browser extensions. One moment of excitement over a good deal can lead to your credit card being stolen, your identity compromised, or your entire device infected with malware.

And the best part for attackers? You never see it coming.

Juniper Research reported that global e-commerce fraud losses were projected to reach $44.3 billion in 2024, increasing to $107 billion by 2029. That number includes stolen credit cards, fraudulent orders, fake stores, and identity theft from compromised accounts. A large portion of it came from small, everyday transactions—things that didn't feel risky at all.

That's what makes this kind of attack so dangerous.

It doesn't take a major breach to hurt you. It takes one click on a fake store that looks real enough. One time reusing a password. One tracking link you didn't double-check. One shared account that was never updated after someone else used it. And before you even realize it, your financial information is in the wrong hands—and your bank account might not protect you.

Scammers use urgency to push you into making mistakes. Limited-time flash sales. Countdown timers. "Going fast—only 3 left!" They use social media ads, fake influencers, and copied product photos. Insikt Group reported a significant surge in Magecart attacks targeting e-commerce platforms in the first half of 2024, with a 103% increase compared to previous periods.

They know what you expect to see—and they give it to you.

Once they have your email and password, they try it across multiple sites. If you've reused it—even once—they can access your real shopping accounts, saved cards, order history, and addresses. And if your device isn't secured, they may install spyware or keyloggers that keep watching what you type long after the purchase is done.

Even legitimate online shopping habits can put you at risk.

Using public Wi-Fi at a café while checking out. Storing your credit card in your browser without a password manager. Skipping the two-factor authentication option because it feels like a hassle. Staying logged in to sites that have access to your billing address and saved cards. Accepting cookies and trackers on every new site without thinking about what they're doing.

And then there's the human factor.

Many people share accounts with family or friends—streaming services, e-commerce platforms, cloud storage linked to receipts. But shared logins mean shared risk. If one person uses a weak password or clicks a fake promo, everyone using that account could be affected.

This chapter will walk you through how online shopping scams actually work, how to spot red flags before you hit "buy," and what you can do to protect your payment methods, personal data, and accounts without giving up the convenience you've come to rely on.

You'll learn what to look for in fake stores, how to verify links, how to use browser tools wisely, and how to protect your identity if your payment information ever leaks. You'll see how to shop smart—not paranoid—and how to make sure your money only goes where you meant it to.

Because the best sale in the world isn't worth it if the price is your identity.

Why It Matters

Online shopping used to be a luxury. Now, it's a daily habit. From groceries and gadgets to digital subscriptions and impulse buys, we've trained ourselves to trust "Buy Now" buttons without thinking twice. But that convenience comes at a steep—and often invisible—price.

Cybercriminals love online shopping. Not because they're browsing for deals, but because it's one of the easiest ways to steal personal data, hijack payment methods, and exploit human behavior. And in 2025, the stakes are higher than ever.

E-commerce scams have surged globally. The Federal Trade Commission (FTC) reported that consumers lost more than $12.5 billion to fraud in 2024, with over $3 billion attributed to scams that started online, with fake shopping websites accounting for the largest single category.

These aren't sloppy scams from poorly designed websites. Many fake e-commerce platforms now look exactly like legitimate ones. They copy logos, design language, reviews, and even real tracking tools. Some clone entire brand websites, using slightly misspelled URLs (like "amaz0n.com" or "n1ke.store") that most people miss entirely.

Once you enter your name, address, and credit card details—everything is harvested. No item ever ships. No customer service ever answers. And your identity is now bundled and sold on dark web forums, often within hours.

But it doesn't stop at fake stores. Even real websites can be dangerous if they've been compromised. Users think they're paying safely, but the form sends their payment data straight to criminals.

Another underappreciated risk? Saved payment details. Many people store credit cards inside browser autofill, mobile apps, or shopping platforms like Amazon, Etsy, or food delivery services. If any one of those accounts is compromised—even through a leaked password or phishing scam—attackers can access your stored cards and start racking up charges in minutes.

The rise of mobile shopping has made the problem worse. Statista's analysis indicates that mobile commerce is expected to generate $2.51 trillion in 2025, with smartphones driving more than 60% of online purchases..

But many users browse on public Wi-Fi, ignore security updates, or download shady coupon apps and "discount extensions" that actually harvest login credentials or inject malware. One tap on the wrong "deal" can infect your device or redirect you to a phishing page that steals your payment info.

And then there's social media—a shopping mall that never closes. Platforms like Instagram, TikTok, and Facebook are flooded with targeted ads for flash sales, mystery boxes, and "going out of business" deals. Some are legitimate. Many are not. A 2024 investigation by the Better Business Bureau (BBB) found that, 40% of online shopping fraud reports originated from ads found on Facebook and Instagram.

Once your information is out there, the consequences compound. Stolen payment credentials are used for fraud, yes—but they also enable identity theft, loan fraud, or tax scams. Your email, your address, your device ID—all become part of a digital profile that criminals can exploit or resell.

Even something as harmless as signing up for an online receipt or loyalty discount can expose you. Many phishing attacks begin with fake emails that look like follow-ups to recent orders. "Track your package" links are a common tactic to infect devices or capture login credentials. If you clicked that button in a hurry, you might've just let someone into your inbox—and from there, your digital wallet.

Online shopping isn't going away. But if you don't take steps to secure your activity, you could lose more than money. You could lose control over your identity, your data, and your peace of mind.

Scams don't look like scams anymore. They look like holiday sales, influencer give-aways, clearance events, or that one-day-only offer you can't resist. That's the trick. And unless you're watching closely, you won't know it was a trap—until the bill arrives, and your account is already empty.

What to Do About It – Your Security Checklist

1. **Use Trusted Retailers Only:** Stick to well-known e-commerce platforms or verified retailers. If you're shopping on a new site, do research first and look for independent reviews.

2. **Check URLs Carefully:** Fake sites often mimic real brands with slight spelling differences. Always verify you're on the legitimate domain before entering any personal information.

3. **Avoid Clicking on Ads or Email Links:** Don't trust promotional links in emails, social media ads, or text messages. Type the retailer's address directly into your browser.

4. **Use Credit Cards or Virtual Cards for Payments:** Credit cards offer stronger fraud protection than debit cards. Some banks also provide virtual cards for safer one-time purchases.

5. **Don't Store Payment Info on Sites:** Skip the convenience of saving your card info in online accounts. If a retailer is breached, your saved data could be compromised.

6. **Be Wary of Deep Discounts and Flash Sales:** If a price seems too good to be true, it probably is. Scammers frequently use fake sales to lure shoppers onto fraudulent sites.

7. **Never Shop Over Public Wi-Fi:** Avoid making purchases on public or shared networks. If you must, use a personal hotspot or VPN to secure your connection.

8. **Use Strong, Unique Passwords:** Make sure your shopping accounts use strong, unique passwords that aren't reused across other platforms.

9. **Enable Multi-Factor Authentication (MFA):** Turn on MFA wherever available for added protection. Choose app-based authenticators over SMS if possible.

10. **Watch for Fake Order or Delivery Notifications:** Phishing emails and texts pretending to be from delivery companies or retailers are common. Go directly to the official app or site to check order status.

11. **Monitor Your Bank and Card Statements Regularly:** Set calendar reminders to review all transactions weekly, and report anything suspicious immediately.

12. **Keep Your Browser and Devices Updated:** Security patches fix known vulnerabilities. Enable automatic updates to stay protected.

Quick Action Plan

1-Minute Fix: Turn on transaction alerts from your bank or credit card provider to be instantly notified of new purchases.

5-Minute Fix: Update passwords for all your online shopping accounts and ensure they are strong and unique.

15-Minute Fix: Audit your browser settings and clear out saved card data and cookies. Remove payment methods stored on e-commerce accounts.

30-Minute Fix: Set up a secure password manager, install an ad blocker and anti-phishing browser extension, and teach family members how to recognize scam shopping sites.

Chapter 32

SIM Swapping: Losing Your Number, and Your Identity

Real-World Scenarios

The Phone Number That Let a Hacker Drain a Bank Account

Marcus was relaxing on the couch after dinner, half-watching TV and scrolling through social media, when he noticed something strange—his phone had no signal. No bars. No data. Just a blank screen and the words "No Service."

At first, he assumed it was a temporary network issue. Maybe a cell tower was down. He restarted the phone. Nothing. Then he opened his laptop to check his bank account, just to make sure a recent payment had cleared.

Access denied! – Wrong password! – That didn't make sense.

Marcus quickly opened his email and was met with a wave of panic: a string of password reset requests from his bank, his PayPal, and his cryptocurrency exchange. Within minutes, he was locked out of every major account tied to his identity.

By the time he reached a support agent at his phone carrier, it was already over.

A hacker had called the carrier, impersonated him, and convinced them to transfer his phone number to a new SIM card—one they controlled. With that number, the hacker intercepted every two-factor authentication (2FA) code sent by text. They reset his passwords, logged into his bank, and drained his savings—all while Marcus stared helplessly at a phone that couldn't even make a call.

He had no idea his phone number—something he used every day for calls and texts—could be weaponized in a matter of minutes.

SIM swap attacks like Marcus's are growing fast. In 2023, SIM swapping caused over $72 million in reported losses in the U.S. alone, according to the FBI Internet Crime Complaint Center (IC3). And the terrifying part? Victims often don't even realize it's happening until it's far too late.

Marcus thought his phone number was just a contact detail.

He didn't realize it was the master key to his financial life.

The SIM Swap That Took Down a Social Media Influencer

Rebecca had spent years building her brand. What started as a small blog turned into a growing online presence—with thousands of followers on Instagram, Twitter, and TikTok. Her audience trusted her. Brands paid her for partnerships. She had finally turned her passion into a real business.

Then, one morning, she woke up to chaos.

Her phone had no service. At first, she brushed it off. Maybe she'd gone over her data cap. But when she opened her laptop, her inbox was flooded with confused and angry messages.

"Why are you scamming your followers?" "Did you really post that?" "Is your account hacked?"

Rebecca's heart dropped. She opened her Instagram and couldn't get in. Her Twitter? Locked. She watched in horror as her entire digital identity was taken over by a stranger.

The hacker had called her mobile provider, posed as her, and convinced them to port her number to a new SIM. Once they had control, they reset her passwords—bypassing all security using the SMS-based verification she had trusted. Within minutes, they were posting fake crypto giveaways, phishing links, and offensive content under her name.

Her credibility was shattered.

Her brand deals pulled out.

And she was left trying to explain what had happened.

Influencers and business owners like Rebecca are prime targets for SIM swaps—because their accounts are public, valuable, and often tied to one simple point of failure: a phone number.

Rebecca thought her accounts were protected by strong passwords.

She didn't realize a single call to her phone carrier could erase everything she had built.

The Crypto Investor Who Lost Everything Overnight

Timothy was no amateur investor. He'd been in the crypto space for years—long enough to see scams, volatility, and rug pulls come and go. He used a secure exchange. Enabled two-factor authentication. And he never clicked on suspicious links.

But even his diligence wasn't enough.

One evening, while checking prices on his phone, the signal suddenly vanished. Calls stopped working. Texts wouldn't go through. He tried to reboot, then switched to Wi-Fi. That's when the flood of alerts hit him.

Your password has been reset.New device login detected.Transfer complete.

Timothy's entire crypto portfolio—worth hundreds of thousands of dollars—was gone.

A hacker had executed a SIM swap, hijacking his phone number and using it to receive all the verification codes protecting his accounts. His strong passwords didn't matter. His 2FA didn't matter. Because it was all tied to a single point of failure: his phone number.

By the time he reached his mobile provider, the damage was done. His Bitcoin had been transferred to a private wallet, with no trace, no reversal, no support. The blockchain doesn't offer refunds.

Crypto transactions are irreversible. And in this case, so was the mistake.

Timothy had done everything right—except for one thing.

He thought two-factor authentication via SMS made him untouchable.

He didn't realize that his phone number had become a backdoor to his fortune.

The Business Owner Who Lost Control of His Company's Accounts

Hector was the founder of a thriving small business. He had built everything himself—his website, his brand, and his loyal customer base. Most of his operations were handled online, and nearly all of his company's accounts were tied to one thing: his mobile phone number.

His email? Linked to his number. His business banking and payroll? Same number. Even his company's social media pages used SMS two-factor authentication for security.

One afternoon, while preparing for a product launch, Hector received an odd email: "Your password has been successfully changed." The problem was—he hadn't changed anything.

Seconds later, his phone went completely silent. No service, no signal. That's when panic set in.

He rushed to log in to his business accounts from his laptop, but he was already locked out. His banking platform showed failed login attempts, and worse—successful ones. Payroll data was being accessed. Funds were being moved.

A hacker had hijacked his phone number through a SIM swap attack, posing as him and convincing the mobile provider to transfer his number to a new SIM card. With control of his number, they reset every password tied to it—taking over his email, draining his business accounts, and even seizing his company's social media presence.

Within an hour, years of work were under threat.

The hacker didn't just steal money—they stole access. They disrupted payroll. They sent fraudulent emails to vendors. They damaged his brand's reputation by posting suspicious messages from the company account.

All because Hector's security depended on a single point of failure: a mobile number.

He thought he had taken the necessary precautions to protect his company.

He didn't realize that one weak link could bring it all crashing down.

What You Need to Know

You use your phone number every day. To receive two-factor authentication codes. To recover passwords. To log in, verify accounts, and prove you are who you say you are. Your number has quietly become one of the most important pieces of your digital identity.

That's why criminals go after it.

SIM swapping—also known as SIM hijacking—is one of the most dangerous and fastest-growing forms of identity theft. It doesn't require hacking your phone or breaking into your accounts. It simply requires convincing your mobile carrier to transfer your number to a new SIM card controlled by someone else.

And once that happens, you lose more than just service.

The attacker now receives your text messages. Your two-factor codes. Your password reset links. They can log into your bank, crypto, email, and social media accounts—because everything tied to your phone number is suddenly theirs.

Most victims don't realize it's happening until it's too late. Their phone signal drops. Their texts stop working. And by the time they notice the service is gone, the hacker has already changed passwords, bypassed authentication, and moved money out of reach.

In just one year, the FBI's Internet Crime Center saw SIM swapping attacks explode—from 320 cases with $12 million stolen (2018–2020) to over 1,600 reports and nearly $70 million in losses by 2021. And that number only includes reported incidents. Many victims never recover their stolen funds. Others never find out how the attack happened at all.

And this isn't just a crypto investor problem. It's not just tech insiders. It happens to freelancers. Small business owners. Teachers. Grandparents. Anyone with a phone number tied to important accounts is a target.

Because SIM swapping isn't technical. It's psychological.

Hackers impersonate you. They call your mobile carrier, claiming their phone was lost or stolen. They use stolen personal details—your name, address, last four digits of your Social Security number—to sound legitimate. And if the support rep isn't careful, they approve the transfer.

That's it. In less than 15 minutes, your number is theirs.

Some attackers don't even need to call. They use fake customer portals. Spoofed numbers. Insider help. In a 2019 case that made headlines, DOJ (Department of Justice) charged a man with bribing AT&T employees more than $1 million to install malware on the company's network, unlock more than 2 million devices.

And once your number is hijacked, recovery isn't easy.

You'll need to contact your carrier, verify your identity (often harder now that your recovery tools are compromised), and hope they can shut down the rogue SIM fast enough to stop the bleeding. Meanwhile, the attacker may have reset your email, accessed your cloud storage, or changed your security questions. They don't just take your number—they use it as a key to everything else.

This chapter will walk you through how SIM swapping works, how it happens, and what you can do to protect yourself. You'll learn how to strengthen your mobile account security, how to recognize the early signs of a SIM hijack, and how to separate your phone number from your most important online accounts.

Because once someone takes your number, they don't just impersonate you.

They become you.

And if they get there before you notice, they won't just steal a few texts or emails. They'll drain your accounts, lock you out, and leave you cleaning up the damage for weeks, months, or longer.

SIM swapping is fast. Silent. And devastating.

But it's also preventable—if you know what to look for.

Why It Matters

Your phone number feels personal—like your digital signature. It's tied to everything from your text messages and social media to your bank account and two-factor authentication (2FA). But what if that number suddenly stopped working, and someone else started receiving your texts and security codes?

That's not a hypothetical. That's a SIM swap attack. And between 2018 and 2025, it's one of the fastest-growing threats in personal cybersecurity.

A SIM swap—also called SIM hijacking or SIM jacking—occurs when a hacker tricks or bribes your mobile carrier into transferring your phone number to a new SIM card they control. Once they have your number, they receive your calls, your texts, and—most dangerously—your verification codes.

From there, it's game over. In a matter of minutes, they can reset the passwords to your email, your bank account, your crypto wallet, and every app that uses SMS-based 2FA. You might not even know it's happening until your phone loses signal—and by then, they're already inside.

Between 2018 and 2021, SIM swapping complaints to the FBI increased by over 400%, indicating a significant rise in such attacks. That figure doesn't include indirect losses like reputational damage, stolen identities, or locked social media accounts. And that's just in the United States.

Globally, telecom regulators are raising red flags. The GSMA (GSM Association) warned that weak internal procedures at mobile carriers—like verifying identities through basic security questions—make it shockingly easy for criminals to hijack a phone number. Some attackers don't even need to speak to a real person. They use automated phone menus or social engineering scripts that work frighteningly well.

In 2025, a growing number of SIM swap attacks are targeting business owners, influencers, and cryptocurrency holders, whose accounts hold either financial value or a large audience. But that doesn't mean regular users are safe. Hackers often start with "low-profile" victims because they're less likely to have account alerts, strong passwords, or security keys enabled.

SIM swap attacks are particularly dangerous because they circumvent one of the most common safety nets people rely on—SMS-based two-factor authentication. Most people feel safe when they enable 2FA, assuming it will protect their accounts even if their password is stolen. But when the verification code itself is hijacked through a SIM swap, the whole system collapses.

Worse yet, many online services still default to SMS as their primary method of verification. That means if your number is compromised, everything from your cloud storage and email to your food delivery and ride-sharing accounts can be taken over in a chain reaction. And once a hacker is inside your email, they can request password resets for dozens of services—all from the shadows.

Some victims report not realizing they'd been attacked until they found themselves locked out of their accounts, with charges appearing on credit cards, messages sent from hijacked Instagram profiles, or emails confirming unauthorized withdrawals. By the time a mobile provider reassigns the number back to its rightful owner, the damage is already done.

Even scarier: many victims don't get their number back at all. SIM swap fraud is not only a technical problem—it's also a bureaucratic one. Phone carriers are not legally obligated to undo the swap quickly, and investigations can take days or weeks. During that time, a hacker has access to everything.

The bottom line: your phone number is no longer "just" a phone number. It's a master key. And if someone else gets control of it, they gain access to every door it opens.

SIM swapping isn't just a hacker trick. It's a full-scale identity takeover—and it's happening to everyday people who never thought their phone could betray them. Protecting your number is no longer optional. It's foundational.

What to Do About It – Your Security Checklist

1. **Set Up a Port Freeze or Number Lock With Your Carrier:** Most mobile providers offer options to lock your number and prevent unauthorized SIM transfers—ask your carrier how to enable it.

2. **Create a Unique PIN or Passphrase for Your Mobile Account:** Never leave your carrier account protected by a default PIN or weak answers to security questions. Use a complex, private passphrase.

3. **Use App-Based Two-Factor Authentication (2FA):** Avoid SMS-based 2FA for sensitive accounts like banking, crypto, and email. Use an authenticator app such as Authy, Duo, or Google Authenticator instead.

4. **Audit Your Accounts for Linked Phone Numbers:** Remove your mobile number as a recovery option from high-risk accounts when possible. Use an email-based recovery or app-generated codes instead.

5. **Enable Login and Security Change Alerts:** Activate notifications for account access, password changes, or number-related activity. These can alert you early if something suspicious is happening.

6. **Avoid Giving Out Verification Codes:** Never read back OTPs or verification codes over the phone—even if the caller claims to be from your bank or mobile provider.

7. **Don't Share Personal Info Online That Can Be Used for Verification:** Avoid posting your birthdate, address, or answers to common security questions on social media or in public forums.

8. **Monitor for Sudden Loss of Cell Service:** If your phone unexpectedly loses signal and displays "No Service," assume your SIM may have been hijacked and contact your carrier immediately.

9. **Protect Your Voicemail With a Password:** SIM swap attackers often access voicemail for verification codes. Set a secure PIN to protect your messages.

10. **Use Different Contact Methods for Critical Accounts:** Consider using a separate VoIP number (like Google Voice) or a secondary SIM strictly for logins and 2FA.

11. **Backup All Recovery Codes and Contact Details Securely:** Store backup 2FA codes and account recovery information in a password manager or encrypted digital vault.

Quick Action Plan

1-Minute Fix: Disable SMS-based 2FA on your most sensitive accounts and switch to app-based authentication.

5-Minute Fix: Set up a port freeze or number lock with your mobile provider and create a strong account PIN.

15-Minute Fix: Audit all critical accounts, remove your phone number where possible, and check notification settings for login or password change alerts.

30-Minute Fix: Set up a secure password manager, store recovery codes, and create a contingency plan for mobile service hijack scenarios.

Chapter 33
Protecting Your Digital Photos and Family Videos

Real-World Scenarios

The Photo That Led to Identity Theft

Isabella had just passed her driving test, and she was thrilled. It felt like a rite of passage—a milestone worth sharing. So she took a photo of her shiny new driver's license, applied a cute filter, and proudly posted it to Instagram with the caption: "Finally legal to drive! Watch out world!"

To play it safe, she blurred out her license number and address, thinking that would be enough. What she didn't hide, however, was her full name and birthdate—both clearly visible in the photo.

She moved on with life, unaware that anyone had noticed. But a month later, something strange happened. Isabella applied for a credit card, only to be unexpectedly denied. Confused, she requested a credit report—and what she found was shocking.

Multiple credit accounts had been opened in her name, with unpaid balances already racking up debt she'd never spent. Someone had used her personal information to impersonate her—and the trail led straight back to that seemingly harmless Instagram post.

Hackers had downloaded the image, extracted the visible information, and combined it with other leaked data available on the dark web. That's all they needed to create a fake identity—and Isabella was now left cleaning up the financial wreckage.

She thought she was simply sharing a proud moment. She didn't realize she was handing her identity to strangers who would use it to ruin her credit and reputation.

The Stolen Selfie That Ended Up on a Fake Profile

Bradley had always been active on social media. One afternoon, feeling good about his new haircut, he snapped a selfie and uploaded it to Facebook. It got a decent number of likes, and he thought nothing more of it.

Until a week later, when a close friend sent him a strange message: "Dude... is this you on a dating app?"

The link led to a profile on a dating site Bradley had never joined. There was his photo, his face, his smile—but it wasn't his name, and it certainly wasn't his bio.

Someone had stolen his image and built a completely fake online persona. Worse, they were using it to lure unsuspecting people into online relationships. As Bradley dug deeper, he discovered the fake profile had already scammed several victims—asking for money, claiming emergencies, even pretending to be in love.

He was horrified.

His photo—taken in a moment of confidence—had become a weapon in someone else's scam. Now, his face was attached to a lie, used to manipulate and deceive strangers for profit.

Bradley had never imagined that a simple selfie could be repurposed in such a disturbing way. He thought he was just updating his profile picture. He didn't realize he was becoming the face of a romance scam he had nothing to do with.

The Family Vacation Photos That Invited Burglars

Charlotte and her family were beyond excited for their tropical vacation. It was their first international trip in years, and from the moment they boarded the plane, Charlotte was sharing every moment online—beach views, food pics, and a daily countdown until they returned home.

She tagged the resort. She posted their travel schedule. She even shared a fun selfie at the airport with the caption: "See you in 10 days, home!"

Halfway through the trip, Charlotte's phone buzzed with a call from a neighbor.

"I hate to tell you this, but I think your house was broken into."

Shocked and shaken, the family returned early to find their front door pried open and their home ransacked. Jewelry, electronics, and important documents—gone.

When the police arrived, their conclusion was chilling. The burglars had monitored the family's social media posts. They knew the house was empty. They knew exactly when the family would return. And with that information, they planned the perfect time to strike.

Charlotte had assumed her friends were the only ones watching her posts. She didn't realize that even with privacy settings, photos can be shared, screenshots can circulate, and information spreads far beyond the original audience.

What started as a fun way to document a vacation had become an unintentional invitation to criminals.

She thought she was simply sharing memories.

She didn't realize she was also announcing that her home was unguarded.

The Baby Photos That Ended Up on the Dark Web

Linda was a proud new mother, and like many parents, she wanted to share the joy with family and friends. She posted sweet photos of her newborn daughter—wrapped in a hospital blanket, yawning in her crib, smiling during her first bath. Every post was marked "Friends Only," and she carefully curated her friend list to include only people she trusted.

She assumed that privacy settings meant safety.

But then, months later, a friend sent her a message that chilled her to the bone.

"Hey Linda... I think I saw your baby's photo on a really creepy forum. Are you sure your account is secure?"

Linda frantically followed the link—and there it was. Her daughter's innocent image, surrounded by disturbing comments from anonymous users on a dark web site known for exploiting stolen photos. The worst part? The picture had been edited, used in ways she couldn't bear to describe. She felt sick.

Despite her account being private, someone had taken screenshots. Maybe it was a former follower. Maybe it was a friend of a friend. Whoever it was, they had saved and reposted her daughter's pictures in places no parent should ever see.

She contacted the platform, filed reports, and tried to have the photos taken down—but the damage was already done. They had been copied, shared, and possibly used to generate AI-manipulated content. Her baby's face had been stolen from a moment of love and turned into something unthinkable.

The practice of parents sharing images of their children online, known as "sharenting," has been linked to increased risks. The Australian Institute of Criminology report (2023) found that 7% of individuals who posted pictures of children online received requests for child abuse material.

Linda thought she was simply sharing sweet moments with people she cared about. She didn't realize she was exposing her child to a world that doesn't play by the same rules of trust and decency.

In an age where anything uploaded can be copied, shared, or twisted—privacy needs to be more than a setting. It needs to be a serious decision.

What You Need to Know

Every family has a digital photo album now. Thousands of pictures stored across phones, cloud accounts, shared folders, social media, external drives, and sometimes—nowhere at all. You take a photo, capture a moment, maybe record a quick video of your child, your parents, your pet, your life. And then you move on.

But the digital world doesn't forget.

Unless you forget to protect it.

Today, our most personal memories are stored on devices and platforms we barely think about. And that's the problem. Because what used to sit safely in a photo album or camcorder now exists in a cloud server, a backup app, or a gallery app that might be sending your photos somewhere you didn't agree to.

It's easy to assume those pictures are safe—until they're not.

In 2023, a Mixbook survey of nearly 2,000 Americans found that half of them never do anything with the photos or videos they capture. Fifty-four percent never even see them again—unless they're scrolling through their phone. No backups. No prints. No cloud copies.

It gets worse.

Most people still keep everything—years of memories—on a single device. No second chances if it breaks, gets stolen, or crashes during an update.

Cybersecurity experts have been warning about this for years. Backup reports say it plainly: storing all your photos on one device is digital roulette. And the odds aren't in your favor.

But it's not just about losing photos. It's about who else might gain access to them.

Hackers target cloud photo storage services. If they breach your account—through a reused password, a phishing link, or a data leak—they can quietly download everything. Private family moments. Screenshots of documents. GPS data embedded in the photo file itself. In some cases, stolen photo albums have ended up on identity theft forums or dark web marketplaces.

You don't need to be famous for your pictures to have value.

In 2023 alone, over 275,000 websites were found hosting child sexual abuse content. And here's the horror: 92% of it was "self-generated." Not because kids wanted to—but because someone tricked, blackmailed, or groomed them into it.

The Internet Watch Foundation says the youngest victims were just three years old.

Yes, three.

More than 107,000 sites showed abuse of children under ten.

Over 2,500 involved children aged just three to six.

This isn't the dark web. It's the internet your family uses.

And the rise isn't slowing down. Because when predators go digital, the playground becomes the device in your child's hands.

And if you've ever shared photos with others—family group chats, shared cloud albums, messaging apps—you've expanded the circle. Now, it's not just your security that matters. It's everyone's. If your uncle's phone doesn't have a passcode, if your child's tablet is logged into your account, if your spouse saves photos to a shared folder without a password—it's all open.

Then there's metadata.

Every photo you take with a phone contains invisible data: time, date, and most importantly—location. Unless you've disabled this feature, most of your images include GPS coordinates. That beach photo with your kids? It tells exactly which beach. That birthday party? It pinpoints the exact house. It's convenient for sorting—but also incredibly useful to anyone trying to track you.

Even deleted photos aren't always gone.

Many cloud services keep deleted files for weeks or months. And if someone else gains access to your account, those deleted photos can be recovered—along with anything else you thought was private. Cloud forensics experts have demonstrated that deleted data, including photos, can often be recovered unless securely overwritten—a common issue in cloud storage systems

This chapter will help you take your photo and video security seriously—not because you need to be paranoid, but because you want to be prepared. You'll learn how to properly back up, encrypt, and secure your digital memories. You'll understand how to manage sharing settings, scrub metadata, and detect when something's not right.

Because your photos aren't just data.

They're your childhood. Your family history. The milestones you'll look back on decades from now. If those memories are worth keeping, they're worth protecting.

And if you wouldn't hand your photo album to a stranger on the street, don't leave your digital one unlocked online.

Why It Matters

Your digital photos and family videos are more than just files. They are your memories—frozen moments of joy, milestones, and history. They represent birthdays, weddings, holidays, first steps, last hugs. But in today's digital world, those memories are shockingly fragile.

Most people don't realize how vulnerable their personal media has become until it's too late. Whether it's a phone that suddenly dies, a cloud account that gets locked, or a data breach that leaks family albums onto dark web forums, once those files are lost or exposed, the damage is deeply personal—and often permanent.

The illusion of safety is what makes this threat so dangerous. People assume that just because they've uploaded their photos to iCloud, Google Photos, or OneDrive, they're safe forever. But cloud services have terms and policies that most users never read. If your subscription lapses, if your account is flagged for violation, or if the company changes its policies, your entire media archive can disappear—without warning.

Backblaze's 2022 Backup Survey exposed a digital time bomb: 54% of users reported losing data—yet only 1 in 10 backs up daily. Backblaze notes that cloud storage users can lose data due to subscription expiration, deletions, or account issues, emphasizing the need for proactive data backup strategies.

And then there's the threat of breach. Cloud storage providers are prime targets for hackers, especially since photo and video files are rarely encrypted on the user's side. If your cloud account is compromised—and you use a reused or weak password—everything inside it is fair game. Your baby's first steps. Your private honeymoon album. Screenshots, scanned documents, personal messages. All exposed.

Major data breaches from 2022 to 2025 have compromised hundreds of millions, and in some cases billions, of individual records, highlighting the significant risk that personal media like photos and videos could be exposed. Some of the files were used to create deepfake content. Others were sold in bulk as part of identity theft kits. Victims weren't public figures. They were everyday people—teachers, parents, retirees—who trusted the platform without ever thinking it could turn on them.

But the danger isn't limited to online threats. Physical devices—external hard drives, USB sticks, smartphones—are still widely used to store and back up personal media. Yet these devices are incredibly easy to lose, damage, or discard.

A study by the University of Hertfordshire found that over 60% of secondhand hard drives purchased online still contained recoverable personal files, including family photos, school records, and medical scans. This was echoed by a 2019 Bitdefender study, which revealed that 41% of used hard drives contained recoverable data, and 15.7% held personally identifiable information (PII), such as documents and photos.

Once those devices leave your home—sold, recycled, or stolen—your memories may be in the hands of strangers. And if you never encrypted or wiped them properly, there's no way to get them back or control where they end up.

Even deleted photos aren't truly gone. Smartphones and cloud services often store deleted files in a "trash" or "recycle bin" folder for 30 to 60 days—and in some cases, indefinitely. That means a photo you thought was erased years ago could be restored by anyone with access to your account or device.

But arguably the most overlooked risk is generational. Families assume they'll always have access to their memories—but what happens if the account holder dies, or if login credentials are lost? Many cloud providers don't allow family members to retrieve files unless there's a legal will or digital legacy setup. Entire family histories can vanish because no one wrote down a password.

Photos and videos aren't replaceable. You can't redownload your child's kindergarten graduation. You can't recreate a lost wedding video. And you definitely can't recover private memories once they've been exploited or deleted.

This is why digital photo and video security isn't just a "tech issue." It's a family issue. A legacy issue. A privacy issue.

If you've never thought of your media library as something worth protecting like a bank account or a passport, it's time to change that. Because to a hacker, a collection of family photos isn't just sentimental—it's valuable. They can use metadata, facial recognition, and geotags to track you. They can use private images to blackmail, scam, or impersonate. And they can sell your most cherished moments for just a few dollars on shady platforms.

Your memories deserve more than casual protection. They deserve a strategy.

What to Do About It – Your Security Checklist

1. **Use Encrypted Cloud Storage Services:** Choose cloud platforms that offer end-to-end encryption for photo and video storage. Avoid free services that don't prioritize security or privacy.

2. **Enable Two-Factor Authentication (2FA):** Turn on 2FA for every account that stores or accesses your personal media—cloud drives, photo sharing platforms, and backup apps.

3. **Avoid Auto-Uploading to Public Folders:** Check your cloud settings to ensure that new media isn't automatically uploaded to public or shareable folders.

4. **Create Local Backups on Encrypted Drives:** Maintain physical backups on encrypted external hard drives or SSDs, especially for sensitive or irreplaceable files.

5. **Watermark or Tag Shared Media:** If you must post baby or family photos online, consider watermarking or using subtle tags to track misuse and discourage theft.

6. **Keep Sharing to a Minimum:** Only share albums or folders with trusted individuals. Always use "view-only" links when possible and avoid granting edit/download permissions by default.

7. **Review Old Shared Links Regularly:** Periodically audit your cloud storage accounts for outdated or forgotten shared links—especially those containing family photos or private videos.

8. **Avoid Oversharing on Social Media:** Don't post real-time updates of your location, daily routines, or identifiable images of children in public feeds.

9. **Use Platforms With Privacy Controls:** When sharing photos with family, use apps or services designed for private sharing rather than public social networks.

10. **Secure All Devices With Access to Media:** Lock phones, tablets, and laptops that store your personal media with strong passcodes or biometric authentication.

11. **Permanently Delete Before Selling Devices:** Use certified data-wipe tools or factory resets with encryption enabled before giving away or recycling phones, computers, or memory cards.

Quick Action Plan

1-Minute Fix: Enable two-factor authentication for all photo storage and cloud accounts.

5-Minute Fix: Review sharing settings for your photo and video folders and disable public links.

15-Minute Fix: Backup important media to a local encrypted drive and remove sensitive files from vulnerable devices or cloud accounts.

30-Minute Fix: Set up secure cloud storage, audit who has access to your shared files, and create a media management routine that includes regular privacy and backup checks.

Chapter 34

The Cloud Isn't as Safe as You Think

Real-World Scenarios

The Private Photos That Went Public

Madison had always relied on cloud storage to keep her digital life organized. It gave her peace of mind knowing her photos, videos, and important documents were safely backed up in one place. She stored everything from childhood memories to scanned IDs and personal notes in the cloud—trusting it was secure.

One morning, she woke up to a message from a friend.

"Hey... did you mean to post these photos?"

Confused, Madison clicked the link her friend sent—and her blood ran cold. Her private photos were circulating on a public image board. Some were harmless, but others were deeply personal—meant only for her eyes.

Panicked, she logged into her cloud storage account. Everything still looked normal... except it wasn't. Her activity log revealed logins from unknown locations. Someone had broken in.

The cause? Madison had reused the same weak password—one she'd created years ago—for multiple accounts, including her cloud storage. That password had been exposed in a data breach from an unrelated website. A hacker had used it to quietly access her files, download them, and post them online.

71% of people now store their photos in the cloud (Threadgold Consulting, 2025) —a clear sign we're trusting our most personal memories to servers we don't control.

Madison never received an alert. No warning. No suspicious login email. Just a quiet, devastating theft of her most personal content.

She had thought her cloud account was a digital vault.

She didn't realize that one weak password had left the door wide open.

The "Deleted" Files That Weren't Really Gone

Charles was meticulous about digital hygiene. He routinely cleaned up his cloud storage—especially sensitive work files, client contracts, and financial reports. One afternoon, needing space for a new batch of files, he carefully selected old documents and hit delete. Gone, he assumed. Out of sight, out of mind.

A few weeks later, while checking an internal company server, Charles found something strange: a folder of documents he had supposedly deleted was back. Not only were they restored, but they had also been moved to a shared workspace by mistake—where anyone with internal access could view them.

Confused and concerned, Charles dug into his cloud provider's policies.

That's when he learned a disturbing truth: many cloud storage services don't permanently delete files when you hit "delete." Instead, files are often retained in backup systems or hidden archive folders for weeks, months, or even longer. These backups exist for recovery purposes—but they're not always private.

Even worse, some cloud providers comply with government or third-party data requests without notifying users. If a backup exists, it can be accessed—even if you thought you erased it.

Charles thought his files were gone for good.

He didn't realize that in the world of cloud storage, deletion doesn't always mean disappearance.

The Shared Folder That Exposed Personal Information

Rebecca was careful with her finances. Each year, she gathered her tax forms, scanned receipts, and financial statements to send to her accountant. This time, she opted for a convenient method: uploading everything to a cloud folder and sharing the link.

She thought she was doing the responsible thing—no more emails or lost attachments, just a secure, digital handoff.

Weeks went by. Then one afternoon, while browsing her cloud account, Rebecca noticed something strange: her shared folder had been accessed dozens of times—far more than just her accountant would ever need. When she dug deeper, her stomach sank.

The folder had been set to public. Anyone with the link could view—and download—everything. Her tax returns, bank statements, even scanned IDs and documents with her Social Security number were all out there. Worse still, she discovered that the folder had been indexed by search engines. That meant complete strangers could stumble upon it with a simple Google search.

She had shared the link with only one person. But the accountant, not realizing the gravity of the setting, had shared it again—and the permissions were never fixed. Rebecca's most sensitive financial information had been floating on the open web for weeks.

She spent the next month freezing her credit, updating her accounts, and watching anxiously for signs of identity theft.

Rebecca thought she was securely sharing a folder.

She didn't realize she had unintentionally published her financial life to the world.

The Cloud Backup That Leaked a CEO's Emails

Hector was the CEO of a rapidly growing tech company. Every day, he exchanged hundreds of emails with executives, investors, and legal teams—negotiating contracts, discussing confidential acquisitions, and outlining future product strategies.

To stay organized, Hector's email account was configured to automatically back up to a third-party cloud storage service. It was a seamless, behind-the-scenes process. He never gave it a second thought.

Until the breach.

Cybercriminals hacked into the storage provider's systems, breaching hundreds of business accounts in a matter of hours. Hector's inbox was among them. Years' worth of confidential communication—emails about funding rounds, patent filings, and internal HR matters—were now in the hands of criminals.

The fallout was immediate.

Investors backed away. Competitors learned about unreleased product features. A rival company mysteriously outbid Hector's firm on a major contract—using language pulled straight from a confidential email. The breach didn't just cause embarrassment; it cost the company millions.

And Hector had no idea it was even happening until a journalist contacted the company to ask about "leaked documents."

He had always assumed cloud backups were safe—encrypted, private, and impenetrable.

But like many executives, he hadn't considered that a weak link in a third-party provider could become a window into everything.

Hector thought his data was safely tucked away in the cloud.

He didn't realize the very tool meant to protect his business had made it dangerously exposed.

What You Need to Know

For most people, the cloud is invisible. A magical place where files go to stay safe, backed up, and always available. You upload, sync, and forget. Your photos, documents, passwords, emails, and memories—all floating somewhere "out there," protected by big tech companies and complex servers you never have to see.

Except the cloud isn't really magic. It's just someone else's computer.

And just like any other computer, it can crash. It can be hacked. It can be misconfigured. Or it can simply lock you out.

According to the 2024 ESG and Normalyze Cloud Data Security Report, 46% of organizations either confirmed or suspected they had lost sensitive data from cloud platforms like SaaS, IaaS, and PaaS within the past year. Not because they did something wrong – but because they trusted the system to work perfectly every time. Spoiler: it doesn't.

The cloud is convenient. It syncs across devices. It saves space. It's always there when you need it—until the moment it isn't. Accounts get suspended. Logins get hacked. Passwords are forgotten. Files are deleted by mistake, or automatically purged after a policy change you didn't notice. And when that happens, many users are shocked to learn that support is limited, recovery is unlikely, and there may be no actual person to talk to.

Cloud accounts are often seen as backups—but they're only backups if you control access and keep duplicates. If your cloud storage is your only copy, it's not a backup. It's a single point of failure.

And hackers know this.

Coordinated phishing campaigns regularly target users of three major cloud platforms. Cloud services are the top phishing bait—responsible for 27% of all clicked phishing links (Netskope, 2025 Cloud and Threat Report)

Why? Because when attackers impersonate cloud providers, people fall for it.

Fake "account suspension" emails tricked thousands into logging into cloned websites, handing over their passwords and multi-factor codes. Once inside, attackers downloaded entire archives—photos, contracts, personal records—and either encrypted them for ransom or sold them on dark web marketplaces.

And the victims? Many had no idea until weeks later, when their files were gone—or leaked.

You don't need to be a business executive or a celebrity to be a target. Everyday cloud accounts contain things that are extremely valuable: tax returns, insurance documents, scanned passports, medical records, personal photos, saved passwords, synced browser data, app keys. Files you uploaded once, forgot about, and now can't remember where they live—or who might be able to access them.

Even well-meaning sharing creates risk. You send a link to a friend or relative. You open up a folder to collaborate on something. But you forget to remove the permissions later. Or the link gets forwarded. Or the wrong file ends up in the right hands... then copied, saved, or leaked permanently.

Search engines crawl millions of "public" cloud links—most never meant to be public at all.

Many contain sensitive documents, photos, even medical records—exposed not by hackers, but by people forgetting to click "private."

One misconfigured setting. One forgotten permission. That's all it takes to leak everything.

And then there's data retention.

Deleting a file from your cloud account doesn't always mean it's gone. Most services keep "deleted" items for weeks—or store them indefinitely in backup servers. That's great for accidental recovery. But it also means your data can outlive your control over it. In legal cases, hacked backups, or insider leaks, even deleted content can come back to haunt you.

This chapter will walk you through how cloud storage really works—not just the tech, but the risks behind the convenience. You'll learn how to secure your cloud accounts, set up proper backups, review access logs, and remove old data that no longer needs to be there. You'll learn how to think differently about "safe" and how to take real ownership of what you store online.

Because trusting the cloud is easy. But protecting what's in it is your job—not someone else's.

Why It Matters

People talk about "the cloud" like it's a magical vault in the sky—eternal, invisible, and immune to disaster. But the truth is much less romantic and far more risky. The cloud is just someone else's computer. And that computer can crash, get hacked, shut down, or deny you access—sometimes without warning, and with devastating consequences.

Today, nearly everything is stored in the cloud: documents, emails, photos, passwords, health records, business data, tax returns, even entire family memories. We upload and forget. We sync and assume. We trust that a folder labeled "backup" or "Google Drive" is enough. But the cloud is not a guarantee. It's a service. And services can fail.

In fact, they do.

In 2021, a major European cloud provider suffered a catastrophic fire at a data center in Strasbourg. Millions of users lost access to their data permanently—not because of a hacker, but because of a hardware failure and a flawed disaster recovery plan. Some businesses never reopened. Some families never recovered years of digital memories.

Cloud platforms are also prime targets for cybercriminals.

According to Abnormal Security's 2024 State of Cloud Account Takeover Attacks report, account takeovers now top the list of concerns for security leaders—outranking even ransomware and spear phishing. A staggering 83% of organizations were hit by at least one takeover last year, with nearly half experiencing five or more. One in five endured over ten attacks.

And it's not just email anymore. From AWS, Google Cloud, and Azure to Dropbox, Docusign, and Gmail—every cloud app is a potential entry point. One compromised account can expose sensitive data, enable fraudulent transactions, or let attackers move laterally across your network. They're not breaking in. They're logging in.

And you might not even know it's happening.

Unlike your personal devices, most cloud services don't give you alerts for unusual activity unless you enable them. Many don't log out sessions on other devices. If a hacker logs in from another country but mimics your usual login behavior, they're invisible. And once inside, they can access years of emails, stored files, metadata, and contacts in seconds.

Then there's the business model. Cloud platforms aren't just storage lockers. They scan, index, and often analyze your files. Some offer AI-powered features that pull information from your documents or photos. That's convenient—until you realize your data is being mined in ways you never explicitly agreed to.

In 2025, multiple investigations revealed that cloud-based AI assistants had inadvertently indexed sensitive user documents while building language models—exposing them in search results to unauthorized users.

Worse yet, your data isn't always deleted when you think it is. Most cloud providers retain backups—even after you empty the trash. Their terms of service often allow them to store deleted content for 30, 90, or even 180 days, sometimes for legal compliance, sometimes "just in case." That deleted tax return or scanned passport photo may be recoverable—by someone who shouldn't have it.

There's also the problem of access control. Many cloud users share folders, links, or documents without checking the permissions. A shared resume folder with "anyone with the link can view" may contain personal info, address, or work history. A public cloud photo album may be indexed by search engines. Once something's been accessed, it can be downloaded, copied, and redistributed without your knowledge—and you'll never know who saw it or where it went.

Even the companies running these services aren't immune. Big Tech has a habit of quietly shutting down platforms, merging services, or changing storage policies. Your free storage may shrink, your files may be auto-deleted after inactivity, or a feature you rely on may vanish without notice. If you don't have a backup outside the cloud, you lose everything.

Legal access is another landmine. If you're incapacitated, pass away, or simply forget your login, your data could become permanently inaccessible. Without pre-arranged legacy access, loved ones can't retrieve your files, no matter how important or personal.

We've become dependent on a system that most of us don't fully understand. And that dependence comes with real risks.

The cloud is powerful. It's flexible. It's essential in many ways. But it's not foolproof. It's not immortal. And it's certainly not private by default.

Relying entirely on cloud storage without layered backups, strong security, and an exit strategy is like building your house on someone else's land—hoping they'll never sell, lock the doors, or tear it down.

Because when it comes to the cloud, what you upload today could disappear, leak, or be sold tomorrow.

What to Do About It – Your Security Checklist

1. **Use Encrypted Cloud Storage:** Choose cloud services that offer end-to-end encryption—not just encryption in transit or at rest. Look for platforms that let *you* manage the encryption keys.

2. **Enable Two-Factor Authentication (2FA):** Always protect your cloud storage accounts with 2FA. Use app-based authenticators instead of SMS for better protection against SIM swaps.

3. **Regularly Audit Shared Files and Folders:** Review who has access to what. Remove access for old collaborators, disable expired links, and turn off public folder settings you no longer use.

4. **Avoid Storing Everything in One Place:** Don't rely on a single cloud provider. Diversify your backups between multiple services and include offline, encrypted copies.

5. **Download Critical Files to Local Encrypted Drives:** Keep important documents and irreplaceable files stored securely offline in case your cloud provider suspends or deletes your account.

6. **Read the Fine Print:** Understand what your cloud provider can access, how long they retain "deleted" files, and under what circumstances they might hand over your data to authorities or third parties.

7. **Delete Files Securely:** Use built-in secure deletion tools or file shredders where available. Empty the trash or recycle bin regularly—many cloud providers retain deleted files for months.

8. **Don't Use Cloud Services for Password Storage:** Avoid saving login credentials in plain text within cloud folders or notes. Use a password manager designed for that purpose.

9. **Backup Cloud Data to a Second Cloud Account:** For extra security, periodically export or sync files from your primary cloud service to a secondary one with a different provider.

10. **Be Wary of Third-Party App Integrations:** Revoke access to any third-party app you no longer use. These often create backdoors into your cloud account.

11. **Monitor Account Activity:** Turn on login alerts, device history notifications, and access logs. Many providers offer these tools to help detect suspicious activity.

Quick Action Plan

1-Minute Fix: Enable two-factor authentication for your main cloud account and set alerts for suspicious login activity.

5-Minute Fix: Review your account's file-sharing settings and remove unnecessary public or shared links.

15-Minute Fix: Create a backup of your most valuable cloud-stored files and save them to an encrypted external drive or another trusted cloud account.

30-Minute Fix: Audit all third-party apps connected to your cloud, secure file permissions, enable encryption settings, and read your provider's data retention and privacy policies.

PART 7 - LOST & HACKED: YOUR EMERGENCY RESPONSE PLAN

Chapter 35

Losing Devices: How to Protect and Recover Fast

Real-World Scenarios

The Lost Phone That Let a Thief Drain a Bank Account

Audrey was finishing up her shopping when she reached into her bag—and froze.

Her phone was gone.

She retraced her steps. Dug through her purse. Checked the store counter. But it had vanished. Maybe it fell. Maybe someone grabbed it. Either way, it was no longer in her hands.

Then came the email: "Your bank password has been changed."

A cold dread filled him.

She raced to her laptop to check her account. But she was already locked out. Too late.

Whoever had her phone hadn't just taken a device—they had guessed her simple PIN code, opened her banking app, and transferred thousands out of her savings. It all happened in under 30 minutes.

Your phone's gone. Your life follows. Millions are stolen every year.

Crack a 4-digit PIN—and it's open season: Bank apps. Emails. Passwords. Everything.

By the time you get the alert, your money's gone—and it's not coming back.

Audrey thought she'd just misplaced her phone.

She didn't realize she had handed over the keys to her financial life.

The Stolen Tablet That Let a Thief Blackmail a Family

Riley used her tablet for everything—video calls with family, managing finances, storing photos of her kids, and checking private emails. It was her digital life in one lightweight device.

After a family dinner at a restaurant, she realized she'd left it behind. She called the staff, went back to check—but it was gone.

She assumed someone would turn it in.

They didn't.

Instead, whoever found the tablet dug into everything. Her private messages. Saved passwords. Cloud backups. And worse—personal photos and videos that were never meant to be shared.

A few days later, she got a message from an unknown number: "I have your files. Pay me $500 or I'll post them online."

She was being blackmailed.

Stolen devices don't just disappear—they're often used to exploit people. Without encryption or remote wipe settings, all that personal data is sitting there, fully exposed. Criminals know this. And they use what they find—photos, chats, documents—to extort, impersonate, or steal identities.

Riley thought her tablet was just a device for staying connected.

She didn't realize it held enough information to be used as a weapon against her.

The Kid's Lost Phone That Let a Stranger Track Their Location

Victor was 12. He brought his smartphone to school every day—mostly for games, chatting with friends, and staying in touch with his parents. One afternoon, the phone vanished. It wasn't in his bag. Not at his desk. Not in the lost and found.

His parents figured it would turn up eventually. It was just a phone. Nothing to panic about.

Until they checked the Google account activity.

Someone had logged in. And not just to browse. The stranger had opened Victor's location-sharing app, pulled up his real-time GPS, and was tracking his movements. They had access to his private messages. His photos. His contacts.

Someone Victor had never met now knew where he lived. Where he went after school. Who he talked to.

Lost devices are dangerous enough. But when a child's phone falls into the wrong hands, the risks multiply. Weak passwords, no screen lock, and automatic logins make it easy for predators to step into a child's digital world. From there, it's not hard to impersonate them, steal their identity, or worse—physically track them.

Victor thought he had just misplaced his phone.

He didn't know someone else was using it to follow him in real life.

The Business Owner's Phone That Fell into the Wrong Hands

Michael ran a thriving online business. Orders, shipping, inventory, payments—it was all managed through his phone. Apps for banking, CRM, customer service, and email were open around the clock.

One night, after a long meeting, he left his phone in the backseat of a taxi. By the time he realized, it was already too late.

The next morning, everything was unraveling.

Unauthorized transactions. Fake refund requests. Scam emails sent to customers. And then—total loss of access. The thief had reset his email, taken over his accounts, and locked him out of his business dashboard.

In one night, his trusted device became a weapon against him.

Business phones are goldmines for attackers. When they're not protected with strong security settings, encryption, or remote wipe capability, they offer everything a hacker needs: customer data, saved payment methods, admin access, and brand trust. Once breached, the fallout isn't just personal—it's professional.

Michael thought his phone was just a tool for work.

He didn't realize it could bring his entire business crashing down.

What You Need to Know

It only takes a second.

You're at a café. A meeting. An airport. You put your phone down—or your laptop, your tablet, your camera. You get distracted. And then it's gone.

Maybe it was stolen. Maybe it was lost. It doesn't matter. Because once that device is out of your hands, everything on it—and everything connected to it—is potentially in someone else's.

And if you haven't planned for that moment, you're already behind.

According to Gartner research, a laptop was stolen every 53 seconds. That number doesn't include phones left in taxis, tablets forgotten in hotel rooms, or USB drives dropped in parking lots. More than 70 million smartphones were lost or stolen globally last year, with fewer than 10% ever recovered (GSMA, 2025).

Most people don't have a recovery plan.

They don't enable tracking. They don't encrypt their drives. They don't use remote wiping tools. Many don't even use a proper screen lock or password. Which means when a device disappears, it's not just the hardware they're losing—it's access to everything they've stored, synced, and signed into.

Emails. Passwords. Bank apps. Work documents. Private photos. Cloud backups. Notes with PIN codes. Saved logins in browsers. Messaging apps still open. One unlocked device can hand over your entire digital life—no hacks required.

Even if the thief doesn't care about your photos or files, they care about what they can do with them.

Resell the device? Sure. But first, they might pull your saved credentials, clone your accounts, or install spyware to track your location and conversations. If the device has access to your cloud accounts—or worse, your password manager—they can gain access to everything else you own, across every other device.

The biggest mistake people make after losing a device is assuming the threat is over.

In reality, the clock is ticking. Fast.

According to a recent study by fintech start-up Nuke From Orbit, nearly 1 in 3 UK adults have been victims of phone theft—a staggering jump from just 17% in 2023.

It's not just the phones that vanished. It's the bank apps, cloud drives, photos, and digital lives they unlocked. Within 30 minutes of being stolen, many phones are already in the hands of someone who knows exactly how to extract data, bypass protections, or clone accounts.

Even if you have a strong passcode, that's not always enough. Not if your email is still logged in. Not if your cloud drive doesn't require re-authentication. Not if your password manager unlocks with a fingerprint—and your fingerprint is cached.

The good news? You can prepare for this.

Losing a device doesn't have to mean losing control. But you have to plan before it happens. Not after.

This chapter will walk you through what to do before you ever lose a device—so that if it happens, you can act fast, limit the damage, and protect your digital life. You'll learn how to:

- Set up tracking tools the right way
- Enable encryption for real protection
- Lock down sensitive apps and data
- Remotely wipe devices that go missing

- Use separate accounts for work and personal access
- Prevent automatic syncing from turning one lost device into a full-blown breach

You'll also learn how to respond quickly when something does go missing—who to contact, what to change, and how to know when a stolen device has led to deeper compromise.

Because most people only think about cybersecurity in terms of passwords or phishing. But physical loss is just as dangerous—maybe more.

If someone picks up your laptop in a coffee shop, they don't need to break into your home network. They're already in. If your unlocked phone is stolen, they don't need to trick you into revealing information. You've already handed it over.

The best way to beat that risk is to expect it. Plan for it. Build a system that doesn't collapse if one device goes missing. One where your data stays protected, your accounts stay locked, and your recovery takes minutes—not weeks.

This isn't about fear. It's about resilience. Because losing a device is inevitable.

Losing everything on it isn't.

Why It Matters

Everyone loses a device eventually. A phone slips out of a pocket. A tablet gets left in a hotel room. A laptop is forgotten in a taxi or taken from a parked car.

It feels like a bad moment. An inconvenience. Something to replace.

But losing a device can also mean losing control—over your data, your identity, your privacy, and sometimes your finances.

Because devices aren't just hardware anymore. They're access points.

A lost phone isn't just a phone. It's your text messages, your email, your banking app, your social media, your location history, your camera roll, your password manager, your calendar, your two-factor authentication codes, your cloud backups—and every app you forgot you even installed.

And if that device ends up in the wrong hands, the damage doesn't stop with the hardware.

According to the Bitglass Healthcare Breach Report (2014), 68% of healthcare data breaches over the past three years were caused by lost or stolen devices—not cyber-attacks. Hacking only made up 23%. Worse? 76% of all compromised medical records came from simple loss or theft.

While this data is now over a decade old and healthcare cybersecurity practices have evolved, it highlights a timeless risk: physical device loss can be just as damaging as a digital intrusion. More recent figures may differ, but the core threat remains relevant today.

No firewall failure. No dark web mastermind. Just a misplaced phone. A stolen USB.

And of those breaches, over half impacted not just the owner, but their workplace or family network as well.

That's because once a thief gets into your phone or laptop, they can:

- Access saved passwords and autofill credentials
- Intercept or reset login information across platforms
- Read private emails, messages, and documents
- Hijack apps tied to financial or cloud services
- Install spyware or ransomware
- Impersonate you using stored photos, contacts, or chats

And yes, it still happens—even with modern security features.

Many users don't enable biometric locks, don't require passcodes for every session, and don't encrypt their local storage. Others leave apps permanently logged in, with payment details, sensitive messages, or personal files just one tap away. And far too many people don't enable remote wipe or tracking features until it's too late.

Despite the risks, many users neglect basic device security; studies frequently show low adoption rates for features like device tracking and remote wipe (McAfee, 2023). That means most lost devices become silent liabilities, slowly leaking access to anyone who can power them on.

But even when a device is returned—sometimes the damage is already done. Because hackers don't need to keep your phone or laptop. They only need it for a few minutes. That's enough time to:

- Clone the SIM card
- Extract cookies and tokens
- Dump credentials from browsers
- Install remote access tools or surveillance apps
- Copy sensitive files to external storage

And unlike account hacks, physical compromises often don't generate alerts.

There's no email from Google saying someone tried to log in. No flag on your banking app. No text from your ISP. Everything looks normal—until it isn't. Until you see unfamiliar logins. Unauthorized purchases. A new phone number on your account. Or worse, nothing at all until your identity is already compromised.

This is why it matters. Because no one plans to lose a device. But almost no one prepares for it either.

You don't want to learn in hindsight that:

- Your backup was six months out of date
- Your password manager didn't require a master login
- Your cloud storage was automatically syncing sensitive data
- Your child's lost tablet was still logged into your email and PayPal
- Your business files were sitting unencrypted on a flash drive in your laptop bag

You want to be ready before it happens. Device loss isn't always preventable—but damage is.

Having strong screen locks, enabling encryption, using device tracking, setting up remote wipe, limiting what apps can access, and backing up data regularly doesn't just protect your privacy. It gives you the power to act—fast—if something goes wrong.

Because when your phone disappears at the airport, or your laptop vanishes during a hotel stay, or your tablet doesn't come back from school, you don't want panic. You want a plan.

This chapter exists to give you that plan. So one lost device doesn't turn into a lost identity.

What to Do About It – Your Security Checklist

1. **Set Strong Locks on All Devices:** Use PINs, biometrics, or complex passwords to lock smartphones, tablets, and laptops. Avoid swipe patterns or weak numerical codes.

2. **Enable Device Tracking Tools:** Turn on "Find My Device" or similar services on all devices. These tools allow you to locate, lock, or wipe your device remotely.

3. **Use Full-Disk Encryption:** Protect data on laptops and external drives with full-disk encryption (e.g., BitLocker for Windows, FileVault for macOS). Without encryption, lost devices can easily be accessed.

4. **Log Out of Cloud and Banking Apps After Use:** Never stay logged in on sensitive apps. If a device is lost, this gives thieves direct access to your accounts.

5. **Set Auto-Wipe on Failed Login Attempts:** Configure your devices to erase data after multiple failed login attempts if supported.

6. **Don't Store Sensitive Data Locally:** Avoid saving passwords, documents, or financial data directly on devices without encryption or proper app security.

7. **Use Password Managers With Remote Lockout:** Choose a password man-

ager that allows remote session termination in case your device is lost or stolen.

8. **Avoid Saving Passwords in Browsers:** Browsers are commonly targeted by thieves and malware. Disable autofill for sensitive credentials.

9. **Label Devices with Contact Info (Cautiously):** On laptops or tablets, use a non-invasive label (e.g., email address only) to help honest finders return your device—avoid including your home address.

10. **Back Up Everything Regularly:** Ensure your data is regularly backed up to secure cloud services or external drives so that physical loss doesn't result in permanent data loss.

11. **Know What's Logged In:** Keep a list of services where your device is signed in (Google, Apple, email, social media) so you can revoke access immediately if needed.

Quick Action Plan

1-Minute Fix: Turn on device tracking and location features like "Find My iPhone" or "Find My Device."

5-Minute Fix: Log out of sensitive apps, enable biometric login, and remove saved passwords from your browser.

15-Minute Fix: Set up automatic cloud backup for your most important files and enable remote wipe functionality.

30-Minute Fix: Create a lost-device response checklist: include revoking session access, wiping the device, and notifying banks or relevant services. Then test your ability to use each tool.

Chapter 36

Managing a Breach: What to Do After You're Hacked

Real-World Scenarios

The Email Hack That Let a Scammer Take Over Everything

Nicholas woke up to a flood of notifications. His phone buzzed nonstop with alerts—password reset requests, login attempts, and security warnings. At first, he assumed it was just a glitch or maybe a phishing scam he could ignore. But then he tried to check his email—and realized he was locked out.

Panic seized him.

In just a few hours while he slept, someone had taken control of his primary email account. At first, it seemed like an inconvenience. But as Nicholas began to assess the situation, it became clear that the consequences were far worse.

His PayPal account had been accessed and used for unauthorized transactions. His social media accounts were showing suspicious activity. Even his cloud storage had been logged into from an unfamiliar location. He began receiving calls from friends asking if he had really sent them strange messages.

The hacker had done exactly what so many cybercriminals do—they started with his email. Once they were in, they used password recovery links to reset access to nearly every account connected to that email. Bank accounts, digital wallets, storage drives, e-commerce profiles—anything that relied on email authentication was now vulnerable.

Nicholas felt helpless. He had always thought of his email as just a communication tool. He didn't realize that it was the digital master key to his entire online identity. The one account he used every day without thinking had now become the source of a massive breach.

By the time he contacted his bank, several transactions had already cleared. By the time he tried to reset his passwords, the hacker had already changed the recovery options and locked him out completely.

It took weeks to regain control—hours of calls, forms, and identity verification. But even then, some accounts were never fully recovered.

Nicholas's mistake wasn't clicking a bad link or falling for a scam. It was assuming that his email didn't need extra protection. He learned the hard way that a weak email password and no two-factor authentication could lead to a total digital collapse.

He thought of email as just another inbox.

He didn't realize it was the front door to everything.

The Bank Account That Was Drained While a Man Slept

It was just after midnight when Andrew's phone buzzed with a text from his bank.

"Did you authorize a $2,000 transfer?"

Still half-asleep, he tapped "No" on the alert, assuming the bank would freeze everything immediately. But by the time he logged into his app to check, the money was already gone.

In less than an hour, someone had drained a significant portion of his savings.

Andrew was stunned. He hadn't lost his card. He hadn't shared his login. But somewhere, somehow, someone had broken in. When the bank's fraud team investigated, the answer became painfully clear: his password had been compromised.

The attacker had used login credentials leaked during a previous data breach—one Andrew hadn't even known about. Worse, his banking password had been weak and reused across multiple platforms. That small lapse in security had made it easy for the hacker to access his account undetected.

Once inside, the fraudster initiated a transfer. The bank's system flagged it, but the automated fraud alert wasn't fast enough to stop it. Andrew's response came just seconds too late.

The money was gone.

Andrew had always believed his banking app was secure. It had a login code, fingerprint authentication, and a trusted interface. But none of that mattered when the weakest link—his password—was already exposed.

He spent the next few days on the phone with his bank, filing claims and disputing the transfer. Some of the funds were eventually recovered, but the emotional toll was lasting. He began to question every app, every login, every platform he had trusted.

He changed all his passwords, added two-factor authentication, and signed up for breach monitoring. But the damage had been done.

Andrew thought his bank account was protected by technology.

He didn't realize that a single weak password could open the vault.

The Cloud Storage Breach That Exposed Private Photos

Allison had always considered her cloud storage account a digital vault—safe, convenient, and accessible from anywhere. Over the years, she had uploaded thousands of personal photos: family vacations, birthday celebrations, candid moments with friends. Alongside those were documents—tax returns, medical records, scans of her ID, even a copy of her lease.

Everything lived in the cloud. And she assumed it was secure.

Then, one morning, she received an email notification.

"Your cloud storage has been accessed from an unrecognized device."

Her stomach tightened. She tried to log in immediately, but her password no longer worked. By the time she regained access using account recovery tools, the damage had already been done.

A hacker had broken into her account, downloaded everything, and left behind a chilling message:

"We have your photos and files. If you don't pay $1,000 in cryptocurrency, they'll be published online."

Allison stared at the message in disbelief. The threat wasn't just financial—it was deeply personal. These weren't just digital files; they were pieces of her life. Pictures she had never shared publicly. Documents containing everything from her Social Security number to her home address.

The hacker had exploited a weak password—one she had reused on other accounts. When one of those services suffered a data breach months earlier, her credentials ended up for sale on the dark web. The cloud account was just one of many vulnerable targets.

Allison reported the incident, contacted her bank, and froze her credit. But the emotional damage was harder to contain. For weeks, she lived in fear that her most intimate files would be leaked. She had to explain the situation to her family, her employer, and even her friends.

She had trusted the cloud to protect her memories and personal information.

What she didn't realize was that the security of that digital vault was only as strong as the key she used to lock it.

The Streaming Service That Led to Identity Theft

Victor was settling in for a quiet night when he received a strange notification.

"A new device has logged into your Netflix account."

He assumed it was nothing—maybe he had logged in from another device earlier or forgotten to sign out somewhere. It didn't seem urgent, so he ignored it.

That mistake cost him more than he ever expected.

Within days, fraudulent charges appeared on his bank statement. His email account locked him out. Then came calls from financial institutions he'd never contacted, asking about loan applications he hadn't submitted. Confused and panicked, Victor started piecing things together—and what he found shocked him.

The Netflix notification hadn't been a glitch.

A hacker had accessed his account using login credentials stolen in a previous data breach. Victor had reused the same password for multiple services, including his email and cloud storage. Once inside his Netflix account, the hacker found his billing details—including a saved credit card. From there, they were able to reset his email password, access sensitive messages, and collect enough personal information to begin opening fake accounts in his name.

It was a classic domino effect. One seemingly harmless breach spiraled into full-blown identity theft.

Victor spent weeks cleaning up the mess—freezing his credit, disputing charges, changing every password he could remember. He reported the incident to law enforcement, but by then, several accounts had already been opened using his name. He had to explain to banks, merchants, and even a debt collector that he had been a victim of fraud.

The experience taught him a brutal lesson: there's no such thing as a "low-risk" account anymore.

He had always thought of his Netflix login as trivial—a convenience, not a vulnerability. But hackers don't make that distinction. They look for any entry point, and once they're in, they go deeper.

Victor thought his streaming account was just entertainment.

He didn't realize it was the front door to his identity.

What You Need to Know

Let's be honest—getting hacked feels awful.

It's confusing. It's embarrassing. It's overwhelming. Maybe you got a strange alert. Maybe your account was locked. Maybe a charge hit your card and you didn't make it. Maybe a friend messaged you, "Did you mean to send me this weird link?" And suddenly, the question hits:

Am I hacked?

The answer might be yes.

In 2024, your odds of staying safe online were slimmer than ever.

According to the Identity Theft Resource Center, over 1.2 billion personal accounts were compromised through phishing, malware, data leaks, and social engineering attacks. At the same time, data breach notices exploded—rising 211% from 419 million in 2023 to more than 1.3 billion in just one year.

Many of these breaches weren't discovered until days or even weeks later, long after the damage had begun. By the time victims realized what had happened, their accounts were drained, identities stolen, and personal data scattered across the dark web.

And make no mistake: the worst thing you can do is nothing.

Hacks rarely stay isolated. A stolen email password can be used to reset your bank login. A compromised social account can be used to scam your friends. A single breached password, reused across accounts, can give hackers a master key to your digital life. That's why managing a breach isn't just about closing one door—it's about making sure all the others haven't been opened.

But here's the good news: you don't have to panic.

You just have to act fast.

What most people get wrong is that they wait. They hope it's nothing. They hesitate because they're unsure what to do—or they don't want to admit what happened. Meanwhile, the attacker has time to move laterally, gathering more data, syncing with more apps, reaching into more systems.

The average hacker doesn't stop at one account. They look for patterns, reuse, and shortcuts. If they compromise your email, they check what other accounts are linked. If they get your phone number, they try SIM swaps. If they grab your cloud drive, they scan for saved passwords and photos of IDs. It's not personal. It's procedural. And it's fast.

That's why a hacked account isn't the end of the story—it's the start of a checklist.

And that's what this chapter is built for.

You'll learn how to recognize the signs of a breach—some obvious, some subtle. You'll understand what to do in the first 15 minutes after discovering a compromise. Which passwords to change. Which accounts to lock. How to check for unauthorized logins. How to secure your devices. How to track where else the breach might have gone. And how to avoid getting hit again.

Because often, a breach happens in silence.

In 2023, IBM reported that on average, it takes 204 days to detect a data breach. That's nearly seven months where someone else could be reading your emails, monitoring your habits, or using your credentials behind the scenes.

For individuals, the window of damage is much smaller—but still devastating.

Stolen passwords are frequently exploited in fraudulent activities shortly after compromise, often within hours—especially when linked to financial or email accounts, according to cybersecurity response patterns.

If your phone is compromised, access to two-factor codes is gone. If your email is breached, password resets for everything else become easy. And if you don't have backups, a hacker encrypting your files could mean losing everything—unless you pay.

The key is not just to respond—but to contain.

Changing your password is good. But not if the attacker still has your device. Securing your account helps—but only if your recovery options (email, phone, backup codes) haven't been compromised. It's not just about fixing what broke—it's about making sure nothing else breaks next.

This chapter is your guide through the fog.

The post-hack playbook.

The calm after the storm.

Because being hacked isn't the end of your security—it's the beginning of your awareness.

What matters most is how you respond. Quickly. Thoughtfully. And thoroughly.

Yes, it's stressful. Yes, it's personal. But it's also preventable—next time. And that's what we'll help you build by the end of this chapter: not just a recovery plan, but a defense plan.

Because once you've been hacked, you don't go back to normal.

You move forward smarter.

Why It Matters

No one wants to believe it'll happen to them.
But eventually, it happens to someone in every household, team, or friend group: a hacked account, a drained wallet, a compromised cloud drive, a stolen identity. It doesn't always come with a bang. Sometimes it starts with something small—a strange notification, a forgotten login, a purchase you don't remember making.

And by the time you realize something's wrong, the damage is already spreading.

A breach isn't always dramatic. It can be slow, quiet, and devastating. The key to surviving one? Acting quickly—and knowing what to do.

While organizational breach detection times are well-documented, individual responses to personal data breaches vary widely. Estimates suggest many consumers take weeks to recognize and react to identity theft or data compromise—giving hackers a dangerous head start. During that window, they can access emails, drain bank accounts, steal cloud backups, impersonate you, or reset your credentials without resistance.

Why does this delay happen?

Because most people don't know what to look for. They ignore subtle signs—a login from a new device, a password reset email they didn't request, an app behaving strangely, a charge for $1.99 that seems too small to care about. But these are all warning signs that the breach is already underway.

And every hour you wait gives the attacker more ground. Hackers move fast. In a credential-based breach, they'll often:

- Change your recovery email and phone number
- Lock you out of your own account
- Turn off security notifications
- Export files, photos, or contacts
- Use saved payment methods to buy gift cards or subscriptions
- Try the same email-password combo on dozens of other sites

In less than a day, a single stolen login can become access to your bank, cloud drive, medical records, crypto wallet, and more. What's worse is that many people make it easier without realizing it.

They reuse passwords. They stay logged in. They link accounts to each other. They skip enabling 2FA. They save passwords in browsers without locking the device. These habits give attackers momentum—and make recovery harder.

That's why it matters.

Because once a breach happens, you don't have time to Google what to do. You need to move—deliberately, fast, and thoroughly. The biggest myth people believe is that "changing your password fixes it." It doesn't.

If your email is compromised, the attacker can:

- Reset other accounts using email verification
- Set up forwarding rules to monitor your messages
- Archive password reset emails so you don't see them
- Use your contacts to launch scams from your name

If your phone number is compromised through SIM swapping, they can:

- Bypass two-factor authentication
- Access banking apps tied to your phone

- Lock you out of accounts—even after you change the password

If your computer is compromised with malware or a keylogger, changing passwords won't stop the attack—because everything you type is still being recorded.

This is why a breach recovery plan isn't just helpful. It's essential.

It should include:

- Knowing your most critical accounts (email, banking, ID services)
- Keeping secure backups of important files and documents
- Using a password manager to create and store strong, unique logins
- Enabling two-factor authentication wherever possible
- Having device tracking and remote wipe enabled
- Keeping copies of recovery codes for key accounts
- Monitoring credit reports and account activity after a breach

A solid recovery plan can be the difference between a bad day and a full-blown digital disaster.

Enabling two-factor authentication and setting up remote account recovery doesn't just speed up your response—it cuts off the damage.

People who prepare don't just bounce back faster—they're far less likely to get hit again. Because once attackers find a weakness, they usually come back for more.

Because when you don't fix the root cause—attackers come back.

This chapter matters because your digital life is more connected than you think. One weak password, one unchecked email, one compromised device can cascade into a crisis that affects your money, your identity, your family, and even your career.

Knowing what to do after a breach doesn't just reduce the damage—it helps you take back control.

Not in panic. Not in fear. But with a system you've already thought through, while your head is still clear.

What to Do About It – Your Security Checklist

1. **Change Affected Passwords Immediately:** Start with your most sensitive accounts—email, banking, cloud storage—and use unique, strong passwords for each one.

2. **Enable or Reset Two-Factor Authentication (2FA):** If 2FA isn't already on, turn it on now. If it is, reset it—especially if SMS was used and SIM swapping is suspected.

3. **Run a Full Malware Scan:** Use a reputable antivirus tool to scan all affected devices for malware, spyware, or keyloggers that may have led to the breach.

4. **Check for Unauthorized Access:** Review login activity for suspicious locations, devices, or changes in settings on your most-used services.

5. **Revoke Suspicious Sessions:** Log out of all sessions or remove unauthorized devices from your accounts (Google, Apple ID, Facebook, etc.).

6. **Notify Your Bank or Credit Card Issuer:** If any financial accounts may be impacted, notify your provider immediately to freeze or monitor your cards.

7. **Freeze Your Credit (if necessary):** If personal identity information has been leaked, place a freeze on your credit reports to prevent new accounts from being opened in your name.

8. **Check for Forwarding Rules or Inbox Filters:** Hackers often set up auto-forwarding rules in compromised email accounts to monitor your activity even after you reset the password.

9. **Review App Permissions:** Ensure no new apps or browser extensions were added without your knowledge. Remove or disable anything unfamiliar.

10. **Update All Software:** Breaches often occur through outdated apps or operating systems. Install all pending updates and enable automatic updates going forward.

11. **Notify Affected Contacts (If Necessary):** If your social media or email was used to send scam messages, inform your contacts to avoid further spread.

12. **Document the Incident:** Keep a record of what happened, when you noticed it, what actions you took, and who you contacted. This helps in any future legal or financial steps.

Quick Action Plan

1-Minute Fix: Change passwords on your primary email and bank accounts, and enable two-factor authentication.

5-Minute Fix: Revoke account access from unknown devices and sessions. Scan your devices for malware.

15-Minute Fix: Notify your bank, check inbox rules, and freeze credit if identity theft is suspected.

30-Minute Fix: Update all apps and operating systems, audit account permissions, and create a written breach report for your records.

Chapter 37

Breached Accounts: Track Them Before Criminals Do

Real-World Scenarios

The Bank Account That Was Hacked Six Months Before the Owner Noticed

Kevin prided himself on being financially responsible. He paid his bills on time, avoided debt, and rarely splurged. But he didn't check his online bank statements regularly. With automatic payments and a modest lifestyle, he felt no urgent need to monitor every transaction. Everything seemed fine—until one afternoon, curiosity prompted him to log in.

What he saw left him frozen.

There were dozens of unfamiliar transactions. Most were small—$5 here, $10 there—easily overlooked. But nestled between them was a $500 withdrawal he hadn't made. His account balance was much lower than it should have been.

Kevin immediately contacted his bank, and what he learned was worse than he expected.

His account had been compromised for over six months.

A hacker had used login credentials from a previous data breach to quietly access his account. Instead of draining it all at once, they started small—testing the waters to see if anyone was paying attention. When no one flagged the charges, they continued. Over time, they siphoned off hundreds of dollars, slowly and steadily.

Kevin hadn't noticed. And that's what the hacker was counting on.

By the time he reported the fraud, the money was gone—and much of it was unrecoverable. The bank could only reimburse part of the loss. The rest had vanished into the digital ether, likely dispersed across untraceable accounts.

Kevin felt violated, foolish, and frustrated. He had always assumed that if something were wrong, the bank would catch it. But in reality, financial institutions rely heavily on customers to flag suspicious activity—especially when the charges are small enough to evade detection.

He changed all his passwords, enabled two-factor authentication, and signed up for transaction alerts. But the damage had already been done.

Kevin thought his bank account was protected by default.

He didn't realize that inattention was all a hacker needed to silently steal from him—for half a year.

The Email Breach That Gave a Hacker Access to Everything

Theresa was used to getting junk emails. So when she received a password reset notification for her primary email account, she assumed it was spam. She hadn't requested a reset, and she didn't click anything. Instead, she ignored it and went about her day.

A few days later, she tried to log in—and was locked out.

Her password didn't work. The recovery options had been changed. Her email, the one she had used for over a decade, was no longer hers.

Panic set in as she realized how much of her digital life was tied to that one inbox. Her social media, her banking, her cloud storage, even her online shopping accounts—all linked to the same email address. And now, someone else controlled it.

A cybersecurity expert later confirmed the breach had started with credentials exposed in an old data leak. A hacker had used those details to access her email, reset the passwords to every connected account, and lock her out of her own digital identity. It had all happened quietly—without a single click or malware infection.

Theresa scrambled to recover what she could. She spent hours on the phone with support teams, proving her identity, requesting account recoveries, and trying to outrun the damage. But in the days the hacker held access, they had already scraped her contacts, changed her financial passwords, and forwarded sensitive emails to a private inbox.

She had thought that one suspicious email wasn't a big deal.

She didn't realize it was the first domino in a chain of digital destruction.

Email isn't just a place for communication. It's the master key to almost every aspect of a person's online life. And when that key falls into the wrong hands, it can open every door.

Theresa now uses separate emails for personal and financial matters, with two-factor authentication on everything. But the experience left her shaken.

She thought her email was just an inbox.

She didn't realize it was the foundation of her entire identity.

The Subscription Services That Were Draining a Man's Bank Account

Henry was reviewing his bank statement when he noticed a $12.99 charge from a streaming service he didn't recognize. At first, he assumed it was a billing error—maybe something his kids signed up for, or a forgotten free trial that had turned into a paid plan.

But when he looked more closely, a disturbing pattern emerged.

There were multiple recurring charges—some for $5.99, others for $14.99—all from various services he'd never used. Music platforms, mobile games, niche streaming sites. Most were small amounts, just enough to fly under the radar.

It didn't make sense. He hadn't signed up for any of them.

Henry called his bank and requested a full transaction history. What he found was staggering. Over the past few months, nearly a dozen subscriptions had been billed to his credit card. Some were international. Others were tied to email addresses he didn't recognize.

A hacker had used his stolen credit card information to create multiple fake accounts across different services. They used his name and card to pay for subscriptions—slowly, consistently—knowing that the small amounts wouldn't trigger immediate fraud alerts.

Henry had become the invisible wallet funding someone else's entertainment.

Because the charges were so small and spread across months, he hadn't noticed them piling up. And by the time he discovered it, hundreds of dollars had already been siphoned away.

The fraud team at his bank confirmed that his card details were likely purchased on the dark web, possibly after being exposed in a previous data breach. The hacker hadn't tried to make a big purchase or withdraw cash—that would have been obvious. Instead, they'd taken the quiet route: death by a thousand microcharges.

Henry canceled the card, filed a fraud report, and spent hours contacting the services to shut down the fake accounts. But the experience shook him.

He thought he was just paying his usual monthly bills.

He didn't realize he was unknowingly funding a hacker's streaming spree—one $12 .99 charge at a time.

The Work Data That Was Stolen and Sold Online

Scarlett had recently transitioned to remote work and, like many employees, used her personal email to access a few work-related platforms. It was easier than constantly switching accounts. Besides, she figured her password was strong, and she wasn't storing anything too sensitive.

Then one day, she received a login alert from a location she didn't recognize.

She dismissed it. Probably just a glitch, she thought.

A month later, her world turned upside down.

Her company's leadership called an emergency meeting. Confidential client files had been leaked online—financial reports, proposals, even internal communications. The breach had been traced back to a compromised login. And the email used to access the platform?

It was Scarlett's.

The hacker had used credentials found in an old data breach—her personal email and password, which she had reused for multiple platforms. With that access, they had logged into the company's cloud workspace, browsed project folders, and quietly exfiltrated sensitive files over time.

No malware. No dramatic ransomware attack. Just a simple login that unlocked everything.

The stolen data ended up on the dark web, bundled and sold to unknown buyers. Clients were furious. Trust was shattered. The company now faced legal scrutiny and reputational damage—and Scarlett was at the center of it all.

She was devastated.

She hadn't meant to put anyone at risk. She had simply used her personal email for convenience. But in doing so, she became the weakest link—a small oversight with massive consequences.

Scarlett spent weeks working with IT and legal teams, trying to contain the fallout. She was never fired, but her role changed. So did the way she viewed digital responsibility.

She thought her personal email wasn't a big deal.

She didn't realize it was the doorway a hacker used to walk right into her company's most private data—and leave with it.

What You Need to Know

Your information is already out there.

That's not an exaggeration. It's not a scare tactic. It's the reality of living in a connected world. If you've used the internet for more than a few years—signed up for an account, ordered something online, joined a social network—your data has likely been involved in a breach.

Not maybe. Probably.

In 2024, over 28 billion records were exposed in data breaches that flooded both the public internet and the dark web.

Emails, passwords, phone numbers, credit card details, even home addresses – nothing was spared.

It wasn't just random leaks; mega-breaches like MOAB and NPD tore open the gates, unleashing a tidal wave of stolen data.

If you think this doesn't affect you, think again.

Your information is probably already out there – waiting to be used against you.

But here's the problem: when a data breach happens, you're rarely the first to know.

The company may not alert you. The leak may go undiscovered for months. And even when a breach is announced, most people ignore the email—or never see it in the first place. Meanwhile, cybercriminals are already scanning the stolen data. They're testing the logins. Trying the passwords. Selling the access. And you're still using the same credentials across multiple sites, completely unaware.

That's how identity theft starts. Quietly.

It's not always a hacker breaking into your system. Often, it's someone logging in using the exact same email and password you've used since 2018—because those credentials were exposed in a breach you forgot about. This is called credential stuffing, and it's one of the most effective and least visible types of attack.

Hackers don't guess your password. They reuse it.

That's why account takeovers (ATOs) are everywhere.

A Security.org survey reveals that 29% of Americans have fallen victim to account takeover fraud (ATO). That's roughly 77 million people.

And the damage isn't small.

In 2023 alone, ATO attacks drained nearly $13 billion, according to Javelin.

One stolen login. One reused password.

That's all it takes to lose everything.

All it takes is one breach. One reused password. And suddenly, the fraudster has keys to your whole digital life.

This is why tracking breaches matters.

Because you can't stop what you don't know about. And if you're not monitoring where your data has been leaked, you're leaving the door open for someone else to walk in.

But here's the good news: it's fixable.

You can't prevent every data breach in the world. But you can control how you respond. You can monitor your email addresses, usernames, and passwords using legitimate breach alert tools. You can set up notifications that tell you if your credentials are exposed again. You can rotate your passwords regularly. Use a password manager. Enable multi-factor authentication. And avoid reusing the same logins across platforms.

Because if a hacker tries to use your old Netflix password on your bank account—and it doesn't work—that's not luck. That's good hygiene.

This chapter will show you how to check if your accounts have already been breached. You'll learn where to look, how to use breach detection tools, how to respond when your data shows up in a leak, and how to take back control—one password at a time.

We'll also cover the red flags of a breach you might not notice at first. Like unfamiliar logins. Unexpected password reset emails. Strange devices showing up in your account activity. Because breaches don't always shout—they whisper. And if you don't know what to listen for, they'll pass you by... until the damage is already done.

You'll learn how to separate accounts by risk—so a breach in one area doesn't affect everything. You'll get smarter about account recovery, email security, and how to use breach data as an early warning system—not just a post-incident regret.

Because the worst kind of data breach isn't the one that happens to a company.

It's the one that silently turns you into a victim—without you even realizing.

Don't wait for a stolen identity, drained account, or locked email to tell you something went wrong.

Track your breaches now, before someone else does.

Why It Matters

You don't always feel it when a breach happens.

Your login still works. Your bank app still opens. Your inbox looks normal. Everything seems fine—until it's not.

Because by the time you notice something's off—a password reset you didn't request, a strange purchase on your card, a friend asking why you emailed them a weird link—someone may have been using your data for days, weeks, or even months.

This is how most breaches unfold.

Not with alarms and flashing screens, but quietly. Silently.
While you go about your life, a hacker might already be going through your accounts.

That's why tracking breaches matters—not after the fact, but before the consequences hit.

In 2024, the Identity Theft Resource Center (ITRC) reported 3,158 data compromises in the U.S., resulting in approximately 1.35 billion victim notices being issued. These incidents exposed a wide range of sensitive information, including names, emails, passwords, Social Security numbers, addresses, medical records, and credit card data.

But not every breach makes the news. And not every company notifies you when your data is compromised.

Some try to contain it quietly. Others delay disclosure for months. And many people don't realize their information is floating on the dark web until something goes terribly wrong. That's what makes proactive breach tracking so important.

Because once your information leaks, it doesn't disappear.

It gets copied, sold, shared, and reused.

It becomes part of credential stuffing databases—used by bots to test your email and password combo on hundreds of sites until one of them works. It gets used to send fake invoices, scam messages, or phishing emails in your name. And if the breach includes your phone number, address, or personal security questions, it may be used for impersonation, identity theft, or SIM swapping.

And the biggest risk? You likely reused that same password somewhere else.

According to Bitwarden's 2024 World Password Day survey, 72% of Gen Z users still reuse the same passwords across multiple accounts—far higher than Boomers, who clock in at just 42%.

That's not a tech gap. It's burnout.

Too many logins. Too many accounts. Too many "create a strong password" prompts.

They call it password fatigue—and it's a hacker's dream.

Because once one account gets breached?

The rest fall like dominoes.

That gap—between awareness and action—is where hackers thrive.

Tools like "Have I Been Pwned," Firefox Monitor, and Google Password Checkup exist for a reason: to help you find out when your data has been compromised. But most people don't check until after the damage is done. Why?

Because breach fatigue is real. There are so many incidents, across so many platforms, that it becomes background noise. You start thinking, "Well, it's probably already out there," and move on. But ignoring a breach doesn't make you safer. It makes you an easier target.

Especially when your breached data becomes someone else's weapon.

In 2024, multiple breaches exposed the login credentials of thousands of users from small e-commerce platforms. Hackers used that data to access PayPal, Amazon, and Apple accounts—because many victims used the same email and password combination everywhere. The breach didn't just cost money—it led to lost files, hijacked accounts, and stolen identities.

That's the hidden cost of ignoring breaches. It's not just what happens on the hacked platform. It's what happens next.

This is why breach monitoring needs to become a routine part of digital life—just like checking your bank account or locking your front door. You don't need to be technical. You just need to pay attention. Here's what matters:

- Signing up for breach alert services using your main email address
- Watching for suspicious password reset emails
- Being cautious about reused passwords or old accounts you forgot existed
- Deleting accounts you no longer use
- Using unique passwords and enabling 2FA—especially after a breach
- Changing credentials immediately if your data shows up in a leak

Because the best time to respond to a breach isn't after you're hacked. It's the moment the leak is discovered.

This chapter is here to reframe the way we think about breach alerts. They're not just warnings. They're opportunities. A chance to slam the door shut before someone walks through it. Because whether it's your email, your passwords, or your personal files, you want to be the one who finds the breach first— not the criminal already using it.

What to Do About It – Your Security Checklist

1. **Check Your Email on Breach Databases:** Use services like HaveIBeenPwned.com or Firefox Monitor to see if your email addresses and passwords have been leaked.

2. **Set Up Data Breach Alerts:** Enable notifications from these services so you're automatically alerted if your email or credentials appear in a new data breach.

3. **Rotate Compromised Passwords:** If your account was exposed in a breach, immediately change the password—even if you haven't seen suspicious activity yet.

4. **Use a Password Manager to Stay Organized:** Store all your credentials securely and receive alerts if any of your stored logins are affected by a known breach.

5. **Avoid Password Reuse:** Never reuse the same password across multiple services—especially for your email, banking, and cloud accounts.

6. **Monitor for Credential Stuffing Attacks:** Check your login history and account activity regularly for suspicious access from unknown IP addresses or devices.

7. **Enable Two-Factor Authentication (2FA) Everywhere:** If hackers get your password, 2FA can still stop them from accessing your accounts.

8. **Secure Your Primary Email Account First:** Since it controls password resets for other services, your main email account must be your most secure one.

9. **Delete Old or Unused Accounts**: Reduce your digital exposure by closing accounts you no longer use—especially those tied to your email or credit card.

10. **Search for Your Personal Info Online:** Occasionally search your name, email, or phone number to see if personal details are circulating on data leak forums.

11. **Request Data Deletion from Sites You No Longer Use:** Some websites allow you to delete your data upon request. Use tools like JustDelete.me to guide you.

12. **Review App and Extension Permissions:** Remove access from any third-party apps that no longer need your data or could be a risk.

Quick Action Plan

1-Minute Fix: Check your email on HaveIBeenPwned and sign up for breach notifications.

5-Minute Fix: Change passwords on any exposed accounts and enable two-factor authentication.

15-Minute Fix: Delete old or unused accounts and audit your password manager for reused or weak credentials.

30-Minute Fix: Review account login histories, clean up third-party app permissions, and search for personal data exposure online.

Chapter 38

Backup and Recovery: Save Your Data Before You Cry

Real-World Scenarios

The Accidental Click That Erased a Family's Memories

Sofia had always been the unofficial memory keeper of her family. Her laptop held it all—baby pictures, school concerts, holiday celebrations, scanned report cards, and even the last voice message from her grandmother. It was a digital time capsule of love, laughter, and legacy.

One evening, while trying to free up space for a new video project, she began clearing old files. She was in a rush—clicking quickly, dragging folders, and emptying the recycle bin without double-checking what she had selected.

It wasn't until days later, while searching for a childhood photo for her daughter's school project, that she realized what had happened. The folder—the one with years of photos and home videos—was gone.

Panic set in. She searched everywhere. Recovery tools, tech forums, professional help. But the files had already been overwritten. They were truly gone—beyond reach, beyond rescue.

Sofia broke down. Birthdays, first steps, family vacations—memories that only existed digitally had vanished with a single misclick.

She had always assumed those files would be there when she needed them. She never thought one routine cleanup would erase years of family history.

The Ransomware Attack That Locked a Man's Life

Owen sat down at his desk one morning, coffee in hand, ready to prepare tax documents for his small business. But when he turned on his computer, instead of the usual desktop, a black screen greeted him with bold red letters:

"All your files have been encrypted. Pay $800 in Bitcoin within 72 hours or lose everything forever."

His hands went cold.

Every file—work invoices, family photos, saved passwords, years of tax records—had been locked. He clicked through folder after folder, helpless as everything he had stored over the past decade was replaced with gibberish.

Desperate, he contacted a cybersecurity expert. The verdict was grim: a ransomware strain had infected his system. Without a backup, there was no guarantee of recovery—even if he paid the ransom. And worse, many victims who do pay never receive their files back.

Owen had always assumed that his computer was enough—that having everything on one device was secure. But in that moment, he learned a painful lesson: one wrong click, one malicious email, one lapse in protection could cost everything.

He didn't just lose data—he lost years of work, personal history, and peace of mind.

The Hard Drive That Died Silently

Walter was the kind of person who prided himself on staying organized. He kept meticulous financial records for his business, spreadsheets tracking every expense, scanned receipts, contracts, and client files—all stored safely on an external hard drive he used religiously.

Or so he thought.

One afternoon, he plugged in the drive as usual, ready to update his books—and nothing happened. No lights. No spinning. No recognition from his laptop. The drive was silent.

He tried different cables, different ports, even a different computer. Still nothing.

Panicked, he took it to a data recovery center. The technician gave him a sympathetic look and said, "This could be a mechanical failure. We'll try, but it may cost over $2,000—and there's no guarantee we'll get your files back."

Walter had no backup. That drive was his only copy of everything.

He had trusted that as long as the drive hadn't been dropped or damaged, it would just keep working. But like many others, he didn't realize that external hard drives can and do fail—often without warning.

In that moment, Walter understood a hard truth: a backup isn't truly a backup unless there's more than one.

The Cloud Account That Was Suddenly Deleted

Rebecca considered herself tech-savvy. She had long since moved away from external drives and local storage, opting instead for the sleek convenience of cloud storage. Everything—from her university papers and tax documents to personal photos and creative projects—was stored neatly in folders on a major cloud platform.

She never worried about data loss. After all, the cloud was supposed to be safe.

But one morning, when Rebecca tried to log in to access an important work file, she was met with an alarming message: "Your account has been suspended due to a policy violation."

Stunned, she checked her email for any prior warnings. There were none. She attempted to contact support, but the responses were cold and automatic: her account had been terminated, the decision was final, and no appeal would be accepted.

And worst of all—her data was gone. Permanently.

She hadn't kept local backups. Why would she? The whole point of the cloud, she believed, was that it was reliable and always accessible.

But what she hadn't realized was that cloud service providers reserve the right to suspend or delete accounts at their discretion. Sometimes it's due to an error. Other times, it's the result of automated systems flagging false positives. Regardless of the reason, once an account is locked or deleted, the data is often unrecoverable.

Rebecca sat at her desk in disbelief. Years of work and personal memories—disappeared in seconds, with no warning.

She thought the cloud was her safety net.

Instead, it became the trapdoor beneath her feet.

What You Need to Know

Every year, millions of people lose something irreplaceable.

It could be 10 years of family photos. It could be a book you were writing. Your wedding video. Your child's first steps. Your graduation speech. Business records. Tax documents. Passwords. Or just the things you thought were safely sitting on your device, waiting for you to need them again someday.

Until one day, they're gone.

A power surge fries your hard drive. A ransomware attack locks your files. Your phone slips out of your pocket and vanishes. Your laptop crashes without warning. Or your cloud provider suspends your account for "suspicious activity" and deletes your files with no appeal. It happens fast, and it happens more often than you think.

In a 2024 survey by ExpressVPN, 38% of individuals across the U.S., UK, Germany, and France admitted they lost important data simply because they didn't back it up.

Not to hackers. Not to ransomware.

Just gone—because they didn't take a few minutes to prepare.

Photos, documents, memories—vanished. In most cases, it wasn't a cyberattack. It was neglect.

The number one reason? No backup. 22% of all respondents reported never backing up their data.

The number two? Incomplete or outdated backups that didn't include the most recent files.

And yet, most people don't back up their data at all.

Why? Because it feels unnecessary—until the day it isn't.

Because they assume someone else is protecting it. Because cloud storage is convenient. Because external drives are clunky. Because backup plans sound boring and technical. Because they've "never had a problem before."

But backup isn't about what already happened.

It's about what will.

Every device fails eventually. Every account can be hacked. Every app can glitch. And when that day comes, you have two options: restore and move on—or start from zero.

The difference between those two outcomes is simple: preparation.

Backing up your data doesn't need to be complex. But it does need to be done intentionally. If your only copy of your important files is on your phone, that's not a backup. If your cloud sync is storing everything in a single folder—without version history or offline copies—that's not a backup. And if your "backup drive" is sitting in the same house as your primary device, unplugged and untouched for two years, that's not protection. That's just false peace of mind.

A proper backup system has three key principles:

1. Multiple copies
2. Multiple locations
3. Regular updates

That means your files should exist in more than one place. At least one of those places should be offline (not connected to the internet). And your backups should run automatically or on a schedule—because a backup that's six months old is just slightly better than none at all.

But backup is only half the equation. The other half is recovery.

Because when something goes wrong, it's not enough to have your files "somewhere." You need to know how to get them back. How fast you can access them. How complete the restore will be. And whether the process will make things worse or better.

A global study by Western Digital and Researchscape found that 35% of people who don't back up their personal data simply don't know how.

Not because they don't care—because no one ever showed them.

In a world where data theft, ransomware, and device failure are daily threats, millions are flying blind, unaware that one accident could wipe out years of digital memories and critical files. Lack of knowledge is now one of the biggest vulnerabilities.

This chapter will teach you how to build a backup system that works for your life—not just your files. We'll walk through tools for personal use, family systems, small businesses, and shared devices. You'll learn how to automate backups, encrypt sensitive data, and restore your system without losing sleep.

You'll also learn about version control—how to protect against mistakes, not just loss. Because sometimes the threat isn't a stolen laptop or fried hard drive. Sometimes it's human error. You delete something you didn't mean to. You overwrite the wrong file. You fall for a phishing scam and don't realize your files are being encrypted in the background.

A good backup plan gives you options. A great one gives you peace of mind.

This chapter won't just help you protect your data. It will help you protect your future self—against panic, against regret, and against the crushing realization that something you can never replace is gone forever.

Because in the digital world, there are two kinds of people: Those who've lost everything—and those who learned from them.

Choose wisely.

Why It Matters

Everyone thinks they'll back up their data tomorrow.
Right after this email. After the next trip. After this semester ends. After the project is done. But the problem with data loss is it doesn't wait for a good time. It just happens.

One moment, everything is fine. The next? Your hard drive won't turn on. Your phone is gone. Your cloud account is locked. Your files are encrypted by ransomware and the only copy is... gone.

And that's when the real cost kicks in.

Because data isn't just "stuff." It's your history. Your identity. Your work. Your art. Your money. Your family memories. Your digital life. And for most people, there's no printed version. No analog backup. No folder in a fireproof box. Just files—living on a few devices that aren't half as reliable as you think.

That's the part most people underestimate.

In 2024, one in four people worldwide experienced data theft or loss—a staggering reminder of how fragile digital life really is. Yet despite the risk, only 66% of global consumers regularly back up their data, according to the Acronis Data Privacy in 2025 survey.

That means millions are just one crash, one hack, or one wrong click away from losing everything—photos, documents, memories—gone in seconds, with no way back.

Let that sink in: the majority of people have lost data. And most still aren't prepared to prevent it from happening again.

Why? Because backing up feels boring. Inconvenient. Easy to delay. Until it's the only thing that could've saved you—and now it's too late.

Data loss comes in many forms:

- A spilled drink on a laptop
- A stolen phone with no cloud sync
- A hard drive failure
- An accidental deletion of an important folder
- A software update gone wrong
- A hacked account where all your emails or photos are wiped
- A ransomware attack that locks your files behind a paywall

The scenarios are different. The result is the same: everything you thought was safe... gone.

That's why backup and recovery isn't an IT department problem. It's a survival skill. Especially now, when everything is digital:

- Work lives in documents, spreadsheets, and cloud drives
- Family photos exist only in smartphone albums
- Medical records, tax forms, and legal documents are sent via email
- Creative projects live in apps and tools, not folders
- Passwords, notes, and financial data are stored in digital vaults

And most of it only exists in one place. One device. One account. One fragile, easily compromised system.

Without a plan, recovery becomes a gamble.

According to the 2024 Handy Recovery Advisor survey, the top causes of data loss weren't hacks or malware—they were accidents. 17% of respondents lost data due to accidental deletion, and 15% blamed device failure.

That's one wrong click, one crash, and it's gone. No hacker needed.

And without a backup? There's no getting it back.

Professional recovery services can cost thousands of dollars—with no guarantee. Even cloud storage isn't foolproof. Files can be overwritten. Accounts can be suspended or deleted. And some providers purge "deleted" files permanently after 30 days.

That's why the key isn't just backup. It's smart backup. It means following a basic rule: "3-2-1"

- Keep 3 copies of your data
- Store them in 2 different formats (e.g. cloud and external drive)
- Keep 1 copy offsite or offline

It also means:

- Automating your backups so you don't have to remember
- Testing your recovery process before a crisis
- Using encrypted drives and secure cloud accounts
- Separating work from personal backups
- Not relying solely on your phone or your browser to store critical data

Because when something goes wrong—and eventually, it will—your ability to recover isn't based on how careful you were yesterday. It's based on the steps you took months ago.

This chapter matters because so much of your digital life is irreplaceable. You might be able to buy a new laptop. But you can't buy back a decade of photos. You might reinstall your email. But you won't recover the message that contained a legal contract, a last goodbye, or a lost password.

So back it up now. Before the power goes out. Before the screen cracks. Before the malware hits. Before you cry.

What to Do About It – Your Security Checklist

1. **Follow the 3-2-1 Backup Rule:** Always keep at least three copies of your data—two on different types of local storage, and one offsite (like a secure cloud service).

2. **Use Automated Backups:** Set up automatic backups on your devices so you don't forget. Choose daily or weekly schedules depending on how often your data changes.

3. **Back Up Critical Files Manually Too:** In addition to automated backups, manually save irreplaceable documents, family photos, and financial records to a separate location.

4. **Choose Encrypted External Drives:** If you use USBs or external hard drives, make sure they're encrypted and stored safely in your home or office.

5. **Use Reputable Cloud Backup Services:** Select cloud storage providers that offer encryption, redundancy, and clear data recovery policies. Avoid free, unverified platforms.

6. **Test Your Restores:** Backups are useless if they don't work. Run test restores every few months to ensure your files can be successfully recovered.

7. **Keep Software Up to Date:** Outdated systems can corrupt backup processes or leave your data vulnerable to ransomware.

8. **Back Up Your Smartphone, Not Just Computers:** Enable cloud backups for phones and tablets—especially for photos, contacts, and app data.

9. **Maintain Backup Logs and Versions:** Use backup software that tracks changes and stores previous versions of files so you can recover from mistakes or malware infections.

10. **Store a Copy Offline:** Have at least one backup stored offline—unplugged and air-gapped—so it's immune to ransomware or power surges.

11. **Document Your Backup Process:** Create a simple plan that family or team members can follow if you're unavailable. Include tools, locations, and access credentials (stored securely).

12. **Clean Out Old or Redundant Backups:** Remove outdated copies to free up space, but do so carefully. Verify that newer backups are intact before deleting anything.

Quick Action Plan

1-Minute Fix: Turn on automatic cloud backup for your phone or laptop.

5-Minute Fix: Identify your most critical files and back them up manually to a USB drive or secure folder.

15-Minute Fix: Set up and test an automated local + cloud backup system on your primary device.

30-Minute Fix: Build a full backup strategy using the 3-2-1 rule, document the plan, and test recovery on at least one file.

Chapter 39

The Right Way to Dispose of Old Devices and Hard Drives

Real-World Scenarios

The Laptop That Wouldn't Die

Gavin felt relieved when he finally upgraded from his old, worn-out laptop. After six long years, the machine had become painfully slow, the screen was cracked from a late-night mishap, and the battery barely lasted ten minutes unplugged. It was, in his words, "basically useless."

Thinking it was time to let go, he listed the laptop on an online marketplace for $150. Within hours, it sold. Before shipping it off, Gavin did what most people would—he deleted his personal folders, ran a quick system format, and assumed the data was gone for good.

That assumption would come back to haunt him.

Three months later, he received an anonymous email with the subject line: "Your old laptop says hello."

Inside was a brief message:

"Hi Gavin. Just wanted to let you know that your laptop is still very useful. I've restored your tax returns, family vacation photos, and a few saved passwords. Don't worry—I won't use them. But others might. Be careful next time."

Attached to the email was a chilling screenshot: his bank's login page—with his saved username pre-filled.

Gavin's hope suddenly vanished.

He had unknowingly handed a stranger his digital identity. Everything he thought he deleted was still there—just buried, not erased. The buyer had used widely available file recovery software to retrieve his data in minutes.

Gavin learned the hard way that a quick format doesn't wipe a hard drive—it just hides the data from plain sight.

If you're selling or discarding an old device, deleting files isn't enough. Without proper data wiping or physical destruction of the drive, you're not just parting with hardware—you may be handing over your entire digital life.

The Printer That Became a Spy

When Quinn upgraded the printer in her small office, it felt like a mundane task. The new model was faster, quieter, and could scan directly to the cloud. Without a second thought, she unplugged the old one and tossed it in the dumpster behind her building.

Weeks passed. Then one of her largest clients called in a panic.

"Someone's been emailing us copies of your contracts," the client said. "Invoices, signatures, even confidential budget reports—everything."

Quinn was stunned. She hadn't sent anything. Her team hadn't either. So how was someone accessing private business files?

The answer was lying in a landfill.

Unbeknownst to her, the discarded printer still held hundreds of scanned documents and printed pages in its internal memory. Most modern printers, especially office-grade ones, include hard drives that store recent activity for quick access or recovery.

That forgotten printer had become a goldmine for whoever found it.

Hackers and identity thieves know this well.

Quinn thought she was just replacing a printer. She didn't realize she was leaving a copy of her company's most sensitive information behind.

Before disposing of office electronics—printers, copiers, or scanners—always check whether they have internal storage. If they do, securely erase it or remove the hard drive entirely. Otherwise, your trash could become someone else's treasure trove of stolen data.

The Smartphone That Wouldn't Stay Erased

Caleb was the kind of person who always stayed on top of tech trends. When his mobile carrier rolled out a limited-time trade-in offer for the latest flagship smartphone, he jumped at the chance. His current phone, though just a couple of years old, had served its time—and the new model promised faster speeds, better cameras, and longer battery life.

Before heading to the kiosk at his local mall, Caleb made sure to back up his photos and contacts to the cloud. Then, like most people, he tapped through the factory reset menu, watched the screen go blank, and saw the device reboot to its welcome screen. To him, it was a clean slate. Done and dusted.

He handed it over to the store associate, got his discount on the new phone, and walked away without a second thought.

But a few weeks later, things started to go very wrong.

He received an alert from his bank: an attempted login from an unrecognized device in another country. Minutes later, his Gmail account was locked due to suspicious activity. Then, friends began messaging him, asking why he was sharing strange links on Facebook and Instagram.

Caleb's heart sank when he opened his crypto wallet app on his new phone—his balance was zero. Every coin, every token, gone.

He began retracing every step and questioning every app. Finally, it hit him: the phone he had traded in.

What Caleb didn't know was that a factory reset doesn't always completely wipe a smartphone's storage—especially if encryption wasn't enabled beforehand. The person who received his "erased" device had used free, widely available data recovery tools to access everything still buried in the phone's memory.

The new owner didn't need to be a genius hacker. All they had to do was scan the device and dig through the remnants. And what they found was a digital treasure chest: cached login sessions, personal photos, saved app credentials, SMS-based two-factor authentication codes, and most importantly—backup access to his crypto wallet.

Caleb had assumed his reset had wiped everything clean. But he hadn't encrypted his phone. He hadn't removed his linked accounts thoroughly. And he hadn't realized just how much data smartphones retain.

He thought he was making a smart upgrade.

Instead, he had unknowingly handed over his entire digital life to a stranger—for the price of a trade-in bonus.

The Smart Home That Became Someone Else's

Miles and Zoe had spent years transforming their home into a fully connected, voice-controlled smart space. From adjusting the lights with a quick voice command to locking the doors remotely from an app, everything was integrated and automated. Their smart home was more than a convenience—it was part of their daily rhythm.

When they finally sold the house to move closer to family, they packed up quickly, eager to start their next chapter. They handed over the keys, waved goodbye to their old home—and didn't think twice about the devices still embedded in the walls: the smart thermostat, the doorbell camera, the voice assistant.

Then, just days after moving, Miles's phone buzzed with a notification: "Front Door Locked." Moments later, another alert: "Thermostat set to 72°F." Confused, he opened the app and was shocked to see live camera footage of the new owners unpacking boxes.

He could see them. Hear them. Track their movements in real-time.

Terrified, Miles tried to revoke access and log out, but the devices were still linked to his account—and still active. His and Zoe's digital fingerprints remained inside the home they no longer owned.

They hadn't factory reset the devices. They hadn't unlinked their accounts. And now, they had unknowingly retained access to someone else's private life—and left their own data exposed.

Smart home devices don't magically reset themselves when a home is sold. If old owners don't manually disconnect their accounts, new residents could end up living inside someone else's digital infrastructure—or worse, hackers could exploit the leftover connections.

Miles and Zoe thought they had moved on.

They didn't realize their old home was still connected—to them, and to anyone else who knew how to exploit it.

What You Need to Know

Getting rid of an old device feels good.

It means you've upgraded. Moved on. Cleared some clutter. Maybe you gave it away, sold it, recycled it, or dropped it in one of those donation bins at the mall. You wiped it, you reset it, you even deleted some folders manually. It felt like enough.

Except it probably wasn't.

Because in the digital world, deleting something doesn't mean it's gone. Formatting a drive doesn't mean it's empty. And a factory reset doesn't mean your data is safe.

Old laptops, phones, tablets, USB drives, hard drives, printers, routers, cameras—even smart TVs—can all contain recoverable data long after you think it's been erased. And that data? It's not just a few leftover selfies or documents. It could be your tax records, passwords, financial spreadsheets, scanned IDs, photos of your kids, cloud credentials, or saved login sessions.

Once that device leaves your hands, someone else can easily get access to everything you forgot was even on it.

A 2021 study by Kaspersky demonstrated that 90% of second-hand devices overall (including computers, phones, and storage media) contained traces of private and business data that could be recovered. Some had files that had been "deleted." Some had been factory reset. But with free recovery software and a little time, researchers were able to pull documents, photos, emails, and browsing history from the majority of the devices tested.

That's not just sloppy—it's dangerous.

Because criminals actively search for old electronics in secondhand markets, public trash, and e-waste recycling facilities. A single discarded hard drive with sensitive information can be sold, cloned, or used for identity theft. A wiped-but-unencrypted phone can be restored and mined for data. Even discarded printers can store scanned copies of every document you've sent through them.

And it's not only hackers. Sometimes it's a curious buyer, a reseller, or a stranger who just happened to find a forgotten device in a drawer at a garage sale.

Your data isn't gone just because you've forgotten it exists.

Most people don't have a clear process for getting rid of devices. They guess. They assume. They delete a few things and move on. They don't realize that unless the drive is securely wiped, overwritten, or physically destroyed, that data can come back to haunt them—or someone else.

There have been documented cases of former employers recovering sensitive corporate data from sold office equipment. Parents discovering that baby monitors and tablets still had login access to their cloud accounts—long after they were given away. And even high-profile breaches caused by improperly discarded storage devices that should have been destroyed but weren't.

And let's not forget your digital footprint doesn't end with storage. Old devices often stay logged into apps—email, social media, cloud storage, messaging, financial tools. If you forget to log out or unlink the device before selling or tossing it, the next person could be posting from your account, accessing your backups, or worse—resetting your passwords.

This chapter will teach you how to dispose of old devices the right way. That means more than just erasing data. It means knowing how to properly wipe a drive, remove accounts, delink services, encrypt storage before deletion, and—when needed—physically destroy sensitive components. We'll also cover what to do with devices you're donating, recycling, selling, or passing down to family members.

Because if you don't take those final steps, everything you tried to protect—your identity, your accounts, your family's privacy—could still be sitting on that "worthless" piece of old hardware.

This chapter will show you how to treat your old tech like what it actually is: A loaded vault you're about to hand to a stranger.

Make sure it's empty before you walk away.

Why It Matters

It's just an old phone.
A cracked laptop.
A USB stick you haven't used since 2016.
A dusty external hard drive shoved in the back of a drawer.

But here's the part most people don't realize: if it ever stored data, it probably still does.

Disposing of old tech is no longer about recycling responsibly—it's about protecting everything that used to live on that device. Because in most cases, that data doesn't actually disappear when you "delete" it.

The danger of data remanence on discarded devices remains a significant privacy concern.

A 2019 study by Blancco Technology Group found that 42% of second-hand hard drives still contained retrievable personal data, with 15% specifically holding personally identifiable information.

That's the myth most people believe:

- Resetting a phone erases everything.
- Formatting a hard drive means it's blank.
- Dragging files to the trash is good enough.

In reality, those methods just remove the "index" pointing to your files—not the files themselves. With freely available tools, hackers or curious buyers can recover years of personal, financial, or professional data in minutes.

This isn't theoretical.

Used devices are a well-known goldmine on the dark web. Identity thieves, blackmailers, and data brokers scan for these items on resale sites and e-waste centers.

And it's not just personal devices at risk.

Small businesses often discard printers, routers, laptops, and USB drives without properly sanitizing them. Many of these contain customer databases, internal memos, contracts, or credentials to cloud platforms. Once tossed, that information can be retrieved, exploited, or sold.

Even old smart TVs, baby monitors, and security cameras may store network passwords and access logs.

The risk doesn't stop when you stop using the device. It stops when the data is unrecoverable.

This is why proper disposal matters.

Because "out of sight" isn't the same as "out of reach." If you don't take steps to destroy or wipe your data properly, it could come back to haunt you—and everyone you were connected to. So what does safe disposal actually look like?

It starts with these principles:

- Encryption before disposal: Encrypt your hard drive or phone storage while the device still works. If the data is encrypted, even if it's recovered later, it won't be usable without the key.

- Certified data-wiping tools: Use secure erasure tools that overwrite your data multiple times. Basic formatting doesn't cut it. Look for NIST-compliant or DoD-grade options.

- Factory reset plus overwrite: On phones and tablets, do a full reset—and then use the device until the storage fills up with nonsense data (like large dummy files or media). Then reset again.

- Physically destroy when needed: If the device is too old or the risk too high, don't sell it—destroy it. Remove and drill through hard drives. Shred USB sticks. Break chips from motherboards. It's not dramatic—it's secure.

- Know your recycling partner: Not all "e-waste" disposal services are equal. Look for certified recyclers that guarantee data destruction and don't ship devices overseas to be resold.

Why go through all this?

Because the cost of doing nothing is much higher than the effort of doing it right.

If an old laptop you sold five years ago still contains saved login tokens, browser cookies, or document fragments—and it gets into the wrong hands—you might never know until it's too late. Your cloud account might get hijacked. Your identity might be stolen. Your business could be compromised. And you'd never connect the dots back to a "dead" device you thought was harmless.

This chapter exists to show you where the real risk lives. Not just in active apps or live accounts—but in forgotten drawers, storage bins, and old chargers.

If it once held your data, it still holds your responsibility.

So don't just wipe and hope. Dispose with purpose. Because what you leave behind might still be traceable—and exploitable.

What to Do About It – Your Security Checklist

1. **Wipe Data Securely Before Disposal:** Never rely on a quick delete or standard factory reset. Use certified data-wiping tools that overwrite the drive multiple times to prevent recovery.

2. **Encrypt Drives Before Use:** If a device or drive is encrypted from the start, even if it's lost or improperly erased, the data will remain inaccessible without the encryption key.

3. **Use Manufacturer Reset Utilities:** For smartphones, tablets, and smart devices, always perform a full manufacturer-recommended reset before selling, recycling, or donating.

4. **Physically Destroy Drives When Necessary:** For especially sensitive data, consider physically destroying the drive—drilling through the platters, shredding SSDs, or using a certified disposal service.

5. **Remove Memory Cards, SIMs, and External Storage**: Double-check that you've removed any additional storage components that could still contain personal data.

6. **Double-Check Cloud Logouts and Account Links:** Make sure you've signed out of cloud accounts (Google, Apple, Microsoft) and removed the device from your connected account list.

7. **Recycle Through Trusted E-Waste Services:** Use certified e-waste recycling services that provide proof of data destruction or follow environmentally safe disposal protocols.

8. **Avoid Donating Unwiped Devices:** Don't donate electronics without thoroughly wiping data. Even charities may pass devices through third parties where data could be extracted.

9. **Track Asset Disposal for Businesses:** If you're managing devices for a company, keep a record of what was wiped, when, and by whom. This is essential for compliance and audits.

10. **Don't Forget Smart Devices:** Smart TVs, speakers, thermostats, and doorbells also store personal information. Reset and delink them just like phones or computers.

11. **Destroy or Reclaim Printer Memory:** Office printers often store scanned documents. Clear memory or wipe internal storage before disposal.

Quick Action Plan

1-Minute Fix: Remove memory cards, SIM cards, and external drives from old devices.

5-Minute Fix: Log out of cloud services and unpair accounts from your old device settings.

15-Minute Fix: Use a secure data-wiping tool (like DBAN or Eraser) to sanitize a hard drive or USB stick before disposal.

30-Minute Fix: Build a checklist for safe device disposal in your home or workplace—include wipe steps, encryption, physical destruction, and recycling options.

Chapter 40

The Cybersecurity Rescue Plan You Wish You Had

Real-World Scenarios

THE FAMILY THAT HAD THEIR WI-FI HIJACKED IN THE MIDDLE OF THE NIGHT

Wesley was a light sleeper. So when he noticed the blinking red light on his Wi-Fi router at 3 a.m., something felt off. His first instinct was that the internet was down—but when he checked, it wasn't. In fact, everything seemed to be working... just a little slower than usual.

Then he noticed the strangest thing.

His smart TV, which no one had used since the night before, was suddenly playing a random show at full volume. Confused, he opened the network settings and saw several unfamiliar devices connected to his Wi-Fi. Stranger still, when he tried to check the feed from his security cameras, he saw the footage had been accessed remotely—and not by anyone in his household.

That's when the panic set in.

A hacker had infiltrated Wesley's home network—quietly and efficiently. They had cracked the router using the default username and password that came with it. Once inside, they gained access to every device on the network: TVs, phones, cameras, even the smart thermostat. Not only had the hacker spied on the family's devices, they had also used the network to mask criminal activity—launching cyberattacks through Wesley's IP address.

By the time Wesley realized what was happening, his home had already become part of someone else's cybercrime operation.

He had assumed Wi-Fi was just a means of getting online.

He never imagined it could be used to turn his house into a hacker's personal playground.

The Phishing Email That Let a Hacker Into a Family's Devices

Tara was rushing through her morning routine when she spotted an urgent email in her inbox. The subject line read, "Immediate Action Required: Internet Service Disruption." The message looked official—complete with a company logo, support phone number, and a payment link to "restore service."

Thinking her bill had been missed, she clicked the link and filled out the form with her name, card number, and account login.

That small action unleashed chaos.

Within minutes, her bank flagged suspicious transactions. Her email logged her out and refused to let her back in. Her phone, normally snappy, started lagging and crashing. Something was clearly wrong.

A hacker had crafted a nearly perfect phishing email. The payment link didn't go to her internet provider—it went to a fake site designed to steal her credentials. Once she entered her info, malware was quietly downloaded onto her computer. That malware spread to other devices connected to her home Wi-Fi, giving the attacker a digital key to her family's entire tech ecosystem.

It didn't stop at her bank. The hacker gained access to cloud storage, photos, smart devices, even the kids' tablets. Everything in the house was compromised—because of one email that looked just real enough to fool her.

Tara thought she was just updating a payment.

She didn't realize she had opened the door to a digital intruder.

The Power Outage That Disabled a Family's Security System

Rose and her husband had invested thousands into their smart home security setup. Their house was equipped with motion sensors, door and window monitors, smart locks, and a full network of surveillance cameras—all connected through Wi-Fi and controlled by an app on Rose's phone.

They felt secure, believing their system would keep them protected from any threat.

But one stormy night changed everything.

A heavy thunderstorm rolled in, and just before midnight, the power went out across their neighborhood. Rose's phone lit up with notifications—then fell silent. The cameras stopped streaming. The alarms stopped responding. The app was frozen.

She assumed everything would reboot once the power returned.

It didn't.

When the electricity came back hours later, Rose realized the cameras hadn't restarted. The entire system had failed to recover. Their home had been left completely unprotected through the night.

Worse yet, she later learned from a neighbor that burglars had been active in the area that night. Nothing happened to their house—but it easily could have. They had no backup power. No offline protection. Just a high-tech system that, without electricity, was useless.

What Rose didn't know was that smart security systems—while sophisticated—often rely entirely on internet connectivity and electrical power. Some burglars even use signal jammers to disable these systems on purpose, knowing there's no manual fallback.

She thought she had installed a foolproof security solution.

She didn't realize she had built a digital fortress with a single point of failure.

The Kid's Gaming Console That Let a Hacker Into the Home Network

Zachary was twelve and obsessed with gaming. When he received a brand-new console for his birthday, he immediately set it up, connected it to the home Wi-Fi, and began exploring online multiplayer games. His parents were happy to see him having fun and didn't think twice when he asked for help downloading a "free" game he'd found online.

The download worked, but the game wasn't quite what Zachary expected. It kept crashing. To fix it, he followed the instructions on a forum and installed a cheat tool that promised to make everything run smoother.

What none of them knew was that the "tool" was actually malware.

Within days, strange things began happening in the household. The Wi-Fi slowed to a crawl. Rose's banking app triggered a fraud warning. Devices around the house began acting oddly—phones freezing, smart lights turning off randomly, security camera footage disappearing.

The gaming console, the innocent birthday gift, had been the hacker's way in. The malware gave the attacker access to the entire network. From there, they could steal saved passwords, monitor keystrokes, and infiltrate any connected device—from phones to laptops to smart appliances.

Zachary had no idea. He thought he was just downloading a cool game.

He didn't realize he'd opened a door to their entire digital life—and invited a hacker inside.

What You Need to Know

Most people think about cybersecurity the same way they think about insurance: something they'll deal with when something goes wrong. Until then, it's background noise.

Until the moment it's not.

The truth is, by the time you realize you've been hacked, targeted, locked out, or manipulated, it's already too late to start thinking about what you should have done. Panic sets in. You try to remember where your backup is—or if you even have one. You scramble to reset passwords. You hope the damage is minimal. And if you're lucky, you regain control. If you're not, you start from zero.

But what if you didn't have to guess your way out of a crisis?

What if you had a plan already in place—the digital version of an emergency kit? Not just for hackers or stolen accounts, but for everyday mistakes. Lost phones. Bad downloads. Suspicious links. Power outages. Account lockouts. Family members clicking something they shouldn't have. Kids oversharing. A suspicious charge. A strange login alert. A breached password.

This chapter is about building that plan—before you need it.

Think of it as your cybersecurity fire drill. Your exit route. Your response strategy. Your step-by-step guide to "What now?" when things go wrong. Because eventually, something will.

Criminals aren't just looking for the biggest targets anymore. They're looking for the easiest. The quietest. The least prepared. If your family has no plan for what to do when a digital problem hits, you are—by definition—one of the easiest.

That's what this chapter fixes.

You'll learn how to create a clear, simple, actionable cybersecurity rescue plan. Something you can refer to in a moment of panic and walk through step-by-step. Something your partner, your kids, your aging parents, or your roommates can understand and follow. Because cybersecurity isn't just about protecting yourself—it's about protecting everyone connected to you.

This isn't just a tech problem. It's a household readiness issue.

The plan you build in this chapter will include:

- How to respond immediately to suspicious activity
- Which accounts to check—and in what order
- How to contact support when you're locked out
- When and how to freeze cards, accounts, or devices
- What tools to use for recovery, backup, and monitoring

- Who to notify—and what to document
- How to reset access across multiple platforms safely
- And how to prevent it from happening again

Because once you've been through a digital emergency, you don't go back to business as usual. You think differently. You act faster. You're more cautious—but more confident, too. And that's the mindset we want to help you build.

A plan doesn't make the danger disappear. It gives you power when everything feels out of control.

It helps you respond with purpose instead of panic. It gives you a checklist when your brain is foggy with stress. It prevents small problems from becoming massive ones. And most importantly—it turns your next crisis into a story with a better ending.

Most people wish they had a plan only after something goes wrong. You're writing yours before it does. And that puts you ahead of 90% of the population.

This final chapter isn't about fear. It's about readiness. It's about saying: "Even if something breaks, I won't." It's about stepping out of the helpless mindset and into the prepared one. Because in a digital world, rescue starts with response.

And your response starts with a plan.

Why It Matters

You don't need a rescue plan until you do. And by then, the damage is often already done.

Cyberattacks are no longer a matter of if—they're a matter of when. And when they hit, they hit fast: money disappears, accounts get locked, private files vanish, strangers impersonate you online. You go from checking your email to calling your bank, your kids, your workplace—and wondering how it all unraveled so quickly.

The worst part? Most people don't even know how it started.

A reused password. A lost phone. A clicked link. A shared Wi-Fi network. One moment of convenience turns into a crisis—and without a plan, panic takes over.

A quick and efficient recovery plan isn't just for businesses—it's a lifeline for anyone with something to lose.

Whether it's a cyberattack, accidental deletion, or device failure, having a plan means you can bounce back fast, with minimal damage.

SentinelOne (What is Cyber Resilience, 2025) puts it simply: the faster the recovery, the smaller the impact.

That's just as true for a global company as it is for a parent with baby photos, a student with a thesis, or anyone storing their life on a screen. No plan? No recovery.

Speed matters. And speed depends on preparedness.

That's what a cybersecurity rescue plan is all about.

It's not a piece of software. It's not a complicated system.
It's a clear, calm answer to a very specific question:
What would I do if I got hacked today?

Most people have no idea. They assume they'll "figure it out" when the time comes. But that delay is exactly what attackers count on. They use that window to deepen the breach, lock you out, cover their tracks, and move onto your other accounts.

Think about it. You probably know where your fire extinguisher is. You probably have a first aid kit. You likely have a plan if your car breaks down or your power goes out.

But what happens when your phone disappears?
Your email is hijacked?
Your bank account is drained?
Your social media starts sending messages you didn't write?

Without a rescue plan, you start from zero. You waste time. You make mistakes. With a plan, you start with a checklist.

And that makes all the difference.

The rescue plan you wish you had includes things like:

- Knowing your most critical accounts and how to access them securely
- Storing recovery codes and passwords in a safe, offline place
- Being able to remotely wipe a lost phone or laptop
- Recognizing signs of compromise before it's too late
- Knowing how to contact your bank, cloud provider, or mobile carrier in an emergency
- Understanding how to freeze your credit or report identity theft

These aren't just nice-to-haves. They're the digital equivalent of knowing how to shut off the gas line.

That's because panic is the hacker's best friend. Confusion gives them more time. Delay gives them more access.

A solid rescue plan limits both.

It also empowers every member of your household. Because cybersecurity isn't just personal anymore—it's shared. A hacked email can affect a spouse. A compromised tablet can infect a work laptop. A breached smart home account can expose a child's location.

A rescue plan isn't just something you make once and forget. It's something you review, practice, and share—just like a fire drill. Because when it's needed, it needs to be ready.

This chapter matters because it's your second chance, written in advance.

It's the calm before the chaos. The structure when everything feels shaky. It's the thing you'll wish you had if you skip it—and the thing you'll be grateful for if you don't.

A breach doesn't have to break you. A hack doesn't have to end in disaster.

But the difference between panic and protection is knowing what to do next. That's what this rescue plan gives you.

So don't wait until something goes wrong. Build the plan now—while you still have time, access, and clarity. Because the moment you need it, you won't have time to write it.

What to Do About It – Your Security Checklist

1. **Create a Personal Cybersecurity Emergency Plan:** Prepare a written plan that outlines what to do if your accounts are hacked, devices are stolen, or sensitive data is leaked. Keep both a digital and printed version stored securely.

2. **Use a Password Manager for Centralized Credential Storage:** Store all your login details in a secure, encrypted password manager to quickly reset or recover access when needed.

3. **Prepare Backup Communication Channels:** If your primary email or phone number gets compromised, make sure you have a backup account and an alternative contact method for recovery.

4. **Enable 2FA on Every Critical Account:** Two-factor authentication is your first line of defense. Prioritize it on banking, email, cloud storage, and social media platforms.

5. **Document Important Account Recovery Steps:** Note the recovery processes for your major accounts (email, banks, work tools) and keep backup codes accessible in a secure, offline format.

6. **Create a Device Recovery Checklist:** Know how to remotely locate, lock, and wipe your lost or stolen devices. Practice this process on your phone, tablet, or laptop.

7. **Develop a Home Cyber Hygiene Routine:** Set reminders to regularly update your passwords, review devices on your accounts, delete old apps, and check for suspicious logins.

8. **Know Who to Call:** Maintain a list of contact numbers for your bank's fraud department, your mobile provider, your cloud service, and any cybersecurity support you may have access to.

9. **Keep Proof of Ownership for Devices & Accounts:** Retain receipts, serial numbers, or registration emails in a secure folder. This can help with law enforcement reports or account recovery.

10. **Train the Family:** Everyone in the household should know what to do in a breach—how to spot phishing, report suspicious activity, and prevent further spread.

Quick Action Plan

1-Minute Fix: Print or export your password manager's emergency access sheet and store it securely.

5-Minute Fix: Set up 2FA on your most critical accounts (banking, email, cloud, work).

15-Minute Fix: Create a contact list for all essential account providers and write down their breach support process.

30-Minute Fix: Build your personal Cybersecurity Rescue Plan document—include backup login methods, device wipe tools, and family instructions.

LAST PART: NOW YOU KNOW - NOW YOU ACT

You've Come a Long Way

Let's take a deep breath together.

You made it.

You've walked through the shady shortcuts, the quiet traps, and the unsettling ease of modern technology. You've looked behind the curtain of "smart" devices and sleek interfaces. You've faced the chilling reality that you've probably already been hacked—and more than once.

But more importantly: you now know how to fight back.

This isn't just the end of a book. It's the beginning of a new way of thinking. So let's step back and look at what you now carry in your digital armor.

From "I Had No Idea" to "Now I Know"

Before this book, you might've thought cybercrime was something that happened to big corporations, celebrities, or careless teenagers downloading sketchy apps.

Now you know better.

Cybercrime isn't out there. It's in here. It's sitting quietly in your inbox. It's in your cloud backup. It's in the router blinking in the hallway. It's in that friendly-looking link from your bank and the app that asked for just a little too much.

You've learned that no one is "too small" to be a target. In fact, the smaller you are, the more likely you'll fall through the cracks—straight into the hands of attackers who automate everything.

You've gone from a passive user to an active defender. And that's a massive shift.

What We Covered – A Chapter-by-Chapter Arsenal

Let's recap what you now know—no jargon, no fluff, just sharp takeaways.

Part I: Everyday Cybersecurity – The Basics

We started by dismantling the illusion of safety. Not to scare you – but to wake you up. You now understand:

- Why doing nothing is the worst possible strategy.
- That ignoring cybersecurity is like leaving your front door wide open with a sign that says "Nobody's home!"
- The anatomy of common threats: phishing, smishing, identity theft, AI scams.

You spot scams quicker. You hesitate before clicking. You've started to question everything—and that's good.

Part II: The Devices You Live With

From your phone to your fridge, everything's online. And that means everything's vulnerable. You learned:

- That smart TVs, smart speakers, and baby monitors can all be exploited.
- That your phone is likely the most dangerous device in your life—because it's the one you trust the most.
- What apps really do with your data behind the scenes.

You now know how to:

- Tame your settings.
- Limit permissions.
- Remove creepy tracking tools.

You're no longer just a user – you're a digital landlord, controlling who gets in and who doesn't.

Part III: Your Digital Footprint

Every search, every app, every login leaves a trace. You learned:

- What your digital shadow is.
- How attackers build profiles without ever meeting you.
- Why data is the new oil and you're leaking it.

You started deleting old accounts. You stopped oversharing. You learned privacy isn't about hiding – it's about having control.

Part IV: The People Around You

Cybersecurity isn't solo. It's a family, workplace, and community affair. You learned:

- How to protect your kids, parents, and colleagues.
- Why human error is the #1 risk—and how to reduce it.
- How convenience (shared accounts, reused passwords) invites danger.

You became the go-to person. The one who says, "Wait – before you click that..." And that matters.

Part V: When Things Go Wrong

We didn't sugarcoat it. Because sometimes—even when you do everything right—it still happens. You learned:

- What to do if your identity is stolen.
- How to report scams.
- Who to contact when accounts are hijacked.

You built an emergency response plan. You're not frozen anymore. You act. You breathe. You recover. And most importantly—you don't blame yourself.

Part VI: Your New Mental Habits

Cybersecurity isn't about fancy tools. It's about how you think.

Here's what's changed:

- You pause before clicking.

- You double-check strange messages—even from friends.
- You use stronger, unique passwords (and maybe installed a password manager).
- You ask: "Does this app really need access to my mic?"
- You stopped saying "I'm not a tech person." You started saying, "I know enough to protect myself."

That's big. That's power. You've developed instincts—the kind you can't buy. The kind that last.

Part VII: Who You Are Now

You're not a cybersecurity expert. Yet. But you are cyber-aware.

That means:

- You don't fall for the easy traps.
- You're harder to fool.
- You make attackers' jobs harder.

You've gone from soft target to moving target. And most of the time, that's all it takes to stay safer than 90% of people. Attackers chase easy wins.

Thanks to what you've learned—you're no longer one of them.

The Hidden Benefit: Confidence

When you understand something, it stops being scary. That's what this book was always about.

Not paranoia—preparation.

Not fear—awareness.

You now live in that sweet spot between knowing what's out there and knowing what to do about it.

That moment when you say: ""**Yeah, I know what this is. And I know what to do.**"

That's cybersecurity confidence. And you've earned it.

Build Your Cybersecure Life

You've got the knowledge. You've seen the threats. You understand how attacks happen, why they work, and where they hide.

Now what?

This is the part where knowing turns into doing.

Because the truth is, cybersecurity isn't about knowing 1,000 things. It's about doing 10 of them consistently.

This part gives you a starter blueprint: a doable plan you can begin right now—even if you're overwhelmed, busy, or tech-shy. We'll keep it real. No buzzwords. No guilt. Just practical steps that protect your digital life and give you back control.

Let's start small. Let's start smart.

Your First 7 Days of Cyber Hygiene

Day 1: Audit Your Passwords

- Make a quick list of the 5–10 most important accounts: email, social media, online banking, cloud storage, shopping.
- Ask yourself: are any of these using the same password?
- If yes, change them—today.
- Use a strong, unique password for each. If you haven't already, install a password manager (like Bitwarden, 1Password, or NordPass). It remembers your passwords *so you don't have to.*

Why this matters: Reused passwords are like using one key for your house, car, office, and safe. One breach opens all doors.

Day 2: Turn on Two-Factor Authentication (2FA)

- For the same critical accounts: go into settings and enable 2FA.
- Use app-based 2FA (like Google Authenticator or Authy) instead of SMS if possible.

Why this matters: Even if someone gets your password, they still can't get in. 2FA stops most automated attacks cold.

Day 3: Lock Down Your Phone

- Go to your phone's privacy settings.
- Revoke microphone, camera, and location access from apps that don't need it.
- Turn off Bluetooth and Wi-Fi when not in use.
- Set up biometric lock (fingerprint, face ID) and auto-lock timer.

Why this matters: Your phone is your digital skeleton key. If it's compromised, almost everything else is too.

Day 4: Tame Your Social Media

- Check who can see your posts, friends list, email, and phone number.
- Remove personal info that doesn't need to be public—birth date, hometown, school.
- Remove access to sketchy third-party apps.

Why this matters: Scammers harvest info from public profiles to trick you or your loved ones. Oversharing makes you a goldmine.

Day 5: Secure Your Home Network

- Log into your router (usually 192.168.1.1 or 192.168.0.1).
- Change the default admin password.
- Rename your Wi-Fi network (SSID) to something *neutral* (not your name, address, or "SmithFamilyWiFi").
- Disable remote management if you're not using it.
- Enable automatic firmware updates if available.

Why this matters: Your Wi-Fi is the gate to your entire digital life. Don't leave it wide open.

Day 6: Clean Your Digital House

- Delete old apps and accounts you don't use.
- Clear out saved payment methods on sites you no longer trust.
- Remove browser extensions you don't recognize.
- Empty your downloads folder and cloud trash bins.

Why this matters: Every unused app or forgotten account is a backdoor waiting to be kicked in. Close them.

Day 7: Teach One Person

- Sit down with your partner, child, friend, or colleague.
- Share one thing you've learned that they don't know yet.
- Help them change a weak password or set up 2FA.

Why this matters: When you teach someone else, you double your impact—and you make the world a little safer.

Quick Wins: Your Cyber Hygiene Checklist

Here's a printable list you can revisit monthly:

- My main accounts all use unique passwords
- I've enabled 2FA on all critical services

- I lock my phone and use biometric security
- I regularly update my operating system and apps
- My Wi-Fi router is renamed and secured
- I don't click links I didn't expect
- I don't download files from random sources
- I review app permissions and privacy settings
- I never store sensitive data in plain text
- I have a plan for what to do if I'm hacked

You don't need to do everything perfectly. But you do need to start.

And you just did.

Create Your "Red Alert" Plan

You're now smart enough to know: even with the best precautions, attacks can happen.

So let's build your emergency checklist—your cyber fire drill.

If You're Hacked:

- Step 1: Disconnect the device from Wi-Fi
- Step 2: Change passwords using a clean device
- Step 3: Enable 2FA on affected accounts
- Step 4: Check bank and card activity
- Step 5: Run a malware/virus scan
- Step 6: Report it (to your bank, service provider, or the relevant cyber authority)
- Step 7: Document what happened for future reference

Knowing what to do *before* it happens is how panic turns into action.

Keep It Going: Monthly 15-Minute Security Rituals

You don't need to live in fear or update your settings daily. But just like brushing your teeth, routine is everything.

Once a month, set a timer for 15 minutes. Then:

- Update all software (OS, phone, browser, apps)
- Check for unauthorized logins on key accounts
- Delete unused accounts and old data
- Review who has access to shared folders or drives
- Google yourself—see what personal info shows up

It's like digital hygiene. Do a little, often.

New Mindset, Not Just New Habits

The big win isn't just ticking boxes. It's that your *mind has changed.*

You're now someone who:

- Asks before trusting
- Acts instead of hoping
- Understands digital risk is real—and fixable

You've moved out of the trap of saying, "I'm not a tech person," and into the powerful space of, "I protect what matters to me."

And guess what? Most people never get this far.

Most people live wide open. They reuse the same password for everything. They leave Bluetooth on forever. They think, "It won't happen to me."

You're not most people anymore.

Tomorrow and Beyond

You don't need to overhaul your digital life in one week. But now, you know what matters. You have a map.

This isn't about being perfect. It's about being harder to hit.

And if something weird happens, you'll know what to do.

You'll pause. You'll think. You'll respond—not react.

Because you've already practiced it.

You're not paranoid. You're *prepared.*

And if you do one thing today—*even just one*—you're already ahead of millions of people who haven't yet opened their eyes.

The journey doesn't stop here. But now, you're walking it with purpose.

Keep Going: Resources and Next Steps

You've built a digital defense line. You've taken control. You're no longer walking around online with your guard down and your data hanging out.

But here's the truth: cybersecurity is not a one-time event. It's a moving target. A living process.

New threats emerge. New scams go viral. New technologies open new doors – for you and for attackers.

So the real challenge isn't just learning cybersecurity once; it's staying alert without burning out.

This part is your compass.

It's here to show you:

- Where to go when you don't know what to do.
- Which tools are worth trusting.
- What to read, watch, or follow—without drowning in tech overload.
- And how to stay cyber-aware without becoming paranoid.

Let's build a sustainable path forward.

The Cybersecurity Mindset: Stay Sharp, Not Scared

Cybersecurity isn't about fear. It's about *awareness.*

You don't need to obsess. You just need to pay attention.

So before we go into tools and resources, let's define your mindset going forward:

- Curiosity over fear: Don't panic when something seems weird—*investigate it.*
- Routine over reaction: Set security habits and check-ins like brushing your teeth—not just emergency fire drills.
- Progress over perfection: If you miss an update or click something dumb, don't freeze in shame. Just take the next step.

The goal isn't to live in a digital bunker.

The goal is to live smarter, safer, freer.

Toolbox: What to Use, What to Ditch

You don't need 50 apps to be secure. You need 5-7 great ones that work for you. Here's a starter kit:

1. Password Manager

Why: Creates and stores unique passwords for every account. No more reusing or remembering.

Try: Bitwarden (free & open-source), 1Password, NordPass

Bonus: Many can generate secure passwords and monitor breaches.

2. Two-Factor Authentication (2FA) App

Why: Adds a second lock to your accounts—like a one-time key that changes every 30 seconds.

Try: Authy, Google Authenticator, Microsoft Authenticator

Avoid: Relying only on SMS—it's hackable.

3. Encrypted Messaging

Why: Regular text messages are not private. Encrypted chats hide your messages from prying eyes.

Try: Signal (best), WhatsApp (good but owned by Meta)

4. VPN (Virtual Private Network)

Why: Encrypts your internet traffic—especially useful on public Wi-Fi.

Try: ProtonVPN (free + paid), Mullvad, NordVPN

Tip: Use when banking, traveling, or on hotel/airport networks.

5. Malware Protection

Why: Defends against viruses, ransomware, spyware, and more.

Try: Malwarebytes (free/paid), Bitdefender, Kaspersky (check regional policies for trust)

6. Browser Privacy Tools

Why: Ads track you. Trackers follow you. Stop that.

Try: uBlock Origin (ad blocker), DuckDuckGo Privacy Essentials, HTTPS Everywhere

Bonus Browsers: Brave, Firefox with hardened settings

7. Backup Tools

Why: If ransomware hits or your device dies, a backup saves your sanity.

Try: External encrypted drive + a secure cloud backup (iDrive, Backblaze)

Where to Learn More – Without Getting Overwhelmed

You don't need a degree to stay cyber-aware. But the right voices can help you stay informed, sharp, and ahead of new tricks.

Websites & Blogs

1. **The Hacker News** - The #1 trusted source for cybersecurity news, delivering real-time updates, threat intelligence, and data breach reports (https://thehackernews.com/)

2. **Dark Reading** - One of the most widely-read cybersecurity news sites and trusted community of cybersecurity professionals covering 13 specialized communities.
(https://www.darkreading.com)

3. **SecurityWeek** - Provides cybersecurity news and information to global enterprises, with expert insights & analysis for IT security professionals.
(https://www.securityweek.com/)

4. **Threatpost** - Independent news site and leading source of information about IT and business security for hundreds of thousands of professionals worldwide.
(https://threatpost.com/)

Mainstream Tech Publications with Strong Cybersecurity Coverage

- **Reuters Cybersecurity** - Global breaking news coverage
- **Forbes Tech/Security** - Daily cybersecurity blogs from staff writers
- **WIRED Security** - Cyberwarfare, dark web, and global cybersecurity news
- **BBC News Cyber-security** - World and UK cybercrime news
- **CNBC Tech Cybersecurity** - Latest major hacks and breaches globally

Podcasts

- Darknet Diaries – True stories of hacks, breaches, and the humans behind them.
- Smashing Security – Funny, insightful look at cybersecurity news.
- CyberWire Daily – Daily short briefings for news junkies.

Books

- *The Art of Invisibility* by Kevin Mitnick – Privacy lessons from a famous hacker.
- *This Is How They Tell Me the World Ends* by Nicole Perlroth – A deeper dive into the cyberwar economy.
- *Cybersecurity and Cyberwar by P.W. Singer & Allan Friedman* – A clear, engaging primer on how cyber issues affect politics, military, business, and your

everyday life.

- *Spam Nation by Brian Krebs* – An exposé into the underground spam empire and the criminal pharma cartels behind it. From the journalist who lives and breathes cybercrime.
- *Hacking the Hacker by Roger Grimes* – Features interviews with ethical hackers and security experts, offering practical advice mixed with personal stories.
- *Cybersecurity Dictionary for Everyone* – A beginner-friendly glossary of 1250+ terms, written in plain English (by—you guessed it—me!).

People to Follow – Cyberheroes on Social Media

Follow people, not platforms. Trust is in humans, not headlines.

X (Twitter)

- @SecBriefs – Demystifying cybersecurity for everyone
- @SwiftOnSecurity – Cybersecurity + sarcasm + clarity
- @briankrebs – Credible breach coverage
- @CyberSecMeg – Great beginner-friendly security tips
- @TheCyberSecHub – Cyber Security Portal with daily fresh news

LinkedIn

- Follow ENISA, CISA, Cybersecurity & Infrastructure Security Agency, Europol Cybercrime Centre for trusted updates.

Tip: Avoid accounts that sell fear instead of giving tools. Real cybersecurity is about *empowerment*, not panic.

Red Flags: What to Avoid in the Cyber Wild West

The internet is full of advice. Not all of it is good. Here's how to spot shady or unhelpful sources:

- They use constant fear and urgency ("HACKERS WILL DRAIN YOUR BANK IN 2 SECONDS!").
- They push miracle tools or ask you to download shady files.
- They promote conspiracy theories or baseless paranoia.
- They never explain why something matters—just tell you to obey.

If you're not sure, ask yourself: "**Does this advice make me feel more *informed*—or just more *afraid*?**"

Go with the one that teaches, not terrorizes.

5 Quick Cyber Questions to Ask Anytime Something Feels Off

1. Was I expecting this? (email, message, pop-up)
2. Is this too urgent or emotional? (threats, rewards, urgency)
3. Do I know the sender—and is the address legit?
4. Does the link look suspicious or unfamiliar?
5. Can I verify this another way? (like calling the real bank or company)

If you hesitate for even a second—*pause*. That pause could save you from a world of trouble.

Build a Circle of Awareness

You don't have to do this alone.

- Share what you've learned with friends and family.
- Start a "cyber hygiene" habit at your workplace or group.
- Join online forums or subreddits like r/privacy or r/cybersecurity101.

Awareness spreads like fire. But unlike a real fire—*this kind saves people.*

Your Cyber-Life Ahead

You now have:

- The tools
- The habits
- The awareness
- The plan

You're not bulletproof—but you're no longer defenseless.

Cybersecurity isn't a product you buy. It's a lifestyle you shape.

And now, you've started shaping yours.

A Final Word: You're Not Powerless

Let's say this out loud together: "I am not powerless."

Because that's what this whole book has been building toward—not a technical manual, not a rulebook, but a shift.

From passive to active.

From "I don't know what to do" to "I know how to respond."

From victim to guardian.

The most dangerous lie in the digital age isn't that hackers are smart or systems are flawed—it's the whisper that says:

"You can't protect yourself. You don't matter. You're not big enough to be a target, or strong enough to fight back."

That's the lie.

And now you know better.

The Power of Awareness

It starts with a gut feeling.

A suspicious email.

A strange charge on your card.

A pop-up that doesn't feel right.

A new device asking for access to... everything.

Before, you might have clicked. Shrugged. Ignored.

Now, you pause. You inspect. You question.

That pause is power. That instinct you've built—it's your internal firewall.

You can't see it. You don't get an alert when it kicks in. But it's real.

And in this world, it may be the most valuable security system you'll ever have.

The Story That Matters Most: Yours

We've told stories in this book—of hacked families, drained bank accounts, Bluetooth breaches, cloud leaks, AI scams, and smart homes turned dumb and dangerous.

But the most important story is the one you're writing now.

Here's a snapshot of what that story might look like in real life:

A True Story – "Something Was Off"

Sarah, a 42-year-old mom of two, had never read a book on cybersecurity before. She wasn't "techy." She used Facebook to keep up with family and Instagram for vacation photos. That's it.

Then one day, she got an email. It said her Netflix account had been suspended and that she needed to update her payment info. The logo looked right. The email sounded professional.

A year ago, she would have clicked.

But this time, something was off.

Instead of panicking, she paused.

She hovered over the sender's address. It was a weird domain.

She checked her Netflix app—it worked fine.

She googled "Netflix phishing email"—boom. Same scam, same subject line.

She didn't just dodge a scam—she rewrote the ending.

No drained card. No stolen info. No stress.

What protected her?

Not a firewall.

Not antivirus.

It was *awareness.*

It was *instinct.*

It was *you*—reading this, building those habits, and sharing them.

That's what power looks like.

You Can Be Someone's Firewall

Every hacker relies on isolation.

They hope you don't know.

They hope your grandma doesn't ask.

They hope your friend trusts that fake invoice.

They hope your child clicks that link.

But now, you're a threat to that silence.

Because you talk. You share. You warn. You might be the person who says:

- "Hey, don't click that."
- "Wait, did you check the URL?"
- "Let's enable 2FA on your accounts."
- "Let me help you set up a password manager."

One moment like that... and you just stopped a hack before it happened.

No dramatic music. No headlines. Just everyday heroism.

Cybersecurity isn't just something you *do for yourself.*

It's something you *pass on.*

You're Already Part of the Solution

Let's flip the script once and for all.

Cybersecurity doesn't belong to IT departments, government agencies, or hoodie wearing hackers in TV shows.

It belongs to:

- Parents who lock down the family tablet.
- Teenagers who recognize a fake DM before replying.
- Freelancers who secure their client files.
- Retirees who delete the scam email instead of clicking.
- Small business owners who care enough to ask, "What if this gets hacked?"

It belongs to *you.*

You are the front line.

You are the firewall.

You are the reason fewer people will get hurt.

Yes, It's Hard Sometimes

Let's be honest.

- You'll forget your new password.
- You'll miss an update.
- You'll slip and click the wrong thing one day.
- You'll feel overwhelmed by the next shiny app that wants your life story.

That's okay. This is not about being flawless.

This is about being *resilient.*

Get tricked? Learn from it.

Feel overwhelmed? Take a break.

Too busy for a full audit? Do one small thing today.

Cybersecurity isn't a sprint. It's not even a marathon. It's more like... flossing your digital teeth. A few minutes a week keeps everything healthier.

And like flossing, once it's a habit, it just becomes who you are.

Let This Be Your New Default

You can't unknow what you now know.

That's a good thing.

You've unlocked a new layer of reality—the part where digital life isn't just shiny, fun, and fast, but also sneaky, messy, and risky.

And that's okay. Because now you have the tools.

Let your new default be:

- Skeptical, not scared.
- Curious, not careless.
- Empowered, not overwhelmed.

Final Words from Me to You

When I started writing *Hack Happens*, I didn't want to write another boring "don't click this" guide. I wanted to write something real. Something that matters.

I wanted you to see that this world isn't just full of threats—but full of *choices*.

That every link, every setting, every permission—is a moment of power.

If you've made it this far, you've chosen well.

And if you ever forget what to do next, come back to this:

"Pause. Think. Then act."

You don't need to panic.

You don't need to be perfect.

You just need to be *aware*—and act like you matter.

Because in the world of cybersecurity, you do.

Now Go Be the Reason Someone Doesn't Get Hacked

This isn't just the end of a book.

It's the beginning of a new role in your life.

You're not a passive user anymore.

You're a protector.

A defender.

A digital guardian.

So go teach someone. Go help someone.

And if the moment ever comes where you stop a scam before it hurts someone else...

You'll smile.

And you'll remember:

Hack Happens. But not this time.

Not on your watch.

The Digital 911: What to Do When You're Under Attack

So it happened.

You clicked the wrong link. Or money just vanished from your account. Or your entire screen got locked with a ransom demand.

First of all—**breathe.** You're not alone. It's not your fault. And there's help available, right now.

This part is your lifeline: who to call, where to report, and how to act before things spiral further.

United States: IC3 and CISA

- **IC3 Statistics**: The FBI's Internet Crime Complaint Center (IC3) received 859,532 complaints in 2024, with reported losses exceeding $16 billion—a

33% increase from 2023.

- **Reporting to IC3**: Individuals can file complaints at IC3.gov. It's advisable to report any cyber-enabled crime, regardless of the financial loss.
- **CISA Contact Information**:
    - **Website**: cisa.gov/report
    - **Email**: report@cisa.gov
    - **Phone**: 1-844-SAY-CISA (888-282-0870)
- **Emergency Situations**: For life-threatening digital threats, call 911. For national security issues, report to tips.fbi.gov or contact your nearest FBI field office.
- **Special Situations**:
    - **Ransomware**: Do not pay the ransom. Gather ransom notes, file names, crypto wallet addresses, and attacker contact details.
    - **Business Email Compromise (BEC)**: Save email headers, bank and wire transfer details, and alert your bank immediately.
- **Response from IC3**: While IC3 may not provide immediate feedback, each report contributes to broader investigations and efforts to freeze funds and track cybercrime patterns.

Canada: CAFC, NC3, and Cyber Centre

- **Canadian Anti-Fraud Centre (CAFC)**:
    - **Phone**: 1-833-292-3788
    - **Website**: antifraudcentre-centreantifraude.ca
- **RCMP's National Cybercrime Coordination Centre (NC3)**: Works closely with CAFC to analyze reports and coordinate cross-border investigations.
- **Canadian Centre for Cyber Security**:
    - **Phone**: 1-833-CYBER-88 (1-833-292-3788)
    - **Email**: contact@cyber.gc.ca
    - **Website**: cyber.gc.ca
- **Local Police**: Report to your local police, especially if the threat is active.
- **Emergency Situations**: Dial 911 for emergencies.
- **Anonymous Reporting**: Contact Crime Stoppers at 1-800-222-TIPS.

United Kingdom: Action Fraud and NCSC

- **Action Fraud**:
    - **Phone**: 0300 123 2040
    - **Website**: actionfraud.police.uk
- **National Cyber Security Centre (NCSC)**:
    - **Email for Phishing Reports**: report@phishing.gov.uk
    - **Website**: ncsc.gov.uk/ actionfraud.police.uk/ ncsc.gov.uk
- **Scotland**: Report cybercrime to Police Scotland by calling 101.
- **Emergency Situations**: Call 999 for immediate threats.

Australia: ReportCyber and ACSC

- **ReportCyber**:
    - **Phone**: 1300 CYBER1 (1300 292 371)
    - **Website**: cyber.gov.au/report
- **Australian Cyber Security Centre (ACSC)**: Provides guidance and support for cyber incidents.
- **Emergency Situations**: Call 000 for life-threatening emergencies.
- **Non-Urgent Reports**: Use the Police Assistance Line at 131 444.

European Union: GDPR and National Authorities

- **GDPR Rights**: Under the General Data Protection Regulation (GDPR), individuals have the right to know, report, and seek compensation if their data is breached.
- **Data Protection Authorities (DPAs)**: Each EU country has its own DPA. Find your country's DPA here: edpb.europa.eu/members.
- **National Reporting Points**: Each country operates its own system for responding to cybercrime, typically involving:
    - **Police Investigation**: National or local police stations.
    - **CERT Support**: National Computer Emergency Response Teams (CERTs) or Computer Security Incident Response Teams (CSIRTs).
    - **Privacy Breach**: National Data Protection Authorities.

- **Examples:**
  - **Germany:**
    - **Cybercrime Reporting**: polizei.de
    - **CERT**: cert-bund.de
    - **DPA**: bfdi.bund.de
  - **France:**
    - **Cybercrime Reporting**: internet-signalement.gouv.fr
    - **CERT**: cert.ssi.gouv.fr
    - **DPA**: cnil.fr
  - **Austria:**
    - **Cybercrime Reporting**: bmi.gv.at
    - **CERT**: cert.at
    - **DPA**: dsb.gv.at
  - **Italy:**
    - **Cybercrime Reporting**: Local Police or Postal Police units.
    - **CERT**: csirt.gov.it
    - **DPA**: garanteprivacy.it
  - **Netherlands:**
    - **Cybercrime Reporting**: politie.nl
    - **CERT**: ncsc.nl
    - **DPA**: autoriteitpersoonsgegevens.nl

NIS2 Obligations for Businesses

- **NIS2 Directive**: Under the Network and Information Systems Directive (NIS2), essential service operators (e.g., hospitals, energy providers) must:
  - Report incidents within 72 hours.
  - Report ransomware payments within 24 hours.
  - Cooperate with national CSIRTs.
- **Non-Compliance**: Failure to comply can result in fines, investigations, and

reputational damage.

What to Include When Reporting

Regardless of the country or agency, prepare the following information:

- **Timeline**: When the incident started, what happened, and when you noticed.
- **Type**: Specify if it's ransomware, phishing, identity theft, etc.
- **Impact**: Detail financial losses, locked accounts, or stolen data.
- **Evidence**: Include emails, phone numbers, fake URLs, and screenshots.
- **Response So Far**: Outline actions taken and entities contacted.

Cross-Border Coordination

Cybercrime often transcends national borders. Local police may escalate significant cases to:

- **EUROPOL** – Europe's law enforcement agency that facilitates coordinated action among member states.
- **INTERPOL** – Handles international law enforcement cooperation, especially in cases with cross-border cybercrime actors.
- **EC3 (European Cybercrime Centre)** – A unit within EUROPOL dedicated specifically to combating online criminal activity, including malware distribution, online child exploitation, and financial cyber fraud.

These agencies don't typically accept direct reports from individuals, but your national police or cybercrime units can forward serious cases to them when international cooperation is required.

Notably, major global operations like the takedown of **Genesis Market** and **Emotet** involved intelligence sharing and joint task forces between:

- The **Dutch National Police**
- **UK's National Crime Agency**
- **RCMP** in Canada
- **U.S. FBI**
- **EUROPOL/EC3**

If your case is part of a larger pattern, it's possible your report could trigger—or contribute to—international law enforcement action.

First Response Checklist (Anywhere in the World)

Whether you're in the U.S., Germany, Australia, or anywhere else—your first few steps matter most.

Do them fast. Do them smart.

1. Freeze financial access

- Call your bank or credit card issuer.
- Enable fraud alerts and temporary blocks.
- Notify cryptocurrency platforms if wallets were affected.

2. Change your passwords

- Start with the breached account, then any reused credentials.
- Enable two-factor authentication (2FA) where possible.

3. Preserve evidence

- Screenshot any messages, ransom notes, email headers, URLs.
- Save copies of files but don't interact with malware.
- Log all timestamps and steps you've taken.

4. Report to the right place

- Use the official platform in your country (IC3, ReportCyber, Action Fraud, etc.).
- Report to your national CERT or DPA if needed.

5. Don't touch infected systems

- If you're unsure, disconnect affected devices from the internet.
- Avoid deleting anything until told to by professionals—it may be needed for forensics.

6. Don't wait

- Timing is critical, especially for wire transfers or ransomware.
- The sooner authorities know, the better your chance of recovering money or stopping spread.

What Not to Do

Here's what to avoid—no matter how urgent things feel.

- **Don't pay the ransom:** Law enforcement and cybersecurity experts strongly discourage it. It rarely guarantees recovery, and in some countries, it may violate laws if paid to sanctioned entities.
- **Don't assume it's too small to matter:** Even a single phishing email helps authorities track larger scams. Your report might be the missing link in a larger investigation.
- **Don't delete or "clean" your system right away:** Unless instructed by a professional, keep the affected environment intact. Wiping logs or reinstalling systems too soon can destroy critical evidence.
- **Don't be embarrassed:** These crimes are designed to fool *anyone*. Billion-dollar companies fall victim. You're not stupid—you were targeted. Now you're informed.

Cyberattacks are confusing, stressful, and violating. But you don't have to be an expert to take control. You just need to know what to do next.

This part gives you that plan.

It connects the dots between panic and power—between the moment things go wrong and the moment you start getting your life back.

Print it. Bookmark it. Share it with your team or your family.

Because the time to act is now—and the sooner you do, the stronger your recovery will be.

Hack happens. But now you know how to respond.

You Deserve to See the Proof

If you've made it this far — thank you. Not just for reading, but for *caring*. About your own safety. About your family. About the world we live in — and the digital threats that surround us daily.

Hack Happens wasn't written for clicks. It wasn't crafted to impress tech insiders or win awards. It was built — from the ground up — to protect people.

People who were left in the dark. People who were told, *"You should've known better,"* while no one ever bothered to teach them what to look for.

That ends here.

This book stands on the shoulders of millions of real voices. Comments. DMs. Cries for help. Shouts of warning. And every so often — a quiet thank-you that stopped us cold.

You weren't just told that. Now, you'll get to see it.

Cybersecurity is full of bold claims, scary stats, and endless warnings. So it's fair — even *necessary* — for you to ask: **"Where's the evidence?"**

That question matters, and you deserve an answer. Not just reassurance. **Proof.**

Throughout ***Hack Happens***, you've seen stories. You've read numbers. You've followed trails of deception, danger, and digital damage.

But none of it was written in a vacuum. This book was shaped by real-world interactions — public comments, private messages, viral posts, and raw reactions that lit up our screens and broke through the noise.

On the next page, you'll find a few tweet excerpts from **@SecBriefs**— shared not to impress, but because you deserve to see them. You've been told that people are waking up. Now you'll see what that looks like. The reach. The replies. The rawness.

And this is just a glimpse. Dozens more — and the full ongoing conversation — are live right now at **@SecBriefs**.

Scam alerts. AI traps. Smart home threats. Identity theft tactics. All rooted in the same mission as this book: **To make cybersecurity real. Human. And survivable.**

As for the data — the statistics, the sources, the hard-to-believe numbers — the same commitment to transparency applies.

Over 200 data points were carefully collected and cross-verified by a small team of three researchers, including myself. We pulled from trusted, public sources: Government agencies. Industry reports. Academic papers. Global surveys.

Still — we're human.

If something feels unclear, if a reference seems missing, if a number shakes you — you're welcome to reach out via **@SecBriefs**. We do our best to share sources, clarify context, and update when needed. While we may not be able to respond to every message, we value every voice — and your questions help strengthen the mission.

Because this was never about being "right." It was about being truthful. Useful. And accountable where it counts.

You're more than welcome to join the **@SecBriefs** community! Not just to follow, but to contribute. Let's fight the darkness — *together.*

Cybersecurity isn't something you should have to figure out on your own. And now, you don't have to.

What follows is just a glimpse. The rest of the story is still unfolding — live — at @SecBriefs.

SecBriefs | Making Cybersecurity Simple
@SecBriefs

Promote

New Leadership, New Priorities!

The old ways are gone. This administration must step up where others failed.

A stronger nation starts with informed citizens.

Start your own cyber awareness journey with the CYBERSECURITY DICTIONARY for Everyone: amazon.com/CYBERSECURITY-...

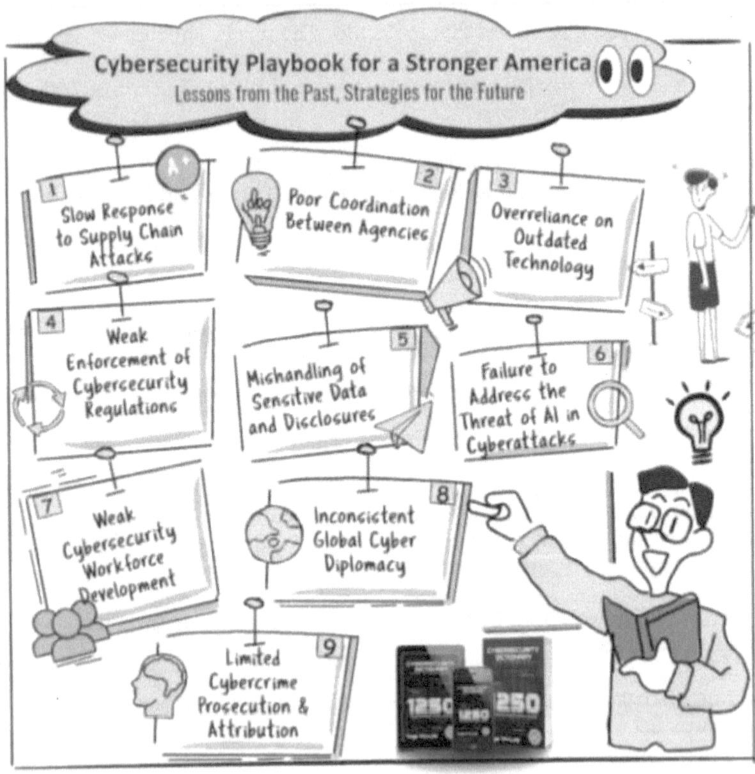

4:13 PM · Feb 8, 2025 · **8.5M** Views

View post engagements

175 782 3.8K 504

SecBriefs | Making Cybersecurity Simple
@SecBriefs

Promote

A New Chapter for America—it's time to put cybersecurity first!

Cybersecurity = National Security

A safer nation begins with informed citizens.

Take the first step to understanding and protecting with the CYBERSECURITY DICTIONARY for Everyone: amazon.com/CYBERSECURITY-...

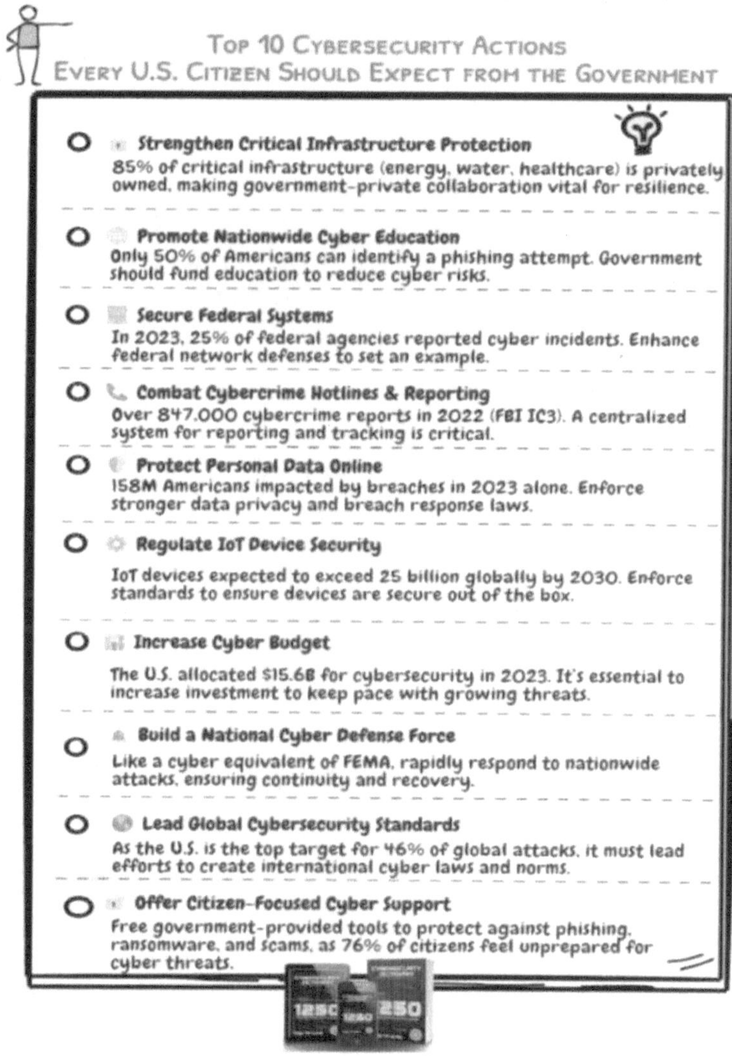

12:09 AM · Nov 16, 2024 · **4.5M** Views

View post engagements

130 902 3.3K 658

SecBriefs | Making Cybersecurity Simple
@SecBriefs

Promote

A cyber breach at 40,000 feet isn't just an IT issue.

Millions trust the skies every day. Only our top cybersecurity experts can keep them safe.

Cybersecurity matters. Learn about it. Demand it.

"Cybersecurity Dictionary for Everyone" on Amazon:
amazon.com/CYBERSECURITY-...

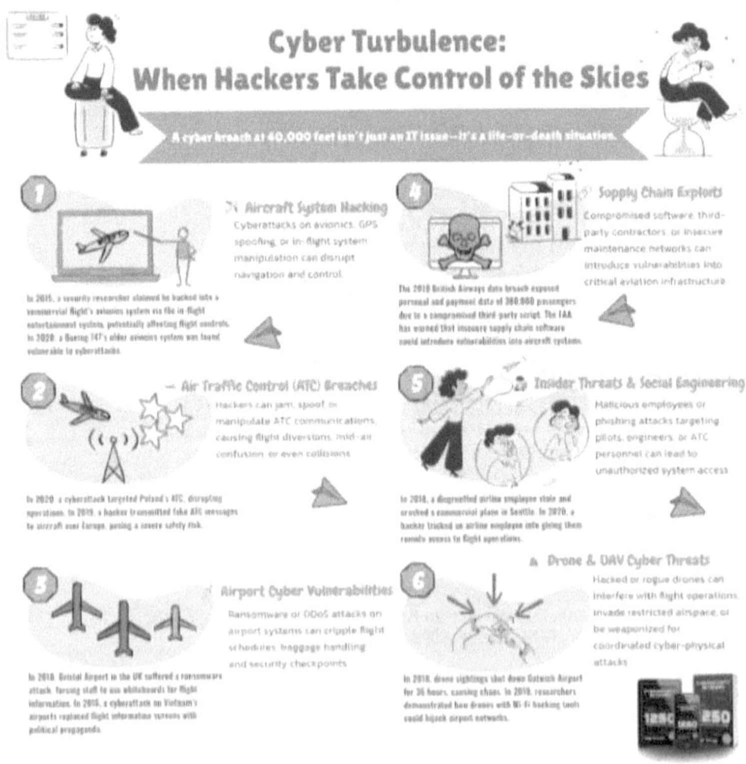

9:39 PM · Feb 1, 2025 · **1.3M** Views

View post engagements

21 232 646 282

SecBriefs | Making Cybersecurity Simple
@SecBriefs

Promote

Don't be a victim; don't wait until it's too late! ❗

Invest in your cybersecurity. It's the best investment you can make for your future.

Educate yourself & your loved ones about online threats with CYBERSECURITY DICTIONARY for Everyone.

On Amazon: amazon.com/CYBERSECURITY-...

8:25 PM · Jan 25, 2025 · **7M** Views

View post engagements

26 207 950 599

SecBriefs | Making Cybersecurity Simple
@SecBriefs

Promote

What to Expect in Cybersecurity in 2025: From AI-driven threats to Zero Trust adoption, the landscape is evolving fast.

Are you ready?

Stay prepared with CYBERSECURITY DICTIONARY For Everyone, on Amazon:
amazon.com/CYBERSECURITY-...

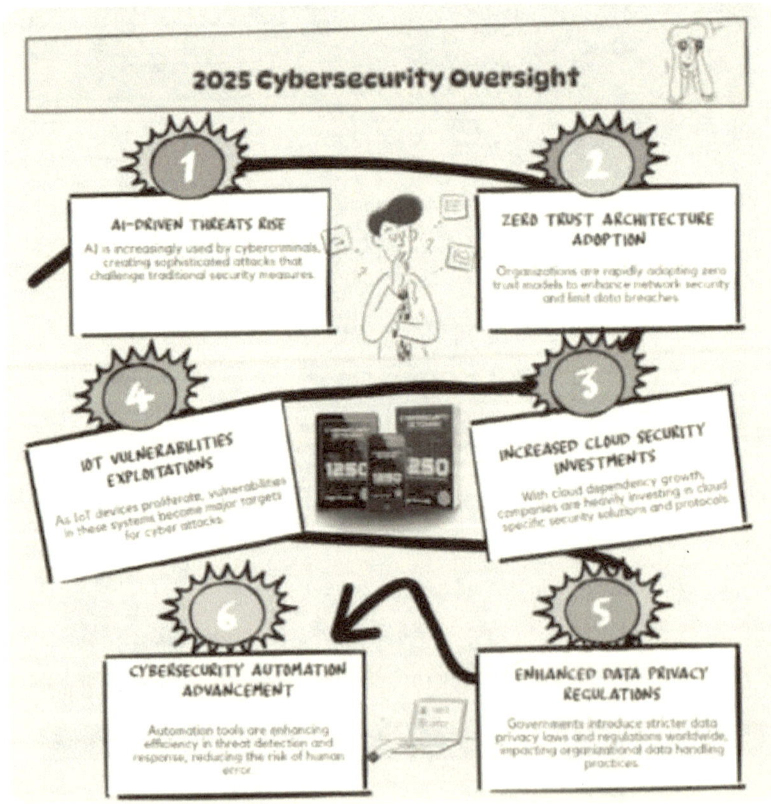

12:14 PM · Dec 29, 2024 · **1.3M** Views

View post engagements

6 63 208 106

In Case You Want to Go Deeper

While writing this book, I came across a number of standout sources — not just data points, but thoughtful research, sharp journalism, and eye-opening investigations that shaped how I understood these topics.

They deserve more than a footnote. Many helped me connect the dots or see things from new angles. If you're curious, working in the field, doing a project, or simply want to better protect yourself and those around you — these are the kinds of resources that truly make a difference.

I've included them here because good work deserves to be recognized. The people behind these materials are doing essential work in cybersecurity education and public awareness — and deserve wider recognition. I'm grateful for what they've created, and if you have the time, they're absolutely worth yours too.

If you've made it this far, you're already ahead. These resources can take you even further:

1. **CrowdStrike 2025 GlobalThreat Report** – https://www.crowdstrike.com/en-us/global-threat-report/

2. **Top Cybersecurity Statistics for 2025** – https://www.cobalt.io/blog/top-cybersecurity-statistics-2025
3. **181 Key Cybersecurity Statistics: Vulnerabilities, Exploits, and Their Impact for 2025** – https://www.indusface.com/blog/key-cybersecurity-statistics/
4. **Significant Cyber Incidents** – https://www.csis.org/programs/strategic-technologies-program/significant-cyber-incidents
5. **Global Cybersecurity Outlook 2025** – https://www.weforum.org/publications/global-cybersecurity-outlook-2025/digest/
6. **10 Cyber Security Trends For 2025** – https://www.sentinelone.com/cybersecurity-101/cybersecurity/cyber-security-trends/
7. **IoT Security Risks: Stats and Trends to Know in 2025** – https://jumpcloud.com/blog/iot-security-risks-stats-and-trends-to-know-in-2025
8. **Ransomware trends, statistics and facts in 2025** – https://www.techtarget.com/searchsecurity/feature/Ransomware-trends-statistics-and-facts
9. **Top 58 Phishing Statistics and Trends You Must Know in 2025** – https://keepnetlabs.com/blog/top-phishing-statistics-and-trends-you-must-know
10. **The Latest 2025 Phishing Statistics** – https://aag-it.com/the-latest-phishing-statistics/
11. **Ransomware Statistics and Ransomware Trends 2025** – https://www.fortinet.com/resources/cyberglossary/ransomware-statistics
12. **AI Cyber Attack Statistics 2025** – https://tech-adv.com/blog/ai-cyber-attack-statistics/
13. **Outsmarting AI-powered cyber attacks** – https://venturebeat.com/security/outsmarting-ai-powered-cyber-attacks-endpoint-defense-2025/
14. **100+ Data Breach Statistics and Trends for 2025** – https://www.stationx.net/data-breach-statistics/
15. **110+ of the Latest Data Breach Statistics** – https://secureframe.com/blog/data-breach-statistics
16. **Data Breaches That Have Happened in 2022, 2023, 2024, and 2025 So Far** – https://tech.co/news/data-breaches-updated-list
17. **Verizon 2025 Data Breach Investigations Report** – https://www.verizon.com/business/resources/reports/dbir/
18. **Healthcare Data Breach Statistics** – https://www.hipaajournal.com/healthcare-data-breach-statistics/
19. **Mobile malware evolution in 2024** – https://securelist.com/mobile-threat-report-2024/115494/

20. **2024 Consumer Cybersecurity Assessment Report** – https://mysecuritymarketplace.com/reports/2024-consumer-cybersecurity-assessment-report/

21. **The biggest data breaches of 2024 in financial services** – https://www.americanbanker.com/list/the-biggest-data-breaches-of-2024-in-financial-services

22. **Endpoint Security Statistics 2025 By Version, Services, Software** – https://scoop.market.us/endpoint-security-statistics/

23. **51 eCommerce Statistics In 2025 (Global and U.S. Data)** – https://www.sellerscommerce.com/blog/ecommerce-statistics/

24. **Cyber attacks in gaming industry 2024** – https://www.hackers4u.com/cyber-attacks-in-gaming-industry

25. **Kids and cybersecurity: what parents should be aware of in 2024** – https://www.kaspersky.com/blog/cybersecurity-threats-for-kids-2024/50188/

26. **SOCRadar ChatGPT Phishing Report** - https://socradar.io/phishing-in-2024-4151-increase-since-chatgpt/

27. **Cybelangel AI Phishing Report 2025** - https://cybelangel.com/rise-ai-phishing/

28. **Tech-Adv AI Cyber Attack Statistics** - https://tech-adv.com/blog/ai-cyber-attack-statistics/

29. **Hoxhunt Phishing Trends Report** - https://hoxhunt.com/guide/phishing-trends-report

30. **CNBC AI Phishing Report** - https://www.cnbc.com/2023/11/28/ai-like-chatgpt-is-creating-huge-increase-in-malicious-phishing-email.html

31. **Harvard Business Review AI Phishing Analysis** - https://hbr.org/2024/05/ai-will-increase-the-quantity-and-quality-of-phishing-scams

32. **Keepnet Labs Deepfake Statistics** - https://keepnetlabs.com/blog/deepfake-statistics-and-trends-about-cyber-threats-2024

33. **The Hacker News Deepfake Defense Report** - https://thehackernews.com/2025/05/deepfake-defense-in-age-of-ai.html

34. **Security.org Deepfake Statistics** - https://www.security.org/resources/deepfake-statistics/

35. **Axios AI Voice Cloning Report** – https://www.axios.com/2025/03/15/ai-voice-cloning-consumer-scams

36. **Keepnet Labs QR Code Phishing Statistics** – https://keepnetlabs.com/blog/2024-qr-code-phishing-trends-in-depth-analysis-of-rising-quishing-statistics

37. **Infosecurity Magazine Report** - https://www.infosecurity-magazine.com/news/qr-codes-used-22-phishing-attacks/

38. **Barracuda Networks Threat Analysis -** https://blog.barracuda.com/2024/10/22/threat-spotlight-evolving-qr-codes-phishing-attacks

39. **QR Code Tiger Statistics** – https://www.qrcode-tiger.com/qr-code-phishing-statistics

40. **Abnormal Security Report** – https://abnormalsecurity.com/blog/data-shows-c-suite-receives-42x-more-qr-code-attacks

41. **Wealth & Finance International** – https://wealthandfinance.digital/with-qr-code-redemption-set-to-surge-to-5-3-billion-in-2025-cybercriminals-will-increase-their-quishing-attacks/

42. **Palo Alto Unit 42 Research:** https://unit42.paloaltonetworks.com/qr-code-phishing/

43. **AirTags becoming 'weapon of choice of stalkers and abusers' as GPS tracker cases rocket by 317%** – https://www.itv.com/news/2024-04-02/airtags-become-weapon-of-choice-of-stalkers-and-abusers-as-cases-rocket

44. Online grooming crimes against children increase by 89% in six years – https://www.nspcc.org.uk/about-us/news-opinion/2024/online-grooming-crimes-increase/

45. **Reuters Cybersecurity** – https://www.reuters.com/technology/cybersecurity/

46. **CNBC Cybersecurity** – https://www.cnbc.com/cybersecurity/

47. **Forbes Cybersecurity** – https://www.forbes.com/cybersecurity/

48. **BBC Cybersecurity** – https://www.bbc.com/news/topics/cz4pr2gd85qt

49. **Tech Crunch Cybersecurity** – https://techcrunch.com/tag/cybersecurity/

50. **Gartner Cybersecurity** – https://www.gartner.com/en/cybersecurity

Bonus: 50 Essential Cybersecurity Terms

To help you feel more confident with the language of cybersecurity, I've included 50 foundational terms at the end of this book. They're written in a clear, friendly style – just like the rest of ***"Hack Happens"***.

These entries are from my other book, "***Cybersecurity Dictionary for Everyone***", an Amazon bestseller that explains 1,250 cybersecurity terms in plain English. If you enjoy the tone and want to go deeper – especially if you're starting a career or just curious about the cybersecurity world - that book is highly recommended.

But if you're just getting started, these 50 terms are a great first step.

No pressure. No jargon. Just a little more power in your pocket.

Access Control

definition: The selective restriction of access to a place or other resource.

explanation: Like a bouncer at a club, access control checks your "ID" (password, fingerprint, etc.) to ensure you're authorized before granting entry.

real-world examples: Passwords, PINs, biometrics, firewalls, and file permissions.

related terms: Authentication, Authorization, Identity and Access Management (IAM)

Adware

definition: Software that shows unwanted advertisements on a user's computer or device.

explanation: It's like those annoying telemarketers who call during dinner - they interrupt your activities and try to sell you something you don't want.

real-world examples: Pop-up ads, banner ads, and unwanted toolbars in your web browser.

related terms: Malware, Spyware, Bloatware

Antivirus

definition: Software designed to detect and remove malicious software from a computer or device.

explanation: It's like a security guard who patrols your computer, looking for and removing any unwanted intruders.

real-world examples: Detecting and removing viruses, worms, trojans, and other types of malware.

related terms: Malware, Cybersecurity, Endpoint Security

Authentication

definition: The process of verifying the identity of a user, device, or system.

explanation: It's like showing your ID to a security guard to prove you are who you say you are.

real-world examples: Passwords, biometrics (fingerprint, facial recognition), security tokens.

related terms: Access Control, Authorization, Identity Management

Authorization

definition: The process of granting or denying access to a resource based on a user's identity and permissions.

explanation: Once you're in the club (authenticated), authorization determines which VIP areas you can access.

real-world examples: Assigning roles and permissions to employees in a company's network, setting file permissions on your computer.

related terms: Access Control, Identity and Access Management (IAM)

Backdoor

definition: A hidden method for bypassing normal authentication or encryption in a computer system.

explanation: It's like a secret passage in a castle that allows someone to bypass the main gate and guards.

real-world examples: Malicious backdoors can be installed by hackers to gain unauthorized access to a system, while legitimate backdoors may be used for troubleshooting or maintenance.

related terms: Malware, Remote Access Trojan (RAT), Vulnerability

Botnet

definition: A network of compromised computers or devices that an attacker controls remotely.

explanation: It's like an army of zombie computers, blindly following the orders of their master.

real-world examples: Launching DDoS attacks, sending spam emails, and stealing sensitive information.

related terms: Bot, Bot Herder, Command and Control

Brute Force Attack

definition: A type of cyber attack that uses brute force to gain unauthorized access to a system or account.

explanation: It's like trying every key on a keyring until you find the one that opens the door.

real-world examples: Attempting to guess a password by trying every possible combination of characters.

related terms: Brute Force, Password Cracking, Dictionary Attack

Clickjacking

definition: A web attack that when users are tricked into clicking on hidden elements on a webpage.

explanation: It's like putting invisible tape over a button, so when you think you're clicking on one thing, you're clicking on something else.

real-world examples: Attackers use it to steal sensitive information, spread malware, or perform unauthorized actions.

related terms: UI Redressing, Web Application Security, Cross-Site Request Forgery (CSRF)

Cloud Security

definition: The broad set of technologies, policies, and procedures used to protect cloud computing environments.

explanation: It's like a comprehensive security system for a virtual city in the cloud, encompassing everything from physical infrastructure to data protection to access control.

real-world examples: Implementing firewalls, intrusion detection systems, encryption, access controls, and other security measures in the cloud.

related terms: Cloud Computing, Cybersecurity, Cloud Service Provider (CSP)

Credential Stuffing

definition: An attack that uses stolen or hijacked credentials to try and gain access to multiple accounts.

explanation: It's like trying a stolen key on every door in a building, hoping to find one that it unlocks.

real-world examples: Attackers use lists of stolen usernames and passwords to try and gain access to online accounts.

related terms: Brute Force Attack, ATO, Password Reuse

Cyber Attack

definition: A malicious attempt that damages, disrupts, or gains unauthorized access to a computer system or network.

explanation: It's like a digital break-in, where hackers try to steal information, disrupt operations, or cause damage to computer systems.

real-world examples: Hacking, phishing, malware infections, denial-of-service (DoS) attacks.

related terms: Cybersecurity, Threat, Vulnerability

Cyber Hygiene

definition: Practices and steps that users and organizations take to maintain system health and to improve online security.

explanation: It's like regular cleaning and maintenance to keep your systems safe from threats.

real-world examples: Regularly updating software, using strong passwords, and backing up data.

related terms: Security Best Practices, System Maintenance, Threat Prevention, User Education

Data Breach

definition: An incident that results in the unauthorized access or disclosure of sensitive data.

explanation: It's like a thief breaking into your house and stealing your valuables.

real-world examples: A hacker gaining access to a company's customer database or a data leak caused by a misconfigured cloud server.

related terms: Data Loss, Cyber Attack, Cybersecurity Incident

Denial of Service Attack (DDoS)

definition: A deliberate attempt to make a machine or network resource unavailable to its intended users, like by temporarily or indefinitely disrupting services of a host connected to the Internet.

explanation: An attack that aims to overwhelm a website or online service with traffic, causing it to crash or become unavailable to users.

real-world examples: SYN floods, ping floods, and other types of attacks that overwhelm a system's resources.

related terms: DoS, DDoS, Botnet

Digital Certificate

definition: An electronic document that verifies the identity of a website or server.

explanation: It's like a digital passport for a website, issued by a trusted authority (Certificate Authority) to confirm its authenticity.

real-world examples: When you see the padlock icon in your browser's address bar, it means the website is using a digital certificate.

related terms: SSL/TLS, Public Key Infrastructure (PKI), Certificate Authority (CA)

Digital Signature

definition: A mathematical technique used to validate the authenticity and integrity of a digital message or document.

explanation: It's like a handwritten signature, but for digital documents. It proves that the document was created by the person who claims to have created it and that it hasn't been tampered with.

real-world examples: Used to verify the authenticity of software updates, emails, and other digital documents.

related terms: Public Key Infrastructure (PKI), Cryptography, Authentication

Encryption

definition: The process of converting information or data into a code, especially to prevent unauthorized access.

explanation: It's like scrambling a message so that only someone with the secret decoder ring can read it.

real-world examples: Used to protect sensitive data, such as passwords, financial information, and personal records.

related terms: Cryptography, Cipher, Decryption

Endpoint

definition: Any device that connects to a network, such as computers, smartphones, and tablets.

explanation: It's like the individual locks on doors in a building.

real-world examples: Using endpoint protection software to secure laptops and mobile devices.

related terms: Endpoint Security, Cybersecurity, Network Security

Exploit

definition: A piece of software, a chunk of data, or a sequence of commands that takes advantage of a vulnerability in software or hardware, causing it to behave in unintended or harmful ways.

explanation: It's like a skeleton key that can unlock a door that wasn't meant to be opened.

real-world examples: A piece of code that takes advantage of a buffer overflow vulnerability to execute arbitrary code on a computer.

related terms: Vulnerability, Zero-Day, Patch

Firewall

definition: A network security system that monitors and controls incoming and outgoing network traffic based on predetermined security rules.

explanation: It's like a security guard for your network, checking every visitor's ID and only allowing those who are authorized to enter.

real-world examples: Used to protect networks from unauthorized access, malware, and other threats.

related terms: Network Security, Intrusion Prevention System (IPS), Security

Hacker

definition: An individual who uses computer, networking, or other skills to overcome a technical problem.

explanation: In the cybersecurity world, a hacker is someone who explores and exploits vulnerabilities in systems and networks. Hackers can be categorized as "black hat" (malicious), "white hat" (ethical), or "gray hat" (somewhere in between).

real-world examples: A "black hat" hacker might steal credit card data, while a "white hat" hacker might work for a security company, testing systems for weaknesses.

related terms: Cracker, Ethical Hacker, Security Researcher

Hashing

definition: The process of converting data into a fixed-size string of characters, which is typically a hash code.

explanation: It's like creating a unique fingerprint for a piece of data.

real-world examples: Storing hashed passwords in a database to prevent easy access if the database is breached.

related terms: Encryption, Cryptography, Data Integrity

HTTPS

definition: The secure version of HTTP, the protocol to transfer data over the web.

explanation: It's like sending a letter in a sealed envelope – the contents are encrypted and cannot be read by anyone who intercepts it.

real-world examples: Used to secure online transactions, protect user privacy, and prevent eavesdropping.

related terms: SSL/TLS, Encryption, Web Security

Incident Response

definition: The process of responding to and addressing the aftermath of a security breach or cyberattack (also known as an incident).

explanation: It's like calling 911 and having emergency responders show up to help you.

real-world examples: Identifying the cause of the incident, containing the damage, eradicating the threat, and recovering normal operations.

related terms: Incident Management, Incident Response Plan, Computer Security Incident Response Team (CSIRT)

Insider Attack

definition: A malicious act carried out by an insider against their organization.

explanation: It's like a wolf in sheep's clothing – an insider who abuses their trusted access to steal data, sabotage systems, or cause other harm.

real-world examples: A disgruntled employee leaking confidential information or a contractor planting malware on the company's network.

related terms: Insider Threat, Sabotage, Data Breach

Internet of Things (IoT)

definition: A network of physical devices embedded with electronics, software, sensors, actuators, and network connectivity enabling them to connect and exchange data.

explanation: It's like a network of smart devices that can communicate with each other and with the internet.

real-world examples: Smart thermostats, wearable fitness trackers, and connected appliances.

related terms: Smart Devices, Connected Devices, IoT Security

IP Address

definition: A unique numerical label assigned to each device connected to a computer network that uses the Internet Protocol for communication.

explanation: It's like a street address for your computer or device on the internet.

real-world examples: Used to route traffic between devices on a network and identify them uniquely.

related terms: IPv4, IPv6, Network Address Translation (NAT)

Keylogger

definition: A kind of surveillance software that records every keystroke typed on a computer.

explanation: It is like having someone secretly looking over your shoulder as you type.

real-world examples: Not only used for malicious purposes, such as stealing passwords or credit card information, but can also be used for legitimate purposes like monitoring employee activity or parental control.

related terms: Spyware, Surveillance, Cybercrime

Malware

definition: Malicious software designed to harm a computer system or network.

explanation: It is like a disease that infects your computer, causing it to malfunction or steal your data.

real-world examples: Viruses, worms, Trojans, ransomware, spyware, and adware.

related terms: Cybersecurity, Virus, Cyber Attack

Man-in-the-Middle (MitM) Attack

definition: An attack where the attacker secretly relays and possibly alters the communication between two parties who believe they are directly communicating with each other.

explanation: Imagine a postman who secretly opens your mail, reads it, possibly changes it, and then reseals it before delivering it to the intended recipient.

real-world examples: Attackers can use MitM attacks to eavesdrop on conversations, steal sensitive information, or inject malicious code.

related terms: Eavesdropping, Packet Sniffing, ARP Spoofing

Multi-Factor Authentication (MFA) / Two-Factor Authentication

definition: An authentication method that requires the user to provide two or more verification factors to gain access to a system or application.

explanation: It is like having multiple locks on your front door – it makes it much harder for someone to break in.

real-world examples: Using a password and a fingerprint scan, or a password and a one-time code sent to your phone.

related terms: Authentication, 2FA, Security

Patch

definition: A piece of software designed to update a computer program or its supporting data, fixing or improving it.

explanation: It's like a band-aid for software – it fixes bugs, vulnerabilities, and other problems.

real-world examples: Software vendors regularly release patches to address security vulnerabilities and improve the functionality of their products.

related terms: Security Update, Software Update, Vulnerability Management

Penetration Testing (Pen Test)

definition: An authorized simulated cyberattack on a computer system to evaluate the security of the system.

explanation: It's like hiring an ethical hacker to try and break into your house to find any security weaknesses.

real-world examples: This helps organizations find and fix vulnerabilities before malicious hackers can exploit them.

related terms: Ethical Hacking, Vulnerability Assessment, Security Assessment

Phishing

definition: A type of cyber attack that uses fraudulent emails, messages, or websites to trick victims into revealing sensitive information.

explanation: It's like a fisherman casting a line with bait, hoping to hook unsuspecting victims.

real-world examples: Emails that appear to be from your bank asking you to update your password, or fake websites that mimic legitimate ones to steal your login credentials.

related terms: Social Engineering, Spear Phishing, Vishing

Ransomware

definition: Malware that encrypts a victim's files and demands a ransom payment to decrypt them.

explanation: It's like a digital kidnapping – your files are held hostage until you pay up.

real-world examples: CryptoLocker, WannaCry, and Ryuk are examples of ransomware.

related terms: Malware, Encryption, Crypto-Malware

Risk Assessment

definition: The process of identifying, analyzing, and evaluating risks.

explanation: It's like a doctor performing a check-up on a patient to assess their health and identify potential problems.

real-world examples: A risk assessment might involve identifying vulnerabilities in a system, assessing the likelihood of a threat exploiting those vulnerabilities, and estimating the potential impact of a successful attack.

related terms: Risk Management, Threat Assessment, Vulnerability Assessment

Rootkit

definition: A set of software tools allowing an unauthorized user to gain control of a computer system without being detected.

explanation: It's like a secret passage in a castle that allows an intruder to bypass security measures and gain access to the inner workings of the system.

real-world examples: Rootkits are often used by malware to hide their presence and maintain persistence on a system.

related terms: Malware, Stealth, Persistence

Sandbox

definition: A secure and isolated environment where programs or files can be executed without affecting the host system.

explanation: It's like a quarantine zone for suspicious software, allowing you to safely test it without risking damage to your computer.

real-world examples: Used for malware analysis, software testing, and web browsing.

related terms: Virtual Machine, Emulation, Malware Analysis

Scareware

definition: A type of malware that uses fear tactics to trick users into buying or downloading unnecessary or harmful software.

explanation: Imagine a pop-up message on your computer warning you of a virus and urging you to click a link to remove it. That link could lead to malware or a fake antivirus program.

real-world examples: Pop-up warnings about viruses or security threats, fake antivirus scans, and messages claiming your computer is infected.

related terms: Malware, Social Engineering, Deception

Session Hijacking

definition: An attack that allows an attacker to take over a user's session on a website or application.

explanation: It's like stealing someone's identity while they're online, allowing the attacker to impersonate them and access their accounts.

real-world examples: Attackers can hijack sessions by stealing session cookies, guessing session IDs, or exploiting vulnerabilities in the session management mechanism.

related terms: Session Fixation, Cross-Site Scripting (XSS), Web Application Security

Shoulder Surfing

definition: A type of social engineering attack where an attacker observes a victim's screen or keyboard input to steal sensitive information.

explanation: Imagine someone peeking over your shoulder as you enter your PIN at an ATM.

real-world examples: Attackers might try to steal passwords, credit card numbers, or other confidential information by watching you type.

related terms: Social Engineering, Eavesdropping, Privacy

Smishing

definition: A type of phishing attack that uses SMS text messages to trick victims into revealing sensitive information.

explanation: It's like a phishing email but delivered via text message instead.

real-world examples: Attackers might send texts that appear to be from your bank, asking you to click on a link or provide your account information.

related terms: Phishing, Social Engineering, SMS

Social Engineering Attack

definition: A type of cyber attack that relies on human interaction to trick victims into revealing sensitive information or performing actions that compromise security.

explanation: Imagine a con artist manipulating someone into giving them money or personal information. Social engineering attacks prey on human vulnerabilities like trust, fear, and greed.

real-world examples: Phishing emails, vishing calls, pretexting, and baiting are common social engineering tactics.

related terms: Phishing, Pretexting, Baiting

Spam

definition: Unsolicited or undesired electronic messages, typically sent in bulk.

explanation: Imagine receiving a flood of unwanted emails or text messages – that's spam.

real-world examples: Spam can be annoying and time-consuming, and it can also contain malicious links or attachments.

related terms: Email Spam, Junk Mail, Phishing

Spoofing Attack

definition: A type of attack where an attacker impersonates a trusted entity to gain unauthorized access or information.

explanation: It's like a con artist who uses a fake ID to gain access to a restricted area.

real-world examples: Attackers might use spoofing attacks to bypass authentication mechanisms, steal data, or spread malware.

related terms: Spoofing, Man-in-the-Middle Attack, Phishing

Spyware

definition: Software that secretly gathers information about a person or organization without their knowledge.

explanation: It's like a spy who secretly records your conversations and activities.

real-world examples: Keyloggers, screen capture tools, and tracking cookies are all examples of spyware.

related terms: Malware, Surveillance, Privacy

Trojan / Trojan Horse

definition: A type of malware that disguises itself as a legitimate program to trick users into installing it.

explanation: It's like a poisoned gift – it looks harmless, but it contains a hidden danger.

real-world examples: Trojans can steal data, install other malware, or give attackers remote access to a system.

related terms: Malware, Virus, Worm

Typosquatting

definition: A type of cyber attack that relies on users mistyping a website's address.

explanation: Imagine typing "Amazom.com" instead of "Amazon.com" – typosquatters register these misspelled domains to redirect users to malicious websites.

real-world examples: Used for phishing attacks, malware distribution, and other scams.

related terms: URL Hijacking, Phishing, Social Engineering

Virtual Private Network (VPN)

definition: A technology that creates a secure, encrypted connection over a public network, like the internet.

explanation: Imagine a tunnel through the internet that protects your data from prying eyes.

real-world examples: Used to access restricted resources, bypass censorship, and protect online privacy.

related terms: Encryption, Tunnel, Remote Access

About the author

Tolga TAVLAS spent 27 years in banking, where cybersecurity mistakes don't just hit systems – they hit lives.

He's also the author of two other books: ***Digital Banking Tips (2015)*** and ***Cybersecurity Dictionary for Everyone (2024)***, an Amazon bestseller that explains 1,250 cybersecurity terms in plain, simple language.

Hack Happens wasn't supposed to be the next book. But something unexpected happened.

While sharing cybersecurity insights to introduce his work, Tolga found himself in thousands of conversations – with people from all walks of life, all over the world. Across millions of impressions and thousands of engagements with real people who had real concerns and expectations about cybersecurity, one quiet message kept coming back:

"No one ever really explained how any of this works. We're not experts. We were never shown how to stay safe."

So he listened. And that's why this book exists.

Tolga wrote **Hack Happens** to make cybersecurity more human.

After hearing from parents, students, veterans, and small business owners, he realized most resources didn't speak their language. This book was created to fill that gap—with clear, practical guidance to help people understand the risks around them and take simple steps to stay safer online.

Tolga believes cybersecurity shouldn't be a mystery – it should be part of everyday life.

www.ingramcontent.com/pod-product-compliance
Lightning Source LLC
LaVergne TN
LVHW090303210926
848480LV00001B/113